When McKinsey Comes to Town

Dear Jiacheng:

May you build noble charater, may God Bless you abundantly!

Love, mom

October, 2023.

in Hong kong

When McKinsey Comes to Town

The Hidden Influence of the World's Most Powerful Consulting Firm

Walt Bogdanich and
Michael Forsythe

Doubleday
New York

www.doubleday.com

Book design by Michael Collica
Front-of-jacket photograph © ppengcreative / iStock / Getty Images
Jacket design by John Fontana

Library of Congress Cataloging-in-Publication Data
Names: Bogdanich, Walt, author. | Forsythe, Michael, author.
Title: When McKinsey comes to town : the hidden influence of the world's most powerful consulting firm / Walt Bogdanich and Michael Forsythe.
Description: First edition. | New York : Doubleday, 2022.
Identifiers: LCCN 2022008480 | ISBN 9780385546232 (hardcover) | ISBN 9780385546249 (ebook) | ISBN 9780385549448 (open market)
Subjects: LCSH: McKinsey and Company—Influence. | Industrial management. | Business consultants.
Classification: LCC HD69.C6 B5749 2022 | DDC 001.068—dc23/eng/20220303
LC record available at https://lccn.loc.gov/2022008480

MANUFACTURED IN THE UNITED STATES OF AMERICA

3 5 7 9 10 8 6 4

First Edition

For Stephanie, Nicholas, and Peter

For Leta, Aidan, and Liam

When McKinsey Comes to Town

Introduction

When McKinsey Comes to Town

In Gary, Indiana, just past the rusting bridges, peeling paint, and railroad switching station sits a green well-tended plot of land that seems oddly out of place. It is a grassy knoll of bushes and trees overshadowed by the drab, hulking remains of a plant run by what was once the world's biggest, most profitable company, the U.S. Steel Corporation.

To the right, a towering furnace and smokestacks rise high against the northeastern sky. Basic steel is made there, forged in heat so intense the metal resembles white-hot lava flowing from a volcano. Nothing is soft or forgiving, only concrete, fire, and metal. To the left, rows of buildings with gabled roofs stretch to the western horizon. This is where steel is treated to make it less brittle before rolling it into massive coils for shipment to places near and far.

Occupying seven miles of lakefront, the steel plant has two hundred miles of railroad tracks, its own hospital, fire department, and police force. In years past, the company did its civic duty by sending workers with good voices and top hats to sing Christmas carols at grade schools across the city.

Inside the green oasis is a granite memorial with a book describing how 513 people died from accidents inside the steel mill. This book of the dead, covered in thick plastic and soot, tells of workers crushed by railroad cars, trucks, and steel. Others fell to their death, were torn apart by explosions, asphyxiated, burned, buried alive, and even drowned. Forty-one died by electrocution. The labor reporter

Joseph S. Pete wrote that steelworker funerals are often closed-casket affairs. The book of the dead explains why.*

Gary once held the promise of twentieth-century industrial America, a melting pot of racial and ethnic groups in pursuit of a better life, money for college, paid vacations, and pensions. From this emerged a solid middle class, two Nobel Prize winners, and the Jackson Five, as well as pollution that befouled the air and waterways.

In the last quarter of the twentieth century, the company's fortunes fell sharply because of cheap foreign steel, old equipment, and suspect management. The workforce dropped below eight thousand. Departments were closed or pared down.

The decay spread to Gary, the city U.S. Steel founded more than a century ago as "a triumph of scientific planning." By the end of the century, Gary had descended into a landscape of abandoned office buildings, stores, and churches. Rather than spend money it didn't have to tear them down, Gary rented the locations to crews filming postapocalyptic and horror movies, including *A Nightmare on Elm Street* and *Transformers.* Even a scene from the miniseries *Chernobyl* was filmed there.

Crime spiked, and Gary's population dropped to 69,000 from a high of 177,000 in 1960. Billboards along the steel mill's southern border reflect a population that had lost its moorings. "Shackled by Lust? Jesus Sets You Free," reads one, followed by ads for a strip club, an injury attorney, and a casino.

The year 2014, however, brought Gary's steelworkers a glimmer of hope. The company's new chief executive, Mario Longhi, hired an elite consulting firm, McKinsey & Company, to inject new ideas into the aging manufacturer. For decades McKinsey sold clients on its reputation as a firm that delivered scientific solutions to complex problems. Blue-chip companies and governments around the world

* In the 1970s, I was one of twenty-seven thousand employees at U.S. Steel. My father also worked there, as did my brother and most of my relatives. Using a long metal hook, I pulled hot steel rods off a roll line, then tied the bundle with metal wires. I knew steelworking was dangerous. Just weeks after I started, a twelve-year employee in my department, Robert Plunk, died after being pinned under a red-hot bar of steel—his suffering unimaginable. —Walt Bogdanich

hired its consultants, as did the CIA, the FBI, and the Pentagon, among others, believing McKinsey had the wisdom and wherewithal that their managers lacked.

McKinsey came to U.S. Steel with the goal of restoring the steelmaker to its iconic status as a company that built the nation's bridges, buildings, and weapons that defeated America's enemies. With McKinsey's help, U.S. Steel promised to recapture that spirit through "a relentless focus on economic profit, our customers, cost structure, and innovation"—all without sacrificing safety or harming the environment. Gary's labor force had little idea of what to expect from these highly paid consultants, some graduates of Ivy League business schools.

But steelworkers would learn soon enough, as did others before them, what can happen when McKinsey comes to town.

Construction on U.S. Steel's Gary plant had begun in 1906 under the direction of the company's chairman, Elbert Gary, a former judge who wanted the city to bear his name, though he did not want to live there himself. Called "a dour moralist" by one historian, Judge Gary cared less about the welfare of residents than about the efficiency and profitability of his steel mill.

Judge Gary sought out European royalty and collected Renaissance art, while steelworkers were stuck living in "the patch," a raw, disease-infected district that had two hundred saloons with names like Bucket of Blood. They worked twelve-hour days, seven days a week. A church group called this eighty-four-hour workweek a "disgrace to civilization," and a congressional committee termed it "a brutal system of industrial slavery." Judge Gary didn't much care. He opposed unions, considered labor leaders his social inferiors, and believed his employees preferred to work as many hours as possible.

The founder of McKinsey & Company, James O. McKinsey, an accountant from the Ozarks, also believed in efficiency and profits. His young company began advising U.S. Steel in the Great Depression. The company quickly became the firm's biggest client; more than forty consultants were assigned to the account. At one point, U.S. Steel generated at least half the billings in McKinsey's New York office. When the Wagner Act of 1935 required companies to negotiate with workers seeking better pay and safer working conditions, McKinsey set up a special unit to advise corporate executives on how to deal with their demands. But McKinsey eventually lost its biggest supporter at the steel company, and in the 1950s the two companies moved apart. Sixty years later, the iconic steelmaker was floundering, and U.S. Steel's new chief executive, Mario Longhi, decided to restore their close relationship.

The Brazilian-born Longhi became CEO of U.S. Steel in 2013. He inherited a company saddled with old, inefficient manufacturing methods. Smaller companies with newer technology had been gouging out big chunks of business from lumbering U.S. Steel, which had not turned an annual profit in years.

Like Judge Gary, Longhi favored a mustache and opulence. He bought a mansion in Florida with ten baths, a guesthouse, a separate gym, media room, and swimming pool. Longhi sold the complex for $9.8 million. He also owned property on Fisher Island, one of the nation's wealthiest enclaves, accessible off the Miami coast only by ferries, helicopter, or private yachts.

Longhi had no experience with a big, fully integrated steel company—most of his previous work experience was at Alcoa—but he knew people who could guide him, and that was his "long time trusted adviser," McKinsey & Company.

At Longhi's direction, McKinsey implemented a "transformational" business plan called "The Carnegie Way," in honor of U.S. Steel's co-founder Andrew Carnegie. The plan was so important to U.S. Steel's future that the manufacturer cited the Carnegie Way forty-nine times in its 2014 annual report. Among the plan's most important goals was finding a more rational, cost-efficient way to maintain the company's aging equipment and infrastructure. There seemed no better firm to manage maintenance costs than McKinsey, widely recognized as the world's premier efficiency experts.

The following January, Longhi told a trade publication that U.S. Steel's transformation was a "phenomenal" success. As proof, he cited his consultants "who have seen what we are doing" and have concluded "there is no deeper, broader transformation effort taking place in the country." Longhi dared anyone to say his company had not considered every option to improve profitability. "We are doing everything that is required—and pretty effectively, by the way."

With a new chief executive and a turnaround plan, U.S. Steel stock began rising, and in 2014 it posted its first annual profit in six years. But the progress was more illusion than fact. The manufacturer posted a $75 million loss in the first quarter of 2015. The downturn impacted workers as well as investors. Nine thousand employees at company plants, including Gary Works, received notices of possible layoffs. Maintenance workers were hit hard: Dozens of them were laid off. Two hundred others were demoted to roving labor gangs at a significant reduction of pay and sent to work in unfamiliar parts of the plant.

Union members came to believe that the Carnegie Way was simply a cover story for the company's plan to cut costs—a plan that workers said jeopardized their safety. Mike Millsap, District 7 director of the steelworkers' union, said McKinsey had no experience running a steel mill or "what it takes to protect the employees from harm."

The warning proved prophetic. In June, workers in Gary found Charles Kremke unconscious with third-degree burns on his head. A U.S. Steel spokeswoman said the employee could not be revived. The coroner ruled that Kremke had been electrocuted, but months would pass without the company's disclosing the cause of his death.

Because of the fatality, the State of Indiana cited U.S. Steel for four safety violations, all deemed serious: failing to "de-energize" the live connection prior to maintenance; failing to adequately train employees to identify a live connection; failing to test equipment to ensure live connections were de-energized before maintenance; and failing to provide protective gear to those working around live connections in a confined area.

The layoffs and safety concerns did not dissuade U.S. Steel from going forward with its plan to issue 21.7 million new shares of stock. This special stock offering, which raised $482 million, occurred in August, the same month the union accused the company of gutting its maintenance department. Angry over safety issues, the union on August 26 led a protest march to U.S. Steel's main gate in Gary. Normally union protests occur only during contract negotiations.

Workers chanted, "McKinsey sucks! McKinsey sucks!" Union members carried signs that drove home their sentiment:

- "Hello Mario! McKinsey must go."
- "McKinsey stole."
- "McKinsey = contract violations."
- "Union yes, McKinsey no."
- "McKinsey steals."
- "Give McKinsey the (picture of a boot)."

In the days after Kremke's death, Jonathan Arrizola, a thirty-year-old navy veteran and father of two young children, worried that his maintenance job was becoming too dangerous, so he began looking for other work. Arrizola told his wife, Whitney, that he had recently received an electrical shock on the job. "He was constantly complaining about the McKinsey group cutting back workers," she told *The Times of Northwest Indiana.* "There was always some kind of close call with someone he worked with."

Then, at the end of September 2016, Arrizola was on a four-person crew troubleshooting an electrical issue on a crane when he came into contact with 480 volts and was electrocuted.

"All they care about is money," his wife said after learning of her husband's death. "I have no husband. My children have no father. I have no idea how I'm going to pay for my house, or my car, any of my bills. I was a stay-at-home mother. I have no experiences. Jon was everything to me." Friends and well-wishers raised $14,000 on her behalf through a GoFundMe campaign.

Billy McCall, president of United Steelworkers Local 1066 during the Carnegie Way, said Arrizola was well liked. "U.S. Steel made all these moves via McKinsey schemes, and ultimately he was moved from one area where he was quite proficient into another area where he was not as proficient," McCall said. "That quite possibly was the direct reason he died."

For the electrocution deaths of Kremke and Arrizola, the government fined U.S. Steel a grand total of $42,000, though that amount was reduced to $14,500 through negotiations with the company. The steelmaker agreed to make ten corrective actions to prevent similar accidents in the future. Adam Finkel, the former chief regulatory official for worker safety under President Clinton, said fines start low and then get "knocked down and down and down." He added, "The fine is bigger for harassing a wild donkey on a national grazing land than for killing a worker."

Union complaints about safety were echoed by U.S. Steel investors who filed a class-action lawsuit, alleging that U.S. Steel misled them on the company's financial health. Based largely on confidential interviews with eleven current or former U.S. Steel employees, many of them managers or supervisors, the investors called the Carnegie Way a "sham," a cover for extreme cost cutting through "massive layoffs and deferring desperately needed maintenance and repairs." They said these policies left the company "with a skeleton crew of inexperienced plant employees who did not know how to maintain or repair equipment, were required to work long hours of up to 90 hours per week, and which resulted in severe unplanned outages."

The company adopted a policy of "don't buy, get by," whereby managers bought items only when absolutely necessary, according to a former U.S. Steel purchasing specialist whose primary job was to order machine parts for the company's American plants. Rather than make needed repairs, the official said, maintenance teams were asked to "jury-rig" failing machines to keep them operating.

Orders for some parts required approval of a "control tower," consisting of McKinsey and the plant manager. "The implementation of the control tower resulted in a significant reduction of requisition approvals," the investor lawsuit stated. A former director of maintenance at another U.S. Steel facility said that McKinsey did not want to hear about "critical" structural maintenance because of the cost and that the consultants played a role in cutting the repair and maintenance budget. (McKinsey and U.S. Steel said consultants had no approval authority over the purchase of parts.)

Billy McCall, the former union official, said he understood that McKinsey received a percentage of what U.S. Steel purportedly saved. In fact, McKinsey's compensation was tied partly to the steelmaker's financial performance, raising questions about the firm's motive in recommending cuts in expenses.

After Donald J. Trump won the November 2016 presidential election, in part by promising to restore blue-collar jobs, Longhi and his second-in-command, David Burritt, decided the time was right to cash in. The two sold a combined $25 million in stock over eight trading days. Longhi told CNBC that he hoped to restore ten thousand jobs, citing a more favorable regulatory environment and lower taxes.

Longhi's optimism carried over to early 2017, when he reassured investors that the worst was over. Days after President Trump took office, he named Longhi as one of twenty-eight business leaders to serve on his Manufacturing Jobs Initiative.

And that's where things stood until three months later, when U.S. Steel reported first-quarter earnings for 2017. Analysts had expected a healthy profit. Instead, the company shocked Wall Street by posting a $180 million net loss, triggering a 27 percent drop in the stock price, the company's largest daily drop in more than a quarter of a century.

Gordon Johnson of Axiom Capital Management called the loss all the more troubling "given that it occurred in a market where U.S. steel prices are high versus previous years." He further noted that the industry had "enjoyed significant protection from imports from both the Obama and Trump administration." Johnson concluded that if the company performed this poorly in good times, then the rest of the year "looks set to resemble a *'Nightmare on Elm Street,'*" an unintended nod to Gary's role in that movie.

Within two weeks of that earnings report, Longhi left U.S. Steel with a $4.54 million bonus. Longhi wasn't the only casualty. His vaunted Carnegie Way disappeared like footprints on Lake Michigan's sandy shore. Whereas the Carnegie Way merited more than forty citations in U.S. Steel's 2016 annual report, it received not a single mention in the 2017 annual report. History had been erased, Soviet-style.

U.S. Steel regrouped and in 2018 created a new plan *and* a new slogan.

"Underlying our efforts," the company wrote, "is our belief that we must operate as a principled company committed to a code of conduct that is rooted in our Gary Principles and our core values." Those core values are "articulated in our **S.T.E.E.L.** principles . . . : **S**afety First, **T**rust and Respect, **E**nvironmentally Friendly Activities, **E**thical Behavior, and **L**awful Business Conduct."

S.T.E.E.L.—with a dash of Ayn Rand. As a Christmas present, the company's new chief executive, David Burritt, gave the former union official Billy McCall a surprise gift—the book *Atlas Shrugged.* "This is the philosophy right now," McCall said in an interview. "This is corporate philosophy, for crying out loud."

With Longhi and the Carnegie Way having passed their expiration dates, McKinsey still remained tethered to the steelmaker, taking in at least $13 million in fees from 2018 through 2020, according to McKinsey records.

Three McKinsey consultants even wrote an article that explained, without a hint of irony, "why maintenance staffing matters." The authors acknowledged that maintenance staffing is easy to get wrong. "Cut too deep and too fast and reliability suffers. And mistakes are tricky to fix."

Especially, they might have added, when people die.

There is no book of the dead at Disneyland, not at a place sold as the "Happiest Place on Earth." Walt Disney designed the park to be pure fantasy. "I don't want the public to see the world they live in," Disney said. "I want them to feel they are in another world." Disneyland offered a mix of past and future, adventure, boat rides, cartoon characters posing for pictures, and theme-based roller coasters. Some rides intended to scare, but not endanger. Under Walt Disney, who died in 1966, the park had an exemplary safety record, earning a reputation as the industry leader for safety.

Several years after it opened, the park had already become a cultural phenomenon. At the height of the Cold War, the Soviet premier, Nikita Khrushchev, tried to visit the "Magic Kingdom" but was denied entry. "I asked: Why not?" Khrushchev said. "What do they have, rocket-launching pads there?"

Buoyed by the success of Disneyland, the company's footprint grew. Other Disney parks opened, including the biggest of all, Disney World Resort in Orlando. The company moved aggressively into filmmaking, publishing, television, and Broadway plays. Then, in 1994, a former toy executive, Paul S. Pressler, became Disneyland's top executive.

Described as handsome, charismatic, and a favorite of Disney's chief executive, Michael Eisner, Pressler set out to leave his mark on the company by hiring McKinsey to thoroughly evaluate the park's operation.

After more than a year of study, on May 13, 1997, McKinsey presented Pressler with its findings in a confidential report titled "Transforming Maintenance: Defining the Disney Standard."

McKinsey professed to have found a way to make Disneyland more efficient and increase profits without sacrificing quality, but that required rethinking how maintenance should be performed. "Intuition or science?" McKinsey wrote in its analysis for Pressler. The correct answer, the firm made clear, was science, as McKinsey defined it.

Maintenance decisions should be based not on the judgment of veteran employees, McKinsey said, but on an analysis of maintenance histories, breakdowns, and cost. Called reliability-centered maintenance, the process originated in the aviation industry, where safety is paramount.

At Disneyland, though, the process evolved primarily into a mandate to cut expenses. Using terms like "cost avoidance," McKinsey recommended cutting back on park maintenance, eliminating jobs, paying some people less, and hiring outside contractors. In a broadly unpopular move, most maintenance workers were transferred to the overnight, or graveyard, shift. To deal with the shock of such a sudden move, McKinsey recommended bringing in counselors to address issues of sleep, nutrition, and relationships. Each overnight worker would also receive a one-year subscription to the *Working Nights* newsletter.

Only a small crew, the Maintenance Response Team, would handle mechanical breakdowns during the day. And even that group, McKinsey said, could eventually be whittled down by 30 percent.

Consultants certainly knew the risk in reorganizing a theme

park, already the envy of the entertainment world. But the reward for implementing the changes, they argued, would be "world class maintenance," eventually saving the company millions of dollars.

McKinsey let no self-doubt dampen its enthusiasm for the changes. "The magnitude of the opportunity gives one pause," the firm told Pressler. "Change of this magnitude is not managed—it is led." To meet this challenge, "leaders must inspire and develop a bench of true change champions."

Finding those "true change champions" might be difficult because McKinsey held a low opinion of many park managers, saying they lacked "critical skills," necessitating the removal or restaffing of 50 percent of the park's leadership. After studying one work area, the consultants wrote, "Meetings, admin and safety using too much time." McKinsey also recommended cost savings through "performance measures based on overhead rate and dollars. Hold shop managers accountable for location overhead."

"There's nothing wrong with saving money," Mike Goodwin, a former maintenance supervisor, told the *Los Angeles Times.* "But not at the expense of your prime objective, which is to keep the place running safely." McKinsey asked another maintenance supervisor, Bob Klostreich, why lap bars on a roller coaster were inspected daily when records showed they never fail.

Klostreich, a twenty-year Disney employee, became incensed. "The reason they don't fail is because we check them every night," he said. Goodwin said Disney viewed not checking lap bars as an acceptable risk. "It's like a pilot saying, 'Hey, we haven't crashed in a while, let's skip the preflight.'"

Five months after McKinsey recommended cutting maintenance costs, Klostreich warned Disney that safety concerns at the park were growing. "As you know," he wrote, "I have expressed to you and others on several occasions my deep concerns over what I feel has been a serious decline in management's readiness, willingness and ability to properly and safely maintain the high speed attractions assigned to the roller coaster team. Our staffing and labor distribution has been and is inconsistent with effective daily preventive management."

Klostreich said he received no response.

The following year, on Christmas Eve, Disneyland experienced a fatal accident that rocked the industry. Luan Dawson, a thirty-four-year-old computer programmer at Microsoft, and his wife, a pharmacist, were waiting to board an old-fashioned riverboat, *Columbia,* which had just finished a cycle through the park. Docking the heavy boat required skill acquired only through training and experience. But on this day, a supervisor filled in for an absent employee even though she had never trained on that boat and had never tried to dock it.

With the boat still moving, too fast as it turned out, the supervisor tied a substitute nylon rope to a metal cleat on the boat. The force of the moving boat tore loose the metal cleat, apparently attached to rotting wood, propelling it like shrapnel from a bomb, killing Dawson and severely disfiguring his wife in front of their son, according to court records filed by a Dawson family attorney, Christopher Aitken. The supervisor was hospitalized with injuries as well.

Aitken said a safer rope that breaks under intense pressure had been used in the past, but wasn't used on this day.

The fatality prompted a national reexamination of safety at the nation's amusement parks and led directly to a new state law in California requiring an independent investigation of serious accidents there. Previously, park officials investigated themselves. The Dawson family reached a confidential settlement with Disney reported to be $25 million.

Aitken said McKinsey's cost-saving measures directly contributed to the *Columbia* accident, among others. At McKinsey's suggestion, Disney had eliminated the higher-paid expert managers on each ride—called ride leads—including on the *Columbia.* They were responsible for ensuring that the rides operated safely. Maintenance also suffered. When employees called mechanics to fix problems, they didn't immediately respond, so they stopped calling, Aitken said. It didn't help, he added, that workers with the most institutional knowledge of rides were "getting forced into graveyard shifts."

In February 1999—two months after the *Columbia* fatality—Klostreich resent his earlier warning to Disney leadership. "I am concerned that the attractions are deteriorating even more so now than at the time I authored the attached memo," he wrote.

Later that year Klostreich was terminated—a move he said was retaliation for being a whistleblower. Disney said he refused to work the graveyard shift for health reasons and no job openings were available during the day. Klostreich filed suit, but it was dismissed.

In July 2000, safety issues became more pronounced. A wheel assembly fell off a ride in Space Mountain, injuring nine people. Poor maintenance was cited as a cause.

Two months later, a four-year-old boy, Brandon Zucker, fell out of the Roger Rabbit ride and was crushed under another car, where he remained for ten minutes. Before his rescue, he went into cardiac arrest, resulting in permanent brain damage. He never walked or talked again. Employees had placed him in a seat that was less safe given his size and failed to fully lower the lap bar. Brandon died at age thirteen. State officials ordered Disney to make significant changes to improve the ride's safety.

David Koenig, who has written extensively about Disneyland in books and articles, said the company wanted a firm like McKinsey because management felt park operations had become too expensive. "They encouraged the Disneyland management to reduce staffing, reduce training, reduce maintenance, reduce, reduce, reduce—reduce everything to the point where it became unsafe," Koenig said. He couldn't say whether the fault rested with McKinsey's recommendations or Disney's implementation of them. "I just know they got the ball started, and we all know where it ended up."

John J. Lawler, who taught in the University of Illinois's School of Employment and Labor Relations, believes management consultants mainly serve to legitimize the goals of their clients. "Clients like to be told they are doing the right thing," Lawler said, adding that management techniques viewed as best practices "are very often propagated by consulting firms and thus these techniques become largely institutionalized in the business world."

The accidents represented a major blow to Disneyland's reputation, but they did not slow the corporate advancement of the cost cutter in chief, Paul Pressler. As reported by the *Los Angeles Times,*

Pressler "enjoyed a meteoric rise, leapfrogging over other executives, including managers of the much larger Disney World in Florida." He joined the inner circle of Disney's CEO, Michael Eisner.

Still, it was a résumé marked by accidents. And it wouldn't be long before new questions arose over the wisdom of Pressler's maintenance policies and McKinsey's role in recommending them.

In the late summer of 2003, Disney employees began hearing strange noises coming from a roller coaster, built to look like a train, as it whizzed through Big Thunder Mountain. Mechanics replaced a guide wheel and put the ride back into service. After the "same unusual clicking sound" occurred again, maintenance once more replaced a wheel. A yellow tag was placed on the train, named I. M. Brave, indicating it should not be used, but it was.

On September 5, 2003, as the temperature climbed toward its high of eighty-seven degrees, Marcelo Torres, twenty-two, and three friends prepared to board the Big Thunder Mountain train shortly after 11:00 a.m. Earlier in the day, Disney employees had continued to hear unusual noises but did not remove the roller coaster for inspection. The yellow tag warning remained.

Torres and his friends did not know they had just boarded a ride with a history of mechanical problems. The previous month, riders had to be evacuated after the train broke down. Of more immediate concern, two retaining bolts had just detached from the axle on the previous ride, causing the wheel guide to fall unnoticed onto the track.

At 11:17 a.m., the crippled train departed with twenty-four passengers on its thirteenth run of the day, a three-minute thrill ride with twists and turns reaching speeds of forty-one feet per second.

When the unusual sounds continued, the decision was made to remove the train for inspection at the conclusion of the thirteenth ride. That proved too late. As the train exited a banked curve, the movement broke an axle rod. The unstable axle eventually wedged itself between the track tie and the locomotive, pushing the locomotive up and back over the first car, crushing Torres inside. He died and ten others were injured. Afterward, state inspectors found parts of the ride scattered all along the track.

The state uncovered significant maintenance and training shortcomings. Employees failed to tighten two screws holding the wheel assembly in place and failed to install a safety wire as part of the "wheel assembly attachment." Ride operators were not trained on how to respond to unusual sounds on roller coasters and did not understand the tagging system used to keep problematic rides sidelined until they were fixed. The maintenance "reliability team" did not follow proper procedure involving the use of tags on other rides. And machinists were allowed to sign for work completed by other machinists.

California required Disney to retrain all outside machinists at Big Thunder Mountain as well as those assigned to the roving "reliability" team, including their managers. The state mandated that all employees get clear instructions on what to do when an unusual noise is detected. Machinists were also forbidden to sign for work they did not perform.

Christopher Aitken's law firm filed suit on behalf of the Torres family, blaming Disney for adopting McKinsey's recommendations. "Disney knew, or should have known, that making extensive cutbacks in their safety and maintenance programs would ultimately have devastating effects on the safety of the public." The lawsuit cited pressure the company placed on employees to keep rides in service, company incentive plans that rewarded money saved, and a "run to failure" philosophy.

Disney reached a confidential settlement with the family, while McKinsey said its work "was not related to the tragic incidents at Disneyland."

Pressler, the Disney executive who solicited and implemented McKinsey's advice, wasn't around to deal with the aftermath of the fatality on Big Thunder Mountain. He left the year before to become chief executive of Gap, the clothing store chain. His mandate: cut costs. He lasted four years before being pushed out.

—

McKinsey was not held to account for what happened at U.S. Steel and Disneyland. No one sued the firm. No government agency accused it of wrongdoing. Consultants were simply doing what they were paid to do: give advice, not orders.

As a result, if something bad happened, the spotlight didn't shine on them. They took no credit publicly when their clients did well, and for years they accepted no blame when their recommendations sent companies off the road into the ditch.

U.S. Steel and Disneyland could not have been more different—one a vestige of a once great blue-collar company, the other a sunny fantasy powered by the latest technology. They were not McKinsey's most lucrative clients or most controversial. Yet they did exemplify the cold cost-cutting advice that turned the firm into the godfather of management consulting.

This core advice is not inscribed in the firm's cherished statement of values, but time and again that is what McKinsey quietly recommended to executives—as workers and communities throughout the world would come to learn when McKinsey came to town.

Chapter 1

Wealth Without Guilt

McKinsey's Values

For the smartest, most accomplished college students, a job at McKinsey & Company can seem like a path to wealth and prestige as well as an opportunity to prove themselves by solving the business world's toughest problems.

As a management consultancy, McKinsey has no peer, and acts like it. When it recruits each year, the firm might attract 200,000 applicants, hiring as little as 1 to 2 percent. A stint at McKinsey, even for a short time, is a lifelong passport to industry and government, thanks to the firm's vast alumni network reaching around the world.

Other top companies dangle promises of riches and the status that comes with them. McKinsey offers that, but also something more—the opportunity for young recruits to use their talents for a higher purpose, to make the world a better place. "Change that matters," McKinsey tells job candidates, a sales pitch of wealth without guilt. "We are a values-driven organization," McKinsey insists.

By portraying itself as a company with a heart, not just a lust for profits, McKinsey appeals to younger, idealistic students concerned about issues like global warming, inequality, and racial justice. It is a potent sales pitch and a strong message to the future wolves of Wall Street that they need not apply. But the firm also offers something just as intoxicating: influence.

For the past century, McKinsey has methodically built its marquee consultancy by selling its philosophy of scientific management to the world's best-known blue-chip companies. At one time or another most Fortune 500 companies have paid McKinsey for advice. So have more than a hundred government agencies around the world.

Because the firm won't identify clients or disclose the advice it gives, Americans and, increasingly, people the world over are largely unaware of the profound influence McKinsey exerts over their lives, from the cost and quality of their medical care to the jobs that pay for their children's education.

A search of records, including internal company documents, found that the firm has advised virtually every major pharmaceutical company—*and their government regulators*—along with health insurers, airlines, universities, museums, weapons makers, private equity firms, casinos, bookmakers, professional sports teams, and media companies, including *The New York Times.* Many of its consultants were just as comfortable advising Trump officials as they were Obama's.

Operating in more than sixty-five countries, they can whisper in the ears of despots and elected leaders alike. In fifteen of those countries, the firm has advised the military, police and defense, and justice ministries. Its consultants have weighed in on the maintenance and support of "armored personnel carriers; minesweepers, destroyers and submarines." Nations hire McKinsey to advise sovereign wealth funds worth more than $1 trillion. McKinsey's own robust earnings make it possible for the firm to run a private hedge fund for senior partners, with large parts of its roughly $31.5 billion in assets under management concealed behind a tangle of shell companies on an island tax haven in the English Channel.

McKinsey's reputation is enhanced by the success of its former consultants, including Tom Cotton, the conservative U.S. senator from Arkansas; Pete Buttigieg, U.S. secretary of transportation; Bobby Jindal, former governor of Louisiana; Sheryl Sandberg of Facebook; Lou Gerstner of IBM and American Express; and James P. Gorman of Morgan Stanley and Merrill Lynch. Outside the United States, McKinsey's alumni have also reached exalted positions, including Kirill Dmitriev, head of Russia's sovereign wealth fund; William Hague, Britain's former foreign secretary; and the former Credit Suisse CEO Tidjane Thiam.

Although the firm is named after its founder, James O. McKinsey, its spiritual leader was Marvin Bower, who joined the consultancy in 1933, ushering in an era of professionalism patterned after the prestigious Cleveland law firm where he once worked. Brilliant but uncompromising, he defined how consultants should work *and* dress. He insisted that McKinsey call itself a firm, not a company; that it run a practice, not a business; and that client work be an engagement, not a job. According to the firm's official history, "The very word *commercial,* when spoken about anyone at McKinsey, is akin to profanity," one consultant said. Because of Bower's principles—the most important being "client first"—the consultancy thrived.

A graduate of Harvard Law and Harvard Business School, Bower believed consultants are best recruited young and trained in-house because "it is easier and more effective to train outstanding people in their formative years." He didn't want consultants offering advice filtered through their prior business experience or, worse yet, their intuition.

Bower also developed the firm's valuable ties to Harvard Business School by aggressively recruiting its prestigious Baker scholars, who earned academic honors and ranked in the top 5 percent of their graduating class. Duff McDonald, who has written deeply reported books about McKinsey and the Harvard Business School, found that as of 2010 roughly five hundred Harvard Business School graduates were working for McKinsey, more than its main recruiting rivals, Goldman Sachs, Google, and Microsoft.

The business school's reputation grew as McKinsey hired more of its graduates and McKinsey gained exposure through the *Harvard Business Review.* Since 1959, the *Review* has given out the "McKinsey Awards" for the best "practical and groundbreaking management thinking" published in the magazine during the year.

If there was an award for squeezing the most out of clients, McKinsey might be the favorite to win it. A senior partner told young recruits that when he started at the firm, a McKinsey manager helped him by offering tips on building client relationships. "Wedge yourself in and spread like an amoeba," he said. "Once in, you should spread yourself in the organization and do everything." In other words, he said, act like "a Trojan horse."

Although based in New York City, McKinsey operates through semiautonomous offices in cities around the world. If New York is the city that never sleeps, so it is for McKinsey, its technical staff ready at any hour to assist consultants in different time zones prepare their findings in the firm's standard format: PowerPoint slides.

McKinsey's sales pitch appealed to Rogé Karma, a Notre Dame graduate. He picked the firm because it emphasized the opportunity to improve people's lives. "That's not Goldman Sachs's pitch. That's not the ExxonMobil pitch," he said. Karma, now a staff editor for the Ezra Klein podcast at *The New York Times,* took the long view. "By coming to McKinsey, you are going to learn a tool kit—a way of operating that will help you to be a change maker when you go out into the world. No matter what you want to do, no matter what impact you want to have, you are going to have this tool kit."

One college graduate worked at Goldman before joining McKinsey, and he said the difference couldn't be more stark. At Goldman, "there was never ever, ever an attempt to be anything other than what they were—'We are the sharks and that's why we are the best and everyone wants to work here because we are the sharks'—and that's refreshing. No one was lying to themselves at night."

McKinsey held itself out to be different. "It is clearer than ever that we need to work with our clients to consider the full impact of our work together, not just on their performance, but on society as a whole," the firm's former managing partner Kevin Sneader wrote in 2018. Toward that end, McKinsey sponsors programs to uplift women, disadvantaged youth, and people of color, as well as other nonprofit work.

Erik Edstrom joined McKinsey to combat global warming. Caitlin Rosenthal, a Rice graduate, joined McKinsey's Houston office not knowing what to expect, but was pleasantly surprised by her compassionate colleagues. "On my first day," she recalled, "I said, 'I don't want to work for any oil companies.'" Karma said he didn't want to work for a pharmaceutical company. McKinsey honored both requests. "My first project was working for a local museum," said Rosenthal, now a history professor at the University of California, Berkeley.

Other companies talk about doing well by doing good. Google once had a simple motto: "Don't be evil." That motto disappeared from the preamble to its code of conduct in 2018 during the tenure of its chief executive, a former McKinsey consultant, Sundar Pichai.

Few companies promote "values" as a recruiting tool with the fervor of McKinsey.

The sales pitch often begins when candidates are asked in interviews to solve business problems, such as how to improve vaccine distribution in Africa, an issue McKinsey actually dealt with in Nigeria. "It was very much made to seem like the kind of work I would get to do regularly if I joined," Karma said.

One Harvard undergrad said he had never heard of McKinsey but applied because his friends did. "No one grows up and dreams of being a McKinsey consultant," he said. But one night after class, while drinking wine from a Solo cup, he decided to fill out an application. After two rounds of interviews, he got an offer. "They do everything to get you to sign up on the spot." And when you do, he said, your McKinsey handlers pop open a bottle of champagne.

In their first year at McKinsey, business school graduates can make as much as $195,000, bonus included, but are often expected to work long into the night, with a demanding travel schedule. "I left after one year," Louis Hyman, an associate professor of economic history at Cornell University's School of Industrial and Labor Relations, said. "One of the feedbacks I got after an engagement was I was too academic. We don't need academics. We need athletes. It's about enduring pain, but it's also about being focused on the team, focused on the victory."

After a short orientation, new hires are assigned to projects run by engagement managers, who are in turn overseen by the firm's partners. If the newbies want to advance, they must develop relationships with partners who can arrange work for high-profile, profitable clients, the kind that senior partners notice. Without a sponsor, employees are "on the beach," meaning out of circulation, either waiting for an assignment or trying to develop their own projects.

"When I was a first-year associate, I experienced a lot of anxiety when I was on the beach while others were staffed on studies," one McKinsey partner recalled. "I would certainly laugh at myself [now] for having resented beach time doing client development work." Without finding new clients, the firm would wither away.

McKinsey employs about thirty-four thousand people, many of whom depart or, in McKinsey-speak, are "counseled to leave" after less than stellar evaluations. Those who remain have demonstrated not only their consulting prowess but also their ability to attach themselves to important people in the firm, opening the way for advancement. A small percentage are eventually elected partners or senior partners, with an income in the millions of dollars.

Leaving McKinsey is not a dishonor. It is more like college graduation, with the gift of high-level connections for future jobs. McKinsey knows that by seeding the business world with former employees, it stands to get new clients in return.

McKinsey's stature allows it to engage, mostly without criticism, in practices that others might view as awkward or inappropriate. It simultaneously consults for companies competing in the same market, so one set of consultants might be telling Company A how to beat Company B while another set is telling Company B how to beat Company A. McKinsey also consults for government agencies that regulate McKinsey clients. In addition to advising the U.S. Food and Drug Administration, McKinsey has consulted for at least nineteen pharmaceutical clients—all subject to FDA regulation.

McKinsey defends these consults on the grounds that sufficient safeguards exist to ensure confidential information is not inappropriately shared.

McKinsey's values are more than a marketing tool; they are the firm's guardian angels, according to McKinsey's noncirculating official history. "Whenever the firm has made mistakes or has allowed its ambitions to run to excess, its values have reined it in," McKinsey says. "A system of values serves as an essential foundation of long-term institutional success."

To drive home the point, McKinsey employees are asked to participate in a "Values Day" organized by offices around the world. Senior partners can use the opportunity to expound on applying McKinsey's values in day-to-day work. In 2019, the Australia managing partner, John Lydon, spoke about how, at a minimum, McKinsey should not work with clients who harm or kill people or cheat their customers.

Just before his death in 1968, the firm's chairman, Gilbert Clee, reflected on the importance of those values. He wrote, "Regardless of an individual's field of interest or what he wants to do with his life, I believe the firm offers two other great satisfactions: the ability to look yourself in the mirror every morning and to say, There's nothing I need to be ashamed of."

Those are the words of a proud McKinsey leader from another era. But there are others, many in fact, who looked and did not like what they saw. In recent years, the firm's actions often seemed to betray its vaunted value system. Beginning in 2018, as one media exposé followed another, McKinsey managers scrambled to counter what had become the gravest threat to the firm's reputation in its long and proud history. Emergency meetings were held, apologies issued, a new managing director took over, and risk management policies were strengthened.

As the firm searched for the reasons behind these problems, one explanation sat front and center, so obvious it was easy to overlook. And it just happened to be the very foundation upon which Marvin Bower had built the firm.

Until recently, McKinsey's website listed fifteen specific values that "inform both our long-term strategy as a firm and the way we serve our clients on a daily basis." Many of those values are routine and obvious, such as "build enduring relationships based on trust" and "bring innovations in management practice to all clients."

Some are directed toward creating a hospitable environment for consultants to thrive, such as "sustain a caring meritocracy." One encourages freethinking: "Uphold the obligation to dissent."

Over time, these values have been updated in small ways, but the first and foremost value—number one on the list—has never really changed: "Put client interests ahead of the firm's." McKinsey had once embraced a more expansive statement where clients came first, the firm second, money third, and personal interest fourth. In time, the money reference disappeared, perhaps because in a place obsessed with professionalism that word appeared unseemly.

Clients felt comfortable with McKinsey's values. And, from their perspective, that's as it should be, since McKinsey charges a premium for its services. When a telecom needed help several years ago, the firm billed the company more than $120 million in two years. For that kind of money, clients should get what they want.

Rosenthal, the consultant who started in McKinsey's Houston office, said the dictum to prioritize client interests sounds selfless but should not be mistaken as public service. "The language around client service makes it seem like serving a client, in and of itself, is valuable without regard for what that company is doing," Rosenthal said. "I found it jarring that client service is so high at the top without any qualifications."

Karma, the podcast editor, sees a difference between working for a manufacturing company and working for McKinsey. At a company, he said, "you are also going to have an allegiance to the product, and an allegiance to the people. You have some sort of other values." At McKinsey, "your entire job is to make shareholders more money."

All this brings into play McKinsey's second value, the imperative to "observe high ethical standards." Does that suggest that consultants, among other things, shouldn't work for clients who engage in harmful behavior or who overemphasize profits to the detriment of their employees? This is no small issue for a consultancy that has often said its main asset aside from its people is its reputation.

What happens if a client sells addictive products known to cause death, or denies immigrants compassionate treatment, or supports corrupt and undemocratic governments? These are not hypothetical questions. In each case, McKinsey had a choice and sided with the clients. "If you want to do ethical work, if that's a priority, then you have to be willing to turn down profitable opportunities. It was never clear to me that McKinsey was ever willing to do that," Rosenthal said.

Seth Green, who joined McKinsey out of Yale Law School, shares her concern. "If we don't bring a moral purpose into these businesses, then the purpose inevitably becomes the client and whatever the client is trying to achieve," Green, now a dean at the University of Chicago, said. In an essay published in *Fortune,* Green asked, "Would having the courage to tell an underperforming tobacco company to pursue more ambitious marketing tactics be an example of our values in action? If so, are these any values at all?"

Garrison Lovely joined McKinsey in part to find ways to reduce violence in prisons. "I came to my job as a McKinsey consultant hoping to change the world from the inside, believing the best way to make progress is through influencing those who control the levers of power," Lovely wrote in a 2019 essay. "Instead of being a force for good, I found myself a party to the most damaging forces affecting the world: the resurgence of authoritarianism and the continued creep of markets into all parts of life."

In decades past, the firm had largely escaped public scrutiny—the most notable exception being McKinsey's role in the Enron debacle. In part because of the constraints of another of the firm's fifteen values: "Preserve client confidences." The public and their government representatives are not in a position to judge if they don't know what McKinsey does or what it says and to whom.

Not until 2018, when the media, led by *The New York Times* and ProPublica, began doing deep dives into the firm's affairs, did many of McKinsey's young consultants first learn that they and their employer had a different interpretation of values. The *Times* wrote, "At a time when democracies and their basic values are increasingly under attack, the iconic American company has helped raise the stature of authoritarian and corrupt governments across the globe, sometimes in ways that counter American interests."

McKinsey's clients included corrupt governments in Russia, South Africa, and Malaysia. There were the Russian companies put under UN sanctions to punish President Putin for seizing Crimea. And state-owned Chinese companies that provide the economic *and military* support for its powerful ruler, Xi Jinping, who most definitely does not abide by McKinsey's "obligation to dissent."

Other controversies followed, including a revolt that erupted inside McKinsey's Washington, D.C., office over the firm's work on behalf of President Trump's harsh immigration policies and a global protest by more than eleven hundred consultants against the firm's extensive work with the world's biggest contributors to rising greenhouse gases.

The most shocking revelation, however, was McKinsey's decision to help companies sell more opioids when the abuse of those drugs had already killed thousands of Americans. Two senior partners discussed possibly purging records, apparently to hide their involvement. McKinsey agreed to pay more than $600 million to settle investigations by dozens of state attorneys general into the firm's role in fanning the opioid epidemic. The firm also issued a rare apology, and fired the two employees, but said it did nothing illegal.

"This is the banality of evil, M.B.A. edition," said Anand Giridharadas, a former McKinsey consultant and author of *Winners Take All: The Elite Charade of Changing the World.* "They knew what was going on. And they found a way to look past it, through it, around it, so as to answer the only questions they cared about: how to make the client money and, when the walls closed in, how to protect themselves."

One former senior partner blamed the opioid fiasco on the inadequacy of the firm's management structure, saying the firm grew too big to be governed as a partnership, which he said is fundamentally based on trust. "It was a great firm, and I say 'it was' because I cannot guarantee what it is today."

McKinsey's troubles eventually became an issue in the 2020 Democratic presidential primaries. With the former South Bend mayor Pete Buttigieg rising in the polls, fresh headlines about the firm prompted questions about a subject he rarely mentioned—his work as a McKinsey consultant. He initially declined to answer those questions, citing a nondisclosure agreement he signed with the firm. But as his silence threatened to overwhelm his campaign themes, Buttigieg sought permission from McKinsey to discuss his time there.

The firm, uncomfortable with the fresh scrutiny it was receiving, took the unusual step of allowing Buttigieg to describe his work, which turned out to be fairly mundane. He told *The New Yorker* he was proud of his work at McKinsey on matters like grocery pricing and renewable energy. "It was a phenomenal learning opportunity," he said.

But reports of McKinsey's untoward conduct—about helping the opioid industry and autocratic nations—left him angry. "It shocks the conscience anytime that a murderous dictator can rely on the legitimacy of a Western consulting company, especially the most prestigious company out there, in order to further their goals." In an interview with the *Times,* Buttigieg also spoke forcefully against McKinsey's preoccupation with shareholder value. "That's not good enough at a time when we are seeing how the economy continues to become more and more unequal, and we are seeing the ways in which a lot of corporate behavior that is technically legal is also not acceptable."

A more emotional response came from one of McKinsey's most famous former consultants—and frequent critic—Tom Peters, co-author of one of the bestselling business books of all time, *In Search of Excellence.* "It's nauseating," he said, referring to McKinsey's work for the opioid industry. "I am shocked. I am appalled and am pissed off."

Peters said that until he heard that McKinsey had recommended "turbocharging" opioid sales, he was still "vaguely proud" to list the firm on his CV. "No more. How do you do that and then pretend you are a values-driven company? How do you have a Values Day and do that shit? It's unbelievable."

An even bigger problem, Peters said, might be the "disinvestment in people" in favor of bigger profits. "I really think the shareholder value maximization thing has done more harm than any single thing maybe in the country. It is the father of inequality, and inequality is the father of Trump."

Several former consultants said they had a hard time understanding how a firm with such kind and caring people could take on such disreputable clients. Green, the university dean, estimates that nine out of ten of his colleagues would not work for a tobacco company or an undemocratic government, yet they would serve them under the name McKinsey.

McKinsey allows consultants to refuse assignments that conflict with their morals. Tobacco and coal-mining companies often top that list. But several veterans of the firm said this only foisted the ethical and moral choices on low-level associates, rather than the firm's leadership. And turning down work can lead to poor reviews and being counseled to leave the firm.

"There was a moral assessment that I saw at the top, meaning the way we talked about great partners—the number of clients they brought in—and I saw them lauded for cases that were at best questionable," Green said, adding that if you take on these tainted clients you have a better chance of advancing. "There's total accountability to the client; there is no accountability to society."

Karma, the podcast editor, said his transformative moment occurred when he was assigned to help a client fire fifteen hundred of its employees worldwide—"not because it was struggling, but because they wanted to make more money," Karma said. "Get them out of the door as quickly and efficiently as possible without any litigation." For him, that marked the end. "I could not come into work every day knowing everything I had worked my entire life for—all of it was being used to make other people's lives worse."

When McKinsey consultants hear over and over again that they are brilliant and the best equipped to solve a company's most complex problems, it can make them feel as though they can do no wrong. Spreadsheets—the lifeblood of number-crunching McKinsey consultants—can further insulate them from the people who might be harmed by their decisions.

McKinsey isn't eager to advertise its reputation as the consulting industry's most prolific job slasher. An orientation booklet for new recruits confidentially discusses this aspect of the business while stressing that it was "written and privately printed for readership by only the personnel of McKinsey & Co." The author, Manish

Chopra, now a senior partner, tells the story of how soon after starting at McKinsey he was assigned to an auto parts manufacturer whose new chief executive wanted a lower head count—a decision Chopra found troubling. Chopra said he had wondered why the firm was not looking to grow revenue, rather than to cut payroll. "I found it unethical to find ways to lay off people, and it was depressing to walk into the client HQ with the employees knowing why we were there."

So Chopra studied ways to boost the client's revenue through more sensible pricing. This, however, led to "countless" arguments with his supervisor. "He was livid, thinking that I was not delivering what I was asked to do." Chopra thought his McKinsey career was doomed, but to his surprise it wasn't. "The beautiful thing about our firm values is that you are obligated, not just allowed to dissent. If you feel something is wrong, it is not an option to stay quiet about it."

That may be so, but Carl Pechman, director of the National Regulatory Research Institute, said other McKinsey consultants are not at all reluctant to recommend firing employees. Pechman tells this story of his McKinsey encounter:

> I'll never forget when a young punk from McKinsey came into my office at the New York Public Service Commission and enthusiastically explained how they were rightsizing one of the state's utilities that was in financial trouble. I said, "You mean lay people off?" He responded that they were not laying people off, but rightsizing. I told him I hope he had the pleasure of being rightsized. Bottom line—these morons rightsized linemen with institutional memory—like where the lines really were—and the utility had to hire them back as consultants.

In February 2018, McKinsey disclosed that 560 senior partners had elected Kevin Sneader, a Glasgow native, as McKinsey's global managing partner. Sneader became just the twelfth partner to lead the firm since its founding.

McKinsey used Sneader's announcement as an opportunity to herald its recent accomplishments, such as doubling the number of partners over the last decade to more than two thousand and strengthening its work in "digital transformation, advanced analytics, design, and implementation." It also acquired a dozen companies in addition to founding a nonprofit organization to address youth unemployment.

"Consistently named the world's most prestigious consulting firm, McKinsey continues to deliver the top management advice [that] leaders have trusted for nearly a century," McKinsey crowed. No longer focused primarily on rendering advice, the firm said it also works "side-by-side with clients, at every level of their organizations, serving as an 'impact partner' to help them build their capabilities and execute their strategies."

Sneader knew he'd have to rebuild the firm's South African office, decimated by its ties to a major political scandal—one that brought down the country's president. McKinsey took in more than one million dollars in fees, but under pressure later agreed to repay the money. Beyond that, though, any problems appeared manageable. "We remain committed to McKinsey's fundamental values," Sneader declared. "The firm you see today is still classically McKinsey, but what we are able to do for our clients, and the impact we have, continues to redefine the profession of management consulting."

Sneader also realized the firm had to reconsider how it operated. So on May 11, 2019, McKinsey adopted a new code of professional conduct, much of which addressed client selection and client behavior. "Each of us has an obligation to maintain the highest professional standards in our client service; create an environment in which our people are respected, inspired and motivated; *consider the wider implications of our actions on society; and uphold the firm's reputation*" (italics added).

Later that year, at a town hall meeting in the firm's Washington, D.C., office, Nora Gardner, a senior partner who sits on an internal committee tasked with vetting new clients, gave the group a progress report. Consultants, she said, were now more aware of the need to more rigorously vet clients, with 30 percent more cases submitted for institutional reviews. "Roughly half of those engagements, roughly 50 percent of them, we debate, discuss, and say, 'Looks okay, proceed.' Thirty-five percent or so get guardrails. 'Please shape it differently.' Stay away from this part of the work et cetera. And about 15 percent have been no go, we're not going to do the work."

McKinsey did not name the clients it rejected.

Old habits, however, can be hard to break, as McKinsey discovered in January 2021.

In a statement, "fulfilling our responsibility to society," McKinsey had emphasized the importance of human rights. "Our commitment to human rights informs whom we serve and on what topics, and we will not do work that supports or enables human rights violations."

But when protests were planned in Moscow over the treatment of the Kremlin critic and poisoning victim Alexei Navalny, McKinsey abruptly banned its employees from supporting the protests. "In line with policy, McKinsey employees must not support any political activity either publicly or privately," the firm stated in a message to employees, according to the online news site *The Moscow Times.*

The order upset members of McKinsey's Moscow office who leaked it to people outside the firm. Under public pressure, McKinsey backtracked and said it regretted sending the message. "Our Moscow office's communication fundamentally misrepresented our policies and values," a spokesman for the firm said. "McKinsey employees are free, in their personal capacity, to exercise their freedom of expression including taking part in civic and political activities."

In terms of numbers, McKinsey's travails haven't hurt recruitment, according to Brian Rolfes, the partner in charge of global recruiting. On February 3, 2021, he shared some good news in a statement posted on the firm's website: "We are aiming to hire more new colleagues this year than any previous year in the history of the firm."

These newcomers, however, will go forward without Kevin Sneader as the managing partner who pressed for all the changes. In February 2021, for the first time in forty-five years, the firm's senior partners voted out a managing partner after just one three-year term.

Seven months later, Sneader joined Goldman Sachs.

Chapter 2

Winners and Losers

The Inequality Machine

As the second half of the twentieth century began, Americans craved one thing more than any other—stability. Having lived through the Great Depression, a world war, and violent confrontations between labor and management, they wanted no more surprises. There were homes to build, children to raise, and prosperity that seemed finally within reach.

The zeitgeist of this era was reflected in a momentous labor agreement reached between the United Auto Workers and General Motors, the world's largest automaker. Known as "The Treaty of Detroit," it gave workers for the first time their ticket to the middle class—health insurance, cost-of-living adjustments, and a pension. In exchange, workers agreed not to strike, allowing General Motors to bank steady profits without disruption. Both sides secured what they hoped was a predictable future. Seeing this, Ford and Chrysler quickly signed on.

While not apparent at the time, the year 1950 would become important for America's workers for other reasons. Sam Walton moved to Bentonville, Arkansas, to open a five-and-ten store, the forerunner of what became Walmart, the nation's largest private employer and a template for building a corporate empire on cheap labor. Marvin Bower became McKinsey's managing partner, turning the firm into the consigliere of America's most powerful corporations. And General Motors executives, seeing what labor had accomplished, began to wonder about themselves: Were *they* being paid enough?

General Motors answered that question by asking McKinsey to study executive compensation at thirty-seven different companies and report back. What McKinsey found was unexpected: worker wages were rising faster than executive compensation.

No one could have predicted how significant that study would become, for it helped spawn one of the most politically charged, corrosive issues in America today: income and wealth inequality. In 1950, the chief executive of a typical large company made 20 times a production worker's income. By 2020, CEOs made at least 351 times as much. And that didn't account for workers who lost jobs from outsourcing and corporate restructuring—business decisions often recommended by McKinsey's stable of well-connected consultants.

The McKinsey study, published by the *Harvard Business Review* and *Fortune,* hit the business community with such force that it reverberated for years to come. For the first time, executives had a feel for the market value of their jobs. "The pay of the individual executive was one of a company's most closely guarded secrets," Arch Patton, the McKinsey consultant who directed the study, wrote. Now executives could learn how they measured up against the competition.

Juan Trippe, founder and chief executive of Pan American World Airways, asked Patton to work on his company's stock options. Other companies quickly followed with similar requests. "People just came from far and wide to get some of Mr. Patton's magic and also get richer," said Mac Stewart, a former member of the firm's management committee.

Executives at railroads, public utilities, and banks were dismayed to learn they were paid less than those in the automotive, textile, and steel industries. One company president in a lower-paid industry wrote to Patton, saying he "set our industry back five years," because it implied their executives were worth less than others. Another executive wanted more income simply for bragging rights. Nobody wanted to be near the bottom, and the race to the top had begun, slowly at first, only to accelerate as each new decade arrived.

Patton made it easier for corporate directors to approve higher compensation by linking high pay to bigger company profits. Corporations that paid bonuses, he said, produced twice the profits of companies that didn't. He also discussed sweetening pay packages through profit sharing, stock awards, including options, and other benefits. Some perks were especially valuable because they helped offset what Patton called "the debilitating effect of the graduated income tax." He cited restricted stock options as the best way for executives to build an estate while increasing company profits.

Patton's studies were not designed to benefit factory workers or service employees. McKinsey was, after all, a management consultant, not a labor consultant. Two years after the Wagner Act of 1935 gave most workers the right to join unions and to collectively bargain with their employers, McKinsey started an industrial relations practice that, according to the firm's internal history, "was no doubt an attempt to capitalize on the sweeping success of labor unions in organizing the shop floors."

The firm's indifference toward workers made news when its founder, James O. McKinsey, evaluated Marshall Field's, a large department store and a revered Chicago institution. To ensure his recommendations were implemented, McKinsey took over as the store's top executive. Then things got ugly. In what became known as "McKinsey's Purge," nearly twelve hundred jobs were eliminated. The fallout from that purge is described unsparingly in McKinsey's own historical archives: "The traditionally paternalistic Marshall Field had become, in the public eye, just another heartless Depression-era corporation that protected its shareholders by firing employees with hardly any severance and no pensions to speak of. It was easy to blame McKinsey for all that and more."

Patton was much more sympathetic to company bosses. He updated his compensation studies year after year in high-profile publications. At a time when McKinsey consultants were supposed to remain in the background, he was one whom companies asked for by name. "His prolific cutting-edge writings on the subject attracted fame for himself and fortune to the firm," according to McKinsey's internal history. Patton eventually accounted for almost 10 percent of the firm's billings. Patton also wedged the door open for other

Contents

McKinsey consultants to slip in and advise companies on other business matters, generating even more income for the firm. "Then I would do the study and find out what their other problems were and obtain their confidence, and then we would go ahead and do another one and another one and another one," one partner recalled.

Patton's work wasn't universally admired in the firm. Peter Walker, who joined McKinsey in 1972 from the actuarial firm Towers Perrin, questioned Patton's conclusions, intimating that he manipulated the numbers "with the general objective of trying to prove that the CEO was underpaid—which I didn't find to be a particularly ennobling process."

Patton's work made colleagues uncomfortable for another reason. They thought it posed a conflict of interest. How could consultants objectively evaluate the worth of executives who hire and pay them? But discomfort is one thing, profits are another, and Patton's executive compensation practice continued for three decades before it was shut down. By then, compensation consultants had become big business, following the example set by McKinsey, conflicts of interest and all. And the compensation trend continued—more money for executives and a growing gap between them and their employees.

Walker almost never got to prove his value to the firm after he questioned why he was asked to analyze country-club memberships for company executives. "What I was asked to do is totally unnecessary," he said. Walker's performance review earned him a zero, and a lecture that captured in a few sentences McKinsey's inflated view of itself, as well as its *own* interest in bigger paydays. "You've got to understand," his supervisor said. "You don't have an MBA, you were a 2.7 math major from Union College. We wouldn't have even interviewed you, if it weren't for your background at Towers Perrin in executive compensation. So if you don't want to do any more compensation studies, then you're not going to stay at McKinsey." Walker promptly switched over to consulting on insurance issues and enjoyed a long and prosperous career at the firm.

As corporations evolved, their priorities changed, including their attitude toward employees. In the 1950s and most of the 1960s—the era of giant conglomerates—CEOs were risk averse, content to take the long view in building for the future. As John Kenneth Galbraith wrote in his 1967 book, *The New Industrial State,* these companies favored stability, not profit maximization, allowing time to develop products that improved people's lives. Within limits, they sought to keep their employees content, if not wealthy. While not everyone got what they wanted, most generally found that their lives seemed more predictable and secure.

The former McKinsey consultant Louis Hyman, an economic historian, described the benefits of this approach: "Paper pushers of the middle class could count on their jobs as their families grew. Working stiffs knew the plant would be open the next year and that their industrial union would get them a raise, but not a revolution."

Stability as a virtue in American life did not last, giving way to the protests of the 1960s, as society addressed festering social problems. And it wasn't long after Galbraith's book that the American corporation began its metamorphosis from a stable pillar of American society into an entity that first and foremost served the whims of Wall Street, often to the detriment of employees and their surrounding communities. Leaner, not bigger, became the goal. And McKinsey was on hand to clothe its clients in the fashion of the moment.

This change grew out of what Hyman called "a new, strictly financial view of corporations, a philosophy that favored stock and bond prices over production, of short-term gains over long-term investment." Consultants, he said, enthusiastically endorsed this change, steering corporations toward rewarding the few over the many, and investors over society. "The corporation under the consultants' helm was no longer an enduring venture; it became a momentary assemblage whose value was not in tomorrow's progress but in today's stock price."

To keep in step with the times, McKinsey steeped itself in the latest management theories, pleasing partners eager to move beyond simple market research into business strategy, organizational design, and difficult analytical problems. This recalibration displeased the McKinsey consultant Tom Peters, who believed that managers had forgotten the basics, such as customer service and recognizing the value of employees.

In a column for *The Wall Street Journal,* Peters unloaded on the firm where he still worked. "In many cases, they have been seduced by the availability of MBAs, armed with the 'latest' in strategic planning techniques." Peters acknowledged that McKinsey did not appreciate his comments, with one partner even suggesting he be fired. That didn't happen; Peters quit before *In Search of Excellence* was published and he went on to write another bestseller.

Executives and their consultants had legitimate reasons for wanting to reimagine the American corporation. Cheap, high-quality Japanese products were challenging U.S. manufacturers, especially in the auto industry, prompting General Motors once again to seek help from McKinsey. But instead of focusing on quality-control issues, a major reason for Japan's success, GM and McKinsey embarked on a massive corporate reorganization, notable mostly for how much it cost and how little it accomplished. In the end, the workers paid the stiffest price for this miscalculation through job losses.

The 1980s brought more instability, sparking a breathless string of stories about sudden riches, corporate raids, leveraged buyouts, and the fading appeal of once stable companies. "Billions could be made by buying up American companies and loading them with mountains of debt," said Les Leopold, director of New York's Labor Institute and author of *Runaway Inequality*. As these raiders got rich off what Leopold called "the deindustrialization of America," their apologists praised them for making corporations more efficient. Some companies had indeed become complacent, but raiders often bought companies to break them up and sell off the pieces, leaving thousands of employees without jobs. "This is not the invisible hand of the market," Leopold said. "This is the financial extraction process."

The Business Roundtable, with a membership of the nation's most powerful corporate bosses, did not believe that companies should have societal interests beyond their own well-being. The business group had a simple philosophy: a corporation should "generate economic returns to its owners." In other words, stockholders. End of story.

The fealty of corporations to Wall Street meant job security became less important. "It was the corporate downsizing of the late 1980s that first broke the traditional covenant that traded job security for loyalty," three McKinsey consultants wrote in their book,

The War for Talent. "Within a few short years, the old taboos against job hopping had evaporated and it had become a badge of honor to have multiple companies on one's resumé." The book included charts with statements like this one: "The old reality: Employees are loyal. The new reality: People are mobile and their commitment is short term."

McKinsey's attitude toward job security is reflected in its own, up-or-out practice, where each individual is regularly reevaluated and those who fail to impress are, in McKinsey's parlance, counseled to leave. The vast majority do leave, mostly because the firm nudges them out, or they disliked the work, or they saw McKinsey as an entrée to managing their own company. But leaving McKinsey is vastly different from blue-collar workers losing their jobs. A résumé that includes a stint at McKinsey almost guarantees another high-paying job. Blue-collar workers, on the other hand, inhabit a grimmer world with fewer options.

In an article, "How McKinsey Destroyed the Middle Class," published in *The Atlantic,* the Yale law professor Daniel Markovits wrote about this loss of loyalty. "When management consulting untethered executives from particular industries or firms and tied them instead to management in general, it also led them to embrace the one thing common to all corporations: making money for shareholders." According to McKinsey, modest profits were no longer acceptable. "Outstanding corporations do win the right to survive, but not the ability to earn above-average and even average shareholder returns over the long term," McKinsey consultants wrote.

To create an "outstanding corporation," managers had to keep their stock price high, and cutting costs through layoffs was usually easier and quicker than boosting revenue. Chief executives benefited from higher stock prices in part because their income was increasingly tied to the value of that stock. Layoffs were often couched as necessary to improve efficiency, and no company could match McKinsey's long record of running up a company's body count. Call it downsizing or restructuring, the result was the same: sending workers home without a job. Duff McDonald, who wrote a history of McKinsey, put this part of the firm's business in context. "There is a distinct possibility," he wrote, "that McKinsey may be the single greatest legitimizer of mass layoffs than anyone, anywhere, at any time in modern history."

Labor unions, with their declining influence, provided little protection. In 1954, more than 34 percent of hourly and salaried employees were union members. By the 1980s, only 20 percent. In 2020, just 10 percent.

With no loyalty to workers, companies began outsourcing good, middle-class jobs to southern states where wages were lower. These job losses were just the beginning. Soon the search for cheap labor expanded into other countries as new technology made it easier to operate a business thousands of miles away. Called offshoring, it had no bigger cheerleader than McKinsey, which had come to see itself as more of an international firm than an American one. "We have unparalleled experience in advising organizations on how, where and with whom to partner for a wide range of global outsourcing and offshoring opportunities," McKinsey boasted.

Steven Greenhouse, the esteemed former *New York Times* labor writer, wrote in 2008 that offshoring, more than any other economic force since the Depression, provoked fear among American workers because it affected blue-collar and white-collar workers alike. "Globalization used to hurt just the Bud crowd, but now it is also hitting the Starbucks crowd."

McKinsey initially focused on India, where it aggressively promoted that country's educated, English-speaking population as a landing spot for U.S. corporations seeking cheap labor. With McKinsey's help, India became the world's top offshoring location, earning the nickname "Offshore-istan." According to Anita Raghavan, who has written about the rising influence of the Indian elite, McKinsey's success in India was due largely to two senior leaders in the firm, Rajat Gupta, the firm's managing partner from 1994 to 2003, and Anil Kumar, who had developed the firm's internet practice in Silicon Valley. Kumar, pompous and abrasive, was not popular in the firm, but he had a powerful ally in Gupta, who shared his desire to spur economic development in India.

McKinsey worked closely with two of India's biggest outsourcing companies: the trade group NASSCOM; and Infosys, which specializes in information technology and business consulting. McKinsey continued to advise Infosys as recently as 2020. Offshoring hurt American workers, but it was very good for India's economy. "Our employee stock options program created some of India's first salaried millionaires," Infosys boasted on its website.

McKinsey, as a matter of policy, does not identify clients, but an offshoring facilitator said the five U.S. companies outsourcing the most jobs to India were five McKinsey clients—Ford Motor Company, American Express, Microsoft, General Electric, and Cisco.

To find the best offshoring locations, the firm evaluated twenty-eight low-wage countries for infrastructure, talent, cost, and business environment. McKinsey praised offshoring in public statements and in a 2006 book, *Offshoring: Understanding the Emerging Global Labor Market.* Among the benefits, the firm said, were economic growth, innovation, and the ability of consumers to buy products at lower prices.

"Companies move their business services offshore because they can make more money—which means that wealth is created for the United States as well as for the country receiving the jobs," McKinsey said. The benefit, the firm said, was a "bigger cake" for everyone to share. McKinsey pointed to how the airlines save money through offshoring: "By leveraging cheap labor, airlines are now able to chase delinquent accounts receivables that they would earlier be forced to ignore."

Even companies with offshore operations were encouraged to do more. "Companies aren't getting the most out of their offshoring programs," McKinsey concluded, especially in finance. But McKinsey praised some General Electric units for successfully offshoring as much as 35 to 40 percent of their finance operations, including accounts payable, regulatory preparation, tax compliance, and cash management.

McKinsey promulgated its views on offshoring through its think tank, the McKinsey Global Institute, which the firm described as independent and highly regarded. How "independent" the institute really was is debatable. In a 2003 report on offshoring, McKinsey said the institute's "primary purpose" was to better understand the global economy "for the benefit of McKinsey clients and consultants."

Josh Bivens, an economist and a research director at the liberal-leaning Economic Policy Institute, views the McKinsey Global Institute with skepticism. The group wants to portray itself as "neutral public intellectuals, just looking at the evidence, and isn't it amazing?" Bivens said. When in fact, he added, the group was trying "to provide an intellectual gloss" on a profit-making endeavor. "They love to focus on the winning side while ignoring or pretending there isn't even a losing side," Bivens said.

Concerned about the loss of American jobs, Congress held hearings on outsourcing, including one on June 14, 2007, where Marcus Courtney, representing tech workers, estimated that between 3.3 and 14 million service industry jobs were vulnerable to offshoring. Courtney cited one published report that said already more than 1.1 million jobs in software, semiconductors, and telecoms had left the country in the previous five years.

McKinsey acknowledged that some American workers may suffer in the short term, but said that shouldn't overshadow the benefits. "Focusing the offshoring debate on job losses misses the most important point: offshoring creates value for the US economy by creating value for US companies," McKinsey wrote. It also produces new revenue and repatriates earnings that indirectly help create jobs for displaced workers. Some displaced workers can move to "other, high value-added activities," McKinsey said.

In any case, McKinsey said, "job losses must be seen as part of an ongoing process of economic restructuring, with which the U.S. economy is well acquainted"—cold comfort for jilted workers trying to feed their families.

The Nobel Prize–winning economist Joseph E. Stiglitz said McKinsey's views on free trade and globalization are flawed. "Even in the best of circumstances," he wrote in *The New York Times,* "the old free trade theory said only that the winners could compensate the losers, not that they would. And they haven't—quite the opposite." Yet free trade agreements retained support because of what he calls "bogus, debunked economic theory, which has remained in circulation mostly because it serves the interests of the wealthiest."

With manufacturing and desk jobs disappearing, McKinsey nonetheless continued to support paying executives more money, citing heightened competition for managerial talent. Although the firm had closed its executive compensation practice, that didn't mean it couldn't advocate very publicly for higher CEO pay. "Talented managers expect to make a lot of money," McKinsey consultants wrote.

So what constituted talent? That was what the three McKinsey consultants tried to answer in their book *The War for Talent.* "Talent is a seductive word, one which people seem to implicitly understand. And they wonder about their relationship to it. Am I 'talent'? How do I increase my talent?" A question, no doubt, for the consultant who wrote that sentence. And then there was this fortune-cookie advice: "Data provide compelling evidence that better talent management results in better performance." Pity the executives who needed McKinsey data to tell them that.

Since McKinsey won't discuss executive compensation at specific companies, its thinking on the matter can be gleaned in part by examining the pay structure at Enron, the failed energy company. Again and again, the firm held out Enron as a model of the modern, successful corporation. It was run by a former McKinsey partner, with help from McKinsey consultants, one of whom even sat in on board meetings. According to *Forbes,* Enron's top five executives took in nearly *$300 million in one year alone* and more than $500 million over a five-year span ending in 2000, most of it from cashing out stock options. Enron eventually collapsed amid allegations of fraud, resulting in the loss of thousands of jobs. (McKinsey was not charged with any wrongdoing.)

Thanks in part to compensation consultants, the offspring of Arch Patton's practice, executive compensation has risen to previously unimaginable heights, prompting a committee of the U.S. House of Representatives to investigate. At a congressional hearing in December 2007, the panel reported that almost half of the nation's 250 biggest public corporations had used compensation consultants with conflicts of interest. Those with the biggest conflicts, the committee's research found, tended to pay their CEOs more. "CEOs don't just get salaries anymore," said Representative Henry Waxman. "They get stock options, restricted stock units, deferred compensation, executive pension plans, lucrative severance packages and a vast array of perks from corporate jets to tax and financial planning services and country club memberships." Roughly 80 percent of a CEO's compensation is stock related, one study found.

The ever-helpful McKinsey published a report in 2002 offering a tip for executives on how to keep their stock price elevated. Executives should spend time, the report said, getting to know their largest investors so that upon hearing of a major new corporate decision, the investors don't panic and dump their shares, sending the stock price lower. But understanding the sentiments of investors without disclosing nonpublic information is tricky. For that reason, McKinsey advised executives to canvass their investors in a way that cannot be construed "as passing insider information." A high stock price, of course, benefits the company *and* the CEO, whose compensation is increasingly linked to the stock price.

As the middle class continued to suffer, and the plight of America's workers became harder to ignore, even McKinsey began to realize that a corporation's myopic fixation on shareholder profits might not be good for society. "While shareholder capitalism has catalyzed enormous progress, it also has struggled to address deeply vexing issues such as climate change and income inequality," McKinsey acknowledged in 2020.

The firm even reconsidered its unqualified praise of offshoring. According to a Bloomberg report, Richard Dobbs, a McKinsey senior partner and a member of the McKinsey Global Institute in London, described his firm's view of globalization as an evolution. McKinsey still supports globalization, he said, but added, "There's a however, and we need to be more aware of the however."

What happens when Walmart plants its flag in a new community is not an unfamiliar story. Cheaper products and market power force local retailers to lower their prices or close their doors while generally depressing wages in the community. But for 1.5 million Americans, Walmart does offer something they need—a job and the self-respect that comes with it. What it doesn't offer is easy passage to the middle class or the certainty of staying there.

By 2005, the average annual salary at Walmart, a McKinsey

client, was roughly $17,500, while the median household income in the United States was almost $50,000. Nearly half the children of Walmart employees, called associates, were on Medicaid or uninsured. Without a union to represent them—the company is rabidly anti-union—the only leverage employees had for better treatment was public exposure, and the pressure that might bring to bear on management.

Reputation was a major Walmart concern in 2005 as the company enlisted McKinsey to look at how it could slow the growth of employee costs, especially health care. "Walmart's healthcare benefit is one of the most pressing reputation issues we face," Susan Chambers, a Walmart executive, wrote in a confidential memo—prepared with the help of McKinsey—to the company's board of directors. She blamed "well-funded, well-organized critics, as well as state government officials," who were carefully scrutinizing Walmart's benefits.

Chambers acknowledged some criticisms were valid, notably that the coverage was expensive for low-income families and that "a significant percentage" of associates and their children were on public assistance. For that reason, a smaller percentage of employees enrolled in the company's insurance plan compared with most national employers. Another problem, Chambers concluded, was perception. "We have not effectively communicated the generosity of our healthcare benefits to the general public."

To address these issues, Walmart asked McKinsey to help lead a fifteen-person team tasked with making recommendations.

One thorny issue uncovered by the task force was that worker tenure at Walmart had grown, seriously impacting the company's finances. Because of longer tenure, more associates qualified for benefits and more paid time off. "An even more important factor is wages, which increase in lock-step with tenure and directly drive the cost of many benefits."

Whereas other companies might celebrate employees for their loyalty and experience, apparently Walmart was not one of them. "Given the impact of tenure on wages and benefits, the cost of an associate with seven years of tenure is almost 55 percent more than the cost of an associate with one year of tenure, yet there is no difference in his or her productivity," the task force found. "Moreover, because we pay an associate more in salary and benefits, as his or her tenure increases, we are pricing that associate out of the labor market, increasing the likelihood that he or she will stay with Wal-Mart." More than anything, this showed how attitudes toward labor had changed since the Treaty of Detroit once held out the promise of a more secure future for workers, one in which their children might have a better life than their parents.

Walmart associates typically spent nearly twice the national average on health care for themselves and their families. Walmart's insurance did not cover routine child immunization. "Governments are increasingly concerned about healthcare costs, and many view Walmart as part of the problem," according to the task force report. Walmart feared states might start requiring companies to report how many of their employees needed Medicaid coverage. In fact, when Minnesota legislators tried to do just that, Walmart lobbied hard against it, releasing a letter stating that the bill was nothing more than a "misguided, destructive assault on a business trying to create 100,000 new jobs this year."

The task force, with the help of McKinsey, recommended that the company increase the percentage of part-time workers, though that would lower the company's health-care enrollment, possibly impacting the company's "public reputation." The group also said management should consider reducing its overall investment in profit sharing and 401(k) programs, lower its company-paid life insurance coverage, and move employees to "consumer-driven" health plans. Finally, to fend off criticism that too many employees needed Medicaid, the task force suggested reframing the debate by suggesting that Medicaid "is everyone's problem, not just Walmart's."

As different as Walmart is from other big companies, it shares one business practice with them. When products or supplies can be purchased more cheaply in low-wage countries, Walmart will do that. In 2005, a longtime Walmart supplier of sprinklers laid off almost all its workers. The company president blamed Walmart for insisting that his company produce the sprinklers more cheaply in China, according to Charles Fishman's book *The Wal-Mart Effect.*

Fishman visited employees who lost their jobs after years of working for the sprinkler company. He found a mixture of bitterness, sadness, and worry.

> ROSE DUNBAR: I went home and cried for a week. I was overwhelmed. I didn't know what to do. I started at Nelson at $4.50. I left at $10.85 an hour fifteen years later. . . . I'm sixty years old. I'm too young to retire. But I'm not desirable. I'm divorced, my daughter lives with me—she doesn't make much—and my two granddaughters.

> TERRI GRAHAM: Earlier this year, they had . . . people walking around the plant and videotaping us working. That was horrible, horrendous. Right in our faces.

> SALLY STONE: Nelson is sending some of the people over to China, like the team leaders, the maintenance men, they are going to China to train the people there and set up the machinery for them.

Those interviews don't fully capture the extent of Walmart's reliance on cheap foreign labor. In the first years of the new millennium, Walmart imported an astounding $30 billion in goods from China alone. Peter Walker, who clashed with Patton half a century ago and has done extensive work in China, told a Fox News host, "If my McKinsey buddies were here today, I think they would say, as I have, that free trade was so the dominant mantra of the time that anything that could be done to foster that and make anything anywhere was pretty much unquestioned."

Fishman reminded readers that Walmart had done other unpopular things. It once locked employees in some stores overnight; forced some employees to punch out and keep on working; and used undocumented immigrants to clean some stores overnight. (McKinsey had no role in these incidents.) In light of all this, Fishman concluded,

> Wal-Mart can't seem to grasp an essential fact: the company has exactly the reputation it deserves. No, we don't give the company adequate credit for low prices. But the broken

> covenant Sam Walton had with how to treat employees; the relentless pressure that hollows out companies and dilutes the quality of their products; the bullying of suppliers and communities; the corrosive secrecy . . . none of these is imaginary or trivial.

Since Fishman's book, Walmart has changed some of its more controversial practices by beefing up health-care coverage, doing more to protect the environment, and behaving in a more socially responsible manner. Following a mass shooting in one of its stores, Walmart banned the sale of handguns and ammunition for military-style weapons. But employees will still struggle to pay their bills. In 2020, Walmart began testing a plan in five hundred stores that raised the minimum wage from $11 to $12 an hour for certain employees.

McKinsey has continued to advise Walmart. In one recent two-year period, the retailer paid the firm more than $5 million in fees, along with $3.2 million to a McKinsey initiative aimed at helping young workers find jobs.

In late November 2017, the chief executive of AT&T, Randall Stephenson, came to the Economic Club of New York on the fiftieth floor of the Empire State Building to praise President Trump's tax cut proposal and to make a promise to his employees. Leaning back in his chair onstage, Stephenson said that if Trump's $1.5 trillion tax cut became law, he would hire 7,000 more workers, invest at least $1 billion in capital improvements, and pay $1,000 bonuses to 200,000 employees. The jobs would not be entry level, he said. "These are 7,000 jobs of people putting fiber in the ground, hard hat jobs that make $70,000 to $80,000."

AT&T explained that the bonuses would go to union members, nonmanagement employees, and frontline managers.

AT&T could afford to be magnanimous. Under Trump's proposal—which Democrats said benefited mostly big corporations that didn't need help—AT&T would save an initial $21 billion in taxes. "If the President signs the bill before Christmas, employees will receive the bonus over the holidays," AT&T said.

—

Three days before Christmas, Trump signed the bill into law and tweeted his thanks to corporations like AT&T. "Our big and very popular Tax Cut and Reform Bill has taken on an unexpected new source of 'Love'—that is big companies and corporations showering their workers with bonuses." A spokeswoman for AT&T said the bonuses were paid as promised.

In the three years after the tax cut, AT&T paid McKinsey more than $35 million. It did not take long for AT&T's promises to unravel. Instead of adding jobs, AT&T eliminated nearly eleven thousand jobs in the first six months after Trump's tax cut became law, according to the Communications Workers of America. And jobs kept disappearing. By June 2020, more than forty thousand jobs were eliminated, the union said. One former McKinsey consultant said the firm earned its money reorganizing parts of the company.

Stephen Smith had worked for more than twenty years at a call center in Connecticut when, with no warning, he learned the company was closing three area call centers, including his. At age forty-six, Smith had to search for a new job. As reported by *The Guardian*, Smith said about ninety employees were offered severance packages or the option of relocating to Georgia or Tennessee—not a viable option for employees with spouses who worked, or who had children in school. Cindy Liddick had worked at the AT&T call center in Harrisburg, Pennsylvania, for twelve years before it closed in 2018. "My husband is very ill, I'm about to lose my health insurance and starting over in the job market at my age is going to be tough," Liddick said.

Joe Snyder, president of a CWA local in Akron, said, "It looks like AT&T is pushing the work to low-paid contractors who do not have the same training, experience, and commitment as CWA members. The money they are saving goes into the pockets of wealthy shareholders looking for short-term profits." Advising AT&T has been extraordinarily lucrative for McKinsey. In just one five-year period in the early 1990s, the company paid McKinsey $96 million.

Another telecom company, Verizon Communications, paid McKinsey a grand total of at least $120 million in 2018 and 2019.

Nearly two hundred McKinsey consultants—*two hundred*—worked on the Verizon account, a former McKinsey employee said in an interview. "We were running fifteen to twenty separate teams," the former employee said, adding that there were similar numbers from other consulting firms. "We were always running into classmates in the lunchroom. It was a running joke."

At times, there were as many consultants as Verizon employees, the former McKinsey employee said. Verizon might have spent at least part of the $120 million to hire permanent employees or upgrade their own staff. Stated another way, Verizon—and AT&T—outsourced their jobs to consultants who would come and go, with little or no loyalty to the companies they advised, beyond pleasing the managers who hired them, ensuring that the next wave of consultants would be as welcome as they were.

By late 2018, more than ten thousand Verizon employees had taken a voluntary buyout. McKinsey said payroll reductions were "not a focus of our work." Even so, Nell Geiser, research coordinator for the Communications Workers of America, said the job cuts were made to meet Wall Street's expectations. "The fastest way to get there is through staff reduction," Geiser said.

Anand Giridharadas, a former McKinsey consultant, believes the nation's failure to address income inequality has turned people against government and against each other. "Many millions of Americans, on the left and right, feel one thing in common: that the game is rigged against people like them," he wrote in *Winners Take All.* "Perhaps this is why we hear constant condemnation of 'the system.' "

A study by the Federal Reserve Board in Washington, D.C., documented that over the last four decades the rising market power of corporations contributed to some of society's most intractable problems: wage growth stagnated as productivity grew; before-tax profit of U.S. corporations rose sharply as income inequality worsened; and household debt rose as financial instability increased. Even the Business Roundtable in August 2019 reevaluated its position that corporations should serve only shareholder interests—a reflection, McKinsey said, "of tensions that have been boiling over."

With offshoring out of favor with many Washington policy makers, the McKinsey Global Institute defended its support of globalization, saying outsourcing and weaker labor unions had been wrongly cited as leading causes of income inequality. The more likely culprits, McKinsey said, were the "boom and bust cycles in the economy" and technological advances. "While much of the public conversation on this issue has been about jobs lost and jobs displaced, the more important story is one about transformation," McKinsey said.

Giridharadas said McKinsey's problem involves more than just whom it advises. "Even at its best, much of the work is about increasing investors' share of the profits by reducing labor's share."

Seemingly every hour, McKinsey peppers the internet with thoughts and suggestions on how companies can cope with the impact of income inequality. They are a veritable catalog of McKinseyisms. "What is your company's core reason for being?" the firm asks. "What's needed is relatively clear: it's deep reflection on your corporate identity—what you really stand for." While the question may be clear, McKinsey said, the answers are not. "How do you pull this off? What are the mechanics of getting it done and making it real?"

McKinsey offered some New Age wisdom: "As you strive to connect the superpower of your business with its impact on society, you're likely to identify a rich constellation of potential purpose initiatives." For people unsure of their beliefs, McKinsey suggested an app through which they can "explore their values and purpose and make workplace connections to enable the pursuit of those aims."

McKinsey rarely apologizes for past mistakes, but it seems appropriate to look back at Arch Patton, who started the march toward higher executive compensation. Later in life, he was asked by a reporter how he felt about the impact of his work.

His one-word reply: "Guilty."

Chapter 3

Playing Both Sides

Helping Government Help McKinsey

In the mid-1990s, a team of McKinsey consultants descended on the Illinois capital of Springfield in pursuit of a utopian dream: to break the cycle of poverty by weaning the poor off welfare with the help of a reorganized state government. The consultants were summoned there by a former partner, Gary MacDougal, who years earlier had left the firm to run a successful business, then turned to politics, helping manage the 1988 presidential campaign of George H. W. Bush.

During an unsettled time in his life, including a divorce, MacDougal had set off on a trek through the Himalayas to ponder what came next. He returned with an idea: maybe he could use his leadership skills and political contacts to reimagine how government might better attack poverty. Like many Republican colleagues, MacDougal believed welfare too often perpetuated poverty, so he vowed to help recipients become self-sufficient.

MacDougal persuaded Illinois's governor, Jim Edgar, a fellow Republican, to authorize a task force, with him in charge, to study poverty programs, set goals, and measure progress. The governor suggested teaming up with his health adviser, Felicia Norwood, an impressive young graduate of Yale Law School who knew her way around state government. Norwood became a trusted confidante.

Given the complexity of his task, MacDougal turned for help to people he knew and respected—his former colleagues at McKinsey. They answered his call with enthusiasm, dispatching a team of seven consultants, including senior partners, who took over a large office next to the Illinois State Capitol. The consultants worked on and off for months, reviewing files on 365 families that received assistance through eighteen programs administered by state agencies and private charities. They interviewed welfare recipients and government officials and visited poor neighborhoods. By the end, MacDougal said, the consultants knew the organizational shortcomings of public assistance better than anyone.

Best of all, McKinsey did everything pro bono, an in-kind contribution with an estimated value in the millions of dollars based on current prices. "The fact that the firm was volunteering their time and had no aspirations to obtain the state of Illinois as a paying client enhanced their credibility," MacDougal said, noting that the firm preferred not to work for the government, believing that real change there was unlikely.

But real change did occur in 1997 when a new law reorganized health services in the state. MacDougal said the welfare caseload dropped 22 percent in the first year under the reorganization. And it happened because of MacDougal and his helpers. "This was the biggest reorganization of state government since 1900," said MacDougal, who went on to chair the Illinois Republican Party and to advise other states on poverty issues.

Later it appeared that the firm's pro bono work may have served a purpose less noble than MacDougal believed. By learning the operational details of pro bono state clients, McKinsey laid the foundation for obtaining work later—this time for profit.

That strategy produced big rewards in Illinois. The state was privatizing Medicaid services through managed care, a system designed to control costs and quality partly by directing patients to certain doctors and hospitals. In early 2017, state officials wanted to expand the program by enrolling an additional 650,000 people but decided it couldn't be done without help. Enter McKinsey. It knew the state, having worked there years earlier with Gary MacDougal.

The new governor, Bruce Rauner, a conservative, pro-business Republican, appointed a former McKinsey official as his deputy governor. And Felicia Norwood, now the state's Medicaid director, knew McKinsey from its previous work reorganizing the state government.

Norwood also worked many years for a McKinsey client, Aetna, in its managed care division.

Governor Rauner, who had promised to cut spending and weaken unions, quickly sailed his administration into the rocks. The state had no budget for more than two years as Rauner faced off with Democratic legislators. To provide a check on the governor's fiscal decisions, voters elected Susana Mendoza as Illinois comptroller.

Small in stature and full of fight, Mendoza visited hospices, nursing homes, and hospitals to see firsthand the impact of the budget impasse on the needy. She found widespread worry and suffering. The state owed $800,000 to one company that provided home care for seniors, forcing the company to slash the number of customers from nine hundred to three hundred.

"They were screaming for help, literally," Mendoza said. "I went to a domestic violence center in Carbondale, the only one in two hundred miles. If they closed, women were going to die." Andrea Durbin, who ran an association that served families in need, said the hardest hit were "the people who are sick, who need the support from the state to be safe and healthy and get back on their feet."

It was during this budget crisis that Mendoza made a startling discovery.

With lifesaving services starving for money, Illinois officials were quietly shoveling millions of dollars out the door to McKinsey consultants. These decisions were often hatched in the dark, without legislative oversight or approval, according to Mendoza. Just three months into her new job, in March 2017, she froze $21.6 million the state had agreed to pay consulting firms for technology advice—most of it earmarked for McKinsey.

Mendoza wanted to know why private consultants "appear to be prioritized for payment ahead of critical services like senior centers, hospice care facilities and educational institutions." She gave the governor five days to answer specific questions, but she said the deadline came and went without answers.

Mendoza did not yet realize the larger story she was helping to uncover—how government became a willing accomplice in McKinsey's effort to build a health-care empire around the idea of playing all sides of the game.

State lawmakers knew little about the consulting payments, prompting a Chicago legislator, Greg Harris, to convene three hearings to learn why the state chose to pay McKinsey more than $75 million with the state in financial distress. Early on he focused on two sole-source contracts totaling roughly $24 million. The state awarded both to McKinsey without as much as interviewing a single other company.

At one hearing, Harris explained his concerns to Norwood, whose office had awarded the contracts: "When you talk about a sole source contract, where there is no bidding, no opportunity to see who else is out there, who might have better experience, better prices, that . . . as you can imagine raises a lot of questions."

No reason to worry, Norwood replied. She and her colleagues were very familiar with McKinsey's work, so there was no need to inquire elsewhere.

"Is there no internal capacity to do any of this work without going out and spending tens of millions of dollars more?" Harris asked.

Norwood said no. "The work definitely can't be done by those employees." Strategizing organizational change was deemed beyond their capabilities.

Legislators were not alone in objecting to the McKinsey contracts. The state's chief procurement officer voided one of them—worth $12 million—because Norwood erroneously concluded that competing bids were not required. One day later Mendoza froze payments on a second McKinsey contract.

Yet it was McKinsey's link to another expenditure that raised the most concern. Norwood, with McKinsey's guidance, arranged to pay $63 billion—the largest procurement in state history—to seven managed care companies to administer and pay for medical services through the expanded Medicaid program. The expenditure bypassed legislative oversight, a decision that Mendoza said was grossly misguided. "That means this proposal is not afforded the same independent oversight as, say, a contract to purchase paper clips," she said.

McKinsey, for one, was not particularly interested in having anyone look over its shoulder, even for its government work. At one hearing, Harris broached the firm's penchant for secrecy with

Norwood. He cited a provision in McKinsey's contract "that neither the state nor McKinsey can refer to each other or attribute any information to the other party in an external communication including news releases pertaining to this contract."

"Is this a standard provision in Illinois contracts?" Harris asked.

Norwood said she thought it was, but couldn't say for sure.

"That does not seem to be very conducive to transparency," Harris concluded.

Once again, Norwood said there was no cause for alarm. She explained that the giant managed care contracts, for example, were put out for bids and would be evaluated by people with no conflicts of interest. "While it is true," she said, "that I have previously worked for a managed care plan, almost 19 years to be exact," neither she nor two colleagues with ties to the health-care industry would participate in the evaluation.

Norwood's answer was accurate as far as it went, but failed to address other vital questions, such as who wrote contract specifications, which have the potential to favor one firm over another. Asked about this, Norwood said McKinsey helped state employees prepare them. Lending a hand, she said, were people from the governor's office, including another deputy governor, Trey Childress, who a year later joined McKinsey's Chicago office. In other testimony, Norwood changed her account to say Childress did not participate. Norwood did not respond to messages seeking an interview.

No one at the hearing thought to ask whether *McKinsey* had any potential conflicts of interest. The firm's client list, a closely guarded secret, would not have been available to state officials. But the authors of this book gained exclusive access to that list, and it showed McKinsey's deep financial ties to the managed care industry.

In recent years, McKinsey billed companies that provide managed care more than $200 million, making it one of the firm's most lucrative sectors. Moreover, four of the seven companies that won parts of the $63 billion Medicaid contract were later acquired by McKinsey clients. And a fifth, the parent company of Blue Cross and Blue Shield of Illinois, was McKinsey's landlord in downtown Chicago. When McKinsey leased three upper-level floors in a building owned by the insurer, *Crain's Chicago Business* called it a big win for the insurance company, which had "a hefty investment to recoup" in the building.

McKinsey did not publicly disclose these ties. A McKinsey spokesman said consultants who acquire confidential information from a client's competitor are forbidden from serving the competitor for "as long as the information has significant competitive value (typically two years)." The firm added: "Clients work with us because they trust that we will keep their confidential information safe."

Legislators wanted to know what McKinsey did to earn monthly fees of roughly $1 million. Or in the lingo of consultants, what were the "deliverables"? Harris, looking over documents at a hearing, saw something that troubled him. "Every month they repeat the same deliverables. So why is this the same without variation?" Harris asked. "I think that's a logical question."

"It is," Norwood replied.

Harris said some deliverables appeared vague, such as helping support and prepare leadership "for provider engagement sessions at appropriate cadence to be defined." At this point, some people began to laugh, he said.

"Do we have a cadence defined?" Harris asked with a touch of sarcasm.

"Is that your question?"

"Yeah, I'm just going through these, just wondering what we have gotten for the million dollars."

"We will go back and get something to you that actually specifically outlines everything we've paid and the deliverables that we've received," Norwood promised.

Six months later, Norwood left her state job for one of McKinsey's biggest clients, Anthem, a large managed care company. McKinsey has billed Anthem more than $90 million since 2018. A significant part of those billings came while Norwood served as president of Anthem's government business division. In addition to Anthem, McKinsey has consulted for at least nine other insurance company clients.

But before Norwood left state employment, another legislator, Representative William Davis, asked whether she was certain that

McKinsey had a clean record doing this kind of work. He was asking, Davis explained, because a company might have an outstanding reputation, "then lo and behold, somebody digs a little deeper and pulls back a layer of the onion" and discovers problems.

"No issues with this company that you are aware of?" Davis asked.

"To the best of my knowledge, Representative, there are no issues with this company that we are aware of."

"Are you sure about that? I want to be certain."

"I'm sure about that, Representative."

If Illinois officials wanted to pull back a layer of the onion, they might have considered a short trip across the Mississippi River to St. Louis, and then another 380 miles to Little Rock. Had they done so, they would have discovered that Missouri and Arkansas had revealing stories to tell about how McKinsey wins government contracts.

As Illinois proved, McKinsey knew not only the fine details of managed care but also how to reach people in power—the decision makers—like the former Missouri governor Eric Greitens.

In January 2017, just days after Greitens was sworn in, he created a new position specifically for Drew Erdmann, a former McKinsey partner who had once been a director with the National Security Council focusing on Iraq and Iran. It wasn't long before Missouri hired McKinsey—again, at no charge—"to assist us with understanding the key leadership and cultural elements that we need to build a high-performing organization."

After McKinsey's pro bono work, the firm stood ready to start collecting money. When Erdmann expressed interest in overhauling Medicaid, the state later that year invited McKinsey and four other consulting firms to bid on a contract to rapidly evaluate the Medicaid program and recommend changes, including ways to combat waste, fraud, and abuse.

McKinsey's submission stood out, most noticeably because it included dozens of pages that were either blacked out entirely or mostly blacked out, making any public analysis impossible. No other consulting firm did that.

A columnist for the *St. Louis Post-Dispatch,* Tony Messenger, became suspicious. He wrote, "Since Erdmann was hired, McKinsey has become a major player in Missouri state government. A key feature of their work appears to be secrecy." The state attorney general said the redactions appeared improper.

The massive redactions foreshadowed what was to come.

The state initially said the winning bidder would be selected based on the following criteria: cost 40 percent, methodology 40 percent, and experience 20 percent. But within days of issuing those specifications, the state suddenly withdrew them and issued a new rating system that de-emphasized cost. Now, instead of the cost being 40 percent, it dropped to only 15 percent. The change allowed McKinsey to more comfortably ask for more money and still achieve a high score.

And that's what happened. McKinsey won the contract for $2.7 million—*three times higher* than the lowest bid or more than the combined total of the three lowest bids. Missouri officials appeared to have copied and pasted identical evaluations in multiple sections, awarding each a 100 percent score. Competitors were judged more harshly, with specific criticisms.

There were other oddities. After submitting its best and final bid, McKinsey requested a meeting with state officials and received permission to revise its proposal—more than a month after the filing deadline. A competitor, Navigant, protested, saying state records establish that McKinsey "was afforded the opportunity to revise and resubmit material that was utilized in scoring." An earlier request by Navigant for more time to submit its original proposal was rejected.

Navigant also objected to McKinsey's extensive redactions, saying it blocked competitors from reviewing the plan "with regard to compliance or substance." Navigant added, "A bid process is required to be open and transparent once completed. This is anything but that." The state said it had no obligation to publish a full bid proposal online, but later removed the redactions. State officials rejected Navigant's protest, saying all applicable rules were followed.

The Missouri House minority leader, Gail McCann Beatty, a Democrat, accused the Greitens administration of rigging the selection process for McKinsey, a charge state officials, including Erdmann, denied. Another house member, Peter Merideth, said the contract didn't pass the smell test. "I don't trust them for a second," he said, referring to McKinsey. Merideth also thought it strange that McKinsey seemed to follow local legislators on social media. "One guy in New York is usually the first to 'like' something I post on social media. Why is it?"

A consumer group, Missouri Health Care for All, also had questions about McKinsey. "We cannot know if McKinsey has any conflicts of interest because we don't know who all their current clients are," the group wrote.

That proved prescient. The three companies Missouri hired to administer the new Medicaid program were either McKinsey clients or soon-to-be McKinsey clients. One of them, the St. Louis–based Centene Corporation, "faced serious charges of mismanagement resulting in at least $23.6 million in penalties in more than a dozen states," *The Des Moines Register* reported in 2018. Those charges, which did not accuse McKinsey of wrongdoing, included "inadequacies" in providing the poor and elderly with access to doctors, according to the newspaper. McKinsey billed Centene more than $50 million in 2018 and 2019.

Shawn D'Abreu, the consumer group's policy director, said Missourians didn't get much for their $2.7 million. While McKinsey's report contained some good ideas, the firm acknowledged that many of its suggestions were already known to state officials.

"Anybody could have gone to the Department of Social Services, interviewed a couple of people, and within a day or so written the exact same report in terms of the things that we identify as good," D'Abreu said. An exaggeration? Perhaps. But the McKinsey report raised other questions as well.

"Nearly all of the major recommendations for 'transformation' can be found in other reports on McKinsey's website," the consumer group wrote. "It's fair to question whether Missouri is getting tailored recommendations for our state or cookie cutter solutions."

McKinsey's evaluation avoided antagonizing Missouri's Republican lawmakers. "The report seems to blame the state's budget woes on the Medicaid program, ignoring the impact of repeated tax cuts," the consumer group wrote. Overall, McKinsey appeared to favor managed care profits over access to health-care services, the group said.

By 2019, Missouri's new vehicle for delivering Medicaid services began leaking oil. A sharp drop in the number of Medicaid enrollments—especially among children—worried Herb Kuhn, chief executive of the Missouri Hospital Association. "When we see over 50,000 children come off the Medicaid rolls, it raises some questions about whether the state is doing its verifications appropriately," he said. Merideth, the state representative, put the number closer to 100,000.

Either McKinsey didn't recommend a plan that would have prevented this, or the state ignored McKinsey's advice. A third possibility is that Missouri's economy improved, but advocates for the poor discounted that explanation. Legal Services of Eastern Missouri put more of the blame on McKinsey's report, which recommended ways to cut Medicaid costs. "Because of its focus on cost savings, the report generally fails to analyze the potential impact of its recommendations on health access and outcomes," the legal services group wrote in a report.

Merideth said managed care failed in another area. "They sold us on saving money," he said, yet Missouri has among the highest per-patient Medicaid costs in the nation. How much responsibility, if any, McKinsey bears for these high costs is an open question.

Managed care if done right can control costs, improve medical outcomes, and deliver better value than the traditional fee-for-service system, which rewards volume over quality and cost. But when managed care doesn't deliver on those promises, the industry has been known to invest in lobbyists to push for more favorable Medicaid rules, according to Dr. Joshua M. Sharfstein, a health policy expert at Johns Hopkins. "I am not opposed to managed care plans in Medicaid, but their engagement is not a magical solution," he said. If the plans are to work as intended, he added, then states must provide "robust oversight."

McKinsey's close ties to insurers were evident in neighboring Arkansas, where Blue Cross Blue Shield took the unusual step of offering the state a $1.5 million grant if it would hire McKinsey to evaluate the Medicaid program. The state took the money, added another $1.5 million, then gave the full amount—$3 million—to McKinsey through an "emergency" sole-source contract.

Several months after awarding the contract, Arkansas had another surprise. Andy Allison, a health economist, tells of interviewing for the job of Arkansas Medicaid director and finding himself in an office with a McKinsey senior partner, David Nuzum. "A McKinsey partner was sitting in my interview," Allison recalled. "They needed advice to figure out if I could do what I was being hired to do." Nuzum declined to be interviewed. But according to McKinsey, Nuzum "was invited in impromptu to speak with Mr. Allison for a few minutes" and played no role in vetting him.

Allison got the job. He came wanting to use Medicaid funds to buy private health insurance for low-income individuals. But it was McKinsey that benefited the most, managing to parlay that $3 million initial contract into state business totaling more than $100 million—without ever having to submit a bid. Quite a haul for one of the nation's poorest states. Later, a legislative audit concluded that the original, $1.5 million Blue Cross–brokered contract, awarded before Allison arrived, was given out improperly and should have been put out for bids.

In an interview for this book, Allison said McKinsey received sole-source contracts because no other firm had the necessary skills to transform Medicaid. "Innovation and payment reform requires a great deal of understanding of the medical market," he said. "No consultancy can pull that off other than McKinsey." Had he sought competitive bids, Allison said, McKinsey would still have emerged as the best. "It would have been the same answer—only much, much slower."

McKinsey must have liked what it saw in Allison, because the firm hired him in 2015, a little more than six months after he left his state job, a development that legislative auditors thought significant enough to include in a highly critical report on the state's stewardship of Medicaid funds.

McKinsey's success in Illinois, Missouri, and Arkansas is more than luck and regional knowledge. The firm's long reach extends well beyond the borders of those states and includes a formidable list of clients spanning the entire health-care supply chain, along with their government regulators. It also creates an almost unquantifiable potential for conflicts of interest.

Recognizing that health care could be a major profit center, McKinsey burrowed deep into state and federal agencies by selling the idea that ordinary government workers lacked the training and experience to understand the nuances of health-care economics. The firm promoted its proprietary analytics, infused with thousands of data sets from clients around the world. No longer the domain of only generalists, McKinsey now had doctors, researchers, and former government regulators on staff.

McKinsey was enormously successful, securing more than one billion dollars in state and federal consulting contracts, often without competitive bidding. Many of those contracts involved advising government agencies that regulate McKinsey's private clients in pharmaceuticals, hospitals, and insurance.

McKinsey's health-care team played an important—and much-criticized—role in the debate over President Obama's signature domestic achievement, the Affordable Care Act, the most significant health-care legislation since Medicare and Medicaid half a century earlier. The law ended years of failed Democratic attempts to help the uninsured. Millions of Americans would now have access to affordable insurance because Medicaid expanded to include not just the poor but also the near poor. Those who did not qualify because of income could use tax credits to buy insurance through a public marketplace and could not be denied coverage because of preexisting conditions.

The law infuriated Republican leaders, who perceived it as a step toward a government takeover of health care. Health insurers publicly supported the legislation but privately tried to kill it by secretly channeling tens of millions of dollars through the U.S. Chamber of Commerce to lobby against the bill.

The insurance industry didn't defeat the Affordable Care Act, but did weaken it by pressuring legislators to remove the "public option," a provision that would have allowed the government to offer competing coverage as a hedge against excessive insurance company profits. President Obama dropped that provision to win the deciding vote of Senator Joe Lieberman of Connecticut, home to several major insurance companies. Congressional Republicans lost the battle but did not stop trying to undermine the new law through court challenges and other means.

In June 2011, Republicans received an unexpected boost. McKinsey shocked Washington by releasing a survey that projected almost one-third of employers "definitely or probably" would stop offering health coverage when the law took full effect in 2014. The study suggested the cure was worse than the illness, threatening to undermine the law before it rolled out.

McKinsey's findings clashed with other studies, including those by the Rand Corporation, the Urban Institute, and the nonpartisan Congressional Budget Office, prompting Democrats to demand that the consultants release their methodology.

For nearly two weeks McKinsey refused, saying its research was proprietary, further infuriating congressional Democrats. "The findings of this survey are so markedly out of sync with the other assessments that it has raised legitimate questions about the product, including how and why it was created," Democrats on the House Ways and Means Committee wrote in a letter to McKinsey's managing partner, Dominic Barton. "The report itself states that McKinsey 'educated respondents' about the implications of the Affordable Care Act, with no indication of the content of this 'education.'" Senator Max Baucus, chairman of the Senate Finance Committee, wrote a similar letter to Barton.

"It isn't every day that the chairman of the Senate Finance Committee and three House committees simultaneously demand that a company cough up the internals of a survey like this one," the *Washington Post* columnist Greg Sargent wrote. "This constitutes real pressure, and underscores how high the stakes have become for Democrats, now that Republicans have been regularly citing the study as a weapon against the health law."

McKinsey finally bowed to political pressure and acknowledged its survey was not comparable to other, more rigorous studies and that it was not meant to be "predictive." That didn't satisfy Senator Baucus, who said the report "is filled with cherry-picked facts and slanted questions." Nancy-Ann DeParle, deputy chief of staff to President Obama, also skewered McKinsey's report, saying that nearly half of the survey's respondents knew little or nothing about an employer's responsibility under the law and nearly a quarter were "not at all familiar" with it. DeParle declined to speculate as to McKinsey's motivation to write such a report.

Had Democrats known how close McKinsey was to health insurers, they might have said a lot more.

The McKinsey report flowed straight from its standard playbook, where the firm identifies a problem lurking around the corner—a problem more serious than people realize, requiring a quick response if harm is to be avoided and prosperity achieved. Solutions are available. And McKinsey can help—for a fee.

To increase its visibility, McKinsey set up the Center for U.S. Health System Reform "to track and model the impact of regulatory change on market and consumer dynamics." The center is unambiguous about its target audience. "We support investors—including strategic buyers and private equity—to understand opportunities emerging from the latest legislative and regulatory reform trends [and] identify attractive investment areas and assets across the healthcare value chain."

"Over the past five years," McKinsey wrote in April 2018, "our healthcare practice has conducted more than 2,500 engagements with healthcare systems, private insurers and government payers, specialist hospitals, academic medical centers and ancillary service providers." That includes twenty of the biggest managed care firms, nine of the largest U.S. hospital systems, and seven of the top ten academic medical centers, "as well as multiple government payers at the federal and state level—including 12 states to transform agency operation [and] enhance their managed care approaches." In addition, the firm serves "leading retail pharmacies, ancillary service providers, industry associations, private equity firms and many of the largest U.S. employers."

With elite clients across the health-care landscape and a lofty reputation, it is easy to imagine how McKinsey could pull government agencies into its orbit.

When President Donald Trump took office in January 2017, it was uncertain how receptive his administration would be to McKinsey's style of solving problems. McKinsey believed most issues, no matter how complex, could be defined one way or another through numbers. Trump believed the best solutions to problems came from loyal friends, especially when they coincided with his own political or financial interests.

There were policy differences. Trump had forcefully opposed Obamacare and supported a failed effort by Republican members of Congress to strip out the guts of the law. In contrast, McKinsey had harvested big profits helping states adjust to the new law. But the firm had both sides of the aisle covered.

In Washington, D.C., where campaign contributions signal who merits attention, McKinsey's four biggest individual donors to political campaigns were leading health-care consultants, an indication of that sector's importance to the firm. Together they accounted for nearly half of all donations from McKinsey's thousands of U.S. employees. Martin Elling, a senior partner and a leader of the firm's pharmaceutical practice, donated the most—nearly $1 million to Democrats from 2015 to 2020. He also solicited money for candidates and used his connections with party leaders to give donors favorable accommodations at the 2016 national convention in Philadelphia, according to emails released by WikiLeaks.

The second-biggest donor was Vivian Riefberg, a senior partner who retired from McKinsey in 2020 after directing the public-sector practice and co-leading its health-care unit in the United States. She gave $346,450, mostly to Democrats. Riefberg oversaw McKinsey's contracts with federal agencies that regulate the firm's commercial clients.

The third-biggest donor, Paul Mango, gave primarily to Republicans. He led a McKinsey unit focusing on health-care reform and became an influential voice on health in the Trump administration after his appointment in 2018 as deputy chief of staff for policy at the Department of Health and Human Services, which includes the FDA.

Overall, McKinsey grabbed more FDA business in four years under Trump—$77 million—than in eight years under Obama. McKinsey has also advised at least nineteen drug companies—all subject to FDA regulation—and three major drug distributors, for which it billed a grand total of at least $400 million during a recent three-year period.

McKinsey, figuring that Big Pharma clients might want more than smart, young Ivy Leaguers, scouted former FDA officials to hire. In one job advertisement, McKinsey sought people with a minimum of five years working inside the FDA's regulatory affairs office. Applicants had to "have knowledge of, and relationships with, investigators and leadership with District Offices." McKinsey did not define "relationships." Job seekers were also required to know pharmaceutical regulations and "the immediate best steps" in responding to an FDA warning letter.

This wasn't McKinsey seeking efficiency experts to slice fat from a bloated budget. It wanted people who could, among other things, help drug companies escape trouble that might have endangered the public's health.

McKinsey insists that advising companies and their regulators does not compromise its objectivity because consultants don't share client information. But it doesn't hurt for pharma clients to know that McKinsey works both sides of the street. McKinsey posted a biography of a Chicago partner, boasting that she "serves pharmaceutical, medical-device, and consumer companies as well as regulators" on quality and compliance issues. This same partner had also developed "a comprehensive action plan" for best practices at an unidentified "major US regulator."

Even if McKinsey doesn't share confidential information, the firm's decision to work simultaneously for drug companies and the FDA puts all parties in an awkward position at best. The FDA had already drawn fire for growing too close to Big Pharma. But it was the agency's close collaboration with the drugmaker Biogen in promoting its controversial Alzheimer's drug, aducanumab, that raised the most pointed questions about the FDA's impartiality.

After two drug trials were stopped because they showed little prospect of helping Alzheimer's patients, the FDA worked behind the scenes to salvage the drug, eventually approving it over the strong objections of its own independent expert advisory panel. Ten of eleven panel members had concluded there was insufficient evidence to show that the drug worked. The eleventh member was "uncertain." Three panel members resigned in protest over the FDA's decision. One of them, Dr. Aaron Kesselheim, a professor of medicine at Harvard Medical School, called the regulator's decision "probably the worst drug approval decision in recent U.S. history."

The stakes were enormous. As many as six million Americans have Alzheimer's, and at an estimated annual cost of $56,000 per patient aducanumab represents a potential windfall for Biogen in the billions of dollars. (Biogen has since lowered the price.) Yet, some health experts say the drug falsely raises hopes of Alzheimer's families, desperate for any kind of treatment, while imposing an almost incalculable financial burden on the Medicare program.

Public Citizen's Health Research Group, an influential advocate for consumers, called the FDA's approval of aducanumab, marketed as Aduhelm, "indefensible" and "reckless" and asked federal officials to investigate.

While the Aduhelm controversy received extensive media coverage, McKinsey's behind-the-scenes role in promoting the drug has remained hidden from the public. Documents obtained in connection with the reporting of this book show McKinsey's strong support for the Alzheimer's drug. In April 2021, months after the FDA's expert panel questioned the efficacy of Aduhelm, Kevin Sneader, then McKinsey's managing partner, praised the drug, calling it a "first-in-class disease-modifying therapy for Alzheimer's." For that reason, he said, Biogen expected "massive public interest in the drug and the disease."

To help with the product launch, McKinsey partnered with UsAgainstAlzheimer's, a nonprofit advocacy group funded in part by Biogen. The result was a web and voice service to support families concerned about the disease, Sneader said. The service, BrainGuide, was developed by a joint McKinsey and Amazon Web Services team and launched on ABC's *Good Morning America.*

The Health Research Group director, Dr. Michael A. Carome, said he was unaware that the FDA and Biogen had a common thread—McKinsey—until the authors of this book questioned him about it. Dr. Carome called that relationship a clear conflict of interest. In 2018, McKinsey billed the FDA $11.6 million for advice on its drug approval process. The firm also billed Biogen nearly $10 million during roughly the same time frame, McKinsey records show. It isn't clear what McKinsey did for Biogen, apart from its work for UsAgainstAlzheimer's.

One month after the FDA's approval of Aduhelm sparked widespread criticism, the acting FDA commissioner, Janet Woodcock, called for a government investigation into how her agency interacted with Biogen before approving the drug. As a result, McKinsey instructed employees in the summer of 2021 "to preserve all materials concerning work we are doing or have done for Biogen relating to Aduhelm."

McKinsey favors a closer working relationship between drug companies and the FDA, according to government records. McKinsey cited relatively recent changes to the drug approval process as one reason the regulator's "relationship with industry has dramatically improved." But more needed to be done, the firm wrote, and it recommended that any additional changes be carried out "with the speed and agility" reflected in the agency's regulation of new drugs.

McKinsey's ties to FDA officials are sometimes developed and nurtured in private settings, like the one in September 2019 where the firm took a leading role at a drug industry conference in New Jersey, home to thousands of drug industry employees. The featured speaker was Dr. Peter Marks, director of the Center for Biologics Evaluation and Research, which performs the vital work of ensuring "the safety, purity, potency, and effectiveness of biological products," including vaccines and gene therapies.

The conference provided an opportunity to meet and hear Dr. Marks, one of the FDA's most important voices, a fact underscored by the meeting's theme: "Because Patients Can't Wait." This concern for patients, however sincere, did not apparently extend to letting patients attend the meeting. No outsiders were allowed, media included. "Please note, no walk-ins will be accepted at the event. Closed to the media," the program states. This private meeting offered drug company insiders a place to network with Dr. Marks and, as noted in the program, to hear "insights from McKinsey." Three McKinsey consultants either spoke or moderated a session.

Earlier that year, McKinsey conducted one of its featured interviews with Dr. Marks, during which he highlighted the FDA's thinking on drug approvals. "We recognize that rigorous clinical endpoints can take much longer to measure," he said, referring to clinical trials. That's why for certain drugs, he said, "we recently issued draft guidance that provides advice on potential accelerated approval."

What conversations McKinsey had with Dr. Marks at the conference are not known, or even if the subject of Biogen came up. But the next year, after the FDA's expert advisory panel had overwhelmingly found Biogen's support for Aduhelm unpersuasive, Dr. Marks joined several other FDA officials in endorsing an accelerated approval process for the drug, which ultimately occurred.

During the Obama and Trump administrations, McKinsey proved extraordinarily successful in winning federal contracts—well over $1 billion, much of it without competition, including at least $130 million with the FDA.

McKinsey pursues these contracts aggressively, sometimes too aggressively, as was the case when it asked a government official for favors later deemed unethical and a possible violation of the law. McKinsey sought the favors after federal auditors threatened to terminate a lucrative McKinsey contract that allowed the firm, for more than a decade, to get millions of dollars in FDA business without bidding for it.

This contract, with renewal options, is prized because once the government vets a company's credentials and sets a fixed price for certain services, federal agencies can buy repetitive goods and services without seeking bids. The downside is that lower prices usually associated with competition may be sacrificed in the name of efficiency.

When McKinsey tried to renew this contract in 2015, government officials insisted on a pre-award audit. McKinsey, however, refused to turn over the requested records, prompting auditors to instruct the contract officer at the General Services Administration—the agency that processes contracts for much of the federal government—to either get the records or cancel the contract.

At this point, the audit process broke down. A division director at GSA intervened at McKinsey's request and removed the contracting officer who had attempted to obtain the audit records. The GSA director then unilaterally awarded the contract to McKinsey, even though parts of it exceeded market prices by as much as 193 percent. As an added bonus, the director tacked on *an additional 10 percent rate increase, and later another 3 percent,* to the already bloated contract, according to a 2019 report by the agency's inspector general. The GSA's unjustified price increase cost U.S. taxpayers an estimated $69 million, and that did not include "any potential costs related to McKinsey's unsupported team-based pricing," a spokesman for the inspector general said in an interview.

McKinsey's success in retaining the contract prompted the firm to seek more special favors from the same GSA director, this time to help secure contracts with three federal agencies—the Centers for Medicare and Medicaid Services, the National Oceanic and Atmospheric Administration, and the Department of the Interior. What made these requests so unusual—and improper—is that all three agencies *operated outside the GSA contracting system,* so the GSA director had no standing to intervene, and in any case should not have advocated for a specific vendor. Nonetheless, the director agreed to help.

"Thank you for yesterday and for talking to NOAA," McKinsey wrote in an email to the GSA director. "We would prefer not to share financials unless asked." In another email, McKinsey wrote, "We really would appreciate your help in talking to the person listed below from the Department of the Interior. She is asking for hourly information that we don't have (as you know well)."

Separately, McKinsey asked the GSA director to help secure a contract that another federal office had repeatedly rejected, calling McKinsey's prices "ridiculous and unsupported." McKinsey was allowed to resubmit its offer and got the contract.

The inspector general was unsparing in its criticism of the GSA director, saying he "failed to comply with laws, regulations, and GSA policies by using invalid price comparisons, relying on unsupported information, and performing insufficient analyses to justify the awarded contract." The IG also said the director "abandoned his role as an impartial contracting officer," creating an appearance of impropriety that potentially gave McKinsey an unfair competitive advantage.

The GSA refused to identify the director, but records show that in 2019 he resigned from the agency before any possible disciplinary action could be imposed.

While the inspector general's investigation was ongoing, McKinsey made a bold, some would say questionable, decision to host educational summits for officials from the GSA and other federal offices. The meetings gave McKinsey an opportunity to interact and socialize with federal contracting officials who one day might be called on to pass judgment on McKinsey's business interests.

A San Francisco session, which McKinsey advertised as the "Innovative Summit on the Future of Government," targeted those "with an aspiration of learning from each other to break down barriers to innovation in government." A couple of months later, McKinsey held a "boot camp" in New York that promised "a fully immersive and interactive 24-hour workshop series focused this year on learning about how to unlock the value of customer experience transformations."

McKinsey, perhaps recognizing the bad optics of hosting an event for federal contracting officials, recommended that GSA employees "consult with your GSA ethics officer as to the appropriateness of you participating." McKinsey hastened to add that the conference had nothing to do with contract procurement, "so we hope it will be fine."

McKinsey closed out the last year of the Trump administration capitalizing on a dire health-care emergency—the coronavirus pandemic that as of March 2022 had killed more than 900,000 Americans. With the country convulsing from the pandemic, protests over police violence, and a bitter presidential election, McKinsey sought to stay in the spotlight by relentlessly churning out COVID-19 position papers, focusing less on how people should protect themselves and more on how companies could use lessons from the pandemic to improve their competitive standing. "From surviving to thriving," read one McKinsey missive.

Even the firm's leader, Kevin Sneader, joined the action, co-writing a locker-room pep talk that cited "innovation"—an all-purpose word in McKinsey's vocabulary—as the reason Brazil's soccer teams regained their swagger after falling on hard times many years earlier. Responding to mass death with cheesy buzzwords, Sneader advised companies battered by COVID to prepare "for the next normal" by adhering to his five *R*s—resolve, resilience, return, reimagination, and reform.

Whatever McKinsey was selling, governments were buying. Within months of the pandemic's arrival, the firm had amassed more than $100 million for advising local, state, and federal officials on how to respond to the crisis. McKinsey's success in lining up COVID work did not come without occasional criticism for, among other things, charging too much and uncertain results.

Jennifer Moon, deputy mayor for Miami-Dade County, emailed a lawyer in the county attorney's office to complain about McKinsey government work. "Apparently, it takes five people with staff support to do what I've been doing myself," Moon wrote in an email obtained by ProPublica. McKinsey has also received COVID-related state contracts in California, Washington, Tennessee, New York, and New Jersey.

Three Democratic U.S. senators took notice, but for other reasons. "Our first concern," they wrote in an April 2020 letter to the White House ethics officer, was that Jared Kushner, the president's son-in-law, was managing a shadow task force on COVID that included private industry and "a suite of McKinsey consultants." Apart from the lack of public accountability, the senators raised questions about who was in charge because Vice President Pence was already leading the official White House coronavirus task force.

The legislators accused Kushner's group of playing "a central role in the federal government's ongoing fiasco of procurement and delivery of ventilators and personal protective equipment." There was a silver lining, however. The task force apparently worked for free.

For a company that expends so much effort presenting itself as a voice for health-care reform, McKinsey has remained silent on some of the most important health issues of our time. It did not lead the fight against cigarettes, vaping, and opioid abuse. (It had clients in all three sectors.) McKinsey did not speak out forcefully against the high cost of drugs or the tsunami of direct-to-consumer drug company advertisements. (Five drug company clients were called before Congress to defend price hikes and executive compensation.) Nor has the firm publicly raised alarms about the consolidation of health-care services. (The firm had clients who presumably benefited from these anticompetitive business decisions.)

McKinsey possesses the expertise and influence to make good on its promise of a more rational, value-based health-care system. And it has achieved a modicum of success in reaching that goal. But making a difference by improving patient health is not its raison d'être. McKinsey is, after all, a for-profit company, and profits it has achieved, sometimes honorably and sometimes not, for itself and for its clients. By that measure, McKinsey is an unqualified success, if not a profile in courage.

Chapter 4

McKinsey at ICE

"We Do Execution, Not Policy"

The late-autumn sun was about to set over Arlington National Cemetery, visible from the rooftop deck, as two hundred McKinsey employees squeezed into a tenth-floor meeting room in the firm's Washington, D.C., office. McKinsey managers had called the meeting on a Friday afternoon—traditionally a travel day for consultants heading home after a week on the road—to discuss an urgent matter.

McKinsey was under assault.

For a company accustomed to always being *in control,* recent events had surprised and unnerved many in its ranks. A year and a half earlier, articles began appearing in the media that questioned McKinsey's judgment and ethics. There was its work for a corrupt power company in South Africa, alleged conflicts of interest in its bankruptcy practice, and an uproar over the firm's work with opioid manufacturers, autocrats, and kleptocrats.

McKinsey had hoped this unwelcome scrutiny would wilt and die in an environment where the media is more accustomed to praising the company than to criticizing it.

But that hadn't happened.

In June 2018, *The New York Times* included a brief mention of McKinsey's work with Immigration and Customs Enforcement—better known as ICE—in a lengthy investigative article about the firm's work in South Africa.

It set off a torrent of criticism inside McKinsey and among its tens of thousands of alumni, tethered to the firm through regular email briefings. Consultants the world over threatened to resign. "It caused a huge issue internally," one London-based consultant recalled.

McKinsey defended its contract with ICE, saying that it primarily involved "administrative and organizational issues."

Kevin Sneader, then just days into his tenure as the firm's managing partner, assured the McKinsey rank and file and its many alumni that the firm stood for something more than making a dollar. "We will not, under any circumstances, engage in work, anywhere in the world, that advances or assists policies that are at odds with our values," he wrote. Besides, he added, McKinsey's work with ICE had ended.

Inside the firm, the controversy over ICE faded into the background.

That changed on Tuesday, December 3, 2019.

That day, ProPublica, a nonprofit investigative newsroom, published a major story in *The New York Times* documenting McKinsey's work with ICE—the federal agency responsible for rounding up undocumented immigrants and deporting them.

For more than a year, the nation had watched reports of screaming children forcibly separated from their parents at the border—sights and sounds impossible to forget. Some were shunted into holding pens, locked inside chain link enclosures no better than cages. One reporter obtained an audio recording of little boys and girls at a Texas detention center, sobbing for their mothers and fathers.

Now consultants in the room had to confront the reality that their firm might have helped to enable these policies.

After Trump was elected, there was an open question about how McKinsey's analytical, highly ordered view of government would mesh with a president who distrusted science, took his cues from ratings-driven television personalities, and embraced conspiracy theories big and small. Trump's operating manner seemed utterly incompatible with McKinsey's data-driven approach to divining the most rational way to run government.

As it turned out, the only thing the Trump administration didn't do was throw McKinsey a party. It awarded dozens of consulting contracts across the landscape of government agencies, producing millions of dollars in revenue for the firm.

But now, in early December 2019, with the president just days away from being impeached, his harsh anti-immigration policies were tearing through the firm.

The article revealed some uncomfortable truths about how far the firm would go in serving clients. According to the article, McKinsey recommended that ICE spend less on food, medical care, and supervision of detainees—proposals that alarmed even some ICE officials who questioned whether the cuts justified the human cost.

Nonetheless, ICE's leadership endorsed the firm's work, saying it brought "a notable decrease in the time to remove aliens with a final order of removal."

The article reverberated outside the firm as well. Pete Buttigieg, then a presidential candidate and a veteran of McKinsey's Washington office, called the firm's actions "disgusting." Another former McKinsey consultant, Andy Slavitt, a former health official under Obama, took to Twitter, calling the recommendations "cruel."

Far more important for McKinsey was how its *current* employees were absorbing the news. Many of the young, idealistic consultants in the room that afternoon had been swayed by McKinsey recruiters, who routinely emphasized the firm's social-sector work. McKinsey hires said they aspired to make the world a better place.

Now they had to come to terms with the darker side of what they had signed up for. Careers were on the line. Speak out and face the consequences? Or stay silent, restrained by the prospect of losing a generous salary and a high-prestige job?

At least two among them had searing personal experiences that stoked their anger. One would speak out that afternoon. The second would follow, days later, with a dramatic mass email to members of the firm. Others, especially senior consultants, were more ambivalent.

For some McKinsey employees, the soul-searching over the firm's work with ICE had actually begun three years earlier during the chaotic opening weeks of the Trump administration.

McKinsey had signed a contract with ICE, worth more than $20 million, and begun work on it during the last year of Obama's presidency. By Trump's inauguration on January 20, 2017, the team was already well into their assignment, embedded at the agency's headquarters near the Potomac River, working in groups of four in windowless offices designed for two people.

But Trump's continuing bluster over immigrants concerned some younger members of the firm.

McKinsey's work with ICE took on added importance because Trump needed the agency to fulfill his core campaign promise to secure the country's southern border. His stance resonated with many white Americans who were receptive to his thinly veiled racist diatribes against immigrants, a theme Trump articulated when he declared his candidacy in the lobby of Manhattan's Trump Tower on June 16, 2015.

"When Mexico sends its people, they're not sending their best," Trump said, two minutes into his forty-five-minute speech. "They're bringing drugs, they're bringing crime, they're rapists, and some, I assume, are good people. But I speak to border guards, and they tell us what we're getting." He continued, telling the Trump Tower audience migrants were coming "from all over South and Latin America" and, he suggested, "probably—probably—from the Middle East."

"And it has gotta stop. And it has gotta stop fast."

Once in power, Trump did move fast. Five days into his presidency, he signed two executive orders. One authorized the building of a wall on the southern border, a promise from that 2015 speech. The other dealt with undocumented migrants already inside the United States, many of whom, he said, "are criminals who have served time in our Federal, State [*sic*] and local jails." He wanted them out and directed ICE to hire ten thousand new officers to make it happen.

With no warning, Trump also banned travel from some Muslim nations, leaving many valid U.S. visa holders and even permanent residents in limbo, unable to enter the country.

McKinsey's Washington office suddenly found itself in the middle of a politically explosive situation. Some members of the team were unlikely to relish making life even more difficult for people fleeing poverty and violence. One consultant helped people who were blind and led a movement for prison reform—*all while in high school.* Another took part in the anti-Trump Women's March the day after the inauguration.

Sensing there might be trouble brewing belowdecks, the project leader, Richard Elder, scheduled an 8:00 a.m. multi-city conference call with members of the ICE team, including senior managers. Elder allowed listeners to voice their concerns. But he also wanted to deliver a message: McKinsey was not going to shy away from this work.

"ICE is changing direction," he announced. "And it's McKinsey's job to change with it."

When his comments triggered new questions, Elder offered a familiar response, one that conveniently allowed McKinsey partners to sidestep tough ethical decisions.

"We don't do policy," he said. "We do execution."

Not everyone bought that explanation, including one young member of the ICE team who spoke up. "With that logic," he said sharply, "you could justify working for any despot, even the Nazis." In poker, his comment was the equivalent of going all in—win everything or lose it all. At that moment, he realized McKinsey was not his future. It was time to leave, and he eventually did, with no regrets.

It wasn't the first time the firm's Washington work had caused dissension among young McKinsey hires. During the late 1960s, several consultants who opposed the Vietnam War refused to work with Robert McNamara's Pentagon.

There would be far more internal turmoil over the ICE contract. But in February 2017, all that was in the future. Elder had done his job. He let the troops air their grievances. Now the work continued.

McKinsey was racing to provide "deliverables" for the Enforcement and Removal Operations division of ICE, responsible for detaining illegal immigrants and deporting them. The project, started in 2016, was dubbed ERO 2.0, and, in the words of an ICE spokesman, the aim was "to review ERO's operations and mission execution, organizational model, and talent and culture management."

A short description of the work on McKinsey's internal website cut through the jargon: "Transformation design to increase arrests. Reduce processing time for detainees, and improve organization health."

As one former senior ICE official described it, McKinsey's consultants acted as a facilitator for the ICE leaders, suggesting ideas, interviewing employees in Washington as well as in field offices around the country, compiling notes, and "running the numbers" on possible initiatives. And, of course, their PowerPoint slides. Hundreds of slides. Binders full of them.

On February 13, 2017, less than a month into the Trump administration, McKinsey delivered a sixteen-page slide deck to ICE titled "Talent Management," a highly redacted version of which became public as a result of the Freedom of Information Act lawsuit brought on by ProPublica.

The presentation reflected the new reality of ICE under Trump, starting on slide 14: "The hiring system can work better and meet additional hiring needs brought on by the Executive Order."

Trump's executive order.

McKinsey's big idea was "super one-stop hiring." This concept was presented to ICE leadership the following month. The plan was to consolidate as many steps in the hiring process as possible into one day, at one location. "We are aiming to reduce time to hire by 30–50% (hundreds of days)," one slide read.

Hiring ten thousand new ICE agents would mean the agency would have to sign on four and a half times more people a year than it ever had. But recruiting qualified agents in a bad economy was hard enough. With America at near-full employment, a quick ramp-up was almost impossible.

"With Trump, who is going to work there now?" the young McKinsey consultant wondered. The answer: a lot of people who agreed with Trump's views on immigration.

Some of McKinsey's suggestions on how to speed up hiring were adopted by ICE, though budget constraints kept the agency from meeting Trump's goal.

McKinsey fought back against the ProPublica report in the *Times,* saying the article "fundamentally misrepresents McKinsey's work." The firm also paid Google to rank its response above the article on web searches, as it had done when it responded to previous *New York Times* articles. McKinsey said that the "scope and goals of our work were established during the prior administration, and they did not change in any material way after the transition in administrations."

But McKinsey's own slides told a different story. The firm was helping ICE carry out Trump's immigration policy. Full stop.

McKinsey had success at ICE doing what it does best—cutting costs. Its consultants claimed ICE could save $385 million a year, mostly from renegotiating contracts for private companies such as CoreCivic (formerly Corrections Corporation of America) that operated many of the more than two hundred detention centers ICE used across the country.

The consultants found six areas where it could trim expenses, and they assigned a number and a letter to each of them. Area 1a was staffing; 1b was "medical." Other items included supplies, capital expenditures, and taxes. One that sparked really fierce resistance inside ICE was 1c—food.

McKinsey had determined that ICE was spending above the "industry standard" on food at some facilities. The problem as McKinsey saw it: ICE's standards for food quality, which had been reviewed and bolstered starting in 2011, were too high, and it backed it up with a slide.

Despite ICE's reputation, key people there actually wanted to improve the quality of life for detainees, and they fought against the McKinsey suggestions. Where McKinsey saw a spreadsheet and the ability to fulfill a KPI (key performance indicator) for a client, they put a human face on what it would mean to cut food spending.

"ICE spends so much on detention—shaving pennies from meals is not the right tactic," a former senior ICE official, who had objected to many of McKinsey's suggestions, said.

That drew the ire of Tony D'Emidio, the McKinsey partner who was in charge of the work. He complained to the boss of the senior ICE official, saying that person was being "obstructionist." D'Emidio denies that this happened.

After the ProPublica article, McKinsey defended itself, saying it was seeking cost savings "without sacrificing quality, safety and mission." That was easy to say. The reality was different.

For example, McKinsey looked at the "daily bed rate" for different facilities and found that some were far cheaper than others. Why not move detainees to the cheaper facilities and fill those beds first? On the surface, it made sense, but the reality was that those beds were cheaper because many were in city and county jails. Rural counties coveted ICE contracts that paid them to house people in otherwise vacant cells, generating much-needed revenue.

"They are cheaper because they are shitty sheriff's jails, and they just want the money," one former Department of Homeland Security official said, calling them "garbage beds."

One of the facilities McKinsey targeted was the ICE family detention center at Dilley, Texas—one of the few places approved to hold mothers and their children—about halfway between the Rio Grande and San Antonio. At one point in 2018 it housed sixteen children under two years old.

In August 2017, emails show that McKinsey consultants met with ICE "leadership" at Potomac Center North—the ICE office building in Washington. The McKinsey team had a PowerPoint presentation they wanted to show.

ICE was paying CoreCivic $157 million a year for it to run Dilley, the biggest family detention facility in the ICE archipelago. McKinsey's slides showed the "should cost" was drastically lower: $40 million, close to a 75 percent cut. Realistically, McKinsey surmised, the agency could push for cuts to the contract of up to $90 million. Where was the fat? The details are redacted, but the cuts came in areas such as "staffing," "food & supplies," depreciation, and "other." An unredacted note on the bottom of the page explained that education and medical "will not be a focus of the negotiations."

ICE officials, helped by phone calls from CoreCivic, successfully scotched the McKinsey plan. The cuts didn't go into effect, but they made some observers wonder how much worse the humanitarian crisis that was about to overwhelm Dilley and other detention centers could have been had McKinsey's proposals won the day.

Dilley was where, in March 2018, a nineteen-month-old girl, Mariee Juárez, had contracted pneumonia, dying soon after being discharged. Her mother filed a $60 million wrongful death claim that detailed a litany of medical shortcomings at Dilley. Only once during Mariee's stay was she seen by a doctor, who gave her Vicks VapoRub for congestion.

Martin Garbus, a well-known human rights lawyer, volunteered at Dilley in early 2019 to help women and their children get through their "credible fear" interview so that they could have a shot at getting asylum in America. Before their arrival, many had been processed through a *hielera* or "icebox," a holding cell run by border patrol agents. They spoke of fleeing the misery of life in Central America, describing rapes, forced prostitution, and brutal gang violence. Many were deeply traumatized. "I never saw anyone as helpless as these women with their kids," Garbus said.

"I saw the South African police brutalize demonstrators, including mothers with children. I saw Southerners in the civil-rights movement attack marchers. I saw Cesar Chavez's members get beaten and shot at," he recalled. "But what I saw in Dilley will stay with me forever."

Some ICE staffers were growing frustrated with McKinsey's presence inside their headquarters building. It wasn't just that it was trying to gut carefully designed standards. The McKinsey team had such high turnover that career staffers were constantly having to explain the agency's inner workings to wave after wave of twentysomething consultants. Worse yet, some ICE staffers had begun to question McKinsey's competence.

Another of McKinsey's "deliverables" to ICE was a "leadership development toolkit," which came in the form of a seventy-eight-page PowerPoint presentation. It dispensed advice like suggesting leadership seminars be held at places such as Civil War battlefields or at the 9/11 Memorial in New York.

By October 2017, McKinsey's contract was up for renewal. Despite the internal resistance, an ICE official wrote in a memo that ERO 2.0 had "quantifiable benefits." Without McKinsey staying on the job, the likelihood of success in seeing these changes through "is very low," the memo said.

The ICE spokesman Bryan D. Cox said that McKinsey had saved the agency $16 million on its contracts "without degradation to service" and that ERO 2.0 had "yielded measurable improvements in mission outcomes."

McKinsey had been trying to speed deportation, but only "once a final legal determination was made regarding someone's case," the firm said.

In April 2018 the Trump administration rolled out its "zero tolerance" policy, vowing to criminally prosecute everyone unlawfully crossing the border. Before zero tolerance, if a family was apprehended, they would typically be released into the United States pending a hearing.

Zero tolerance, with parents in criminal detention, meant children had to be separated from them, since they could not be held in such facilities. Trump immigration hard-liners hoped that this draconian step would scare off most people from even trying to make the crossing. Instead, by mid-June, at least twenty-five hundred children, including more than a hundred under the age of four, had been ripped from their parents and in some cases moved hundreds or even thousands of miles away from them. The images—and the sounds of sobbing children—shocked a nation.

They shocked people inside McKinsey as well. But after the initial furor, McKinsey began working with another immigration-enforcement agency, U.S. Customs and Border Protection.

On the evening of Tuesday, December 3, 2019, Scott Elfenbein was in a taxi, heading to a dinner in Manhattan with his soon-to-be in-laws, reading the ProPublica/*New York Times* story on his phone. He wondered how McKinsey's management would explain this. It was hard to dismiss the report's findings, backed up as they were by hundreds of pages of McKinsey's own PowerPoint slides and emails.

Elfenbein was a newly minted McKinsey associate with the classic pedigree—a Harvard undergraduate degree and a Wharton MBA. The firm's recent bad publicity bothered him, but because of the firm's focus on client confidentiality—even between McKinsey consultants—he hadn't been aware of the extent of McKinsey's involvement with ICE, work that involved some of his colleagues.

The new article shattered whatever peace he'd made.

Twelve years earlier, Elfenbein had received a call in the middle of the night from his best friend, who he asked not be named.

"Elf, I'm being deported and I wanted to call and say goodbye," the friend told him.

Elfenbein hung up, thinking his friend was playing a really bad joke on him.

He called again: "Don't you dare hang up on me! Listen, I've been arrested and I'm being deported. I'm calling to say goodbye."

Elfenbein's friend was a star student at their high school in Miami, with a near-perfect GPA and the top score on eleven Advanced Placement examinations. Both had just graduated. Elfenbein was bound for Harvard. But his friend, who came to America when he was two years old, was undocumented; his Colombian parents had overstayed their visas. Ineligible for financial aid, he enrolled at the local community college. Now even that was being taken away after ICE agents raided their home, throwing the family in a detention center while they awaited the inevitable: a one-way ticket to Bogotá.

It was, Elfenbein recalled years later, the first time he had ever heard of ICE.

Elfenbein and his classmates, outraged and heartbroken, sprang into action. They talked to immigration lawyers and were told nothing could be done. They asked their local representatives to the U.S. Congress for help. Again, no luck.

But there was this new website—Facebook—that was catching on. They wrote posts saying how great their friend was, and a Fox affiliate in South Florida picked up on it. "Apparently a bunch of teens using technology to call attention to a social injustice resonated with one local station," Elfenbein said.

Then CNN ran a story. Now those same members of Congress got back to them. Maybe there was something his friends could do after all. Fresh out of high school, they traveled to Washington, sleeping in a cramped basement. Their plan was simple: roam the halls of Congress.

They got a senator, Chris Dodd of Connecticut, and a Florida congressman, Lincoln Díaz-Balart, to sponsor private bills, delaying the day of reckoning for Elfenbein's friend and his older brother, though their parents were soon deported.

His friend went on to graduate—with honors—from Georgetown.

The case got national attention, including stories in *The New York Times.* It also helped to build momentum for the Dream Act—which aimed to legalize the hundreds of thousands of young people across the country who were undocumented only because of decisions their parents made when they were children. Elfenbein went on to found an immigration-advocacy group at Harvard.

Reading the article, Elfenbein knew that McKinsey was in conflict with what was until then the defining arc of his life. His fiancée—Elfenbein was days away from his wedding—was blunt. "If you don't quit right now, you don't stand for anything," she said.

He called his old friend, now a successful banker in Brazil, who was equally blunt: "Don't go fuck up your life because of me."

Elfenbein knew that if he quit, "my tiny little voice wouldn't matter."

That Friday, he walked into the meeting room at the D.C. office. His voice would soon matter very much.

The many navy veterans in the D.C. office had a ready phrase for what was happening: this was an all-hands-on-deck event.

Normally, no more than fifty to eighty people would show up at these "town hall" meetings. That day—December 6, 2019—there were about two hundred, or almost half of the McKinsey workforce in the nation's capital. They crowded into a space created by removing the dividers between several conference rooms.

It was a drill that was becoming routine. At other town halls aimed at countering negative press, the troops were inevitably told that the reporters writing the stories had an agenda, that the work done for Regime A or Company B was legitimate, and that the firm was taking action to remedy any shortcoming.

But this was different. First of all, the work with ICE was done by people in this office. Even more important, this wasn't the first time the firm had been confronted from within about its work with ICE. Sneader, the firm's managing partner, had addressed it the year before.

The new article, backed by the McKinsey slides, raised questions about Sneader and the firm's leadership. Sneader made clear from the outset that his stewardship would be different from that of Dominic Barton, his predecessor. Barton, tall and urbane, whose first wife hailed from the Labatt beer family, became Canada's ambassador to China after stepping down as the firm's managing partner. Sneader, short and combative, was from gritty Glasgow—a biographical detail he liked to mention in television interviews. He wasn't going to turn the other cheek when his firm got bad press. But he didn't ignore problems and earlier that year had overseen the rollout of a new screening process for potential assignments designed to help the firm avoid future damaging headlines.

The room filled up. Facing the crowd was Nora Gardner, a senior partner who led the Washington office. Also present that afternoon was D'Emidio, the partner who had overseen the day-to-day ICE project, as well as two more junior managers, Ed Barriball and Jonah Wagner, who worked on the Customs and Border Protection account.

"Many of us share very, very strong beliefs and feelings," Gardner said, opening the meeting. "First, strong passion, belief, and respect for immigrants, for human rights, for the immigrant experience." Acknowledging the anger many consultants were feeling about the firm's work with ICE, she appealed for understanding: "We do have a shared value system, and I'd urge us to express care in our colleagues and assume best intent in our colleagues."

Barriball spoke next. He made the point of saying that he was a registered Democrat and "wondered if this [ICE] was an agency I wanted to serve."

Back in the Obama administration, he said, McKinsey had been hired by ICE to help improve a deeply demoralized institution that consistently ranked near the bottom in a survey ranking job satisfaction in federal agencies. Barriball and his colleagues were exploring ways for ICE to recruit better people and to stop being "absolutely gouged by their vendors," especially the private prison companies that housed so many detainees. McKinsey had never advocated for lower-quality food for detainees, he claimed. The firm, he said, was only asking why contractors were charging wildly different prices for the same food in different locations.

In addition to procurement and recruiting, there was a third assignment. Barriball brushed over it very quickly.

"It was very hard for them to do their job on a day-to-day basis," Barriball said of ICE. He said most people McKinsey worked with at ICE were "concerned primarily with finding and arresting folks who had committed very serious crimes in the country" and that this was something McKinsey could "help them with."

"Obviously the context changed quite a bit in the new administration," he added.

Wagner, in describing McKinsey's work with CBP, said it was "in line with things we were personally proud of and I think we can all feel proud."

The partners then took questions.

For Mobasshir Poonawalla, a junior consultant in the audience, the comments by Barriball and Wagner stung. He grew up on welfare, living in a two-bedroom apartment with his parents and four siblings. He studied hard and was admitted to Wharton. His older brother wasn't as fortunate. He was an undocumented immigrant who had come to America as a child. Under Obama, he had some protection as a Dreamer, but Trump's crackdown on immigration and his zeal to kill DACA meant Poonawalla's brother faced the real chance of being deported. To him, McKinsey's public explanation that it was only helping ICE with deportations of people already on "final legal determination" was infuriating, because that was his brother's status. He raised his hand.

"We've lived our entire life hiding him when the doorbell rang," Poonawalla said. Then he offered a suggestion.

"Instead of citing bipartisan political support which I very much disagree with, why don't we clearly outline that this is something that we no longer do, not because of the political or the optics of it, but because we are values driven," he said.

That drew some applause. "Full of empathy," Gardner responded. "Thank you for sharing that. I know that there are others in the room who are similarly touched and having a similar experience. Just a lot of gratitude for that. I think you'll appreciate that it is hard for our firm to take a political stance on that, on what is a very charged issue."

Elfenbein, assigned to the Philadelphia office, didn't think it was proper to speak out at the time. But the meeting left him upset. He felt that McKinsey had failed to address a deeply human issue with any sense of humanity and was angered that the firm had the gall to say that helping what he considered the most polarizing government agency was not political.

Elfenbein and the other McKinsey consultants in the room were being told not to believe what was in the article, but McKinsey's own slides—hundreds of them—were also published as attachments, and despite the heavy redactions they backed up the article's content.

Elfenbein found it hard to focus on his work. The day before the town hall meeting, he was given talking points on how to communicate with McKinsey recruiting prospects from Wharton's MBA program in ways that avoided the ICE issue or assuaged them. He was told not to initiate discussions about ICE with potential recruits.

"That's when the figurative levee broke," he said.

That night, he sent an email to some of his Wharton MBA classmates who had also joined McKinsey as well as some of McKinsey's top recruiters for the school. He pointed out the disparity of what McKinsey was saying publicly and the evidence available internally, including project descriptions on the biographical pages of some of the ICE project consultants.

The next day he was at the town hall meeting in D.C. The unapologetic way that D'Emidio and Barriball justified the work made him even angrier. The Monday after the Washington meeting, Elfenbein added to his initial email, this time addressing it to far more colleagues—about twelve hundred—including Sneader and Liz Hilton Segel, the head of North America for the firm. He was testing the limits of McKinsey's long-held principle that everyone had an "obligation to dissent."

"I hope you'll read my note as coming from a heart in a good place while it feels like I'm personally in a rough place," he began. He then wrote of a friend who was "ripped from his bed at 3 AM and placed in a horrific ICE detention center that still gives him nightmares."

"From my observation we have not demonstrated leadership in crisis nor even demonstrated that Our Values hold true under duress," he continued.

He laid out his recommendations in bullet points. Among them: a demand that McKinsey make a public apology for working for ICE and "stop saying we would do this work again." Another: "Stop using legality as the barometer for ethicality." On this, he was particularly biting, adding a parenthetical phrase: "If we helped southern states 'improve agricultural asset yield' in the 1850s would we still stand behind that? Our guidance so far would indicate the answer is 'maybe.' "

He also wanted to give back any money in his paycheck that could be attributed to the work for ICE and set up a company email address, TakeItOutofMyPay@mckinsey.com, for his colleagues to contribute as well.

The email also informed McKinsey consultants across the world that the firm in his opinion was not leveling with them on the extent of its work for ICE.

He pressed send.

"I felt like I was going to throw up."

Elfenbein waited. Two minutes, maybe three minutes went by.

His phone rang.

On the line was a well-respected leader at the firm, who told him how after years at McKinsey he had stopped being the person who stood up for principles. Elfenbein's email had moved him. Then he said, "Watch this."

He wrote, "I'm with Scott. Take it out of my pay." And hit reply all.

Hundreds followed his lead, writing to him from places around the world, including Germany, Ireland, the U.K., and Japan. They offered messages of support and forwarded Elfenbein's email to thousands more people at McKinsey. "It was a rebellion," said another person who attended the Washington town hall. "A rebellion occurred at the firm between junior consultants and associate partners and above."

A few days later, D'Emidio, the partner in charge of the ICE project, sent a mass email of his own. Subject: "Call for reconciliation and healing."

In bullet points, he wrote of his deep sympathy "for those of you whose families and friends live in fear of my client," as well as guilt "for having been the cause of so much angst, shame, mistrust, and anger for so many of you."

But then his email took a turn as he described how hurt he was "by the stinging words of some emails accusing me of having no sense of ethics, purpose, or values," anger at the "vilification" of his colleagues on the ICE project, plus "frustration" over what he said were "inaccurate portrayals" of the team's work. He then said he was proud of the "impact" his team had. D'Emidio called for dialogue "with the hope that we can heal each other's wounds."

Elfenbein didn't lose his job, and Sneader even let him know that his email was "appropriate." But another senior partner called and asked him a very McKinsey-like question: Did he know how much money in lost productivity his email had caused?

The experience left Elfenbein, who resigned from McKinsey in late 2021, with a jaundiced view of the firm he had so enthusiastically joined, buoyed by the promise from recruiters that he would be "uniquely positioned to do something that does on occasion help move society forward."

"It might be oversold," he said.

Chapter 5

Befriending China's Government

In late 2013 a fleet of Chinese dredging vessels descended upon Fiery Cross Reef, more than six hundred miles south of China proper. Among the ships was the *Tian Jing Hao,* the largest dredger in Asia, capable of sucking more than a million gallons of sand an hour from the seafloor. Over two years, satellite photos tracked the reef's transformation from an uninhabitable outcropping barely poking above the water's surface into a 677-acre island.

China's government insisted that Fiery Cross, and a clutch of neighboring reefs turned islands in the South China Sea, wouldn't be militarized. But on September 25, 2015, the world learned otherwise. The respected *Jane's Defence Weekly,* using satellite photos, reported the completion of a 3.1-kilometer-long airstrip on the reef capable of handling long-range Chinese bombers. Missile systems would soon follow.

That same day, two thousand miles to the north, Chen Fenjian, president of China Communications Construction Company, the owner of the *Tian Jing Hao,* gathered members of his leadership team in Beijing for an important meeting.

China Communications is no ordinary company. It is one of the ninety-six state-owned enterprises that, because of their importance to China's national security and economic vitality, are managed by the central government in Beijing. These companies make China's weapons, grow and distribute food, operate phone and internet networks, refine oil, forge steel, mine coal, and, like China Communications, build bridges, roads, and ports around the world as an instrument of Chinese foreign policy. Chen and other top executives at these essential "central enterprises"—the *zhongyang qiye*—are handpicked by the Communist Party's Organization Department.

To help guide him, Chen hired an American firm, McKinsey. In recent years, McKinsey has advised at least twenty-six of the ninety-six companies designated by Beijing as *zhongyang qiye*.

In all, 702 people took part in the meeting, some via videoconference from the company's far-flung field offices across the globe. Their aim: discuss how the company would fit into the Chinese government's five-year economic blueprint. Even after almost four decades of economic reforms, this relic from the days of Chairman Mao holds great sway, directing massive government resources into favored industries.

That day, a McKinsey team presented recommendations. Though the specifics are a secret, China Communications eagerly advertised its connection to McKinsey—*maikenxi* in Chinese—where the country's highly educated elite dreamed of landing a job. McKinsey analyzed China Communications' "market environment" and made recommendations on the company's "overall strategic goals" as well as its "business portfolio strategy," the state-owned company said in a statement.

Landing China Communications as a client was a coup for McKinsey. The state-owned company had been winning Chinese-government infrastructure contracts around the world as part of a strategy to burnish China's influence. It even considered a foreign stock market listing for its booming dredging business.

For McKinsey, China Communications, one of the world's biggest engineering companies, meant one more revenue source. But for the United States, the company's island building had fundamentally altered the balance of power in the Pacific Ocean.*

* Mike Forsythe was an officer in the U.S. Navy from 1990 to 1997. As navigator on a guided-missile cruiser, he made several transits of the South China Sea. In those days, years before the Chinese naval buildup, the biggest worry was the depth of the water; at times it can be alarmingly shallow. The idea that his ship's passage could be challenged by the Chinese navy was the furthest thing from his mind.

These days, U.S. warships that pass close to the new islands are regularly tailed and harassed by Chinese navy vessels and auxiliary ships, vastly increasing the likelihood of a deadly mishap between two nuclear-armed powers. In one incident, a Chinese warship came within forty-five yards of the bow of a U.S. destroyer near one of the new islands, forcing the American ship to maneuver to avoid a collision. A Washington think tank said the sea "will be virtually a Chinese lake" by 2030. "China, with its authoritarian system and its determined incursion into the South China Sea and globally, presents a constant naval threat," President Biden's navy secretary said during his confirmation hearing.

McKinsey's work with a Chinese government-owned company that built islands in disputed waters conflicts with the goals of a far more important client: the Pentagon. McKinsey has taken in hundreds of millions of dollars from the Defense Department in recent years. Internal McKinsey records show that from 2018 until early 2020, the U.S. Defense Department was among McKinsey's top tier of clients. No Chinese company ranked among the firm's top revenue earners during that time.

In 2015, the same year McKinsey was advising China Communications, it was also studying how the U.S. Army could reduce costs in sustaining America's industrial base for manufacturing ammunition. McKinsey has also worked with the Naval Surface Warfare Center in Dahlgren, Virginia, which helps develop the weapons that would be used in a conflict with China. In 2019, the navy awarded McKinsey a $15.7 million contract to work on its "affordability campaign" for the F-35 fighter.

The firm's consultants also regularly take Pentagon posts. One partner, Eric Chewning, was chief of staff to Mark Esper, a defense secretary during Trump's presidency. In 2020 he returned to McKinsey. McKinsey's Jesse Salazar was named deputy assistant secretary of defense for industrial policy in the Biden administration.

For McKinsey, it had been a long journey from advising the captains of American free enterprise to advising a Chinese state-owned firm building military bases for America's chief strategic and economic rival.

By the time that South China Sea airstrip became operational,

McKinsey had shown its willingness to help clients that others might have avoided. Successive generations of McKinsey's managing partners had steered the firm to jobs with various levels of the Chinese government. McKinsey even set up a Communist Party cell in its Shanghai office, according to an account in the party's official *People's Daily,* as did other foreign companies. McKinsey says it is "generally unaware of and does not track the private political affiliations of its employees."

Two developments helped lead McKinsey into the arms of some of China's most strategically important government-owned companies. First was the firm's increasing appetite for government work after Nancy Killefer, newly returned from the Clinton administration's Treasury Department, had set up a public-sector practice in 2000, opening up a new line of revenue for the firm. Second was McKinsey's relentless international expansion. By the 1980s its non-American partners outnumbered the U.S. partners. The firm opened new offices around the world, including in Moscow, Dubai, and Johannesburg.

The biggest international prize of all—at least the one with the most potential—was China. For centuries the world's most populous country had also been home to the planet's preeminent economy. It had gone through 150 troubled years, marked by foreign occupation, revolution, war, and famine, but by the early 1990s, with its economy booming and its leaders keen to overhaul its sclerotic state-owned industries, China needed McKinsey's business know-how. And with the firm's most lucrative clients, like Volkswagen, staking their futures on China, McKinsey's leaders felt that they had to be there.

It wasn't always so. When China was still stuck in the Marxist mire, McKinsey didn't see the country as a vital business opportunity. In the 1970s, Bank of China had approached the firm about help with restructuring, and in 1985 the Chinese government had asked McKinsey to help overhaul its Soviet-era steel industry. In both instances, the firm turned down the work, "in each case on the grounds that Firm leaders didn't believe they could have an impact," according to an account in McKinsey's official history book.

But China's scorching economic growth in the early 1990s—GDP grew 14.2 percent in 1992 and topped 13 percent the following two years—captured the world's attention. The country's political reforms had been put on ice following the bloody 1989 crackdown in and around Beijing's Tiananmen Square, but on the economy Beijing's leaders were opening the country up to foreign investment, tolerating the rise of aggressive new private companies, and looking to overhaul the country's decrepit state-owned banks, refineries, phone networks, steel mills, and shipbuilders.

McKinsey had set up shop in Hong Kong in 1985, and like so many Western companies it used what was then a British colony as a base to venture into the mainland. In quick succession, McKinsey opened offices in Shanghai and Beijing in the midnineties. The firm invested millions of dollars in training its global cadre of consultants for success in China. Many Chinese hires were sent to Europe to learn the basics of the craft there. Meanwhile, to master Chinese, some McKinsey-bound MBAs from U.S. business schools enrolled at Beijing's Tsinghua University.

McKinsey's early work in China focused on helping its global clients set up operations there. The 1990s were a time when the large multinationals, like General Motors and 3M, were scrambling to profit from the world's fastest-growing major economy. McKinsey consultants were there to help guide companies through the complexities of doing business in China, recalled Olivier Kayser, a former senior partner who was based in Shanghai and Beijing in the late 1990s.

It was an electrifying time to be in China. The economy was opening up to Western businesses, and Chinese students flew off by the hundreds of thousands to get a first-class education in the United States. China's burgeoning and largely uncontrolled internet was bursting with entrepreneurial talent. Despite the political pall that descended over the country after the 1989 crackdown, on a personal level Chinese people enjoyed freedoms unimaginable just a few years earlier. They were no longer tied to an assigned work unit and could instead work and shop where they wanted and marry whom they chose. Soon the country would join the World Trade Organization, and many hoped the economic liberalization would lead to demands for more political rights.

"The genie of freedom will not go back into the bottle," President Clinton said in 2000 as he drummed up support for China's accession to the WTO.

The McKinsey team in China shared that optimism. "There was a feeling that economic development would lead to democracy, that the Communist Party would eventually loosen its grip on society, and that China would soon become like Hong Kong," Kayser recalled from his time in China. "The general direction of history was clear."

Early China-based McKinsey consultants, including Kayser, Gordon Orr, Jonathan Woetzel, and Tony Perkins, an American who is now an elder in the Mormon Church, knew that for the China practice to succeed, they had to attract local clients, including the state-owned companies overseen by the Communist Party that dominate the commanding heights of the economy.

So they set up talks at hotel conference rooms in Shanghai and Beijing for company executives, offering free advice on company strategy and organization, attracting large crowds.

They landed a Shanghai-based government-owned conglomerate with hundreds of thousands of people on the payroll. Almost a quarter century after the work and eighteen years after Kayser left McKinsey, he wouldn't divulge its identity. But the company, along with many other state-owned enterprises, was facing obsolescence. China was opening up the state sector to competition, from both domestic and international companies. Millions of redundant workers faced unemployment.

"There was a race against time. Deregulation was on the way," Kayser said. "The employment losses were going to happen; whether the employment gains would make up for it, you had to hope."

Kayser and his colleagues focused on ways to "ring the cash register" rather than be the foreign consulting firm telling a Chinese state-owned company whom to fire. With a decrepit socialist-era sales force, it was relatively easy to make some basic improvements that brought in new revenue. "Once we had established our credibility, they could say look, this is the money we made off of McKinsey," Kayser said.

After two years on the ground in mainland China, McKinsey landed what was to become one of its best clients: Ping An Insurance.

McKinsey took on Ping An in 1997 and stayed there for the next quarter century, helping what was a backwater regional company grow to become the world's second-biggest insurance company by market capitalization. McKinsey consultants liked working with Ping An, because "they just did what McKinsey told them to do."

"Once the project is over, they just execute, no questions asked," the former McKinsey consultant, a Chinese national, said in an interview.

Peter Walker, one of the firm's barons who lorded over the global insurance sector, spent an increasing amount of time in China as the relationship with Ping An deepened and McKinsey took on more Chinese insurance companies as clients. Louis Cheung, a McKinsey consultant who helped lead the Ping An work, moved over to Ping An and was named the company's president ahead of its 2004 initial public offering in Hong Kong. Years later he would found a private equity firm with the grandson of China's former president Jiang Zemin.

The Ping An IPO also showed that even as McKinsey worked with private-sector clients in China, the firm—wittingly or not—courted the all-powerful, pervasive Chinese government. McKinsey had hired a top graduate of Harvard's MBA program, Liu Chunhang, the son-in-law of China's soon-to-be premier, Wen Jiabao. As vice-premier until 2003, Wen had overseen the financial services industry, including Ping An. Wen's wife acquired an enormous stake in Ping An ahead of the IPO, hiding much of it in the name of Wen's elderly mother. McKinsey has said that it hired Liu based on his qualifications, not his connections. "Any suggestion that Mr. Liu was hired or employed for improper purpose is false and extremely misleading," the company said in 2018.

The fact that Premier Wen's son-in-law joined McKinsey shows just how prestigious the firm had become to China's Western-educated elite. The firm moved from success to success. From starting out with a few dozen consultants in China in the mid-1990s, after a decade it had more than three hundred. And as China's big state-owned firms prepared for global stock market share sales, McKinsey was there to help them.

Not everyone at McKinsey was thrilled that the firm was devoting so much time to working with governments and parastatals. To them, a McKinsey consultant should be advising CEOs in the private sector.

Ron Daniel, the firm's managing partner from 1976 to 1988, who well into his nineties kept coming into the firm's midtown Manhattan office each day, was one of them. One day, he took aside Ian Davis, who led the firm from 2003 to 2009, telling Davis how he wasn't keen on all this "public sector stuff."

Davis's tart reply: "Ron, you mean we shouldn't be working in China?"

The answer was obvious.

As China's economic growth accelerated, McKinsey dove right into that "public sector stuff"—the Communist Party–controlled *zhongyang qiye.*

In the first decade of this century, China's leading state-owned companies were shedding years of Soviet-style central planning, restructuring by adopting Western-style "best practices" (a McKinsey specialty) and unlocking massive efficiency gains that helped spur Chinese growth. In 2007 the economy grew at 14.2 percent, matching its torrid pace from 1992. Companies such as Apple, General Motors, McDonald's, Volkswagen, and Boeing were finally realizing what had been a mostly unfulfilled dream of Western merchants for centuries: they were making a lot of money in China.

For multinational companies—McKinsey's core clients—it defied common sense to stay out of a market that became, in rapid succession, the world's biggest cell-phone market, the world's largest car market, the world's top exporter, and, by 2010, the world's number two economy after the United States.

McKinsey kept adding marquee state-owned firms to its client roster, including China Mobile, China Telecom, and the oil giants Sinopec and PetroChina, as well as coal, steel, banking, foodstuffs, and shipping conglomerates.

Local governments and Beijing ministries also sought McKinsey's advice. Shanghai hired the firm to help with urban planning. In 2009, Ian Davis traveled to Beijing to sign an agreement with China's Commerce Ministry. That same year, McKinsey was asked by the government to help plan its economic stimulus program to counter the effects of the global financial crisis. McKinsey's role was small—involving figuring out if price cuts to televisions would stimulate demand—but Dominic Barton, who succeeded Davis that year as the firm's managing partner, presented McKinsey's findings to the National Development and Reform Commission, the powerful planning agency that oversees China's industrial policies.

One former McKinsey consultant who worked in China said that the firm's successful push to attract state-owned enterprises as clients, sometimes by offering them discounts on consulting fees, resulted in "a transfer of intellectual property from the West" that served "to build China and build the SOEs."

"Now we have a big competitor. For me personally it was not all that inspiring to be working for an SOE at cut rates."

As McKinsey's work deepened in China, the country's state-owned companies and its government offices eagerly told everyone they had hired the world's most prestigious consulting firm.

McKinsey's name was so well known that it even attracted a Chinese copycat, Chengdu McKinsey Management Consulting Company. In 2009 the phony McKinsey actually won a contract to advise the Sichuan provincial government on its economic plan.

The ruse fooled the official *China Economic Weekly,* which likened McKinsey—the real one—to an octopus extending its tentacles of influence. It called the firm the "foreign brain behind the 12th Five-Year Plan," highlighting the fake McKinsey's work in Sichuan.

While McKinsey and its global clients expanded in China, the country's human rights record drew international condemnation. China threw activists like the Nobel Peace Prize laureate Liu Xiaobo in jail, where he died. The Communist Party cracked down on any group that might pose a challenge to its rule. But people still hoped, as Clinton did in 2000, that China's economic boom would eventually bleed over into the political sphere. In 2008, China hosted the Olympic Games. Tens of millions of young Chinese were discovering that they could voice their opinions on the country's dynamic social media platforms. Relations between the United States and China, though often testy, were at times cordial.

That would soon change. In November 2012, Xi Jinping, son of one of the founders of the People's Republic, took over leadership of the ruling Communist Party.

Xi saw the world very differently from the bland apparatchik he replaced. To Xi, the party was tottering on the brink of collapse, hobbled by corruption and the influx of Western ideas such as press freedom and rule of law. Xi didn't want to be China's Gorbachev and preside over the demise of the Communist Party. Only days into his rule, he gave a speech chastising the Soviet party's collapse in 1991, blaming it on the fact that "nobody was man enough to stand up and resist." Xi jailed human rights defenders and feminists. China's free-for-all social media platforms were reined in by aggressive censorship. Xi began a ruthless crackdown against the Muslim Uyghurs in Xinjiang, involving mass detentions and forced sterilizations that the American government would soon label a genocide.

To bolster his power, the official media, controlled by the Communist Party, portrayed him in heroic terms not seen since the days of Mao Zedong. Relations with the United States deteriorated. But for McKinsey, it was business as usual.

While it's true that multinationals like BMW, Apple, Boeing, and Starbucks also stayed the course in China, the cars, phones, airplanes, and coffee they sell differ from McKinsey's flagship product. By dispensing its know-how to state-owned companies such as China Communications, the builder of the South China Sea islands, McKinsey was bolstering the power of the Chinese state and the ruling Communist Party. Xi made clear that there was no distance between the Communist Party and leading state-owned enterprises like China Communications, telling party cadres that "adhering to party leadership and strengthening party building is the glorious tradition of our country's state-owned enterprises."

In the fall of 2013, Xi launched a Maoist-style party "rectification" campaign, strangling what semblance of free speech remained on social media platforms. But McKinsey at this point not only advised state-owned Chinese companies and even government agencies—it went one step further and began to champion some of Beijing's signature policies, including several that put China at odds with the United States and Europe.

One such program was the Belt and Road Initiative. Invoking the Silk Road, the caravan route of centuries past, the trillion-dollar plan sought to extend China's influence by building ports, roads, bridges, railroads, and other projects across Asia, Africa, and beyond.

The plan quickly raised alarms in Washington and other Western capitals. Leaders feared China's government would use the initiative as a stealth plan to expand its own military influence, to entrap poor nations by lending them money that they couldn't repay, and to bind those nations in a Beijing-dominated sphere of influence. "These roads cannot be those of a new hegemony, which would transform those that they cross into vassals," France's president, Emmanuel Macron, said on a visit to China.

McKinsey took a different view. Barton, then McKinsey's managing partner, made Belt and Road the theme of a keynote address in Beijing in March 2015 at an annual meeting where companies seeking business there mingle with China's top leaders. Barton said that McKinsey was very excited about the Belt and Road strategy. He also publicly dismissed concerns that the initiative would be a tool to expand China's influence.

McKinsey convened senior government officials to discuss the initiative and amplify the government's message that China was embarking on this "not out of self-interest, nor out of geopolitical intentions."

"The world is waiting for the 'One Belt, One Road' grand blueprint to move from dream to reality," Barton and his colleagues said in a post on the company's Chinese website in May 2015. "We are willing to work with governments, enterprises, and think tanks to conduct more detailed research on the above proposals and contribute a little to the expansion of the prosperity of human society!"

Soon, McKinsey consultants began flogging the importance of China's Belt and Road to clients. In 2015, the Malaysian government hired McKinsey to make an economic feasibility report for one of the biggest public-works projects ever envisioned in the country: a rail line connecting the ports on the eastern side of peninsular Malaysia to its prosperous cities on the western side.

In a slide presentation, McKinsey consultants wrote that Malaysia taking on the project would "build the nation-to-nation relationship" with China because of the project's importance to the Belt and Road Initiative. The consultants said China had "geopolitical reasons" for its interest in rail lines in Southeast Asia. Another slide pointed out that Chinese financing of a rail line in Indonesia came with generous terms for that country. McKinsey called it a "game changer."

In 2016, China Communications Construction, the very same McKinsey client that was building the islands in the South China Sea, won a $13 billion contract to build Malaysia's railroad. An aide to the prime minister at the time said that Malaysia had offered China Communications the rail contract as part of a scheme to pay off debts run up by a corrupt government investment fund.

McKinsey said that its role in the project "was limited to studying socio-economic impact and financial feasibility" and that the firm had no role in the Malaysian government's decision to hire China Communications Construction. "To portray us as working behind the scenes to advance any government's agenda—across independent client teams and projects—is simply untrue," McKinsey said in a December 2018 statement following a *New York Times* report about its work on projects related to the Belt and Road Initiative.

For McKinsey, touting the Belt and Road Initiative was good business. Nine of the top fifteen Chinese contractors for the BRI have been McKinsey clients.

McKinsey also focused on China's controversial industrial policy, Made in China 2025. First introduced in 2015, the plan aims to make China the dominant player in industries such as electric vehicles, biopharmaceuticals, and aerospace by focusing hundreds of billions of dollars in state-backed lending to those areas. China's top trading partners fear it is a path for China to control entire industries and supply chains, undermining their own economies and eventually pushing foreign companies out of China's own massive market. In March 2021 the Biden administration called it one of China's "more far-reaching and harmful industrial plans."

McKinsey produced at least ten reports in Chinese about Made in China 2025. But in May 2018, facing a barrage of criticism from its most important trading partners, China's government ordered the country's media to stop writing about it. McKinsey also stopped mentioning the policy.

While controversial in some parts of the world, to many if not most McKinsey consultants in China this work is normal and acceptable. The vast majority of McKinsey's staff in China are local hires, and an increasing number are becoming partners and senior partners, giving them the power to take on new clients.

Many of these Chinese consultants have advanced degrees from places like Harvard and Stanford, but they are part of China's elite—the biggest beneficiaries of China's one-party rule. And they include people like Chen Guang, a partner who joined McKinsey in 2007 after earning a doctorate in optical engineering at Shanghai's Jiao Tong University.

In December 2017, Chen spoke at a meeting in Shenzhen of the China Merchants Group, one of the biggest contractors for Belt and Road and a strategically important state-owned firm. The main focus of the gathering was "building a high-quality professional cadre team"—a requirement stemming from the just-finished Communist Party Congress, a once-every-five-years event that anoints the country's top leaders. In his talk, Chen drew comparisons between the military and business, and his slide deck showed a picture of a soldier holding a rifle.

Another controversial project that McKinsey pushed in China focused on "smart cities." The idea of smart cities is to make urban areas more livable by using networked cameras to better manage traffic, or to reduce water and electricity use through "smart" meters that can send information back to a central location. McKinsey promoted this idea around the world.

McKinsey took part in a 2018 smart cities conference in southern China alongside a government commission that descended from the Mao-era state planning bureaucracy. In 2019 the senior partner Sha Sha, one of the firm's first local hires, spoke at the China Smart City Expo. McKinsey partnered with its most reliable China client, Ping An, to help the insurer implement smart cities systems in the southern Chinese city of Nanning to monitor financial fraud.

But the idea of smart cities encompasses far more than using technology to better manage traffic or to save on electricity and water use. It also covers policing and the use of predictive analytics to help prevent crime, a fact McKinsey made clear to its audience in Chinese.

"Police patrols cannot be everywhere, for instance, but predictive analytics can deploy them in the right place at the right time," McKinsey wrote in a global report about smart cities, which the firm translated into Chinese. It received widespread coverage in China's state media.

In an authoritarian state like China, where police have few constraints and there is no rule of law, that sentence takes on a very different meaning than it would in London, Tokyo, or New York City. A report issued by a U.S. congressional panel on China said that Chinese security officials are using smart cities technology to "expand, improve, and automate information collection and analysis for mass surveillance."

Nowhere is that more true than in China's far west, where the Chinese government has imposed the world's most intrusive network of surveillance cameras and security checkpoints, what the *New York Times* reporters Chris Buckley and Paul Mozur call a "virtual cage" that complements the vast network of detention camps designed to make the region's Muslim minorities "into secular citizens who will never challenge the ruling Communist Party."

It also happens to be the region where, in September 2018, McKinsey's Greater China team gathered for their annual retreat.

It was a sumptuous affair. At one event, a filigree of red carpets laced around sand dunes and open tents where the young McKinsey men and women lounged on prayer rugs and throw pillows. At another, consultants dined alfresco in an ancient Silk Road city and, as the sun set, were treated to a light show featuring multicolored two-humped camels projected onto the face of the crenellated city wall.

They also gathered for speeches—and the inevitable PowerPoint slide presentations—at yet another venue: this one an ornate banquet hall resembling a sultan's palace. A sign overhead captured the mood: "I can't keep calm, I work at McKinsey & Company."

Usually corporate retreats don't make headlines. But a photo of this one—complete with the red carpets and sand dunes—appeared on the front page of *The New York Times* on December 16, 2018. The reason: the McKinsey consultants were partying in Xinjiang, just four miles from a detention camp, one of hundreds in a vast archipelago of gulags in western China housing upwards of one million ethnic Uyghur Muslims and other minorities.

By the time the McKinsey consultants gathered in Xinjiang's ancient Silk Road city of Kashgar, the detention camps were well known. In 2016 the Communist Party boss in the region, Chen Quanguo, had imposed a harsh system of mass surveillance and checkpoints over about half of Xinjiang's twenty-five million people after a surge in violence between the Muslim minorities and majority Han Chinese. Doctors, musicians, teachers, business executives were all caught in the dragnet, which by 2018 had metastasized into the mass detention system. Days before the McKinsey Xinjiang gathering, a United Nations panel called on China to "immediately release" people who had been wrongfully detained.

Children, whose parents were detained in the camps, were dispatched to indoctrination schools that instilled obedience to the Communist Party. Women were detained for the crime of having too many children and subject to involuntary sterilizations and even abortions. As the rest of China relaxed birth control measures, in Xinjiang birthrates plunged as the government created "a climate of terror around having children," according to an Associated Press investigation.

The United States says this amounts to genocide. A March 2021 U.S. State Department report said that genocide and crimes against humanity, including rape, torture, and forced labor, had been committed against the Uyghurs and other minority groups in Xinjiang by the Chinese government.

All that was lost on the McKinsey consultants, who captured their Disney-like experience on Instagram. A couple—garbed like extras from the live-action *Aladdin* movie—posted a photo of the two of them leaping off the crest of a perfect sand dune. Many rode camels in the desert, one flashing the peace sign. The head of McKinsey in the region, the Harvard-educated Joe Ngai, posed for a snapshot with his employees—in the background, female Uyghur performers in flowing yellow gowns, dancing underneath a sign emblazoned with the meeting's theme: "Connecting Together."

While McKinsey isn't responsible for the Chinese government's actions in Xinjiang, hosting a party there put McKinsey on the defensive. "I'm surprised they didn't catch on to the horrible optics," said James Millward, a professor at Georgetown University who studies the region. "Somebody should have been reading the news and said, Wait a minute, we don't want our corporate logo there."

Peter Walker, the former McKinsey senior partner who now describes himself as an expert on U.S.-China relations, tried to explain Beijing's policy toward the Uyghur minority in an April 2020 interview on Fox News.

Walker told Tucker Carlson that despite mass detentions most people in Xinjiang "are materially better off in terms of the quality of life," he said, explaining in his view how Chinese leaders think. "Do I agree with that? No, I don't agree with it," he said.

In response to the *Times* account of the Xinjiang retreat, McKinsey said it would "be more thoughtful about such choices in the future."

In a sign of how important McKinsey considers China to the firm's future, two of its recent managing partners—Barton and Kevin Sneader—both headed the Asia practice before being elevated to the top post. Barton lived in Shanghai, and Sneader, even after taking the firm's top job in mid-2018, based himself in Hong Kong.

In Hong Kong, massive pro-democracy protests erupted in 2019, continuing into 2020, often taking place near McKinsey's office in central Hong Kong. Millions of people took to the streets to demonstrate against Beijing's increasingly heavy hand over the former

British colony, which until then had enjoyed liberties not available to people in mainland China, including freedom of assembly, freedom of the press, and freedom of religion.

McKinsey didn't take out ads or sign any letters in support of the Hong Kong demonstrators, and likewise raised no public objections when Beijing extinguished Hong Kong's democracy movement, and with it the city's civil liberties, with a draconian new national security law.

In contrast, when massive protests erupted across the United States after the murder of George Floyd, McKinsey was quick to ally itself with the cause. The firm was among the signatories of a full-page ad in *The New York Times* dedicated to Floyd's memory. Sneader's name appeared under the company's logo.

It was an inconsistency not lost on a young McKinsey associate in the United States who had spent time in China.

"Kevin Sneader is based in Hong Kong," the consultant said. "In one instance he can speak passionately about racial justice, but aren't there folks outside his front door who could also benefit from the same forthrightness?"

As relations between China and the United States spiraled downward during the four years Donald Trump was president, McKinsey's work in China attracted bipartisan scrutiny. In a June 2020 letter to Sneader, Senator Marco Rubio, a Florida Republican, asked the firm to identify its work with the state, the Communist Party, and any companies in China in "areas of critical national interest to the United States," which he defined as covering a broad range of industries, including health care, telecommunications, pharmaceuticals, and military or civil defense.

Rubio's office said that McKinsey did get back to the senator but declined to disclose the names of its Chinese clients.

Had McKinsey divulged its Chinese client list, here's what Rubio would have learned: From 2018 to early 2020, among McKinsey's fifty-four mainland Chinese clients that could be identified, nineteen were state owned, according to internal company records and announcements by Chinese companies. One of them, the State-Owned Assets Supervision and Administration Commission, is the government agency that oversees the state's ownership stake in companies. Chen Guang, the McKinsey partner who spoke to the China Merchants Group session about the Communist Party Congress, was one of at least two partners supervising that work, the records show. McKinsey says it has not served SASAC and says that China's central government "is not a client of McKinsey, and to our knowledge, has not ever been a client of McKinsey." That statement doesn't mention McKinsey's work with lower levels of China's government. In 2020 McKinsey was invited by SASAC in southwestern China's Yunnan province to give strategic advice to some of the region's biggest state-owned companies, local media reported.

The clients include the big state-owned commercial lenders China Construction Bank and Industrial and Commercial Bank of China, Shandong Steel, and the petrochemicals maker Shanghai Huayi Group. Also on the list, China Telecom, Sinopec, First Auto Works, and the coal company Shenhua, all of which are among the ninety-six strategic state-owned firms: the *zhongyang qiye.*

In the wake of reporting in the *Times* about McKinsey's work in China, Saudi Arabia, Russia, and other nondemocratic countries, the firm announced a change in the way it would accept new clients. Every new prospective client would now be evaluated by a panel made up of McKinsey staffers and outside experts. Partners soliciting new clients were told to prescreen them to make sure they were appropriate. And the firm said it would no longer accept work advising the military, intelligence, police, or justice officials in authoritarian states, nor would it do work for political parties or political advocacy groups, and it wouldn't engage in lobbying. McKinsey says that policy applies to China because the country belongs to a group of nations that scored six points or below on a democracy index published by *The Economist* magazine, which ranks countries on a ten-point scale.

Several current and former McKinsey employees said they were skeptical that McKinsey would follow through on this new policy, citing the wide berth the senior partners around the world have in taking on new clients and the failure of past screening efforts to prevent the firm from taking on controversial work, such as with the drugmaker Purdue Pharma.

And two former senior partners said the very success of such a policy risked undermining McKinsey's business model, which they said depends on putting an enormous amount of trust on its corps of partners to make important decisions.

"The quid pro quo is you had integrity," said George Feiger, a former senior partner in the London office.

Chapter 6

Guarding the Gates of Hades

Tobacco and Vaping

The reckoning was a long time in coming. For nearly half a century, the cigarette industry had used lies and deception to escape accountability for selling the most lethal consumer product in American history. Year after year, study after study, evidence mounted that cigarettes addicted and killed smokers. Aggrieved parties filed lawsuits and legislators proposed laws—all unsuccessful—as tobacco lawyers and friendly politicians ensured that the men who ran tobacco companies stayed in the shadows, answering only to stockholders.

On April 14, 1994, that all changed inside room 2123 at the Rayburn House Office Building. A House committee did the previously unthinkable: it summoned executives of the seven biggest tobacco companies to stand before them and for the first time answer questions under oath about their products. The hearing followed new revelations that tobacco companies were designing cigarettes to sustain addiction.

No longer would the debate over smoking center just on whether cigarettes caused heart disease or cancer—an attack manufacturers parried by saying if adults knew the risks and still smoked, that was their choice. New disclosures raised questions about whether smokers really had a choice. What if manufacturers manipulated an addictive drug in cigarettes—nicotine—to keep people smoking?

Witnesses accused cigarette companies of essentially dosing their product with enough nicotine to ensure addiction. Ammonia was added to enhance the drug's impact. High-nicotine tobacco plants were grown, and different leaves were blended to achieve desired nicotine levels. One major cigarette manufacturer wrote that it was in the company's long-term interest "to be able to control and effectively utilize every pound of nicotine we purchase."

Tobacco companies had secretly studied the pharmacology of nicotine and knew that without it people wouldn't smoke. "Think of the cigarette pack as a storage container for a day's supply of nicotine," one Philip Morris researcher wrote. "Think of the cigarette as a dispenser for a dose unit of nicotine. Think of a puff of smoke as the vehicle for nicotine." Tobacco stocks plunged amid worries of an outright ban on smoking. Philip Morris tried to intimidate the media by filing a $10 billion lawsuit against two reporters and their employer, ABC News, for their landmark investigation of nicotine manipulation in cigarettes. But it was too late. The tide had turned.

The April hearing, televised live to the nation, reached an emotional climax when seven tobacco executives stood next to each other, hands raised, swearing to tell the truth. They denied what most of America knew to be true—that cigarettes were addictive and harmful. The hearing "played to a deep popular anger about corporate dishonesty and greed," Allan M. Brandt, a Harvard history professor, wrote. Tobacco companies suddenly began losing court cases, setting the table for the industry a decade later to pay more than $200 billion in what was then the largest civil litigation settlement in U.S. history. "The hearing ushered in a public health victory for the ages," *The New York Times* editorialized. Big Tobacco had become one of the nation's most reviled industries.

McKinsey & Company watched this rising tide of condemnation, knowing full well that for decades the firm's consultants had been helping the biggest tobacco companies sell more cigarettes. It was handled in typical McKinsey fashion—in secret. McKinsey's name did not figure in the congressional hearings on tobacco, or in two major books totaling fourteen hundred pages, or in media investigations of the industry.

Secrecy benefited both McKinsey and its tobacco clients. Cigarette makers did not want consultants sharing marketing strategy, and McKinsey did not want its reputation sullied as an enabler of companies that sold a deadly product. Were that to happen, prospective hires might wonder how cigarettes squared with the firm's "values," a word often used among new employees and clients.

Cigarette companies, despite their reputation, were attractive clients for one reason: they had mountains of cash. As the investor Warren Buffett once said, "I'll tell you why I like the cigarette business. It costs a penny to make. Sell it for a dollar. It's addictive. And there's fantastic brand loyalty." Like so many chain-smokers, McKinsey could not resist the lure of cigarettes. The profits were too addictive.

The story of McKinsey's extensive work for Big Tobacco has never been told, the details buried deep in fourteen million pages of industry documents. That relationship can be traced back to at least 1956, when McKinsey did a wall-to-wall examination of Philip Morris's operation. Consultants visited its plants, interviewed managers, and studied sales figures. Among McKinsey's recommendations: eliminate jobs and expand research facilities to capitalize on rapidly changing technology in manufacturing. A year later McKinsey produced another report, this one marked "highly confidential," that recommended how the research department, including an experimental pilot plant, should be structured.

But the report also did something else: it foreshadowed the industry's transformation from selling a largely agricultural product into one that scientifically engineered cigarettes through chemistry, nicotine manipulation, and smoke analysis. McKinsey cited, for example, the introduction of "reconstituted tobacco," a process that turns tobacco scraps into paper-like sheets, which are then chopped up and added to the cigarette. Along the way, nicotine is removed with other substances. But, significantly, nicotine is later added to achieve the desired nicotine content.

By the mid-1950s, cigarettes were already under assault after a stream of disturbing reports linking smoking and lung cancer. As researchers, doctors, and public health officials tried to warn Americans that smoking can be lethal, Philip Morris joined an industry-led disinformation campaign aimed at discrediting critics. No evidence can be found in industry records indicating that McKinsey played a role in this deception, but for a company so deeply involved in Philip Morris's business, it strains credibility to believe the consultants were not aware of it.

One fact is undeniable. McKinsey knew about the health risk of smoking because it recommended that Philip Morris designate a unit to carry out two assignments: "coordinate all research that bears on the problem of smoking and health," and recommend studies on "the physiological effects of cigarette smoking." After reading McKinsey's 1956 report, the cigarette company's vice president for manufacturing, Andrew C. Britton, wrote this in an internal company memo: "I think continuous attempts should be made by research to find out exactly what the smoker consciously or unconsciously may want that we can provide to him." One pleasure smokers "unconsciously" wanted was nicotine.

Any lingering doubts about the safety of cigarettes were dispelled one Saturday morning in 1964, when the U.S. surgeon general, Dr. Luther Terry, reported that numerous studies had confirmed the link between lung cancer and smoking. Recognizing the impact of such an announcement, Terry held his press conference on a weekend to minimize its effect on stock prices. And while smoking was not yet widely shunned—that would come later—it is unlikely that McKinsey, known for its exhaustive research and business savvy, would fail to grasp the reputational risk of taking on or keeping such a client.

If McKinsey consultants were concerned, they did a good job of hiding it. As warnings about cigarettes intensified, McKinsey took on new tobacco clients, including R. J. Reynolds, Lorillard, Brown & Williamson, British American Tobacco, and even Japan Tobacco International. The firm also sought to boost cigarette sales in Germany and Latin America.

Tobacco companies did not hire McKinsey to put a shine on their corporate logos. They viewed the firm as a valuable ally and strategist. In 1985, McKinsey wrote a confidential thirty-six-page memo to William Campbell, soon-to-be president of Philip Morris, proposing how the company could remain competitive when tobacco use had peaked due to health concerns. It was a pivotal moment for both the company and Campbell. Philip Morris had just overtaken its longtime nemesis R. J. Reynolds as industry leader, and Campbell was in line for a promotion. (He later became one of the tobacco executives who testified that nicotine was not addictive.)

Several options for boosting or at least sustaining cigarette profits were not available. Philip Morris refused to devalue its product by offering steep coupon discounts. Advertising, particularly for its flagship brand, Marlboro, had reached a saturation point. And the company's manufacturing plants were already efficient and modern. McKinsey told Philip Morris that the only remaining options were to expand, refocus the sales force, and improve "the merchandising and display programs." Philip Morris spent more than $80 million on product displays and shelf space, but that was still much less than its chief competitor, R. J. Reynolds.

Finding ways to energize a sales force played to McKinsey's strength. "In the last three years we have served the majority of the top 25 U.S. packaged goods manufacturers and half the leading retailers," McKinsey boasted. To lead its team, McKinsey offered one of its stars, Andrew John Parsons, a British-born overachiever who, after two degrees at Oxford, enrolled at Harvard Business School and became a Baker scholar. The firm added two senior partners—Charles Shaw, who developed McKinsey's South American business, and Tom Wilson, who led its North American consumer goods practice. McKinsey also planned to add research analysts and systems consultants. "We propose to employ three organizational devices that we have found useful in similar projects," McKinsey said. "Namely a task force, a steering committee and frequent workshops."

Mark LeDoux, a young McKinsey consultant assigned to the tobacco team, had the job of dealing with smaller retailers who had begun to question whether selling cigarettes was worth the hassle. Companies kept adding new brands to already crowded display shelves, and some customers objected to any cigarette sales at all. On top of that, thieves were shoplifting cigarette cartons, or even breaking into stores during off-hours to steal them, putting pressure on their razor-thin profit margins. McKinsey told retailers not to worry. "We crunched the numbers and found that cigarette sales accounted for 40 percent of a typical store's profits," LeDoux said in an interview. "They didn't realize that." In fact, cigarettes kept some stores afloat.

How much McKinsey charged Philip Morris is confidential, but the firm lifted the veil ever so slightly when, for another cigarette client, the firm outlined its philosophy and fee structure. "We put client interests ahead of firm or individual interest," McKinsey promised. "We vigorously protect client confidentiality." And the firm only undertakes projects "that have a significant multiple of value creation to fees—typically at least 10 times." Of course, "value creation" can be defined in many ways. And McKinsey's vow to put client interests over all else sounded reasonable, but not for this industry. Moreover, how could McKinsey justify advising hospitals and government agencies on how to reduce health-care costs while their tobacco clients were filling hospital rooms with the sick and dying?

McKinsey stuck with cigarette clients even as internal industry documents surfaced in legal proceedings that cast Big Tobacco as a predator bent on fooling the public about the safety of its products. In 1992, the federal judge H. Lee Sarokin became so outraged reading industry memos in a liability lawsuit that he cast aside judicial restraint when he wrote, "All too often in the choice between the physical health of consumers and the financial well-being of business, concealment is chosen over disclosure, sales over safety, and money over morality. Who are these persons who knowingly and secretly decide to put the buying public at risk solely for the purpose of making profits and who believe that illness and death of consumers is an appropriate cost of their own prosperity."

For his strong words, Judge Sarokin was removed from the case. But they would be echoed a decade later when another federal judge expressed the same conclusion after presiding over the government's Racketeer Influenced and Corrupt Organizations Act (RICO) case against Big Tobacco.

Anyone seeking to justify taking money from cigarette companies could always find a way. Big Tobacco did employ tens of thousands of workers. In 1990 a *Fortune* magazine survey of top executives, outside directors, and analysts ranked Philip Morris as America's second most admired company, largely because it had pleased investors. A hospital and a children's zoo bore the name of the Tisch family, owners of Lorillard, a major McKinsey client. And across from New York's Grand Central Terminal, Philip Morris's corporate headquarters featured a branch of the Whitney Museum, which the company cited as an example "of how private enterprise can address the public interest to the betterment of society."

Murray H. Bring, a senior Philip Morris lawyer, said the industry had nothing to apologize for. "We know that we are manufacturing a lawful product," Bring said. "We also know that we are honorable and honest people." Geoffrey Bible, a senior Philip Morris executive, cautioned against banning cigarettes, using words not likely to end up in a McKinsey slide:

> What do you think smokers would do if they didn't smoke? You get some pleasure from it, and you get some other beneficial things, such as stress relief. Nobody knows what you'd turn to if you didn't smoke. Maybe you'd beat your wife. Maybe you'd drive cars fast. Who knows what the hell you'd do.

The domestic cigarette industry was under siege, but millions of Americans still smoked, and new customers were needed to replace the ones who quit or died. This meant money remained available for consultants. Lorillard's chief executive, Andrew Tisch, personally implored his employees to cooperate with McKinsey because competitors and government regulators had changed market dynamics. Lorillard needed to rethink strategy, he said, and McKinsey consultants were "renowned for their ability to solve problems and create opportunity."

Any successful McKinsey strategy had to involve Lorillard's Newport brand, the nation's second most popular cigarette behind Marlboro. With one of the highest nicotine yields on the market, Newport was especially popular with Black customers, in part because it was marketed aggressively where they lived. In 1978, Lorillard used James Brown's hit single "Papa's Got a Brand New Bag" for its marketing message that "Newport is a whole new bag of menthol smoking."

More than two-thirds of young Black smokers preferred Newport's menthol cigarettes. Blacks also suffered disproportionately from tobacco-related illness. Whether by design or happenstance, McKinsey in the early 1990s sent Pamela Thomas-Graham, the firm's first Black female partner, to help lead its Lorillard team.

McKinsey's much bigger client R. J. Reynolds—run for a time by a former McKinsey partner, Lou Gerstner—was struggling under debt from a leveraged buyout made famous in the book *Barbarians at the Gate*. To boost profitability, McKinsey suggested two of its favorite perennials: offshoring and paying workers less. "Offshoring parts of products could result in huge savings," McKinsey told the company. "Embedded labor—coupled with low labor rates in emerging markets—drives savings opportunity." Savings for stockholders, perhaps, but a potentially devastating blow for the displaced workers. As proof of its ability to squeeze profits from labor, McKinsey cited its "global network" of offshore manufacturing experts.

RJR's big moneymaker, Camel, appealed to younger smokers mostly because of an advertising campaign that featured a cartoon character, Joe Camel. Using a cartoon to sell cigarettes infuriated tobacco critics because if smokers did not start young, they most likely would not start at all. RJR cynically marketed Camel as great for people who do "what's right" and embrace a "lust for living."

McKinsey followed up on RJR's themes by invoking a technique called "funnel analysis" to reach potential customers in certain demographics, including "trendy 20s in urban areas or African Americans." (Funnel analysis charts interactions consumers have with a company before buying their products.) The firm also lapsed into well-worn McKinsey-speak, offering to dip into its "robust tool kit of innovative ideas," including an unexplained "killer idea approach," a phrase either ill-advised or perfect for a cigarette company.

International markets were also a growing concern for Big Tobacco. With the antismoking movement on full boil in the United States, cigarette companies worried that sentiment could spread overseas. Once again, McKinsey stepped in to help. In Germany, where RJR's Camel was losing market share, McKinsey counseled the company to pour all its resources into revitalizing the brand. But RJR had to act fast, McKinsey advised, before new regulations, aimed mostly at reducing underage smoking, could hinder certain promotions and advertising.

In the late 1990s, Philip Morris executives entertained a more ambitious international strategy. They joined two other tobacco giants, British American Tobacco and Japan Tobacco International, on a secret mission to construct a code of conduct that would convince the world that Big Tobacco could self-regulate and stop youth smoking. By doing so, they hoped to circumvent a major threat—the World Health Organization's first global public health treaty. Since the three companies controlled about 41 percent of the world market, they had the resources to hire not just McKinsey but also other consultants, lawyers, and even Kissinger Associates, the firm founded in 1982 by the former U.S. secretary of state.

The companies called their undertaking Project Cerberus, after the three-headed dog that guards the gates of Hades in Greek mythology.

From 1999 through 2001, the Cerberus team hashed out their plan in a series of meetings in London, Geneva, and New York City. These were not budget-conscious affairs. The tobacco executives met in London at the historic Grosvenor House hotel, overlooking Hyde Park and Mayfair, the high-end shopping, dining, and art district. McKinsey helped organize strategy sessions and recommended ways the three competing companies could work toward a shared goal.

After a meeting in London, McKinsey wrote a confidential summary of what the group hoped to accomplish, including ending the industry's isolation, regaining its voice in tobacco control discussions, and achieving a stable business environment. To appear credible, the group initially considered hiring an independent audit body to ensure that the companies fulfilled their promises. But that provision was discarded amid discord over how the oversight should work.

Project Cerberus's grand ambition was never realized. When the industry's proposal was finally revealed to the public, it attracted virtually no attention, because on that day, September 11, 2001, terrorists crashed hijacked planes into the World Trade Center and the Pentagon, killing thousands.

Project Cerberus did not stop the WHO antismoking campaign,

but the cigarette companies did not surrender. Instead, they sought to weaken tobacco control measures in countries around the world. An investigation of Project Cerberus, published in the *American Journal of Public Health,* concluded that the project showed yet again that health professionals should not trust the industry. "This lesson is particularly important in developing countries, where governments, policymakers, and the general public are vulnerable to the tobacco industry practices and often poorly prepared to contest their influence," the authors wrote.

By the late 1990s, the U.S. Justice Department had finally begun training its guns on Big Tobacco, accusing it of violating RICO by fraudulently hiding the risks of smoking. After a bitter battle that resulted in six years of litigation and a nine-month trial, the federal judge Gladys Kessler settled the issue once and for all.

In August 2006, Judge Kessler issued a ruling of more than sixteen hundred pages that gave voice to health officials who for decades fought to expose the industry's dishonesty. Four major McKinsey clients were defendants. Kessler's finding cast Big Tobacco companies as racketeers, a term usually associated with organized crime. Then in words that echoed Judge Sarokin, she wrote that the industry had "marketed and sold their lethal product with zeal, with deception, with a single-minded focus on their financial success, and without regard for the human tragedy or social costs that success exacted." She also put an end to the notion that tobacco executives did not know their products were addictive and deadly. Kessler wrote,

> Defendants have known many of these facts for at least 50 years or more. Despite that knowledge, they have consistently, and repeatedly, and with enormous skill and sophistication, denied these facts to the public, to the Government, and to the public health community.

A full ten years after the court's devastating takedown of the industry, McKinsey was still trying to help Philip Morris, now called Altria, to sell more cigarettes, according to internal company documents. "We are one team, working side-by-side," McKinsey said in a business proposal. As a tobacco teammate, McKinsey expressed its "deep commitment" to deliver "a pragmatic, actionable loyalty program that works for Altria"—in other words, a program that rewards customers for buying more of their cigarettes, including the company's iconic Marlboro brand.

McKinsey is also a teammate of the FDA, which since 2009 has had the authority to regulate tobacco products, including Altria. In other words, McKinsey plays both offense and defense, a dubious practice that has long remained secret. Since 2009, the FDA has awarded McKinsey more than $11 million for advice on regulating tobacco and for organizing the FDA office that includes tobacco regulation. During much of that time, McKinsey also consulted for the world's biggest cigarette companies without disclosing this potential conflict of interest to the FDA, two senior former officials of that agency said.

As of 2019, McKinsey's tobacco clients included Altria, Philip Morris International, Imperial Tobacco Group, British American Tobacco, and Japan Tobacco Inc. For Altria alone, McKinsey billed more than $30 million in 2018 and 2019. Serving the regulator and the regulated has been part and parcel of McKinsey's modus operandi, especially in the federal government.

"We have served the FDA on over 30 initiatives," McKinsey wrote in winning $1.1 million in contracts to advise the agency's Center for Tobacco Products. McKinsey's tasks included "risk identification and mitigation" as well as "influencing the behaviors, opinions, and practices that are contrary to the goals and objectives" of tobacco regulators. Presumably, that included McKinsey's cigarette clients.

Eric N. Lindblom, former director of the FDA's Office of Policy for the Center of Tobacco Products, said he was "startled and surprised" to learn of McKinsey's long record of consulting for cigarette companies. "We didn't think, duh, they are also going to serve the industry," Lindblom said. "I just don't remember this coming up or talking about it."

Dr. Lawrence Deyton, the center's first director, said he was also unaware that McKinsey had served tobacco interests. "That should have been disclosed," Dr. Deyton said. "If one of those potential vendors has a relationship that might have an impact on their work, I would hope that would be part of the discussion for qualifications."

For half a century, McKinsey consultants helped tobacco companies peddle their toxic products without penalty and made a fortune doing so. Management consultants face ethical questions all the time about whether to take on a risky client, and they handle these matters differently. At McKinsey, individual employees can turn down assignments if they have moral qualms about a particular client. But if a partner still wants that client—and they are under great pressure to find new revenue streams—then assembling a team of willing employees is usually easy. The firm's decentralized management structure gives partners enormous latitude in making decisions. Individual consultants can assuage their consciences, but the firm still profits. (McKinsey said it now screens clients more carefully and that within the last two years it has stopped consulting on tobacco issues.)

The firm also knows there is no shortage of suspect companies in search of a quick fix to their problems, sometimes at the public's expense. Soon, nicotine would come calling again, this time in a different product. And once again, McKinsey was there to open the door.

The tobacco industry was bloodied but hardly defeated. Millions of Americans continued to buy cigarettes, though nowhere near as many as in previous decades. The percentage of young smokers, so critical to the industry's continued profitability, was plummeting, eventually landing in the single digits. Millennials had a different set of values from their parents, and standing outdoors to fill their lungs with cancer-causing smoke held little appeal.

President Obama sought to build on these changing attitudes by signing legislation in 2009 that explicitly gave the FDA the authority to regulate cigarettes, tobacco, and any new product that the agency "deemed" a tobacco product. The law would be enforced through a new office, the Center for Tobacco Products, with nicotine a major focus. To help the office operate more effectively, the FDA chose to revamp its regulatory philosophy. No longer would the agency just react to events; it would proactively seek to identify health risks before they became a full-blown crisis. Given this fundamental shift in strategy, the tobacco office decided it needed an outside adviser skilled in carrying out major government reorganizations.

The FDA turned to a familiar name—McKinsey & Company. In securing the FDA contract, McKinsey acknowledged the importance of adopting a proactive mindset, rather than "the more reactive form of management that is too common among similar organizations in the federal government." The names of McKinsey's senior leaders handling the contract were redacted in government records on the grounds that they were trade secrets, an expansive if questionable use of that exemption.

McKinsey's work got an early test with the appearance of electronic cigarettes, handheld devices that delivered nicotine vapor through battery-generated heat, not combustion. For adult smokers, e-cigarettes provided a safer way to satisfy their nicotine addiction without the harmful effects of smoke. Under the law, the FDA could have quickly "deemed" e-cigarettes a new tobacco product and taken steps to regulate them. But it did not. Instead, the agency waited six years before even beginning the process, a decision that would have serious consequences for teenagers and raise questions about the FDA's new "proactive" mindset.

E-cigarette manufacturers could not expect to openly market their nicotine devices to nonsmoking teenagers, but selling them to adults as less harmful than cigarettes might garner wide support. E-cigarette companies faced two major problems, though. Their products had to deliver uniformly high levels of nicotine without a harsh taste, something they could not yet do, and they needed to slip through or around a presumably more vigilant FDA. The first problem was a matter of technology and chemistry. The second was political.

It wasn't until 2015 that a new product solved the technical problems and in the process transformed the industry. It was called Juul. With a sleek design, and a battery that could be recharged in a computer portal, Juul became known as the iPhone of vaping. This high-tech product appealed to millennials and even younger potential customers. It was also powerful, delivering some of the highest nicotine yields in the industry—the equivalent of twenty cigarettes. As a bonus, the nicotine taste could be masked in fruity, child-appealing flavors. Its small size made it easy to hide from parents and teachers, and unlike cigarettes it left no telltale smell of smoke on their clothes.

Juul smartly spread the news of its new e-cigarette through a social media campaign, emphasizing lifestyle, an approach tobacco companies had used successfully to capture young smokers. Juul also bought face-to-face access with teenagers, paying $134,000 to a charter school group to set up a summer camp, according to *The New York Times.* "Other schools across the country were offered $10,000 from the e-cigarette company for the right to talk to students in classrooms or after school," the *Times* reported.

In just a few years, the vaping industry had sown the seeds of a teenage nicotine epidemic—exactly the type of threat that the FDA's revamped tobacco unit was supposed to identify early and address.

The Illinois senator Richard Durbin, a veteran of the tobacco wars going back decades, was among the first members of Congress to raise alarms over vaping. Durbin's father, a two-pack-a-day Camel smoker, died at an early age from lung cancer, and the senator hadn't forgotten it. "Losing precious market share, Big Tobacco put their researchers and marketers to work," he said. "They needed a new product that did not carry the moral taint of cancer-causing tobacco—even better if it looked like a USB flash drive and could easily plug into a kid's laptop."

Had Durbin and his colleagues examined the roster of Juul employees, they would have discovered an army of former cigarette company employees—thirty-nine of them—from five tobacco companies, all former McKinsey clients.

Medical professionals expressed deep concern about vaping's sudden popularity with adolescents. Dr. Jonathan Winickoff, a practicing pediatrician at Massachusetts General Hospital, said many of his young patients were unaware of "JUUL's massive nicotine content and do not understand the dangers of nicotine." Once his patients started vaping, Dr. Winickoff said, many of them found it "nearly impossible to stop."

Senator Durbin responded by challenging the foundation on which Juul was built—as a smoking cessation product for adults. "More than 20 percent of children under the age of 18 are using e-cigarettes, compared with less than 3 percent of adults," Durbin said. "JUUL knows exactly where their profits are coming from and it's not from adults looking to quit smoking . . . it's from our children."

Where was the FDA? he wanted to know.

In 2013, two years before Juul even hit the market, five U.S. senators had already written to the FDA urging the agency to assert its regulatory authority over vaping. Nothing was done. Senators would write more letters; health officials would raise more alarms—again, without result. Through it all, Juul kept selling flavored nicotine, which appealed to its young customers. "Pediatricians are reporting their teenage patients are putting e-cigarettes under their pillows so they can vape overnight," Dr. Sally Goza, president of the American Academy of Pediatrics, said.

Despite their popularity, little was known about e-cigarettes. Could underage vaping pave the way for smoking as adults? No one knew. What other chemicals might be in Juul's nicotine cartridges or in nicotine vials that customers of other brands load into their open-system e-cigarettes? There were reasons aplenty for society to have demanded answers to these questions, especially because the adolescent brain is particularly vulnerable to nicotine addiction.

This lack of vigilance resulted in what a former deputy commissioner of the FDA, Dr. Joshua Sharfstein, called a "full-blown catastrophe."

The FDA didn't create the crisis, but it did little to stop it. Agency officials said they struggled to find the right balance between helping adults to stop smoking—still the nation's leading cause of preventable death—and keeping e-cigarettes away from children. The FDA also complained that unfavorable judicial rulings had undermined its oversight, though that ignores the agency's decision to invoke its own "regulatory discretion" to delay by years the vetting of e-cigarettes. Senator Durbin blamed the FDA for acting less like a watchdog and more like a willing accomplice, "delaying commonsense regulation of the e-cigarette industry," refusing to remove illegal products from the market, and "staying silent in the face of false health claims."

The *Times* offered its own harsh assessment of the FDA:

> In dozens of interviews, federal officials and public health experts described a lost decade of inaction, blaming an intense lobbying effort by the e-cigarette and tobacco industries, fears of a political backlash in tobacco-friendly states, bureaucratic delays, and a late reprieve by an F.D.A. commissioner who had previously served on the board of a chain of vaping lounges.

Under great public pressure, the FDA announced in July 2017 that it would place nicotine and addiction "at the center of its tobacco regulation efforts." Two months later, the FDA created a nicotine steering committee, staffed mostly with senior leaders from the FDA's drug evaluation office and the Center for Tobacco Products. Both units were McKinsey clients. Some might say better late than never, but to the parents of addicted teenagers the delays were inexcusable.

There was a lot of ground to make up. By the end of 2017 more than 2 million middle and high school students were using e-cigarettes. That number would grow to 5.4 million in 2019. And McKinsey, with Juul as a client, played a role in helping that company achieve success.

One fact spoke most convincingly about the FDA's regulatory record. Not a single Juul device in the United States had been sold legally, according to congressional testimony in late 2019. A vaping device to be sold legally would need pre market review by the FDA, and as of 2019 that had not happened. Nonetheless, Juul's sales of e-cigarettes totaled $1 billion in 2018, giving the company an estimated valuation of $38 billion, more than Ford Motor Company. McKinsey's specific advice to the FDA could not be determined, but the fact remains that the agency failed to identify and "proactively" address vaping as a looming threat. (By the end of 2021, only three vaping products—none made by Juul—were approved for sale by the FDA.)

While the FDA did little to stop the spread of underage vaping, McKinsey was busy consulting for the two most powerful forces seeking to dominate the vaping market—Juul and the tobacco giant Altria. Each company had its own vaping product, but Altria ultimately decided to support Juul, the market leader. So in 2018, Altria invested nearly $13 billion in its former competitor. To sweeten the deal, the tobacco company distributed $2 billion in bonuses to fifteen hundred Juul employees.

Working for Juul proved profitable for McKinsey as well. In less than two years of work, Juul paid McKinsey between $15 million and $17 million, Alfonso Pulido, a McKinsey partner, stated in a deposition in a product liability case in the U.S. District Court of Northern California.

Neither the parents of addicted teenagers, nor government regulators, knew of McKinsey's conflicted relationships. McKinsey said internal conflict of interest rules prohibit the sharing of confidential information between consultants for clients with competing interests. In Pulido's deposition, he was asked how those rules are enforced, but he sidestepped the question. "They are enforced by processes and procedures that dictate how we staff our teams and organize our teams and serve our clients," he said.

McKinsey consulted for Juul on highly sensitive topics, such as surveying which flavor names appealed to thirteen- to seventeen-year-olds, though the firm said that work was in support of the company's effort to prevent youth vaping. McKinsey even offered to study the "risk framework" of Juul's developing a product for the marijuana market. McKinsey's research raised no red flags within the firm, one partner who worked on the Juul account said.

Juul employees recalled seeing McKinsey consultants in and out of the company's San Francisco headquarters on Pier 70, a renovated shipyard in the Dogpatch neighborhood, a trendy mix of warehouses and art galleries. Strategy sessions were held in a "war room" with to-do lists and important issues taped to the wall.

Asked whether McKinsey worked on FDA issues, an employee with direct knowledge of these meetings replied: "Oh my God, McKinsey helped JUUL write their FDA submission—dead serious." Pulido in his deposition confirmed that McKinsey helped prepare Juul's response to the FDA's inquiry into the company's marketing practices.

McKinsey said it stopped consulting for Juul in the spring of

2019 because of rising regulatory uncertainty and "increased awareness of youth use."

Juul knew it had a large target on its back. So the day after the FDA expressed concern about nicotine flavors attracting younger users—hardly a new concern—Juul stopped accepting orders from its ninety thousand retailers for mango, fruit, crème brûlée, and cucumber. But not mint and menthol. The decision promised more than it delivered, according to Siddharth Breja, a former senior vice president of global finance at Juul. In a wrongful-termination lawsuit, Breja said the company "always knew that its sales would not suffer because the mint pods, given its fruity flavor, would make up for any lack of sales of the other flavored pods." And how did Juul know? "This was confirmed through research conducted by McKinsey & Co," the lawsuit alleged. (Juul later stopped shipping mint, but not menthol.)

Juul further strengthened its ties to Big Tobacco by elevating K. C. Crosthwaite, Altria's former chief growth officer, to CEO in September 2019. The company took the position that Altria, formerly called Philip Morris, wasn't a bad actor. But some employees found the company's close ties to the cigarette company troubling. One engineer characterized the company's outlook as "split between mission and money." At the highest levels, the engineer said, "it was growth, profit. Stuff about health was just a cover."

One of McKinsey's major competitors in the consulting business decided it could not work for Juul, a company selling an addictive product favored by minors. A McKinsey partner, Michael Chui, posted a public comment expressing concern about vaping. "In just a few years," Chui wrote, "vaping has wiped out two decades of work getting teens to quit (or never start) cigarette smoking." Chui did not single out Juul or his firm, though he might not have known that McKinsey had Juul as a client. (Another major consultancy, Bain & Company, also had several teams working for Juul.)

So why did McKinsey take on this controversial client? According to confidential internal company documents, Juul apparently had a big supporter in the firm, a leader so influential and respected that senior partners in 2021 would elect him managing partner, the top post in the firm. His name: Robert Sternfels, who is listed on internal documents as McKinsey's director of client services for Juul. McKinsey said Sternfels knows Juul's former owner, but did not work on any "client engagements" with Juul.

McKinsey also consulted for a group widely viewed as a tobacco industry front group—the Foundation for a Smoke-Free World. Founded in September 2017, the nonprofit organization asserted that its goal was to reduce deaths and disease from smoking while assuring potential donors that its board was independent with no ties to the tobacco industry. That statement was noteworthy for what it did *not* say—that Philip Morris International *started* the group with donations of $8.4 million. Of that, more than $400,000 went to McKinsey. PMI was the group's sole donor, and McKinsey was the sole consultant.

"Our mission is to end smoking in this generation," the group wrote on its home page. "We also support the development of alternative products and methods that may reduce users' current health risks and help them to stop smoking entirely." The foundation promised to fund research and promote ways "to accelerate progress in reducing harm and deaths from smoking."

Health officials weren't buying it. In a letter to the British medical journal *The Lancet,* researchers at the University of Bath reported that the foundation spent more money on public relations than on research. This expenditure, the researchers wrote, "does not match the picture the Foundation paints of itself as a scientific body, but instead supports the growing consensus that the Foundation provides a key public relations function for Philip Morris." Indeed, the World Health Organization and "hundreds of public health organisations globally have taken a strong stance in rejecting collaboration with the Foundation," according to the researchers.

In 2017, the same year McKinsey took money from the tobacco-financed foundation, President Trump's FDA awarded the consulting firm another contract, this one for $1.2 million, to revamp hiring in the tobacco and medical products units. Two years later, the FDA gave McKinsey a $1.5 million contract for developing "curiosity, creativity and innovation" in the tobacco unit's science office.

Trump personally weighed in on the dangers of vaping in September 2019. Seated in the Oval Office with the first lady, Melania Trump, he announced that his administration was moving to ban all flavored nicotine vapors, except menthol. "We can't have our kids be so affected," Trump said. Two months later, he backed off, saying the issue needed more study, after being warned of the political fallout.

The backlash against Juul continued to build. In late November 2019, Altria said it had devalued its investment in the company by $4.5 billion, citing bans on vaping in certain areas and the increasing likelihood that the FDA would ban nicotine flavors.

Then, on January 2, 2020, Trump reversed himself again and announced a ban on most nicotine flavors. Menthol was not included. The order also did not apply to vape shops, which made most of their money selling vials of nicotine for so-called open-tank devices, where consumers add their own nicotine. Addiction researchers criticized the announcement, especially the decision to leave menthol on the market, since they said menthol enhanced nicotine's impact, making quitting more difficult. Its cooling sensation also masked the harsh taste of nicotine, making it more appealing to children, said Dr. Goza of the American Academy of Pediatrics. "The idea that menthol is an adult flavor is just plain wrong."

The FDA did not publicly protest. Two weeks later, the *New York Times* Editorial Board declared the agency to be in distress and in need of fixing or risk becoming a regulator without influence. The editorial did not mention McKinsey's behind-the-scenes work on behalf of the FDA.

The firm had silently profited in the service of not just tobacco and vaping but also, as evidence would show, opioids. McKinsey even ventured into another area of potentially addictive behavior—gambling—when it advised a major casino on how to keep gamblers at the table when they were about to leave.

As McKinsey discovered, addiction offered big rewards—and dangers—depending on whether you were selling or buying. And McKinsey partners were most definitely selling.

Chapter 7

Turbocharging Opioid Sales

The year was 2002, and McKinsey was on the hunt for new clients, this time in the target-rich field of pharmaceuticals, already a major income source for the firm. McKinsey planned to stimulate interest by publishing an article contending that Big Pharma had been leaving money on the table by mishandling its sales force in the field.

While most clients hire McKinsey because of reputation or referrals, the firm also seeks new business by writing thought pieces suggesting that companies have problems in need of fixing. The article's lead author, Martin Elling, a Harvard law grad, would become a major force in McKinsey's pharmaceutical practice.

Elling's article admonished drug companies for relying on "the 'pinball wizard' sales model," where drug reps bounce from one doctor's office to another. The most successful sellers earned roughly the same as the less productive ones for a simple reason: their employers couldn't distinguish between the two. McKinsey called it "equal pay for unequal performance," which bred disillusionment and morale problems.

McKinsey wrote that drug companies could fix the problem simply by doing a better job of analyzing prescription data. "When a patient fills a prescription, the order is stored in a database that can be matched for drug, producer, and physician," the firm explained. This information could then be used "to target physicians who are most likely to prescribe more of a given drug over time, no matter how much or how little they prescribe at the moment." It also allowed companies to identify high-performing sales reps and reward them.

The article did not go unnoticed. One predatory drug company, Purdue Pharma, apparently liked McKinsey's ideas. From 2004 to 2019, Purdue paid McKinsey $83.7 million in fees for marketing advice that made its billionaire owners even richer by stoking the nation's appetite for the painkilling drug OxyContin.

McKinsey assembled a formidable team to advise Purdue, including Elling and two medical doctors, one of whom also had a PhD.

OxyContin had first hit the stores in 1996. Because the drug could continuously treat severe pain, patients were now able to sleep through the night with a low risk of addiction, the company said. Both claims were soon revealed to be overstated or false. Some patients found that the drug, a powerful opioid, stopped working sooner than advertised, prompting them to take more of it. Purdue also started offering OxyContin in higher doses, increasing the risk of addiction.

The drug rendered some users euphoric, sending them on a chemical high that they wanted again and again. Sales jumped. A rise in crime followed. When addicts couldn't get OxyContin, they stole it or in later years turned to heroin and fentanyl, a synthetic opioid similar to morphine except exponentially more powerful.

By unlocking the power of data analysis to find doctors most likely to prescribe the opioid, Purdue had created a monster that would tear holes through families, schools, and communities. Many died. Reputations were ruined.

In the end, the casualties included Elling and his colleague Arnab Ghatak, a medical doctor—both fired by McKinsey after internal records showed they had discussed purging records to hide the firm's involvement. The consultancy, which for decades had mostly kept its name out of the news, suddenly found it on the front pages of America's newspapers, leaving an ugly and lasting reputational scar. To settle government investigations into its role in helping Purdue "turbocharge" opioid sales when thousands of people were dying of overdoses, the firm agreed to pay more than $600 million even as it denied any wrongdoing.

Purdue filed for bankruptcy, after agreeing to pay $8 billion to settle government investigations. Its owners, the Sackler family, agreed to pay $4.5 billion in exchange for a legal shield against any further opioid litigation. A federal judge later ruled that the bankruptcy court lacked the authority to grant that protection.

The real losers, of course, are the 750,000 people who died in an epidemic kick-started, the government said, by the sale of OxyContin. As of late 2021, opioid deaths showed no sign of abating.

Looking back, it is easy to see how this tragedy unfolded. The FDA approved OxyContin without a proper review. Purdue exaggerated its benefit and downplayed its risk. The drugmaker bought doctor loyalty by hosting more than forty pain management training conferences, some at warm-weather resorts. Upwards of five thousand physicians, pharmacists, and nurses attended these all-expense-paid meetings where Purdue recruited and trained them to speak on matters important to the company, according to the *American Journal of Public Health.*

Purdue also benefited from a movement that it helped finance, aimed at convincing doctors that their unjustified fear of opioid addiction caused them to undertreat pain.

OxyContin first sank its teeth into the poorer communities. "From a sales perspective, OxyContin had its greatest early success in rural, small town America—already full of shuttered factories and Dollar General stores," Beth Macy wrote in *Dopesick,* her powerful account of opioid addiction and abuse. Within the first two years of the drug's release, 24 percent of high school juniors in a small western Virginia town said they had tried OxyContin along with 9 percent of seventh graders.

Doctors were being arrested for improperly prescribing pills that were resold on the streets and in schoolyards. The U.S. attorney in Maine grew so concerned that in February 2000 he took the extraordinary step of alerting the state's doctors of this gathering menace. Other companies, instead of seeing the potential for tragedy, saw a path to bigger profits. The opioid market was expanding, and they wanted a piece of it.

Still OxyContin remained a predominantly local story, but not for long. Bob Cole, an investigator for the State of Ohio Board of Pharmacy, called an editor he knew at *The New York Times* with a story tip: county medical examiners along the Ohio River were finding the same opioid—OxyContin—in a surprising number of dead bodies brought in for autopsies. The editor asked a reporter, Barry Meier, to investigate, and in the spring of 2001, Meier co-authored a front-page story that helped turn OxyContin into a national story.

Purdue did not hold back in defending its turf. As Meier reported in *Pain Killer,* his seminal book on OxyContin, Purdue "used money, job offers, and other favors to co-opt, influence, or defeat its critics or potential opponents."

With Purdue increasingly under scrutiny, the drugmaker hired McKinsey to help protect its opioid franchise, not an unreasonable expectation given that McKinsey calls itself the leading consultancy for medical product companies, handling as many as forty-five hundred projects in a single five-year period.

Equally important, McKinsey knew the opioid business.

McKinsey had already been advising a Purdue competitor, Johnson & Johnson, a pivotal player in opioid production and one of McKinsey's most lucrative clients through the years. Best known for its baby products, J&J also sold its own opioid drug.

But J&J's biggest contribution in the field of pain treatment came from its ownership of two companies that processed the starting material for opioids, which came from a mutant strain of Tasmanian poppy plants. J&J sold the product to opioid manufacturers, including Purdue, prompting law enforcement to call J&J the opioid "kingpin," an embarrassing moniker for a company that built its reputation as a family-friendly company.

McKinsey helped J&J sell its signature opioid, a narcotic patch called Duragesic. In PowerPoint slides, McKinsey recommended that J&J target "high abuse-risk patients (eg males under 40)" and move physicians who were "stuck" in prescribing less potent opioids into prescribing stronger formulations. Another slide asked, "Are we properly targeting and influencing prescription behavior in pain clinics?"

The McKinsey slides provided ammunition for a lawsuit the Oklahoma attorney general filed years later against J&J—but not McKinsey—accusing the company of "embarking on a cunning, cynical and deceitful scheme to create and feed the need for opioids, engineer a mutant poppy to amplify the need they created, overstate the effectiveness and minimize the risk of these drugs."

In the first trial of an opioid lawsuit, a J&J witness twice tried to distance the company from McKinsey's slides, saying they were "McKinsey's words," not J&J's. Asked by a lawyer for the state whether the company fired McKinsey, the witness said no and acknowledged that McKinsey continued to consult for the company. The judge ruled in favor of the state and ordered J&J to pay a $465 million penalty, citing the company's "false, misleading, and dangerous marketing campaign" that led to addiction and overdose deaths. The Oklahoma Supreme Court ultimately threw out that ruling, saying the state's legal strategy in pursuing the case as a public nuisance was flawed.

J&J and McKinsey might seem unlikely to have ended up in the seamier side of the narcotics business. Both sought to imbue their quest for profits with a higher purpose—McKinsey through its "values" and an obligation to dissent and J&J through its corporate "credo," which held that its first responsibility was "to the patients, doctors and nurses, to mothers and fathers and all others who use our products and services." Employee complaints and suggestions, the credo stated, should not be discouraged.

McKinsey's work had far less impact on J&J than on Purdue Pharma.

By the time McKinsey took on Purdue as a client in 2004, the drugmaker already knew it was vulnerable. The company's legal team had instructed its sales reps to avoid using terms such as "addiction" and "abuse" in their reports. That same year, the FDA sent Purdue a stern warning letter that said its advertisements "grossly overstate the safety profile of OxyContin by not referring in the body of the advertisements to serious, potentially fatal risks."

McKinsey's consulting team at Purdue Pharma had the backing of three senior partners—the highest rank short of managing partner. All three had extensive experience in pharmaceuticals. Their accomplishments reflected McKinsey's admirable qualities as well as its contradictions, from serving the less fortunate to helping companies profit at the expense of the health and safety of their customers.

McKinsey's team included Arnab Ghatak, a cum laude graduate from Princeton, who also earned a joint medical and MBA degree at the University of Pennsylvania. Ghatak's interests included improving health care in developing nations, a mission that did not square with helping Purdue push more narcotics out the door in the midst of an opioid epidemic. He married a woman of similar intellectual heft who oversaw philanthropy projects at McKinsey's other opioid client, J&J. Their union merited a breezy article in *The New York Times* telling how they met.

The other senior partners on the team were Elling, the Harvard Law School graduate and a leader of the firm's North American pharmaceutical practice, and Robert Rosiello, who sat on McKinsey's Partner Compensation and Client Risk Committees. Rosiello would later become the chief financial officer at Valeant, the former McKinsey client accused of price gouging on lifesaving drugs.

At least twenty-four other partners consulted for Purdue. To have seven partners on the same contract, in addition to a support staff, signaled this wasn't a rogue unit flying under the radar of the firm's risk managers. The size and duration of the job guaranteed the firm steady revenue, not something the higher-ups would be inclined to disrupt.

McKinsey began consulting for Purdue when J. Michael Pearson led the firm's pharmaceutical practice. An intense, sometimes profane senior partner, Pearson did not fit the stereotype of lean and disciplined McKinsey consultants. Yet his record at the firm was impressive. In his nearly quarter of a century at McKinsey, he consulted for many of the top drug companies, guiding them through consolidations, mergers, and other matters. Pearson, who became Valeant's CEO, came to believe that drug companies spent too lavishly on new drug development without getting much in return.

McKinsey's elite roster of corporate clients and its supreme confidence convinced Purdue that its opioid franchise was in good hands.

But because the firm works in secret, the drug company couldn't publicly cloak itself in McKinsey's respectability.

With government investigators circling, Purdue needed a counterweight, someone important enough to give it cover. That someone turned out to be the former New York City mayor, Rudy Giuliani. "We believe that government officials are more comfortable knowing that Giuliani is advising Purdue Pharma," one senior Purdue official said.

"America's mayor" had a difficult assignment. Federal prosecutors in Virginia had prepared a damning prosecution memo of more than a hundred pages that the author Patrick Radden Keefe described in his book *Empire of Pain* as "an incendiary catalog of corporate malfeasance." Prosecutors wanted felony charges brought against three Purdue executives.

Purdue hired Giuliani to make those charges disappear, and they did, Keefe reported. In 2007, a Purdue affiliate agreed to pay a $600 million fine to settle federal charges stemming from its early deceptive marketing practices. Three Purdue executives also pleaded guilty to a single "misbranding" charge and agreed to pay $34.5 million.

The absence of jail sentences infuriated Purdue's critics, especially families who lost children to the epidemic. The judge himself expressed regret that the terms of the plea deals precluded prison terms.

Purdue's public relations problems were not going away, however. The mothers of children who died of opioid overdoses were rallying public support. So in June 2009, Purdue's future chief executive, Craig Landau, asked McKinsey to find ways to counter these emotional messages. One possible solution: round up OxyContin users to speak out in favor of the drug.

To hold back the tide, Purdue employed a two-part marketing strategy: make what seemed like reasonable concessions to the public health community while continuing to put pills in the hands of as many people as possible. The company removed its most powerful dose, the 160-milligram pill. It supported prescription monitoring and suspending shipments to Mexico because those pills often ended up back in the United States. And under pressure, Purdue decided to reformulate OxyContin so addicts could not crush it to release the active ingredient all at once, rather than slowly over an extended period.

The reformulation, however, needed FDA approval, so McKinsey lent its expertise, arranging for the firm's "FDA expert" to speak for two hours with a top Purdue official. "It was extremely helpful to get insights on how they are crafting the response," Maria Gordian of McKinsey wrote to her colleagues in an email.

On January 20, 2009, Gordian reported that McKinsey and Purdue "had a very good FDA rehearsal yesterday," attended by several members of the Sackler family. "The team did an outstanding job on the study, preparing the client and executing the mock meeting. We are off to DC today for the actually [*sic*] FDA meeting tomorrow."

Purdue eventually got FDA approval for the reformulation, but it did not change the fact that the drug remained highly addictive and was being prescribed to people for whom less risky options were available. "The real problem with opioids from the public health perspective is addiction," said Dr. Lewis Nelson, a specialist in emergency medicine and an FDA adviser. "These pills in the reformulated version don't do anything to reduce the likelihood or magnitude of addiction."

Addicts who could no longer obtain OxyContin turned to the street. A hundred-tablet bottle purchased at a pharmacy for $400 sold for $2,000 to $4,000 on the black market. As pills became even more scarce, addicts turned to heroin, triggering what became known as the second wave of opioid abuse. Highly addictive and unregulated, the narcotic was sometimes spiked by street dealers with a synthetic opioid, fentanyl, which is fifty to a hundred times more powerful than morphine. Users didn't always know that fentanyl had been added or in what amount, and many died from unintended overdoses.

To combat a decline in prescriptions, Purdue expanded its sales force, prompting one of Purdue's owners, a member of the Sackler family, to ask why the company had predicted a decline in OxyContin sales, when he thought they should be rising. At moments like this, Purdue executives again turned to McKinsey.

To boost sales amid the strengthening opioid epidemic, McKinsey had to cook up radical new ideas. One suggestion was to promote

OxyContin as a drug that gave patients "freedom" and "peace of mind," along with the "best possible chance to live a full and active life." OxyContin could also reduce stress, making patients more optimistic and less isolated, McKinsey said, a suggestion health officials called ludicrous.

McKinsey also suggested that Purdue pay more attention to nurse-practitioners and physician assistants, who are not doctors but can influence prescribing practices. "They have the greatest sales rep access and are increasingly important in large group practices," McKinsey said. The two groups registered double-digit increases in OxyContin sales, another target of opportunity.

Purdue, meanwhile, organized a sales contest to identify and reward its top sales reps—not a new concept, but in line with McKinsey's recommendations from years earlier.

OxyContin use was still rising in parts of the country, giving Purdue hope. "Despite a national decline, micro market analysis suggests important pockets of growth that Purdue should focus on," McKinsey wrote in 2013. "It is encouraging that at a zip code level, roughly 40% of zips are actually growing their OxyContin prescription volume."

One growth pocket was Fort Wayne, Indiana. But an examination of those "encouraging" sales figures revealed a trail of abuse and misery. Opioid-related deaths were surging in the Fort Wayne area, with heroin and fentanyl contributing to that rise.

At a Fort Wayne pain clinic, Dr. Michael Cozzi wrote more opioid scripts than any doctor in the state, eventually leading the state to suspend his medical license. Seeing up to 120 patients per day, Cozzi wrote sixty-four thousand prescriptions for controlled substances in two years. Of those, almost three million dosage units were for oxycodone, the opioid and main ingredient in OxyContin. When patients didn't have cash, Cozzi accepted guns as payment. In one month, he prescribed controlled substances for 1,700 patients.

The sales boom benefited at least one Purdue field rep as well. In 2012, during what the Indiana attorney general called the peak of opioid prescribing, that sales rep ranked first among 525 sales reps nationwide in selling the company's pain medicine. She alone accounted for $2 million in OxyContin sales during the first quarter of 2012. Her reward: a vacation to Aruba and a first-quarter bonus of $36,000.

Purdue could have used this sales data for more than Aruba vacations. Indiana authorities said in legal papers that the drugmaker "knew the identities, practices, and prescribing volumes of every health care provider the company visited, and therefore was well-situated to identify suspicious prescribing. Yet Purdue did not use this information to protect patients and the public." McKinsey might also have used its sales data to warn Purdue of dangerous prescribers.

Still, OxyContin sales remained a concern for Purdue. Higher-strength pills, the company's most profitable ones, were in decline, as were the number of pills per prescription. Purdue's sketchy reputation made it possible for competing companies to sell their opioids just by saying their drugs were not OxyContin.

The situation had deteriorated to the point where in the early summer of 2013, Purdue instructed McKinsey to find a way to stop the hemorrhaging. Superficial marketing gimmicks be damned.

This was war, and McKinsey began viewing those who challenged Purdue as the enemy. Attempts to curb the epidemic had gone too far, the firm asserted, making it difficult for patients who truly needed pain relief to get help. To fix this, McKinsey needed to descend into Purdue's engine room, figure out what was broken, and come up with a plan—a major undertaking, not just because of client expectations, but also because of the mission's urgency.

Known for its analytical skills, McKinsey asked Purdue to buy more data, right down to how many milligrams of OxyContin each prescriber wrote. The consultants didn't just sit around their computers and spreadsheets; they ventured into the field, interviewing physicians, nurse-practitioners, and pharmacists. They did ride-alongs with sales reps and studied techniques for keeping patients on opioids longer, according to law enforcement records.

The consultants used McKinsey-speak to communicate, discussing "field force execution," benchmarks, and the firm's proprietary "corporatized provider network connector." Presumably, Purdue knew what all that meant.

"Lastly our work builds upon our prior experiences serving Purdue that go back 10 years," McKinsey wrote. This institutional knowledge gave the firm the credibility that other consulting firms lacked. McKinsey reassured Purdue by saying it was "pursuing 20+ distinct opportunities" to boost sales.

On July 18, 2013, McKinsey presented the Purdue Pharma board with its much-anticipated market analysis. It was preliminary but sobering. Some problems were obvious. To stem the flow of opioids, the Drug Enforcement Administration and the Justice Department had begun pressuring different links in the supply chain, including wholesalers and pharmacies. That led to patient complaints about problems filling their opioid prescriptions.

"The retail channel, both pharmacies and distributors, is under intense scrutiny and direct risk," McKinsey wrote. "We see clear disruption impacting patients and it is spreading. The range of obstacles include entire pharmacies being shut off by distributors, pharmacies themselves imposing tablet limits . . . and pharmacies choosing to not stock OxyContin." These measures posed a "clear and direct threat to patient access," McKinsey concluded. "This requires an urgent response."

The worst access problems were at retail pharmacies, especially Walgreens, which had abruptly changed policies after admitting it broke the law by not properly monitoring prescriptions. The drugstore chain's new safeguards flagged suspicious patients and imposed dose limits.

McKinsey recommended a counterattack. The firm suggested lobbying Walgreens leaders "to loosen up." The most audacious recommendation was to create an alternative drug delivery system. The plan, McKinsey said, was to deliver OxyContin directly to patients through mail-order pharmacies to circumvent retail pharmacy restrictions on high-dose, suspicious prescriptions.

Another option, McKinsey said, was to "fight back" against steps that the DEA, the Department of Justice, and others were taking to address opioid overuse. Purdue also needed a clear strategy to respond to influential groups like Physicians for Responsible Opioid Prescribing.

It was time, McKinsey said, to "turbocharge" Purdue's sales engine.

McKinsey's recommendations were well received by the company. But Russell Gasdia, Purdue's vice president of sales and marketing, privately questioned at least one of the conclusions in an email to Arnab "Arnie" Ghatak at McKinsey. "Arnie, some venting. . . . I have some real concerns with the thought that our issues center on a need to turbocharge sales."

Ghatak emailed another McKinsey partner and tried to put him at ease about Gasdia's qualms. "FYI . . . think it is just stress, will try to see him live tmw."

McKinsey still had to present its turbocharge plan to Purdue's owners—members of the Sackler family. After the meeting, Ghatak reported that the board meeting "went very well—the room was filled with only family. . . . We went through exhibit by exhibit for about 2 hrs. They were extremely supportive of the findings and our recommendations." Elling agreed: "The findings were crystal clear to everyone and they gave a ringing endorsement of 'moving forward fast.' "

The most important takeaway from McKinsey's July 2013 analysis was this: while drugstores and law enforcement officials were trying to limit how much OxyContin was coursing through the nation's bloodstream, McKinsey was doing just the opposite, even suggesting ways to get around those safety measures.

Then, a little more than a week after McKinsey suggested ways to boost sales of OxyContin, the FDA—the agency most responsible for ensuring the safety of the country's drug supply—rewarded McKinsey with a $2.6 million consulting contract with the Center for Drug Evaluation and Research, which regulates prescription and generic drugs, including OxyContin. The FDA contract called for McKinsey to "work with the office leadership, the program managers, and other key personnel to design, develop, and implement an operating model that ensures good communication both internally and externally."

In the following weeks, McKinsey rolled out ever-stronger recommendations to keep the OxyContin pipeline flowing, such as targeting the heaviest prescribers, sharply increasing prescriber visits by sales reps, using patient advocacy groups to push back against efforts to limit "appropriate" access, accelerating efforts to set up an alternative drug distribution channel, and engaging in high-level talks with Walgreens.

"Rather than addressing the pieces individually," McKinsey wrote, "we recommend you take actions to 'Turbocharge Purdue's Sales Engine' and optimize across all elements of the winning sales model—from targeting, to territories, to incentive compensation." The firm invoked words from the Vietnam War, stressing the importance of "winning the hearts and minds" of the sales force and permanently changing how the company operates. Purdue later rebranded its "turbocharge" campaign, realizing it might not sit well with families that lost children to opioids. The new name: "Evolve to Excellence."

In 2017, McKinsey made a suggestion that stunned the healthcare community when it later became public. The firm thought Purdue should consider giving distributors a rebate for every OxyContin overdose attributable to pills they sold. As a guide, McKinsey estimated how many customers of these companies might overdose. It projected that in 2019, for example, 2,484 CVS customers would either overdose or develop an opioid use disorder. A rebate of $14,810 per "event" meant that Purdue would pay CVS $36.8 million that year. CVS is also one of McKinsey's biggest clients. McKinsey said that Purdue never implemented the rebate program.

As the decade came to a close, McKinsey announced that it would no longer take on opioid manufacturers as clients. By then, 400,000 Americans had died from abusing prescription or illicit opioids. Along the way, Purdue's owners had removed $10 billion from their company.

Should there be any lingering question about the importance of McKinsey's work, one of its partners, Maria Gordian, a lead "counselor" to the drug company's chief executive, answered it clearly and forcefully in an internal memorandum she wrote in 2009.

When McKinsey arrived, Gordian explained, Purdue was facing "an unstable and challenging situation." Fortunately for the drug company, McKinsey came to the rescue. "Through a series of efforts, *we secured the future of the crucial OxyContin franchise*" (italics added).

Doubtful she'd put that on her résumé now.

Other embarrassing documents surfaced as government investigators closed in, including this email that Elling sent on July 4, 2018, to another senior partner on the Purdue case, Dr. Ghatak: "It probably makes sense to have a quick conversation with the risk committee to see if we should be doing anything other than eliminating all our documents and emails. Suspect not but as things get tougher there someone might turn to us."

"Thanks for the heads up," Ghatak replied. "Will do."

"Have a great fourth," Elling replied.

McKinsey fired both men without specifying a reason, except to say they violated the firm's professional standards.

On February 4, 2021, Kevin Sneader, the firm's managing partner, sent out a company-wide memo announcing that McKinsey had reached a settlement with forty-nine state attorneys general. "Indeed, while our past work with opioid manufacturers was lawful and never intended to do harm, we have held ourselves to a higher bar. We fell short of that bar. We did not adequately acknowledge the epidemic unfolding in our communities or the terrible impact of opioid misuse and addiction, and for that I am deeply sorry."

Sneader made no mention of McKinsey's consulting work for the different links in the opioid supply chain, like the retail drugstores and the major drug distributors. Some of those entities ended up paying millions of dollars to settle government investigations into their handling of opioids. The nature of McKinsey's advice to these companies could not be determined.

By August 2021, McKinsey had paid about $641 million to settle claims from states and U.S. territories, but that didn't end the litigation. A McKinsey lawyer said at a federal court hearing in California that the firm was facing fifty additional lawsuits filed by cities, counties, Native American tribes, union health benefit plans, and schools, among others.

McKinsey also set out to mitigate the problems it helped to create.

In 2018, Tom Latkovic, a senior partner in Cleveland, coauthored an article titled "Why We Need Bolder Action to Combat the Opioid Epidemic." Latkovic also co-authored a McKinsey article that offered ten "insights" into the opioid crisis. One warned that opioids are frequently prescribed to patients "with known or potential risk factors for abuse."

McKinsey also supported a nonprofit group, Shatterproof, dedicated to ending the stigma of drug addiction. Its founder, Gary Mendell, whose son killed himself after struggling with addiction, gives emotional speeches, including one at a McKinsey health-care conference, about how the stigma of opioid addiction delayed the quest to defeat the epidemic.

Latkovic offered a similar message: "As we've done more work on opioids, we have come to appreciate the deep and really nefarious role that stigma plays in the crisis."

Latkovic's efforts to combat the stigma of drug addiction were laudable. But an attack on stigma holds society responsible. An attack on opioid manufacturers, distributors, and physicians is different: it is bad for business. For years no one at McKinsey dared to publicly criticize the firm for helping Purdue Pharma sell more opioids.

McKinsey did, however, boast about creating the Center for Societal Benefit Through Healthcare. The firm wrote, "We have honored that mission by serving our clients effectively and investing in issues deeply relevant to society, such as social determinants of health, rural health, maternal health and behavioral health—including mental health, substance use and the opioid crisis."

Purdue is not solely to blame for the opioid epidemic. Doctors overprescribed OxyContin, pharmacists collected bonuses for filling prescriptions they shouldn't have, the FDA and DEA allowed the epidemic to take shape, and lawmakers failed to enact laws to safeguard the public.

"We didn't get ahead of it. Nobody got ahead of it," the FDA commissioner, Dr. Scott Gottlieb, said at a medical conference in October 2017. The FDA should have limited OxyContin's use to only certain patients, but it didn't, nor did it issue strong early warnings of the drug's high risk for addiction. The FDA official who led his agency's review of OxyContin's drug application took a job at Purdue two years after leaving the FDA.

Dr. Michael Carome, director of Public Citizen's Health Research Group, said the FDA too often made decisions "that placed the financial interests of opioid manufacturers over protecting public health."

A *New York Times* headline offered this harsh judgment: "As Tens of Thousands Died, F.D.A. Failed to Police Opioids." The agency was supposed to oversee a program that required the makers of OxyContin and other long-acting opioids to finance the training of physicians on their safe use and then evaluate whether the program worked. But the FDA dropped the ball, a medical study concluded.

"Even when deficiencies in these efforts became obvious through the F.D.A.'s own review process, the agency never insisted on improvements to the program, called a risk evaluation and mitigation strategy, or REMS," *The New York Times* wrote. The senior author of the study, Caleb Alexander, said he was surprised that "the design of the program was deficient from the start."

Here again McKinsey's dual role as an adviser to the regulated and the regulator came into play. In 2011, the FDA awarded McKinsey a $1.4 million contract to reorganize the office overseeing the flawed programs that were the focus of the study.

Informed that McKinsey had consulted for the FDA while advising Purdue, Dr. Andrew Kolodny, a senior scientist and co-director of opioid policy research at Brandeis University, expressed surprise. "It is a very obvious conflict of interest," he said in an interview. "That never should have been allowed, never should have happened."

On Capitol Hill, senators wanted to know whether McKinsey's close relationship with the FDA had contributed to the government's failure to recognize and rein in the opioid epidemic. On August 23, 2021, a bipartisan group of six senators wrote to the FDA, asking about the agency's extensive contracts with McKinsey.

"While working with the FDA, McKinsey also worked for a wide range of actors in the opioid industry, including many of the companies that played a pivotal role in fueling the opioid epidemic that our country now faces," the letter said.

At least seventeen of the contracts awarded to McKinsey by the FDA between 2008 and 2021—worth more than $48 million—called for the firm to work with the Center for Drug Evaluation and Research, the letter said. That division was responsible for approving certain drugs, including prescription opioids.

In 2010 and 2011, the senators noted, the FDA had awarded more than $2.4 million in contracts to McKinsey to design a system called "track and trace" to enhance the agency's ability to identify drugs harmful to consumers. Those contracts "strongly suggest that McKinsey, while representing the FDA, was actively engaging with its private-sector clients that were the targets of this new regulatory process—an obvious conflict of interest," the letter said.

McKinsey's ties to federal health officials went deeper than the senators realized. In March 2022, *New York Times* reporters were the first journalists to obtain a new cache of McKinsey documents that showed how the firm quietly courted the man who became the nation's most influential health-care official, Alex Azar, Trump's secretary of Health and Human Services.

After Azar left Eli Lilly, where he served as president, he asked McKinsey for advice in finding a job. His main contact there was Elling, who, along with Ghatak, was instrumental in advising Purdue Pharma to turbocharge OxyContin sales in the midst of the opioid epidemic.

"I'd really value sitting with you guys and talking through ideas you may have and advice on how to look at and for opportunities," Azar told Elling in an email.

Elling responded immediately. "We'd love to sit and learn of your aspirations and provide any thoughts that might be helpful."

"Wonderful," Azar replied. What exactly was discussed when they got together isn't known, but seven months after their meeting Azar got the job as HHS secretary.

"Thanks guys," Azar wrote to Elling. "Very grateful for all your help. Let me get my sea legs over there and we can chat about the practice and connection to HHS."

In the days before Azar's Senate confirmation, a rift developed in McKinsey's office over what to tell him in a memo about the opioid crisis. Ghatak sought to downplay the danger, even going so far as to say that the words "crisis" and "epidemic" were hyperbole, a colleague said.

Tom Latkovic, a senior partner, wanted to strengthen the warning. "I'm trying to highlight the hornet's nest you are entering," he wrote in an internal memo.

With little time to resolve the conflict, McKinsey removed a strongly worded section that Ghatak found objectionable.

A spokesman for Azar denied that McKinsey helped him get the HHS job.

While opioid addiction and fatal overdoses affected wide swaths of society, they fell heaviest on the working poor, struggling to survive in rust-belt cities where factories closed, salaries stagnated, and jobs were outsourced. The epidemic contributed to the further fracturing of the middle class while diminishing the prospects of those aspiring to join it.

In a review of the book *Deaths of Despair and the Future of Capitalism,* Atul Gawande wrote that the authors, two Princeton economists, explored a vexing question: why so many members of the working class without college degrees were dying from drug and alcohol abuse or suicide. The numbers had reached such a level that life expectancy in the United States as a whole dropped three years in a row.

Opioids played a role, but as Gawande observed, they did not create the conditions that spawned the despair.

> We all but load the weapons of self-destruction for people in misery. The U.S. has . . . embraced automation and globalization with greater alacrity and fewer restrictions than other countries have. Displaced workers here get relatively little in the way of protection and support. And we've enabled capital to take a larger share of the economic gains.

Gawande wrote that the book put numbers "on a long-simmering but inchoate sense among many people that something had gone profoundly wrong with the American Dream."

As opioid abuse tore through America, many of its enablers—doctors, distributors, and regulators—were publicly exposed. Yet for years one vital player managed to escape public scrutiny in congressional hearings, books, newspapers, documentaries, and medical journals. That player was McKinsey, the consigliere of health-care companies and their regulators, a font of business school wisdom that promised to reimagine the future of medical care for the benefit of all.

It was not until 2019 that Maura Healey, the Massachusetts attorney general, revealed that her office had been digging through the drugmaker's confidential files and discovered McKinsey's deep involvement with Purdue. Healey was the first attorney general to sue Purdue's owners, and her staff's investigation of McKinsey led the way for other state attorneys general to hold the firm accountable.

The states are now able to use their shares of the $600 million settlement to pay for treatment, prevention, and recovery. McKinsey also agreed to limit its work with manufacturers of addictive narcotics and pledged to put tens of thousands of pages of documents related to its opioid work into a public database.

Despite heavy media coverage of McKinsey's role in fanning the flames of the opioid epidemic, many government officials remain loyal to the firm. In Healey's own state, Governor Charlie Baker hired McKinsey to handle a study into the "future of work" while McKinsey was paying the state for the harm it caused from opioids. Healey called the governor's decision to hire McKinsey "outrageous."

The Boston Globe reported that the state's health department had already paid McKinsey more than $18.6 million since the beginning of 2020.

Just hours after *The New York Times* published an article about Healey's findings, a private chat room for present and former McKinsey workers registered their reactions. Several were expletive-laced expressions of outrage. Others talked about the duty to serve the client's bottom line within moral and ethical boundaries. Another wrote that it was fine to maximize shareholder value "but not at all costs, not at the cost of our moral values and our society's well-being."

After the *Times* published those responses, the website was shut down.

Chapter 8

"Turning a Coal Mine into a Diamond"

The swag is abundant. Charge your cell phone with an ExxonMobil-branded battery. Spread out in the cool Colorado mountain air on a blanket that folds into its own carrying case, courtesy of the Mount Sinai hospital system. Pick up your free Cotopaxi backpack from the company whose motto is "Gear for Good." Make the world more beautiful with "wildflower seed bombs" from Standard Industries, the building materials company that planted thirty-five hundred trees in honor of this annual jamboree of the great and the good. Welcome to the Aspen Ideas Festival.

At Aspen, and its Swiss cousin, the World Economic Forum in Davos, an invitation validates your importance, a recognition that you have something wise to say, that you belong in the company of the wealthy and the powerful. Vitally important issues get aired here in courteous panel discussions often moderated by prominent journalists who treasure the spotlight. Facebook's Mark Zuckerberg spoke there in 2019 to an audience free from hecklers accusing him of undermining democracy.

The year Zuckerberg spoke, attendees were treated to an event by the rapper Common, who wore a white T-shirt emblazoned with the slogan "Let Love Have the Last Word." The Aspen Ideas Festival is partly underwritten by Paul E. Singer, founder of the hedge fund Elliott Management, anointed "the world's most feared investor" by Bloomberg News. Another underwriter is ExxonMobil. Throwing executives, scientists, celebrities, and journalists into the same room "can generate ideas capable of transforming our world," ExxonMobil gushes.

Occasionally, a heretic slips in on the list of invitees. Such was the case with the Dutch historian Rutger Bregman, who famously skewered the Davos attendees in January 2019 for flying hundreds of carbon-dioxide-spewing private jets into an event "to hear David Attenborough speak about how we're wrecking the planet." He quickly pivoted to the topic of rich people not paying enough taxes, an issue he thought was central to solving a host of society's problems but, he said, received scant attention at Davos. "It feels like I'm at a firefighters conference and no one's allowed to speak about water."

Bregman wasn't invited back in 2020.

McKinsey, another Aspen underwriter, has no such worry. The firm's partners are invited back year after year. It's their night at the Oscars. Institutionally averse to publicity, McKinsey views Aspen and Davos as opportunities for its consultants to meet potential clients, show off their research, and perform the subtle art of convincing corporate bosses and government agencies that they have problems they may not realize. And McKinsey can solve them.

In June 2019, the last pre-COVID meeting of the Aspen festival, McKinsey came in force. André Dua, a senior partner from the Chicago office, spoke about automation in the workplace. Lareina Yee, the firm's chief diversity officer, focused on women in senior corporate positions. Michael Chui, a McKinsey Global Institute partner, emceed a panel on technology and trust.

Then there was Dickon Pinner, a senior partner and co-founder of McKinsey's sustainability practice. He was the main attraction on a three-member panel called "Climate Breaking Points: Business Strategies to Mitigate Economic and Social Risks."

Lean, eager, and prone to framing talks with three bullet points like so many of his McKinsey colleagues, Pinner spent most of his career in the firm's semiconductor practice. He also was a former engineer at Shell, the giant oil and gas company. Another panelist, a former McKinsey consultant and Oxford scholar, Cameron Hepburn, serves on an advisory board for Shell and is a senior research fellow at an oil-industry-funded think tank. The third speaker, Phil Waldeck, an insurance executive, has no apparent background in climate studies. But his company, Prudential, does have a $5 million partnership with Aspen. If he lacked world-changing ideas, Waldeck did serve as the Greek chorus. "Double-click on that," he'd say to emphasize a conversation point.

Pinner came armed with PowerPoint slides charting carbon dioxide levels and temperature going back 350,000 years. It showed dramatic swings, with both moving in tandem. Then, about 10,000 years ago, the line flattened out. What followed was the flowering of human civilization, which, he said, "was predicated on climate stability." In the last 40 years, that stability ended, with carbon dioxide levels soaring to levels not seen in more than 3 million years. Even with the growth of solar and wind power, global temperatures are set to rise 3 to 4 degrees Celsius (5.4 to 7.2 degrees Fahrenheit) under current policies.

"We are not on the right path right now," he said.

Pinner was making a cogent and urgent case for action, playing to one of McKinsey's strengths—its ability to quantify problems.

Gillian Tett, the *Financial Times* reporter moderating the session, called his presentation "absolutely chilling," adding that she would challenge anyone "to just say, 'whatever' " and walk away.

The world was running out of time. Months after Pinner's talk, rising temperatures and drought fueled massive wildfires that devastated parts of Australia. Then, as the seasons turned, the fires moved to the Northern Hemisphere, engulfing the American West and turning the sky over San Francisco a Martian orange. More than four million acres burned. The California fires were small-scale compared with the infernos that erupted in Siberia in 2021. It was Russia's biggest fire season ever, burning an area about the size of Tunisia.

With warmer air able to hold more moisture, tropical deluges came to New York City. Central Park recorded its most hourly rainfall ever between 10:00 p.m. and 11:00 p.m. on August 21, 2021, a record that was smashed only eleven days later as the remnants of Hurricane Ida flooded the city. Scientists said that Greenland's million-year-old ice sheet was melting so fast it might have passed the point of no return, meaning even if global warming stopped, it would continue to melt, threatening to inundate the world's coastal cities.

Anyone reading the barrage of urgent calls from McKinsey to reduce carbon emissions might get the impression that the firm is a Very Green Company. It deploys "green teams" in its offices across the world, ferreting out ways to reduce the firm's carbon footprint, from reducing paper use to cutting back on travel through more videoconferencing. The firm invests in projects such as solar cookstoves in China and rain-forest preservation in Panama to offset its emissions. McKinsey even calculates its own total carbon emissions, which take into account the air travel logged by McKinsey's road-warrior consultants.

Being green is part of McKinsey's official mantra, memorialized in its code of conduct: "As a firm, we take seriously our responsibility for the environmental sustainability of our operations and our offices take steps to reduce our environmental footprint. We also serve private, public, and social sector clients across the world on steps they are taking to address climate change."

The message McKinsey wants to convey is clearly laid out on its website: "We are committed to protecting the planet."

McKinsey is an evangelist—in public—on the need for its clients to take urgent action on climate change. In one year, from August 2019 to August 2020, the firm put out at least fifty-six reports or emails on the topic. Titles included "Earth to CEO: Your Company Is Already at Risk from Climate Change," "Sustainability Under the Sea," and "Fashion on Climate: Look Closer at How the Fashion Industry Can Urgently Act to Reduce Its Greenhouse-Gas Emissions."

Those McKinsey reports don't downplay the crisis. In one slide deck from 2019, McKinsey predicts that climate change is "expected to be as severe in impact as weapons of mass destruction."

One reason McKinsey is so passionate in public about climate change is that the thousands of young, supremely well-educated, and environmentally conscious people it recruits expect it. Their children will likely live well into the next century, when the melting ice caps in Greenland and Antarctica could submerge many coastal cities, while the Middle East and parts of the Indian subcontinent may become too hot for human habitation.

McKinsey wants prospective hires to believe that they are joining a company that cares about the climate. Its online testing system challenges applicants to make the right environmental decisions in a computer simulation. "You are the caretaker of an island where plants and animals live in a variety of diverse ecosystems" was one recent scenario. The test taker is then tasked with building a healthy coral reef and finding the right vaccine to cure a flock of birds from a "hideous virus."

In its many public reports, McKinsey is clear-eyed and appropriately alarmist about the looming environmental threat. In 2020, the year after Pinner's appearance in Aspen, he co-authored a *McKinsey Quarterly* article that laid out the ways the world could limit the global temperature rise to 1.5 degrees Celsius above preindustrial levels. That's the level set by the UN's Intergovernmental Panel on Climate Change, beyond which, the panel concluded, it will become increasingly difficult for humans to adapt.

Pinner and his colleagues argued that the world was running out of time to reach that goal, and mapped out three scenarios on how to get there, all requiring reductions in emissions from the oil and gas industry, electric utilities, agriculture, and the tailpipes of cars and trucks.

"The good news is that a 1.5-degree pathway is technically achievable," the McKinsey consultants wrote. "The bad news is that the math is daunting. Such a pathway would require dramatic emissions reductions over the next ten years—starting now."

What companies cannot do, McKinsey says, is to engage in public relations, focusing on "feel-good initiatives" without really changing the behavior of a company, from climate change to mentoring women and minorities. "Our challenge to our clients is: how can you go from words on a page to facts on the ground? How do you move from branding and slogans to something that is lived in the day-to-day?"

That was the challenge Gillian Tett, the moderator in Aspen, posed to Pinner. Given the urgency of the crisis, she asked a logical question: "Have you tried to take this to Washington? Have you tried to take it to the White House?"

Pinner said no, repeating the line McKinsey uses to justify working with controversial clients like ICE and the Saudi government.

"I think from our point of view, we don't really have a role to play on the policy side," Pinner said. "Where we think we can add value is by converting the science into numbers that expose the risk and put them in a form that decision makers can make decisions." Besides, he intimated, government wasn't the answer. "We think the big issue here is around capital formation and allocation," he added.

That was Pinner's big focus: to show how markets weren't properly accounting for the risk of investing in offshore oil rigs, pipelines, and even coastal real estate in Florida, assets sure to take a big hit as temperatures and sea levels rose and the world moved away from fossil fuels.

When pressed at the panel for something—anything—he would be comfortable recommending to policy makers, the furthest he would go was this suggestion: "How might you incentivize the private sector to redirect capital flows into assets that are less risky." He wasn't asking for specific policies that might affect oil or coal production but instead calling for markets to somehow work their magic.

Despite Aspen's lofty aspirations, the "solutions" that usually emerge have a common theme: they involve little or no sacrifice from the world's billionaires or big corporations. Instead, they focus on the private sector "doing well by doing good"—with small measures to address pressing problems that often call for collective action. It's good PR.

That's the critique offered by Anand Giridharadas, a former McKinsey consultant and a former Aspen fellow. In a 2015 speech to his fellow fellows, he questioned the entire premise of the organization, saying it makes the rich and powerful feel virtuous about the incremental good deeds their companies do under the banner of "corporate social responsibility" while their core businesses continue to inflict harm.

Giridharadas called it "the Aspen Consensus," a belief that "the winners of our age must be challenged to do more good." But there was a caveat, he said. "Never, ever tell them to do less harm. The Aspen Consensus holds that capitalism's rough edges must be sanded down and its surplus fruit shared, but the underlying system must never be questioned."

—

Take ExxonMobil. At the 2019 Aspen conclave, Vijay Swarup, the oil company's head of research and development, extolled the virtues of "carbon capture," a technology that can pump smokestack emissions back into the ground. ExxonMobil said it was "all the buzz." But ExxonMobil had been buzzing about carbon capture for more than a decade by this point, and the technology remained mired in the pilot stage. But carbon capture does nothing to address ExxonMobil's biggest contribution to global warming, namely the tens of millions of cars and trucks around the world burning its gasoline. Months before he spoke, ExxonMobil forecast that its emissions by 2025 would be 17 percent higher than in 2017, adding twenty-one million tons annually of carbon to the atmosphere, about what Greece emits each year. The company kept that forecast secret.

Three weeks after Pinner spoke in Aspen, the departing McKinsey associate Erik Edstrom took aim at the "feel-good initiatives" that companies use to give the appearance of being environmentally focused without taking the painful measures necessary to really make a difference. But the focus of his ire wasn't an oil company, or a coal miner, or an automaker: it was McKinsey itself.

In many ways, Edstrom fits the profile of an ideal McKinsey hire. Like many of the firm's consultants, he is a military veteran, having led a U.S. Army platoon in Afghanistan and served on the honor guard at Arlington National Cemetery. In a company that values physical prowess, he was among the fittest of them all—a triathlete and, at West Point, the top scorer in the army's physical fitness test. After the army, he went to Oxford, alma mater to many of McKinsey's top leaders.

But Edstrom's time in Afghanistan brought out another side of him, one that questioned the wisdom of the senior military and civilian leaders who kept America in a war for a generation: a war that brought untold suffering to Afghan civilians and killed or wounded thousands of American soldiers. "If a millennium of the dead could speak: There is no betrayal more intimate than being sent to kill or die for nothing, by your own countrymen," Edstrom wrote in a book about his war experience.

While in the army, Edstrom was deeply affected by the former vice president Al Gore's campaign to raise awareness about man-made climate change, capped by the 2006 Oscar-winning documentary, *An Inconvenient Truth.* He wanted his professional life to focus on helping to solve this existential problem. At Oxford, Edstrom earned a master's in environmental change and management, in addition to getting an MBA. Edstrom eventually settled in Melbourne, working first for Boston Consulting Group and then, starting in early 2018, for McKinsey.

Like all new associates, Edstrom was given two books. One was Marvin Bower's *Perspective on McKinsey,* written in 1979, which expounds on core values and principles that shaped McKinsey. The other was *A History of the Firm,* a readable internal company history.

From the history book, Edstrom learned that McKinsey owed much of its success to consulting for fossil fuel companies.

Mobil Oil was McKinsey's first mega-client in the early 1950s, a time when it also served Union Oil and Sun Oil. In the mid-1950s, at the recommendation of Texaco, McKinsey took on work with Royal Dutch Shell, first in Venezuela in 1956. Shell was so pleased with McKinsey that the following year it asked the firm to conduct a global restructuring, helping McKinsey plant roots on the European continent, according to the firm's official history. By 1960, Texaco was McKinsey's biggest client.

McKinsey then took on work with government-owned oil giants such as Pemex in Mexico, PDVSA in Venezuela, and Saudi Aramco. Coal-mining clients also came early on. When the firm opened its office in Melbourne in 1963, the place Edstrom would work more than half a century later, among its first clients was Broken Hill, now BHP, the world's largest mining company by market capitalization, which mined coal in Australia. The head of the Melbourne office in the 1960s, Rod Carnegie, went on to head the Australian branch of Rio Tinto, now the second-biggest mining company. Both companies are McKinsey clients to this day, and many of Edstrom's colleagues in Melbourne were working on those accounts.

McKinsey's early work with oil companies needs historical context. The knowledge that rising carbon dioxide levels can heat the atmosphere was not widely known in the 1950s, when Mobil and Texaco were driving the firm's revenues. But, just like with tobacco, any work done for fossil fuel companies over the last quarter century by the highly educated cadre of McKinsey consultants was done with the full knowledge that the product their client sold was irreparably harming the world.

Although Edstrom had hoped to work on environmental issues, that proved difficult in Australia, where big, politically influential mining companies have turned the country, and Indonesia, into the world's two biggest exporters of coal. In a resource-dominated society, where per capita carbon emissions exceed even American levels, there wasn't much demand for highly paid environmental consultants. At BCG and then McKinsey, Edstrom advised a private equity company, a bank, a telecom provider, a beer marketer, and a childcare company. He also studied prison-bed management for the Australian state of New South Wales.

While environmental work was scarce, Edstrom soon discovered that there was work aplenty in the coal industry, and contrary to the firm's public line that it was "committed to protecting the planet," McKinsey took pride in helping coal companies become more profitable.

One day, the Australia office sent around an email with an attached video. The subject line: "What we do matters: See an inspiring client impact story."

Edstrom clicked play, and a slide popped up titled "Turning a coal mine into a diamond in 6 months." Set to peppy music, the video, since taken down, describes a recent McKinsey job for what appeared to be an Asian client that resulted in a coal mine increasing production by 26 percent, he said. Despite the global climate crisis, despite the fact that burning coal for power contributes nearly a third of energy-related carbon emissions, someone at McKinsey thought this work was praiseworthy.

This was "one of the most profitable projects in our company," the head of the coal-mining company said on the video clip, according to Edstrom.

Mark Shahinian had a similar experience. Like Edstrom, he had an advanced degree in environmental science and hoped to harness those skills at McKinsey. He worked out of the Boston office, rising to become an engagement manager—the mid-level managers who perform a role akin to a platoon sergeant in the army.

Shahinian is proud of the environmentally focused work he did at McKinsey, especially an influential study about how the price of lithium-ion batteries—the kind that power electric cars—was set to drop dramatically. But, he said, McKinsey and its competitors depend on big multinational companies doing projects that last for years or decades. Oil companies fit that bill. Solar equipment startups generally do not, and there just wasn't that much work for him in green energy. McKinsey follows the money.

McKinsey says it is working with its clients around the world to "address climate change," but as of 2020 there was no green-energy company among any of its biggest clients, though it does advise carbon-free electric utilities such as Mercury in New Zealand, and Albemarle, which mines lithium, the key component in batteries. Vestas, a wind power company, is also a client, but tiny compared with the big oil and coal companies.

"They can't invent billable hours that don't exist," Shahinian said of McKinsey. But there are billable hours at the big oil, gas, and coal companies, work that offers opportunities for junior consultants to advance their careers.

Australia is one of the few developed countries that is actively planning to open new coal mines, especially in the vast Galilee Basin in the northeastern state of Queensland. An associate partner invited Edstrom to work on a coal project in Queensland, but he declined, in keeping with the McKinsey policy that allowed consultants to turn down assignments if they had ethical qualms. But in passing on the assignment, Edstrom lost a chance to build ties with senior managers, and that ultimately led to more time "on the beach," McKinsey-speak for a consultant with no client work.

Edstrom believed the policy of letting consultants opt out of projects on ethical grounds was a cop-out, freeing McKinsey as a whole from taking a stand.

If he couldn't work in his chosen field, at least Edstrom could raise awareness among his colleagues of the looming climate threat. He joined the "Green Team," where consultants around Australia discussed environmental issues, and looked for ways to influence management's thinking on the subject.

On a corporate retreat to the Great Barrier Reef, he and his fellow consultants saw firsthand the ravages of rising carbon dioxide levels. "It was dying out incredibly fast," Edstrom said. "It looked like the ashy logs from a leftover campfire." Internally, the Green Team raised the possibility that the dying reef was due, in part, to McKinsey's service to fossil fuel clients. "But that message fell on deaf ears. After the trip, people went back to their normal client work, including working for coal mines with predictable outcomes for the environment."

Edstrom questioned his superiors about the disconnect between McKinsey's public statements about curbing carbon emissions and its work with coal companies. In response, he was told, "If we don't serve coal clients, BCG [Boston Consulting Group] will."

Edstrom was becoming increasingly disillusioned. The cognitive dissonance came not only from client work but also at corporate social events such as the 2018 Australia Values Day, held in the executive meeting rooms overlooking Sydney's premier horse-racing track.

After the usual pep talks and the corporate bonding games such as a putt-putt golf competition on a course made from nonperishable food (donated to the needy, of course), the consultants were treated to the evening's entertainment McKinsey's own Australia-based band, the Marvins, named after the firm's legendary de facto founder, Marvin Bower, famous for putting the firm's interests above his own.

For a band named after such an honor-bound and parsimonious man, the core members of the Marvins—a partner and two senior partners, millionaires many times over—chose to play an unexpected set of songs. There was "Common People," a 1995 hit by the British band Pulp, about a rich girl who wanted to experience life among England's working class.

> You'll never live like common people
> You'll never do whatever common people do
> Never fail like common people.

Then there was "Killing in the Name" by the alternative metal group Rage Against the Machine, sung by a band made up of the whitest of white-shoe consulting firms, whose partners regularly cycle in and out of government. The song ends with this line: "Fuck you, I won't do what you tell me" (repeated sixteen times) followed by a "Motherfucker."

The following year, the Australian office's Values Day went down market—part of a firm-wide reaction to the 2018 *New York Times* report on McKinsey's lavish corporate retreat in western China, just miles from a sprawling detention center housing Uyghur Muslims. In response to widespread criticism, McKinsey had said the firm "would be more thoughtful about such choices in the future." In 2019, the partners' speeches were heavy on values and ethics. But after the Australia managing partner, John Lydon, had finished speaking about how, at a minimum, McKinsey didn't serve clients who harmed people or cheated customers, Edstrom felt he had to speak out. Someone handed him the microphone.

What if, Edstrom asked, McKinsey served arms makers who made weapons used to bomb the home country of other McKinsey consultants? Was that in keeping with the company's values?

Soon afterward, his job at McKinsey came to an end. His lack of good assignments—exacerbated by his turning down the coal project—contributed to a poor performance review. He was, as McKinsey puts it, "counseled to leave." He suspects his outspokenness was also a factor.

Just before he was asked to leave, Edstrom finally did get to work on an environmentally focused project. It was for the New Zealand electric utility Mercury, which uses only green energy. Helping the company retain customers and get new ones was successful and satisfying. But by then, his fate was fixed.

As he was heading out the door in mid-July 2019—three weeks after Pinner spoke at Aspen—Edstrom sent out what became the mother of all farewell emails. It ricocheted around McKinsey offices across the globe.

There's nothing unusual about an employee, at McKinsey or any company, sending around an email upon leaving. It's an epistolary form that rarely burns bridges. At McKinsey that's doubly so, because a McKinsey consultant never really leaves the firm. The formidable alumni network, institutionalized at McKinsey, keeps people tethered to the firm for decades after they leave, with emails, reunions, and, most important, job prospects. Speak out against the firm and you risk being cut off from a lifetime of networking opportunities.

That's exactly what happened with Edstrom.

A few paragraphs into his email, it was clear Edstrom wasn't sticking to the script of expressing gratitude for the honor of working at McKinsey and sadness at the prospect of leaving it. So, after briefly thanking several colleagues, his email took a sharp turn, striking at the heart of McKinsey's ethical foundation—its values.

"My short time at the Firm," he wrote, "has shown me how much impact McKinsey can achieve in a short amount of time. I'm immensely proud of having played a very small part in that. However, creating impact is not an absolute good." And doing good work, he added, doesn't equate to doing good. "I believe it's time for McKinsey to take precedent-setting action around client selection. As an organisation, McKinsey seems to talk a lot about values and principles without taking a valued or principled stand for much of anything."

Then, to make sure his message wasn't lost, he used words rarely directed at McKinsey's leaders. "In my mind McKinsey is an amoral institution." He said McKinsey regularly took on clients who brought harm to others. "There are many cases where I believe this causes detriment to society, McKinsey's reputation, and the planet."

Edstrom took aim at two sectors in particular, McKinsey's work with the military, the focus of his Values Day critique, and its work with coal-mining companies. "Coal kills," Edstrom wrote. "The longer coal companies stay in the black, the more irreparable damage will be done to the environment."

But that is exactly what McKinsey was doing for its many coal clients, he wrote, making them more efficient and profitable, putting off the day when the market forces described by Pinner would finally put them out of business. Plenty of companies are "amoral," he said, but McKinsey's amorality doesn't just affect itself. As the world's most influential consulting firm, it shapes the practices of thousands of clients.

"There is a commonly used phrase for hypocritical eco-marketing used to make a business or product appear more 'sustainable' than it actually is: 'greenwashing.' "

Edstrom cited the example of McKinsey boosting production at a regional coal company by 26 percent. As proof, he attached a link to the video. A small group of McKinsey consultants were enabling this single client—not identified in the video—to supply the world with coal that would add *megatons* of carbon dioxide.

"Think about it," he continued. "Is there a worse client to serve than those directly responsible for putting us on the incomprehensible fast-track to planetary omnicide?"

In the hours after he sent the email, dozens of McKinsey consultants from around the world wrote back to him. One colleague, also in Australia, said that when he had objected to working with a coal client, he was told "it was OK, there were plenty of other associates who would do the job."

Another wrote, "Too often we become willfully blind for the sake of sanity, but over time that's not OK." Still another: "For what it's worth I do think we have a lot of reflection to do."

Edstrom wasn't the only McKinsey consultant in Australia taking a stand on the environment. A few years earlier, several consultants had left a project with a Canadian gold-mining company in nearby Papua New Guinea that for decades had been the focus of complaints because the mine dumped its waste, or tailings, directly into rivers, one former McKinsey employee said.

Because McKinsey fiercely guards its secrets, even internally, Edstrom did not know the true extent of McKinsey's work with the world's biggest polluters. In the firm's nearly century of existence, no reporter has obtained access to McKinsey's client list. But in the course of reporting this book, we have.

For a firm "committed to protecting the planet," McKinsey counts at least seventeen mining and fossil fuel companies among its biggest clients. Collectively, those clients earned McKinsey hundreds of millions of dollars in recent years, according to internal records.

Since 2010, McKinsey has worked for at least forty-three of the hundred companies that have pumped the most carbon dioxide into the atmosphere since 1965, based on a list of polluters compiled by the Climate Accountability Institute, a nonprofit that raises awareness about how corporations are contributing to climate change. Those forty-three companies, when accounting for the customers who use their products, were responsible for more than 36 percent of the *planet's* greenhouse gas emissions from fossil fuels in 2018.

Number three on the historic polluter list, Chevron, one of McKinsey's biggest clients, generated at least $50 million in consulting fees in 2019. Saudi Aramco, number one on the list, has been a McKinsey client since at least the 1970s.

During that half a century, Chevron's total emissions came to 43.7 gigatons (43 billion tons) of carbon dioxide. In 2019, energy-related emissions for the entire planet amounted to about 33 gigatons, according to the International Energy Agency.

Other top McKinsey fossil fuel clients include ExxonMobil, BP, Royal Dutch Shell, Russia's Gazprom, and Qatar Petroleum.

If McKinsey was advising these companies on how to reduce their carbon emissions, the work would reflect McKinsey's corporate values. But that does not always appear to be the case. Projects, or "studies," that McKinsey has recently done for Chevron indicate that reducing carbon emissions was not the focus of its work. There was, for example, the "Upstream Oil & Gas—Digital Roadmap." The biggest project centered on a "product solution" for Chevron's Mid-Continent Business Unit, a region encompassing oil-producing areas in the southern United States, including the Permian Basin in Texas, where Chevron is the top producer.

A case can be made that oil companies like Chevron *need* the smart cadre of McKinsey consultants to guide them through an existential threat to their business model: the global push to move away from fossil fuels. BP and Shell, for example, are scrambling to expand their clean energy businesses.

So with an army of McKinsey consultants advising them on strategy, what approach did Chevron choose? Drill, baby, drill.

In July 2020, just as the global pandemic was decimating demand for Chevron's gasoline, the company's CEO, Mike Wirth, speaking to the Texas Oil & Gas Association, said that the global push for clean energy "doesn't mean the end of oil and gas," *Bloomberg Businessweek* reported. Wirth said that Chevron would "find ways to make oil and gas more efficient, more environmentally benign."

The contrast with the European oil companies couldn't be more dramatic. A few weeks after Wirth's remarks, BP said it would reduce oil and gas production by 40 percent in a decade. BP and Shell have cut their dividends to help pay for their transition away from fossil fuels.

As of early 2022, McKinsey said it had undertaken more than two thousand "sustainability engagements" with clients. One example McKinsey cited was helping a "major energy provider" that it didn't identify cut its carbon dioxide emissions by 82 percent.

Yet in recent years, McKinsey continued to acquire new fossil fuel clients, making them more profitable and more efficient at extracting carbon from the ground.

Just as Edstrom was saying goodbye to his colleagues in Melbourne, McKinsey consultants in Canada were filing into the corporate headquarters of a big new client: a Vancouver-based coal-mining company.

The Elk River passes through the pristine wilderness of the Canadian Rockies as it winds its way south. Upriver, deep in the mountains near the British Columbia–Alberta border, the untrampled scenery gives way to what resembles a war zone. Some of the soaring peaks have been blasted away, filling the surrounding valleys.

This is the Greenhills Mine, one of the top-producing coal mines of Teck Resources, the biggest producer in North America of metallurgical, or coking, coal. Steel mills use this coal in blast furnaces to remove the oxygen from iron ore, producing the metal used to make steel but also producing large quantities of carbon dioxide, so much so that steelmaking accounts for about 7 percent of the world's greenhouse gas emissions.

Teck, one of the world's biggest exporters of steelmaking coal, sells much of what it mines to Asian customers. Factoring in the coal its customers burn, Teck accounted for seventy-three megatons of carbon dioxide in 2019, the equivalent of about one-tenth of Canada's total carbon dioxide emissions that year.

The open-pit mining technique at Greenhills, akin to the mountaintop removal mining in the Appalachians, unearths naturally occurring toxins such as selenium, which seeps into the upper Fording River, part of the Elk River watershed. Scientists say the runoff is killing and deforming fish downstream as far south as the Montana border and contaminating drinking water, according to a 2019 article published by the Yale School of the Environment. At high concentrations, selenium can cause nausea, fatigue, skin lesions, and neurological disorders in humans.

In the fall of 2018, Teck got a new chairman, possibly the most prominent Canadian in global business: Dominic Barton, who until July of that year served as managing partner of McKinsey, where he touted the firm's green credentials. Immediately before Barton joined Teck, McKinsey appeared to do little or no work for the company, according to internal records. After Barton became chairman, that changed. In 2019, McKinsey, by one internal measure, took in about $20 million in fees from Teck, making the coal company one of McKinsey's biggest clients.

A review of work McKinsey did for Teck found one job that focused on "Coal Processing Optimization" at the Greenhills mine. Another was "Pit to Port Model and Control Support." Another McKinsey project left little to the imagination: "Drill and Blast."

After a year on the job at Teck, Barton was appointed Canada's ambassador to China, which produces half of the world's steel, and with it significant pollution. Some of that steel is made with Teck coal. China's sovereign wealth fund owns Teck stock, and a former senior Chinese diplomat sits on its board of directors. Teck says it is aiming to be carbon neutral by 2050.

Barton left Teck, but McKinsey consultants remained and continued to collect millions of dollars in fees.

In 2021, as the world economy recovered from the COVID-induced slowdown, carbon emissions bounced back as well. The leading polluter, generating more than a quarter of the world's total, was China. The planners in Beijing stimulated the economy by stoking a construction boom, leading to big increases in steel production and electricity generation, both highly coal intensive.

In China, McKinsey was advising some of its biggest steelmakers, hungry for coking coal from its big Canadian client, Teck. Among the firm's client roster, Hebei Jinxi Steel, the state-owned Shandong Steel, and Shanxi Liheng Iron & Steel. The firm in recent years has also advised the two biggest oil companies, China National Petroleum Corporation and Sinopec, and in August 2019 McKinsey presented a report to the board of the third biggest, CNOOC.

Much of the coal powering Chinese industry came from Southeast Asia, where McKinsey was working with some of the region's biggest coal-mining companies. One of the firm's major clients in recent years was Banpu, a Thai energy company with mines across the region.

In Indonesia, the world's second-biggest coal exporter after Australia, McKinsey has recently counted two major coal miners as clients, and the firm also works with PT Pertamina, Indonesia's second-biggest oil producer.

The work, at odds with McKinsey's public statements on the urgency of combating climate change, speaks to the nature of the firm itself: at McKinsey, the senior partners, scattered across the globe, have called the shots on business in their area.

By 2021, Dickon Pinner's thesis on the magic of the market cutting pollution, argued so poignantly at Aspen two years and more than sixty gigatons of greenhouse gas emissions earlier, was proving woefully inadequate. American coal exports, both for power plants and for steel furnaces, were soaring. So too were coal prices, which more than doubled from August 2020 to August 2021.

McKinsey's own coal barons—the partners overseeing work in the business—were not only rewarded; they were lauded. In Indonesia, Vishal Agarwal won a promotion to senior partner. An internal announcement for the Global Energy and Materials team honoring him came with a graphic that appeared to riff off the *Outlander* television series. Agarwal was the "Outstander."

"Vishal the Great, the story of the leader that turns GEM industries in Indonesia into the champions that take on the world," it read.

In the background of the graphic—eating into a mountainside—an open-pit mine.

Anger and frustration were mounting among McKinsey's rank and file, younger consultants facing a lifetime of increasingly dire climate catastrophes. Among 465 people responding to an internal survey on priority issues for McKinsey to address, 369 named "climate change and carbon emissions," far and away the most of any issue. In contrast, only 79 picked "compensation and benefits."

On March 23, 2021, a group of about a dozen junior and mid-level consultants sent an open letter to the firm's leadership. Several members of the group had read Erik Edstrom's 2019 farewell note and were inspired by it. Their letter built on some of his ideas, taking it to a new level.

"The climate crisis is the defining issue of our generation," they wrote. "Our positive impact in other realms will mean nothing if we do not act as our clients alter the earth irrevocably."

The group warned that McKinsey's continued work to help polluters profit "poses serious risk to our reputation, our client relationships," and the firm's ability to attract talented people. "For several years, we have been telling the world to be bold and align to a 1.5C emissions pathway; it is long overdue that we take our own advice," they wrote.

The group said that by 2030 McKinsey should remove all the carbon the firm has emitted since its founding in 1926, by buying carbon offsets. Much more important, the group said McKinsey should disclose information about its clients' total emissions, push all of its clients to align with the UN's pathway of 1.5 degrees Celsius, and use the firm's reputation and influence "to convene broad coalitions and guide the orderly transition from a carbon-centric economy."

Within two weeks, more than eleven hundred McKinsey employees had signed the letter. Pinner and another senior partner, Daniel Pacthod, the co-leaders of McKinsey's sustainability practice, set up a phone call with the letter writers.

Pinner was sympathetic. He supported the idea of ending McKinsey's work with coal companies, but, given the firm's powerful regional senior partners, he had little chance of changing the course of the firm. "Without senior partners from the Middle East, central Asia, Africa, Australia, and South America this conversation is lopsided," one of the participants on the call said.

Pacthod said, "We have to be pragmatic, I mean, we're not a nonprofit."

Pinner had one, urgent request: "Please don't take this to *The New York Times,* we are so close."

Two weeks after the letter came out, Sneader and his newly elected successor, Bob Sternfels, responded, telling the group that they "share your view that the climate issue is the defining issue for our planet and all generations" and scheduling an "ask me anything" company meeting on the topic for Earth Day, April 22, 2021.

Two days before Earth Day, McKinsey announced the formation of "McKinsey Sustainability," a platform aimed to help its clients meet the goal of cutting the world's carbon emissions in half by 2030 and achieve net zero emissions by 2050. "Our aim is to be the largest private sector catalyst for decarbonization," Sneader said.

The Earth Day talk by the firm's leaders reiterated that notion. Sneader, then still heading the firm, and Sternfels, joined by a few other senior partners, including Pinner and Pacthod, answered questions. The message from the firm's leadership was blunt: McKinsey would continue to serve the big polluters because, they said, the firm couldn't help them decarbonize if they didn't have a relationship. "How can we not serve fossil fuel clients if we're going to be relevant?" There was no commitment to public disclosure of McKinsey's work with polluters. It was a key demand. Without disclosure, McKinsey "had license to prolong climate change because they can hide behind the curtain of confidentiality," the participant said.

Two months later, on June 30, a massive fire laid waste to the town of Lytton in British Columbia. The day before, the temperature surged to 121 degrees Fahrenheit, shattering Canada's heat record and surpassing the all-time high temperature in Las Vegas.

A few weeks later, Sreevatsa Praveen, a mid-level McKinsey consultant in Dubai, put out a call for help. An Asian power company was planning to build an 800-megawatt coal-fired power plant and was looking for contractors to supply equipment, such as boilers and coolant systems. Could anyone share some contacts?

Rizwan Naveed, a mid-level McKinsey consultant who helped to draft the climate letter, let loose in a farewell email to colleagues on the yawning gap between what McKinsey was saying publicly and what it was doing with clients, all under the cloak of confidentiality. "Just reading our own publishing on the topic makes it clear that by continuing to help our most polluting clients expand emissions unabated, we are in effect aiding and abetting the destruction of our environment," he wrote.

"Any global conversation about sustainability at McKinsey that does not account for our work with polluters amounts to greenwashing, with our sustainability clients, colleagues, and their impact being used as the detergent," he wrote in the email, dated July 30, 2021.

Naveed, who noted that his work at McKinsey focused on measuring the emissions of the firm's clients, wrote of his frustration that senior partners, who listened with a sympathetic ear, said the right words about curbing emissions, then ultimately avoided doing anything to alter McKinsey's work with big polluters.

In late October 2021, *The New York Times* published an account of the letter and the internal debate it had sparked. The sympathy senior McKinsey partners had shown was mostly gone. In its place, an unapologetic defense of the firm's work. Writing his rebuttal in *The Wall Street Journal,* McKinsey's new managing partner, Bob Sternfels, said, "Companies can't go from brown to green without getting a little dirty. And if that means some mud gets thrown at McKinsey, so be it.

"To us, the case is straightforward: The bigger the player, the bigger the possible reductions," he wrote. "Abandoning those that are contributing the most to emissions doesn't advance the cause."

One of the writers pointed out that Sternfels was making a strawman argument: they were asking not that McKinsey abandon these clients but rather that the firm disclose the total carbon emissions from these clients and that it focus on helping them cut those emissions. Sternfels did not address the fact that McKinsey made many of these companies browner, not greener, and that they brought in hundreds of millions of dollars for the firm.

One retired McKinsey senior partner, Carter Bales, saw things differently. In an interview almost three years before the letter was drafted, he foreshadowed their alarm over ever-rising emissions and McKinsey's role in advising polluters.

Few McKinsey veterans loved the firm more than Bales, one of the most successful consultants the company ever produced. An ardent conservationist, Bales founded the firm's environmental management practice. A year before his death in 2019—his voice ravaged by throat cancer—Bales reflected on McKinsey's decision to advise major polluters.

"It's a long-term terrible idea."

Chapter 9

Toxic Debt

McKinsey on Wall Street

The financial time bomb that would devastate the American economy was already ticking by the time Mayor Michael Bloomberg and Senator Chuck Schumer arrived at New York City Hall on the morning of January 22, 2007. They had come to the Blue Room, standing shoulder to shoulder before an oil portrait of Thomas Jefferson, to warn that too much government regulation threatened prosperity on Wall Street. Both political leaders had long benefited from their association with the city's financial markets. As they spoke, certain Wall Street practices were starting to generate headlines—practices that would soon cost thousands of families their homes, their jobs, their savings, and their middle-class way of life.

To make their case, Bloomberg and Schumer presented a study they had commissioned from McKinsey. Since the 1930s the firm had worked closely with some of the most consequential leaders in finance: men like Walter Wriston of Citibank and David Rockefeller of Chase Manhattan. McKinsey, the gold standard of management consulting, said the economy was threatened by *too much* regulation, not *too little.*

McKinsey warned that without changes in policy New York might lose its standing as the financial capital of the world. Should that happen, talent and capital would migrate to Europe—London in particular—and jobs would be lost, with consequences rippling across the nation. "I'm obsessed with this issue," Schumer told reporters.

In fact, regulation of financial institutions and markets had actually eased in recent years. The Depression-era rules separating securities firms and commercial banks—meant to keep lenders from making risky investments with depositors' money—had been tossed aside nearly a decade earlier. Financial markets were free to experiment with exotic new products, generating immense profits. Mortgage lenders could now easily sell off the loans they made, freeing up capital to make still more loans. Home loans were bundled, then sold and resold. This securitization of credit spurred private borrowing but had a significant downside. Because Wall Street had a seemingly insatiable desire to buy mortgages and auto loans, especially higher-yielding subprime loans, loan officers increasingly didn't care whether a borrower was creditworthy.

Easy money ruled the day. Credit ratings that were supposed to provide a check on irresponsible lending instead falsely certified high-risk investment products as safe. The world's biggest insurer, AIG, eagerly sold financial instruments, called credit default swaps, intended to protect investors against doomsday losses that its top executives were convinced would never come.

As the mayor and the senator spoke, Wall Street's transformation into a giant casino had yet to seep into the public consciousness, though the evidence of it was there for those who wanted to find it. Home prices in the hottest markets, like California and Nevada, were doing the unthinkable: falling. At 85 Broad Street, a fifteen-minute walk from city hall, Goldman Sachs bankers were scrambling to reduce the firm's exposure to what would soon be called toxic debt.

But on this day, Bloomberg and Schumer had other priorities, and criticizing the financial markets wasn't one of them. Bloomberg, a former bond trader, became one of the nation's richest men by selling financial information to Wall Street. Schumer, as a New York senator, represented no more powerful constituency than the securities industry, tapping them for nearly a quarter of a billion dollars in campaign donations for Democrats. He supported a legislative amendment that blocked the Securities and Exchange Commission from regulating credit-rating agencies. He also backed Wall Street's request to reduce its funding of the SEC and to allow commercial banks and investment banks to merge.

By hiring McKinsey, Bloomberg and Schumer had selected a firm skilled at navigating Wall Street. McKinsey partners not only consult for the biggest banks; they often end up running them. In 2007, McKinsey veterans occupied top positions at Lehman Brothers, Morgan Stanley, and UBS. McKinsey's former managing partner Rajat Gupta had joined the board of Goldman Sachs the previous November, days after retiring from the firm.

To show the depth of its research, McKinsey boasted that its consultants personally interviewed more than fifty CEOs in financial services and surveyed another three hundred senior managers. Labor and consumer groups were also contacted, but for them no numbers were given.

The firm concluded that Europe was beginning "to embrace U.S.-style credit terms," threatening American dominance in the "leveraged lending" and subprime markets. One business leader expressed concern that the United States was being marginalized in derivatives. "The more amenable and collaborative regulatory environment in London in particular makes businesses more comfortable about creating new derivative products," McKinsey wrote.

One bright spot: America still led the world in securitizing credit, McKinsey said, "but the seeds of change are already germinating" as the concept became increasingly popular in Europe.

The consultants recommended weakening parts of the Sarbanes-Oxley Act of 2002, a law designed to prevent the type of corporate fraud that resulted in the bankruptcy of Enron, at the time the biggest in U.S. history. Enron's chief executive, a former McKinsey senior partner, went to prison for his role in that scandal.

Barely a year after Schumer and Bloomberg showcased the McKinsey report, it disappeared. And no one wanted to resurrect it as Wall Street slipped ever more deeply into an economic abyss not experienced since the Great Depression. News articles, bestselling books, and award-winning documentaries have explored the origins of this catastrophic breakdown. The culprits are many: bankers with a lust for bigger profits, regulators ignoring those they were supposed to protect, and compromised politicians.

These autopsies seldom mention McKinsey.

In its early years, McKinsey worked on the periphery of the financial system, doing glorified white-collar grunt work. During the Great Depression, McKinsey earned modest fees from investment banks by conducting what were then called "bankers' studies," a requirement before a bank could underwrite bonds on behalf of clients. James O. McKinsey saw this straightforward work—looking at a company's sales, assets, people, and organizational structure—as key to getting even more business.

But those assignments were never at the core of McKinsey's work, which for much of its early history rested firmly with mainstream American business: companies like General Motors, U.S. Steel, and Texaco. They could afford McKinsey's fees. They were the kinds of clients that generated new work year after year. They were the kinds of clients where McKinsey could really make its mark.

Banks, highly regulated after their central role in exacerbating the Great Depression, were years away from reclaiming their role as a central driver in McKinsey's revenue stream.

American banks were hobbled by myriad state and federal laws that effectively meant that their business ended at state lines. In 1933, a new law, the Glass-Steagall Act, split commercial banks and investment banks. Congress and the new president, Franklin Delano Roosevelt, wanted to make sure that panics on Wall Street never again led to runs on banks across the nation. The Federal Deposit Insurance Corporation protected savers' accounts from bank failures. Big New York City lenders like Citibank and Chase couldn't even legally open branches in neighboring Westchester County until 1960.

The banks that survived the Depression were like highly regulated, boring utilities. The joke during those years was that bankers operated on the 3-6-3 rule. Pay depositors 3 percent interest (the government regulated interest rates), lend the money out at 6 percent (often by simply buying Treasury bonds), and tee off by

3:00 p.m. The spread between deposit and lending rates guaranteed that even a poorly run bank could turn a small profit.

With modest profits came modest salaries. In 1980, the highest-paid banker in the United States was Roger Anderson, the chairman of Continental Illinois. He made $710,000 that year, or $2.24 million in 2021 dollars. In 2021, James P. Gorman, a former McKinsey senior partner who was chief executive of Morgan Stanley, made $35 million, tied for the top spot with David Solomon, the Goldman Sachs CEO.

All this meant that most American banks couldn't evolve into the giant corporations that, in the years after World War II, became dependable mega-clients for McKinsey. That began to change in the late 1960s. The big money-center banks in New York and Chicago were emerging from their post-Depression shell as the world economy continued to boom, focusing on their thriving corporate clients and chasing them across the globe.

In 1967, Walter Wriston, the new chief executive of New York's First National City Bank, concluded that his institution—better known as Citibank—had outgrown its old organization. He asked his close friend the management expert Peter Drucker what he should do. Drucker said he should hire McKinsey, and he did just that.

The consultants recommended reorganizing the bank around business sectors, like corporate or retail banking. The McKinsey partner Dick Neuschel warned Wriston the change would turn the bank's staff against each other. "You don't have the guts to do that," Neuschel said. Wriston thought that was a bizarre and annoying sales pitch, but hired McKinsey anyway. The day the McKinsey men walked through the doors of Citibank at 399 Park Avenue, the days of the 3-6-3 rule had effectively ended.

On Christmas Eve 1968, Citibank started rolling out the McKinsey plan. Fifteen months in the making, it organized the bank into functional rather than geographic lines, with new divisions for big corporate accounts, small and medium-sized businesses, and retail customers.

The system was called "matrix management," and Drucker likened it to "trying to play basketball, tennis, and soccer on the same court with the same people at the same time," the banking reporter Phillip Zweig wrote in his 1995 biography of Wriston.

The idea was to decentralize decision making, much as GE and GM had already done with help from McKinsey. In banking that meant enabling lower-level bankers to make bigger loans. The goal: to ensure that Citi's corporate customers were served by bankers who understood their industries, not by generalists who handled a diverse set of clients. In a complex organizational structure, it made sense to rationally deploy the bank's resources where and when they were needed. As Wriston put it, Citibank had to have a system where "when you need the clarinet player, he's there. But you can't have a clarinet player in a hundred countries, so you devise a matrix."

One of the effects, Zweig writes, is that the McKinsey plan, accompanied by Wriston's aggressive earnings-growth targets for each of the bank's profit centers, dehumanized the company.

"Before the changes that Wriston wrought, employees felt an assurance, implied if not written, that if they performed well, they would not have to worry about their next job."

But measured solely by profit growth, McKinsey's work was a success. In 1972, Citibank, with its McKinsey-designed organizational structure, overtook Bank of America as the most profitable American lender. McKinsey was soon selling matrix management to banks across the country, including to David Rockefeller's Chase, Wriston's archrival. Wriston fired McKinsey. He kept the matrix.

By the 1970s the banking industry was waking up from its comfortable slumber. Wriston's rivals longed to match his 15 percent targets for annual profit growth. But to do that, they needed to reorganize, devolving lending decisions to battlefield lieutenants who knew their industries. Banks across the country followed the lead of Citi and Chase, hiring McKinsey so that they too could unlock the secrets of the matrix.

The McKinsey-ization of Wall Street was afoot.

But, in banking as in investing, past performance is no guarantee of future results. In Chicago, McKinsey's matrix helped set off a chain of events that contributed to what was then the biggest bank failure in American history and the worst financial crisis since the Great Depression. At the center of this crisis were three big

McKinsey clients, Continental Illinois, Chase, and Seattle-First, or Seafirst, all of which had eagerly imbibed the McKinsey Kool-Aid.

Continental Illinois was once the largest bank between the East and the West Coasts. It was a paragon of conservatism with a lowercase *c*—run for a quarter century from 1934 by Walter Cummings, a New Dealer who had led FDR's bank stabilization program. The bank's loan book skewed strongly to the world's safest investment: U.S. Treasuries. Reporters quoted Cummings as saying that the only good loan was one that had been repaid.

Under his successors, Continental became more willing to embrace greater risk, to compete in the same league as the big New York banks. So in 1975, a squad of McKinsey consultants—described by one bank officer as "stony-faced guys"—slipped past the Ionic columns gracing the entrance of 231 South LaSalle Street and on to Continental's banking floors. They would stay for more than a year, interviewing the bank officers from a prepared questionnaire.

"The McKinsey people seemed a little wistful, maybe bored," wrote James P. McCollom, a bank officer at the time who later wrote a book about Continental's rise and fall. "They thought a lot, going down the list of questions; they noted the answers, but more with patience than with curiosity."

"Because obviously they *already knew* the answers."

By January 1977 the bank—with McKinsey's help—was ready to implement matrix management. McKinsey called for the bank to reorganize, giving individual business units, and more junior bankers, more power to sign off on big loans. This decentralization seemed to work at Citibank, so why not at Continental?

For a few years, Continental's McKinsey-led reorganization appeared successful. By 1981 the bank was the biggest commercial and industrial lender in the United States, its share price surging even as stocks of other big banks remained stagnant. In 1978, *Dun's Review* lauded Continental as one of the best companies in the country alongside stalwarts like Boeing and GE.

But warning signs of trouble ahead had been ignored. Lending surged, but deposits didn't keep up, meaning banks became more leveraged, the FDIC wrote years later. Many of those new loans would turn sour, most notably in what had been called Group U, the energy lending division. In 1977, Continental's Group U became the new home of John Lytle.

Until McKinsey's matrix changed his life, Lytle was anything but a star at Continental. After two decades of barely venturing beyond Chicagoland, he ran a portfolio of about $20 million in the bank's small-business division. Despite no background in the highly specialized field of energy lending, he soon found himself overseeing $600 million and newly empowered to make big lending decisions.

In 1978, Lytle was introduced to the head of energy lending at an upstart Oklahoma City bank based in a shopping mall of the same name, Penn Square. Owing to its small size, Penn Square was limited on how much money it could lend to the state's booming oil and gas industry, so it invited far bigger institutions like Continental, Chase, and Seattle-First to participate in what is called upstreaming.

Lytle hit it off with the Penn Square executive, and Continental's work with the shopping-mall bank took off. Along the way, he personally borrowed more than $500,000 from Penn Square. In the late 1970s, skyrocketing oil and gas prices masked Penn Square's shoddy lending practices. Lytle advanced up the ranks and kept acquiring more loans. By 1982, Continental owned more than $1 billion in Penn Square–originated loans. But when energy prices plummeted amid the sharpest economic downturn in decades, the loans started going bad, prompting federal bank regulators to shut down Penn Square that July. Continental reported its first loss since the Great Depression.

Continental had the most exposure to Penn Square, but Chase and Seattle-First—both McKinsey matrix clients—were also hit hard, along with many smaller institutions. A year later, Seafirst collapsed and was acquired by Bank of America. Then, in the spring of 1984, Reuters published rumors that Continental faced bankruptcy. The rumors became a self-fulfilling prophecy as many of Continental's big corporate customers pulled their deposits. By July, the federal government bailed out Continental by taking a majority stake. It was the biggest bank failure in American history until 2008. It also gave rise to the "too big to fail" doctrine, which guided financial regulators in the recession that would come later.

Lytle got three and a half years in prison for defrauding Continental of $2.25 million. The judge said that Lytle was "someone in way over his head." Chase would spend years trying to extricate itself from millions in bad Penn Square loans.

McKinsey's banking work earned the ire of Paul Volcker, the Fed chairman at the time of the Continental rescue, who quipped to the president of the Federal Reserve Bank in Dallas that "in his day he knew a bank was headed for trouble when it grew too fast, moved into a fancy new building, placed the chairman of the board as head of the art committee, and hired McKinsey & Co. to do an incentive compensation study for senior officers."

The Fed chairman wasn't alone in questioning McKinsey's advice. Warnings were coming from inside the firm as well. In their book *In Search of Excellence,* Tom Peters and Bob Waterman wrote that the best companies avoided using the matrix or had abandoned it. Calling it "the modish but quite obviously ineffective structure of the seventies," Peters and Waterman said the system just didn't work because it siphons away creativity and responsibility in the service of a mathematical model.

Continental's McCollom went a step further, saying, "McKinsey had sold us matrix management, the very snake oil that the excellent companies avoided."

It turned out that another prominent McKinsey consultant came to a similar conclusion.

Lowell Bryan had a visceral understanding of how a poorly run banking system could hurt people in Middle America. When he was a boy, his father told him about how the failure of four banks in dust bowl Oklahoma had spelled an end to the family fortune.

A football player and star wrestler at Davidson College in North Carolina, Bryan earned an MBA from Harvard in 1970 and spent time after his graduation training the South Vietnamese to run their telecommunications system. It was one of the safest jobs in the country, he said, "because the North Vietnamese did not want to destroy the system they knew they would be taking over."

After working for a time at State Street, the big Boston-based asset manager, Bryan was hired by McKinsey as a banking consultant, the same year that the firm began reorganizing Continental Illinois. Bryan regarded McKinsey's banking work as "amateurish." The big jobs with Citi, Chase, Seafirst and Continental Illinois were carried out in part by McKinsey consultants who specialized not in banking but in organization and marketing.

"I was just shocked that we were trying to serve clients with as little knowledge as we had," Bryan recalled years later.

Bryan would soon become one of the intellectual giants at a firm full of Rhodes scholars. When he was hired, the firm's banking practice was small, only about 3 percent of its client work in 1975. But that soon changed. By 1983, McKinsey's Financial Institutions Group, made up of banks and insurance companies, took up 25–30 percent of the work in New York and London, McKinsey's two biggest hubs.

In one sense, McKinsey just rode the wave. The financialization of the American economy was well under way. The Depression-era regulations that had neutered the commercial banks and had tamed Wall Street began to loosen. Companies increasingly bypassed commercial banks to raise money, issuing commercial paper or junk bonds. Savers got much better rates with money-market accounts that invested in commercial paper. By 1986, the caps on the interest banks could offer for savings accounts were a thing of the past.

Financialization meant that the days when the best-paid bankers in the land made less than $1 million a year were over. With Wall Street salaries and bonuses rising ever higher, McKinsey began to lose some of its stars. As the firm's official history put it, "There was a growing sense of frustration among some partners, especially younger partners in the countries with great financial centers, that the potential for wealth creation at McKinsey could not match what they might find in careers like investment banking."

To make a McKinsey career more attractive, the firm overhauled its compensation system, allowing its partners to make more money. In 1985, McKinsey set up its own investment company, the McKinsey Investment Office, which managed pension funds and the investments of its top consultants. Not only was McKinsey putting its stamp on Wall Street, but Wall Street was putting its stamp on McKinsey. One senior partner lamented that these expectations of higher salaries were changing the culture of the firm, "and not for the better."

There were plenty of opportunities for McKinsey partners to justify those higher salaries. Commercial banks had lost the cushy, government-mandated interest rate margins that had for decades given their executives the freedom to hit the links by 3:00 p.m. Now banks had to adapt or die. "They were on a highway to nothing," said George Feiger, hired by McKinsey in 1981 as a banking consultant.

Some turned to McKinsey for advice, but, increasingly, companies were looking elsewhere, especially to the upstarts Bain and Boston Consulting Group, because McKinsey was serving up cookie-cutter formulas and selling them to one client after another. Ron Daniel, the new managing partner, wanted the firm to be a font of ideas that could be used to deepen ties with existing clients and draw in new ones. "We can't just be a Firm of takers and appliers," he told his fellow directors in Vienna in 1980. "More of us must be givers and creators of new thinking and new ideas."

Lowell Bryan thought he had a solution, an idea so big that in the annals of financial history it ranked right up with the invention of double-entry bookkeeping in fifteenth-century Venice. If McKinsey could own this new idea—he called it a "technology"—banks all over the world would be clamoring to hire the firm.

Bryan's big idea: the securitization of credit. While he did not invent securitization, he became one of its biggest, most visible promoters.

It was also the logical response to the wave of bad loans that McKinsey itself had helped to create with matrix management and decentralization. In theory, securitization would enable banks to avoid that fate by off-loading the loans, and the risks, to investors. But just as traditional bank lending is fraught with risks, so too is securitization.

Until the late 1960s, America's home-lending industry pretty much worked the way George Bailey, played by Jimmy Stewart, explained it to the panicked customers of Bailey Building and Loan in the 1946 classic *It's a Wonderful Life.*

"You're thinking of this place all wrong as if I had the money back in the safe," Stewart tells his customers, desperate to withdraw their money when they see a run on the town bank. "The money's not here. Why, your money's in Joe's house, that's right next to yours. And then the Kennedy house and Mrs. Macklin's house and a hundred others. You're lending them the money to build and then they're going to pay it back to you as best they can."

Like the Bailey Building and Loan, America's banks and thrifts were constrained on the mortgages they could issue until they found more depositors. Securitization solved that problem.

In 1968, Fannie Mae, a company created by an act of Congress to promote home ownership, was given the power to buy up conventional home mortgages from banks, bundle them into tradable securities, and sell those securities to investors. It injected a big shot of liquidity into the mortgage market. Banks, thrifts, and a new breed of companies specializing in mortgage originations such as Countrywide Financial could now make home loans from borrowed cash and then sell them off to Fannie Mae or its twin, Freddie Mac. Rinse, repeat.

By the early 1980s, Wall Street firms, led by First Boston and Salomon Brothers, were fast getting into the business of loan securitization, applying the idea to big mortgages not covered by Fannie, as well as to other debt instruments such as auto loans and credit card debt. But the idea was slow to catch on. It needed an intellectual champion to make it respectable. Lowell Bryan filled that need.

In 1986 he inaugurated the "Securitization Project" at McKinsey. The point, he explained, was "to improve McKinsey's ability to serve its extensive client base of financial institutions, including money center banks, securities firms, and insurance companies."

McKinsey consultants began churning out articles and books that extolled the benefits of credit securitization. In 1988, the firm published Bryan's *Breaking Up the Bank,* which put securitization at the center of a completely overhauled banking system. A second book, *Securitization of Credit,* by the McKinsey consultants James

Rosenthal and Juan Ocampo, offered a how-to guide for companies and banks that wanted to employ the "technology."

The McKinsey trio of Bryan, Rosenthal, and Ocampo also published journal articles that would soon be cited by the Federal Reserve as it explored the new phenomenon of securitization. The *Journal of Applied Corporate Finance* devoted its Fall 1988 issue to securitization, with McKinsey consultants writing three of the nine articles.

Securitization, Bryan said, could free companies—not just banks, but any company—from the straitjacket of their balance sheets. A company need only set up a "special purpose vehicle," inject the assets—anything that borrowers had to repay over time such as mortgages or auto loans—then sell those assets as a security to investors.

For banks, getting loans off balance sheets was especially attractive. The more loans on the books, the more cash reserves they were required to hold. Securitization freed up capital that could be used to make more loans. "Securitization's potential," Bryan said, "is great because it removes capital and balance sheets as constraints on growth."

But that wasn't all. To McKinsey, securitization was not only more efficient but potentially a safer way to lend money. This was partly because of what the industry was calling "credit enhancement," essentially a guarantee on the product issued by a bank or an insurance company. This would allow credit-rating agencies like Moody's and S&P to issue favorable ratings for the product.

These credit guarantees "can raise the credit risk of a pool to investment grade levels," Bryan wrote. "This in turn allows individuals, pension funds, and other classes of investors who have neither the skill nor the desire to assess credit risk to invest in the securities issued by the special purpose vehicle."

To Bryan, a system where the originator, the "credit enhancers," and the ratings agencies all scrutinized the loans was obviously better than the old way of lending money.

"In the securitized credit process, *three* parties, rather than one, concern themselves with credit quality," Bryan wrote.

Rosenthal and Ocampo, working under Bryan, wrote in their how-to book that with credit securitization banks that make more bad loans would naturally be shunned, creating a virtuous circle where the system weeds out bad lenders or forces them to improve. "Over time this will lead to better credit decisions at the point of origination," they wrote.

There were, of course, the obligatory notes of caution. Bryan acknowledged that securitization wasn't simple. Its success depended on the competence and, to some extent, the good faith of all parties and that "if too many deals are poorly underwritten and if large defaults and losses result, this promising new technology could, at worst, hasten a credit collapse."

The books and articles by McKinsey's Rosenthal, Ocampo, and Bryan helped Wall Street sell the idea of securitization. McKinsey partners then fanned out across the globe, spreading the good news about special purpose vehicles, asset tranches, and credit enhancement to the uninitiated.

Because the structured securitization deals were so complicated, lawyers played a big role. Few were more important than Jason Kravitt, who founded the securitization practice at Mayer Brown. Kravitt read Rosenthal and Ocampo's book and said it gave the idea some intellectual heft.

"Back in the '80s and '90s, we were all on a voyage of discovery. We thought we were going to make the world a better place," Kravitt said three decades later. "I think the McKinsey book gave the idea and the product and industry a lot of credibility."

For bankers, the people who needed convincing were the issuers—companies that generated so-called receivables, such as GM's auto loans or Banc One's credit card accounts. They made the raw material.

"The McKinsey book helped with credibility with issuers," William Haley, who worked for Salomon, told Bloomberg's Mark Pittman in 2008. "It wasn't that easy in the beginning. Conferences now have thousands of people, but I remember once in Beverly Hills, I gave a speech and there were maybe 25 people in the audience."

Salomon and First Boston didn't need McKinsey's help on securitization. McKinsey started generating fees—the original idea behind Bryan's project in the first place—with commercial banks and securities firms that wanted to join the securitization game.

McKinsey's partners told clients that setting up a securitizations department wasn't simply a matter of poaching talent from rivals. In many instances, the hierarchical culture of a buttoned-down commercial bank had to change in order to accommodate the risk-taking culture of investment bankers who specialized in such loans, recalled Feiger, a senior partner in McKinsey's European banking practice in the early 1990s who went on to head what became the investment banking arm of UBS, the Swiss banking giant.

McKinsey advised the commercial banks on how to change their organization to accommodate more risk to get higher returns. Sometimes that involved setting up a trade finance division, or a push to internationalization, or a specialty in asset securitization. "We helped them get into something feasible," Feiger said.

Another former McKinsey partner who worked on Bryan's securitization project said that once word got out about McKinsey's work in the area, banks became interested. "The largest banks in the world came to us and asked questions about what they could do with it and what they could do with their specific assets."

By 1990, the Federal Reserve, realizing that securitization was sweeping the financial markets, issued a report, the bibliography of which is studded with McKinsey references. Of the Rosenthal and Ocampo book, the Fed noted that while it was "informational in nature, the authors are clearly pro-securitization."

Because the United States had invented securitization, it had a big head start over rivals in Europe and Asia. McKinsey saw a market opportunity in educating bankers around the world about the concept. In mid-June 1991, experts in the field met in London for a conference organized by the *Financial Times* and chaired by George Feiger.

While Feiger's presentation set forth the benefits and potential pitfalls of securitization, it was clear what side of the ledger the firm he represented was on. His paper began by explaining why a financial institution should want to securitize its assets. He also hinted at just how deep the concept had penetrated McKinsey's thinking, saying the firm has "given advice to industrial companies in terms of restructuring balance sheets, and also to financial institutions in terms of business strategy and balance sheet strategy, and securitization of assets has been a key component of all of these activities."

Bryan tried to sell the idea to lawmakers. To him, the introduction of securitization was nothing short of a revolution. Bryan estimated it would take ten to fifteen years for securitized credit to "displace completely the classic banking system." That wasn't long, he said, since "the fundamentals of the banking system have remained essentially unchanged since the Middle Ages." He compared the introduction of securitization to the transition from vacuum tubes to transistors and then to integrated circuits.

"The longer we at McKinsey have thought about it, the more convinced we have become that structured securitized credit is a superior technology," Bryan wrote.

At the time, the American financial system was reeling from multiple crises. The collapse of Continental Illinois, the failures of scores of savings and loan institutions, and billions of dollars in bad loans made to Latin American nations led to calls for a shake-up. Bryan thought he had the solution: putting securitization at the heart of a new concept for American banks. He proposed splitting the banking system into "core" banks, ones that specialized in taking government-insured deposits, and "wholesale" banks that focused on lending and used securitized credit.

Bryan's core bank idea won some supporters in Congress, and in 1991 the concept came up for a vote. A forty-year-old representative from Brooklyn, Charles Schumer, introduced the measure and spoke out in favor of it at a House Banking Committee hearing that June. Banks generally hated the measure, however, and so did the thirty-eight-year-old Treasury undersecretary for domestic finance, Jerome Powell, who, along with Bryan, also testified that day. The measure was defeated.

Bryan would continue advocating for securitization well into the 1990s. In 1996 he and a colleague, Diana Farrell, wrote a book, *Market Unbound: Unleashing Global Capitalism,* a paean to market supremacy over government, that noted the spectacular growth of the stock of securitized loans—which had grown from $100 million in 1980 to $1 trillion in 1992. The McKinsey duo predicted further growth into the new century, especially outside the United States.

"Going forward, loan securitization will be more important to the absolute growth of the world's liquid financial stock than it was over the past decade," Bryan and Farrell wrote.

Bryan had good reason to say that. One of McKinsey's former consultants, Jeffrey K. Skilling, was putting Bryan's ideas of securitization into practice in Houston, where he was transforming a staid natural gas distributor into an energy trading company called Enron. At McKinsey, Skilling had been "deeply influenced" by Bryan. Now, as the CEO of Enron, he had the power to put Bryan's words into action. And he did.

On December 2, 2001, Enron filed for Chapter 11 bankruptcy protection. Outside Houston, few ordinary Americans suffered from the company's collapse. But even as Enron was unraveling, bankers on Wall Street were spawning mutated versions of securitized mortgages that within a few years would spark the biggest economic crisis since the Great Depression.

With interest rates after the 9/11 attacks the lowest in decades, bankers went hunting for higher yields. Working with the big mortgage originators like Ameriquest and Countrywide, they began securitizing home loans that Fannie and Freddie avoided—the subprime mortgages made to risky borrowers. Credit agencies, dependent on those same Wall Street firms for fees, didn't see—or didn't care—that people across America were defaulting on their mortgages.

Many of those foreclosures involved loans to people who were not creditworthy. But Wall Street needed subprime loans to create mortgage-backed securities and the ever more exotic derivatives built from those securities. To entice borrowers, they offered mortgages with adjustable rates, interest-only payment options, and teaser rates that, after two years, rose sharply.

The "*three* parties" Bryan said would make securitized loans superior to conventional lending instead worked in concert to pump more and more toxic debt into the global financial system. Between 2001 and 2008 more than $27 trillion was securitized, an amount equal to almost twice the U.S. GDP in 2007.

Trillions of those dollars would soon disappear.

Weeks after Schumer and Bloomberg spoke at city hall, the unraveling became very public with the bankruptcy of New Century Financial, a subprime lender, followed in July 2007 by the collapse of two Bear Stearns hedge funds that invested in securitized mortgage debt.

By the following March, Bear Stearns, America's fifth-biggest investment bank, was absorbed by J. P. Morgan in a government-brokered fire sale. But the dam really broke in September when Lehman Brothers and Washington Mutual declared bankruptcy. The federal government had to bail out AIG—swamped with billions of dollars of claims for the "credit enhancements" that it couldn't pay—to the tune of $182 billion. And the longtime McKinsey clients Merrill Lynch and Wachovia, both fatally crippled by their subprime holdings, were sold off to stronger rivals.

The common denominator: toxic securitized debt.

All this occurred less than two years after Schumer and Bloomberg touted the McKinsey study that warned against heavy-handed regulation and the risk that Europe could catch America on asset securitization.

"In theory, securitization should serve to reduce credit risk by spreading it more widely," Secretary of the Treasury Tim Geithner and Larry Summers, Obama's top economic adviser, wrote in 2009 as they were making the case for new regulations. "But by breaking the direct link between borrowers and lenders, securitization led to an erosion of lending standards, resulting in a market failure that fed the housing boom and deepened the housing bust."

For Wall Street bankers, it was a game, and their pain was short-lived. A few months after the meltdown, many Wall Street bankers were receiving annual bonuses. By 2013, the S&P 500 index hit record highs. But millions of ordinary Americans never recovered from the Great Recession. Unemployment climbed to the highest level in a generation. In 2013, the Government Accountability Office said that the downturn resulted in $22 trillion in losses for the economy.

If they hadn't fallen prey to predatory subprime lenders and too-good-to-be-true home refinancing deals, the cratering economy meant that many Americans soon slipped into financial insolvency. Millions of foreclosures—disproportionately affecting minorities—peaked in 2010, two years after the markets crashed.

In 2018, a decade after the financial crisis, *The New York Times* revisited some of the people its reporters had interviewed at the time.

In Marietta, Georgia, Meg Fisher lost her job as a legal secretary in mid-2009. A college graduate, she had always been able to find steady work in the past, but this time was unable to. She and her husband filed for bankruptcy in 2009, and they lost their suburban home to foreclosure a few years later. "I probably will never be officially full-time employed ever again," Ms. Fisher, then fifty-six, told the *Times.*

Guillermo Gonzalez declared bankruptcy and lost his Miami-area home to foreclosure in 2008 when the cratering economy cut his commissions as a liquor distributor. A decade later, he was slowly recovering. "We're doing it one step at a time."

It wasn't just America. In China, twenty million migrant workers suddenly found themselves without a job as exports collapsed. Ireland's unemployment soared to 16 percent from less than 5 percent before the crash. Iceland's banks, heavily invested in U.S. securitized assets, lost $330,000 for every man, woman, and child in the country.

"Securitization was based on the premise that a fool was born every minute," Joseph Stiglitz, the Nobel Prize–winning economist at Columbia University, said in October 2008. "Globalization meant that there was a global landscape on which they could search for those fools—and they found them everywhere."

If McKinsey or Bryan felt any remorse for proselytizing securitization for so many years, they certainly didn't show it. In 2009, Bryan, who had long pushed for lighter government oversight of the markets, said the collapse occurred because regulators "basically chose not to regulate."

"If you look at securitization from the 1970s until roughly 2000, you see mostly benefits from it," he wrote in the *McKinsey Quarterly*. "The reason it became unsound is that we allowed too much credit risk to enter the system."

McKinsey doesn't deny that it played a role in the spread of securitization: "McKinsey did help develop the concepts behind securitization, which today remains beneficial and widely used in the financial system and broader economy." But in the 1980s securitization was a "nascent concept that bore little resemblance to the complex instruments at issue in 2008" and to even "indirectly attribute the 2008 financial crisis to McKinsey's work" would be "deeply misleading," the company said.

Feiger, the former McKinsey director who helped spread the idea of securitization in Europe, says that McKinsey always explained the good, the bad, and the ugly about securitization to its clients. "What you're dealing with is a chain of trust," Feiger says of the concept. "To work, all parties have to have integrity and competence. What happened in the financial meltdown is that they weren't competent or honest."

Ocampo, the co-author of *Securitization of Credit,* left McKinsey as a partner in 1995. Like Bryan, he said that the "technology" had been abused.

Bloomberg's Mark Pittman was one of the few Wall Street reporters to see the coming of the financial meltdown. In the weeks after the bankruptcy of Lehman Brothers and the massive bailout of AIG, he wrote about the origins of the securitization craze. That led him to Ocampo's book and to the Enron special-investment vehicles set up under Skilling. "It's a powerful technology that has been driven beyond the speed limit," Ocampo told Pittman in late 2008. "For the last five years, instead of going 65 mph, they've been gunning it up to 140 mph, 150 mph."

Chapter 10

Allstate's Secret Slides

"Winning Will Be a Zero-Sum Game"

On a late summer day in 2000, Dale Deer was driving west on Interstate 70 in central Missouri when traffic stopped because of construction work.

Behind him, Jason Aldridge, a twenty-year-old college student, was on a cross-country road trip from Kentucky to Las Vegas with a friend. Aldridge was trying to adjust his cruise control and did not notice that traffic had stopped. Seconds later, his Mercury Cougar slammed into the rear end of Deer's Chevy pickup truck, severely injuring Deer's back and neck.

Accidents like this occur every day on America's roads, which is why drivers are legally required to carry insurance. Aldridge's policy was with one of the nation's best-known insurers—Allstate, a venerable company that collected his premiums in exchange for the promise of protecting him from major, unexpected financial loss.

Both Deer and Aldridge expected that would be the case here, too. Facing a stack of bills, Deer submitted a claim for $24,000, well below the $100,000 maximum on the policy. And that's where the process took a strange turn. The Allstate adjuster on the case, Mary Greene, inexplicably chose not to process Deer's claim, saying later that she decided to take a "pass." Tired of waiting, Deer sued Aldridge.

Back at college in Kentucky, Aldridge opened the door one day to a police officer serving him a court summons. He was being sued for $2 million. "I really thought my life was over," said Aldridge, who had once lived in a trailer park. "I just gave up." He stopped going to classes.

Aldridge eventually sued Allstate, alleging that the insurer acted in bad faith by not paying Deer's claim. Only then did his lawyers make an important discovery: a management consulting firm, McKinsey & Company, had been advising Allstate through PowerPoint slides on how to save money on claims. So they asked Allstate to produce the slides. After Allstate refused, the judge in the case, Michael Manners, ordered Allstate to turn them over.

Allstate refused. Judge Manners found Allstate in contempt of court and fined the company $25,000 a day until it complied with his order. Allstate still refused. In late 2007, the Missouri Supreme Court followed up by also ordering the insurer to produce the slides. Again the insurer declined, and by the middle of 2008, Allstate had run up more than $7 million in fines. Manners later said he had never seen anything like it in nearly thirteen years on the bench.

What could possibly be in those slides that Allstate would ignore court orders and risk millions of dollars in fines to keep them secret?

This was also a question being asked by David J. Berardinelli, a former prosecutor in New Mexico who was the first plaintiff's lawyer to write about the existence of the McKinsey slides. A lover of high-performance cars, fur coats, and fine wine, Berardinelli had learned of the slides while representing an elderly couple—Allstate customers for more than three decades—who were severely injured in 2001 when a drunk driver forced them off an icy road and into a ravine.

As part of his investigation into why Allstate rejected their claim, Berardinelli found that McKinsey had helped the insurer overhaul its claims system and that a secret slide deck explained it all. He asked for it. Allstate refused, claiming the slides contained trade secrets. Eventually, Allstate was compelled by the court to release them to Berardinelli, but only on the condition that he not make them public. Allstate even put a watermark on them, rendering scans or photocopies unreadable.

When a New Mexico appeals court gave Berardinelli permission to publicly release the slides, he returned the old ones to Allstate, with the expectation that he'd get more readable copies. But Allstate had sprung a trap. They kept Berardinelli's old slides and then refused to give him replacements.

Not ready to give up, Berardinelli entered into the court record a three-hundred-page summary of the slides that he had compiled earlier. Allstate tried to have the summary placed under seal, but the court said no. Meanwhile, word of these internal documents—more than twelve thousand pages, and slides—spread throughout the American legal community, prompting one lawyer to describe them as "a kind of holy grail" for plaintiff lawyers.

"They were willing to wait for years, tie up our court systems, and spend an inordinate amount of money in legal fees—all to keep this quiet," Berardinelli wrote.

Upon hearing of Allstate's insurance practices, the Florida insurance commissioner began an investigation, and he, too, found Allstate unwilling to produce requested documents. "If Allstate is willing to pay $25,000 per day in fines to a Missouri court for its ongoing failure to provide similar documents, it's obvious to me that it will take more than a monetary sanction to get them to comply with our subpoenas," the commissioner said.

The commissioner suspended Allstate's license to sell auto insurance until the company produced the slides. That got Allstate's attention because only California and Texas have more cars on the road than Florida. In 2008, Allstate relented, briefly posting the slides on its website.

Why did Allstate fight so long and so hard? The most succinct explanation comes in the title of a book written by Berardinelli: *From Good Hands to Boxing Gloves.*

Since 1950, "You're in good hands with Allstate" has been the slogan of the Allstate Corporation, one of the longest-running and most recognizable taglines in American business. For decades, under the ownership of Sears, Roebuck and Company, those words meant something: Allstate would, year after year, pay out the vast majority of its premium income in claims, usually generating a modest profit. The company's agents would even make house calls—called pop-outs (as in "pop out" of the office)—to deliver claims checks in person.

That changed in 1995, after Allstate completed its spin-off from Sears. As a new publicly listed company, its executives eagerly embraced the increasingly financialized economy where massive increases in share-based compensation became a major goal—unimaginable in the staid environment at Sears. In anticipation of the spin-off, a team from McKinsey met with Allstate's management in late 1992.

Three years later, they were ready to roll out their plan to boost profits using the McKinsey slides as a road map. "It worked. It paid off for them," Judge Manners, who presided over the Aldridge case, said of McKinsey's work with Allstate. "I guess they make a lot of money doing this."

In one slide, McKinsey told Allstate to try to settle 90 percent of its claims as quickly and as cheaply as possible. For the other 10 percent, policyholders or third-party claimants who didn't take the Allstate offer or, even worse, hired a lawyer, the "boxing gloves" treatment was in order. They would fight in courts, for years if necessary, wearing down anyone who dared to sue.

McKinsey designed a system—the Claims Core Process Redesign—that pushed adjusters to make quick, lowball offers rather than allow them to come up with settlements that they considered fair. Adjusters, now tethered to a computerized claims system called Colossus, were reduced to little more than call-center workers reading prepared scripts. Pop-outs became rare. For homeowners' claims, it was another computer program—Xactimate. But the idea was the same. Push claimants to accept less than the covered amount. Allstate says this characterization is "false and misleading" and that it overhauled its claims system in the 1990s to "pay claims more promptly and accurately." McKinsey declined to comment.

Most McKinsey slides, at first glance, seem anodyne, filled with phrases such as this: "The way we approach claimants and develop relationships will significantly alter representation rates and contribute to lower severities." But Allstate employees understood what it meant, because it was explained to them in plain English.

Here's how Maureen Reed, an attorney for Allstate from 1992 to

2003, described a meeting on the topic with senior Allstate executives:

> We were told at this meeting that McKinsey had concluded that Allstate was "paying too much for claims" which had created a corporate culture of claimants expecting to be paid for claims. This was presented as a bad thing. McKinsey advised Allstate that to increase profits, Allstate needed to pay less on claims.

Central to the goal of reducing payouts was preventing policyholders from hiring lawyers, she said, because "represented" clients on average got payouts multiple times bigger than claimants who didn't hire legal help.

"We were told that Allstate was going to change the way claims were handled so that claimants could not get lawyers," Reed said. In other words, beat down the opposing counsel by fighting every motion in court, making it so time-consuming and expensive that lawyers would reconsider filing suit against Allstate. This was the "boxing gloves" part of the strategy.

"More people without representation would mean larger profits for the company," she said. McKinsey was telling Allstate to *turn its claims center into a profit center.*

The words merit italics because what McKinsey did at Allstate fundamentally altered America's insurance industry.

Americans have had a love-hate relationship with insurance companies for decades. They love their local insurance agent, typically a pillar of the community, a coach for Little League baseball or Pop Warner football. But they hate dealing with insurance *companies* that bombard them with paperwork requests and sometimes deny what they see as legitimate claims. Until McKinsey appeared on the scene, the profession was dominated by experienced claims adjusters bound by law to offer fair claims. The "claims man" was an honorable and coveted profession in postwar America.

Insurance is absolutely vital to guard against unexpected loss, and sometimes very costly recovery, whether from a car accident, a flooded home, a sudden debilitating injury, or the death of a family breadwinner. With insurance, you're indemnified; there's a solemn, very comforting promise: you'll be "made whole."

Without insurance, the financial ramparts that keep millions of people in the middle class can quickly crumble. "Insurance is the great protector of the standard of living of the American middle class," writes Jay M. Feinman, a law professor at Rutgers who studies the industry. "But only when it works."

For decades in America, it did. People bought policies. Insurance companies invested that premium money and paid out the claims that the policies—contracts—stipulated. The industry was profitable most years but not extraordinarily so. Skilled people—adjusters—mostly evaluated claims on their merits.

McKinsey had been consulting insurance companies since at least the 1950s. In the 1980s the senior partner Peter Walker, who later went on to focus on China, built a fiefdom of the firm's insurance consulting business, publishing an industry book each year that compared the performance of each of the big companies. It made the perfect gift for ambitious insurance executives.

McKinsey was focused on its traditional role of making businesses more efficient—cutting costs. For the claims department, that meant controlling the expense of handling claims, known in the industry as loss adjustment expense, or LAE. This could be anything from culling excess employees, cutting down mailing expenses, negotiating better prices for copier paper, or reducing overtime costs.

But tinkering around the edges, streamlining offices, and cutting expenses could get the company only so far. What insurance companies spend on claims processing is a small fraction of what they pay out in claims themselves. In 2018 the property and casualty industry paid out $365.9 billion in claims, spending $64.6 billion in processing fees, meaning insurers on average spent about 17 percent of what they paid out for administration expenses.

By the 1990s, with McKinsey-led financialization sweeping the economy and ever-increasing pressure from activist shareholders for companies to boost profits, the firm pushed a big new idea to its clients: reducing the amount paid out in claims. In McKinsey-speak:

"After years of squeezing the cost side, management recognized huge opportunities to rebalance and invested cautiously in LAE to capture indemnity savings." The new approach to boosting profit was to curtail what insurance companies saw as unjustifiably high amounts paid out to some claimants. To control what it called "leakage."

McKinsey was telling Allstate to essentially declare war on a sizable proportion of its policyholders. One slide proclaimed, "Winning will be a zero sum game." In other words, Allstate's gains come at the expense of its policyholders. Another featured an image of an alligator. Why? Because, like an alligator, Allstate would just "sit and wait" for its victim—the claimant—to give up. "The money came from the only place it could come from—the pockets of Allstate policyholders and claimants," Berardinelli wrote.

Before McKinsey, there were still angry policyholders. Before McKinsey, insurance companies lowballed claims. But McKinsey systematized it. And because the firm has no qualms about advising multiple companies in the same industry, its ideas metastasized. As competitors saw Allstate's profit soar and its executives become wealthy, other insurers hired McKinsey. This is the McKinsey way and has been since the firm's early days. With McKinsey, there's no promise of exclusivity. It takes on work with multiple companies in fiercely competitive industries, from tobacco to banking to drugmakers.

Following Allstate's adoption of the McKinsey system, State Farm, the biggest property and casualty insurer, signed up for the same magic elixir. Its McKinsey-designed "Accelerating Claims Excellence" system was first introduced to its field offices in mid-1995. AAA followed a few years later. Liberty Mutual also became a McKinsey client.

"It has been common knowledge within the casualty insurance industry since at least 1995 that McKinsey was openly selling the same redesign methodologies and claim handling processes it developed in the early 1990's for State Farm and Allstate to their competitors," Stephen Strzelec, a former manager for State Farm, said in a 2008 affidavit.

"They set a trend," one former McKinsey partner said of the firm's work with Allstate. "The claims process was just evil, and I think what's happened now is that more insurance companies have followed that."

At Allstate, profit soared more than sixfold in the decade after McKinsey's program was put in place. Its share price more than quadrupled, handily beating out the broader markets. The pay of Allstate's top five executives, tied to the share price just as the McKinsey partner Arch Patton had envisioned half a century earlier, shot up. In 1994 their combined compensation amounted to $2.95 million. A decade later it had reached $19.3 million. In 2020 the top five executives made a combined $38.2 million, led by the CEO, Thomas Wilson. By 2021 the average salary of an Allstate worker was about $62,000, barely keeping up with inflation over twenty-five years.

Meanwhile, the percentage of premiums paid out on claims declined. Allstate executives and shareholders were becoming fabulously rich by reducing payouts, preventing many policyholders from getting all the money to which they were entitled. It was, said Russell Roberts, a former management consultant who is spending his retirement studying how McKinsey has altered the insurance industry, "reverse Robin Hood."

The surge in Allstate's share price was accompanied by a dramatic fall in the "pure loss ratio," the measure of claims payouts divided by premium income, before factoring in operating costs. In 1987, Allstate paid out 70.9 cents in claims for every dollar it took in. By 1997, two full years into the McKinsey makeover, the ratio had fallen to 58.2. By 2006, after spiking a year earlier amid huge claims resulting from Hurricane Katrina, it was 47.6.

Congress wanted to know whether policyholders were being harmed by Allstate's quest for higher profits. In 2007, J. Robert Hunter, an insurance expert with the Consumer Federation of America, told members of the Senate Judiciary Committee that McKinsey's advice was leading to lower claims payouts. Hunter urged the committee to examine whether hiring the same consultant—McKinsey—was tantamount to collusive behavior on the part of insurers, who have a limited exemption from antitrust laws. Few private-sector industries get such exemptions, akin to those enjoyed by Major League Baseball.

"The use of these products to cut claims payouts may be at least part of the reason that consumers are receiving record low payouts for their premium dollars as insurers reap unprecedented profits," he said.

That was certainly the case at Allstate. Even as the company was fighting to keep the McKinsey documents secret, its executives were touting the success of its new claims model to Wall Street. At a 2006 investors' conference, Allstate's then chief executive, Ed Liddy, said that from 1993, when McKinsey first proposed its Claims Core Process Redesign, to 2005, the amount of money Allstate had paid out in bodily injury claims had fallen by 10 percent.

Liddy shared in that wealth. In 2006, he was paid $24 million.

Roberts, the former management consultant, estimated that the McKinsey system resulted in the transfer of $94 billion from policyholders to Allstate coffers from 1995 to 2018. Add in State Farm and other companies that adopted the McKinsey system, and the total approaches $374 billion, Roberts calculated. "So much of this is driven by the whole McKinsey mentality and their constant drive to extract more money from individuals while giving them less value—taking that money and redirecting it to themselves, and to executives and to shareholders," Roberts said.

Roberts began researching McKinsey's influence on American society, especially the insurance industry, after serving as an expert witness in 2009 for Berardinelli, the lawyer who brought the slides to the public's attention. In that case, the judge ruled in favor of Berardinelli's client, citing in part Allstate's abuse of the legal system. Allstate calls Roberts's analysis "simplistic and invalid," saying it is impossible to extrapolate figures from the time of McKinsey's work in the 1990s because the claims processes have changed over time. Allstate says ninety-five cents of every dollar it takes in goes to pay claims or operating costs.

The McKinsey claims system extended far beyond Allstate and far beyond personal injury claims.

In 2007, *Bloomberg Markets* magazine published a searing investigation into how Allstate, State Farm, and other insurers, using the McKinsey method, were routinely lowballing offers to homeowners whose homes had been damaged or destroyed by natural disasters. The most famous irate claimant: the Mississippi Republican senator

Trent Lott, who sued State Farm when the company wouldn't pay for damage to his home from Hurricane Katrina. State Farm said the damage was from water (not covered), rather than wind (covered).

A 2003 fire in the San Diego area destroyed more than two thousand houses, but insurers, including Allstate and State Farm, refused to reimburse policyholders for the amount needed to replace their homes, sometimes hundreds of thousands of dollars below replacement value, Bloomberg reported. They were not being made whole.

Under state laws across the country, insurance companies are obligated to pay the fair value of whatever benefits their policyholders are entitled to. An insurance policy is, after all, a contract. But what makes the duty of insurance companies even more pressing is the fact that many kinds of insurance aren't optional. Every driver is required by law to have auto insurance. Mortgage companies require people to buy homeowners insurance. An industry where the government compels people to buy their product is especially obligated to carry out its fiduciary duty.

"Delay, deny, defend violates the rules for handling claims that are recognized by every company, taught to adjusters, and embodied in law," Feinman, the Rutgers law professor, said.

Shannon Brady Kmatz comes from an Allstate family. Her father worked at the company for thirty-seven years. As a little girl growing up in New Mexico, she would sometimes tag along on pop-outs, especially if it involved a trip to Ruidoso, a mountain village and ski area a few hours southeast of Albuquerque. She was proud of her dad. When someone asked where her father worked, she'd thrust her palms out and say two words: "Good Hands."

But in 1997, when Brady decided to follow her father's footsteps and accept a job offer from Allstate, he told her to reconsider. He had retired a year earlier because the company had changed, and not for the better.

She lasted three years. During that time, she met a grand total of two policyholders face-to-face. Then there was the third one, who paid a visit to her office in Albuquerque. He charged into the second-floor reception area carrying a sawed-off shotgun, angry that

Allstate was slow-walking his claim. "You know that stuff could happen because you have a lot of angry claimants out there," she said.

Brady doesn't suffer fools. After leaving the insurance industry, she became a police officer. She answers questions with "yes, sir" and "no, sir." But her three years at Allstate tested her. The place was far different from where her father had spent his working lifetime.

Brady describes the life of a McKinseyfied Allstate adjuster in Hobbesian terms: nasty, brutish, and short.

The ten adjusters were jammed into a second-floor room, competing with each other for bonuses, and even for the chance to keep their jobs. Each adjuster was rated for how many claims they closed for low dollar amounts. Brady's group was called the "unrepresented unit" because the claimants hadn't hired lawyers. It was her job, in line with McKinsey's recommendations, to keep it that way.

Brady, who became an expert witness for attorneys suing Allstate, said in a sworn statement that it was "common knowledge at Allstate" that people who hired lawyers got settlements that were on average two to three times those of people who weren't represented.

So Brady said she lied to the policyholder. It wasn't her words; it was from a McKinsey script they called "attorney economics." "Some people choose to hire an attorney, but we would really like the opportunity to work directly with you to settle the claim," the script read. "Attorneys commonly take between 25–40% of the total settlement you receive from an insurance company plus the expenses incurred. If you settle directly with Allstate, however, the total amount of the settlement is yours."

Or, as a McKinsey slide stated in all caps, "WIN BY EXPLOITING THE ECONOMICS OF THE PRACTICE OF LAW."

Time was of the essence. The McKinsey system laid out strict rules for closing out cases—most within thirty days, still more within sixty, and all of them by ninety days—or passing them on to the "represented" unit, or to the fraud division. And do it for as little money as possible. Close them fast, close them cheap, and bonuses and promotions were there for the taking. Fall behind, give the policyholders more money, and you'd soon find yourself being put in JIJ—Job in Jeopardy—by the manager.

Each Monday morning, Brady and her colleagues would find a

printout of their 30/60/90 progress on their desks. A whiteboard on the wall tracked the office progress, allowing everyone to see how they measured up against their colleagues.

Adjusters knew that their greatest ally in meeting their 30/60/90 goals were the poor and uneducated policyholders. The ones with poor English, the elderly living on Social Security, or the ones in desperate need of the money to pay bills. "If you knew they were living paycheck to paycheck, they were a prime target," Brady said. If Allstate sent them a lowball check in the mail and they cashed it, that was tantamount to settling. "If they cash the check, it is full and final. Kind of scary, isn't it?"

The goal was to settle as many claims as possible, even before the claims had been evaluated, and do it for less than the authorized amount.

The insurance adjuster's role had been greatly diminished. During her father's time, setting a value for a claim had been a skill. Under Allstate's new system, the computer would spit out an estimate. This was Colossus, a program that analyzed hundreds of different injuries entered by adjusters like her. As Brady soon learned, Colossus had been tweaked to lowball claims amounts. It was then her job to persuade the policyholder to accept a claim even lower than the one disgorged by Colossus.

Mark Romano, one of the people responsible for tweaking Colossus so that it favored the insurer, worked out of Allstate's headquarters in Northbrook, Illinois. "I could turn the knob, so to speak, and increase the values of cases, or I could turn the knob down and decrease the value," he said.

When payout data indicated something was amiss, Romano took to the road to find out what was going on. He and his colleagues discovered that adjusters were entering an unusual amount of herniated disk injuries into Colossus, a far more valuable claim than a "soft tissue" claim like whiplash. Romano was told to "calibrate" the claims teams across the country, telling them to reduce the number of herniated disk claims "regardless if a neurologist or an orthopedic surgeon or a radiologist or whomever said it was a herniated disk."

For Romano, who already had severe misgivings about his job, this was, in his words, "the straw that broke the camel's back." He had voiced his concerns about Colossus to Allstate lawyers who were preparing a defense against a class-action lawsuit. He began experiencing severe headaches. Doctors couldn't figure out why. He went on disability. When he came back, he was reassigned and effectively told he had no future at the company. Romano took early retirement in 2009. "I had become a liability," he said.

The headaches went away. The following year, he joined the opposition: the Consumer Federation of America, where he worked to inform consumers about the new reality in America's insurance industry.

When he started out in insurance, back in his native Florida, he saw it as a way to make an honorable living while helping people cope with financial loss. "I felt really good about what I was doing."

In the beginning, he said, the claims division wasn't viewed as a cost center, just a necessary part of the business. "It was one of the few opportunities to actually interact with your customer, and so they wanted to make sure it was a positive experience," he said.

"It evolved over that time to becoming a profit center, so to speak, which it never was intended to be," Romano said. "And a lot of that, as I learned toward the end, was a result of a lot of these programs that were being put into place by McKinsey."

Allstate says courts "did not identify institutional issues involving underpayment of claims" from the Colossus system, adding that "McKinsey was not involved in the implementation of Colossus."

After years of legal battles, both Dale Deer and Jason Aldridge won settlements from Allstate. Deer was awarded $750,000 plus interest, which Allstate paid in October 2007, more than seven years after the accident. The following year, Aldridge won his own settlement against Allstate. The terms were confidential.

Chapter 11

"The Enron Astros"

At 7:08 p.m. under an overcast sky, Octavio Dotel of the Houston Astros threw the game's first pitch, marking the official opening of Houston's quirky new baseball stadium. It had the league's first retractable roof with a massive glass window that gave fans a view of the city's office towers. The inside featured an actual train and an artificial hill deep in center field with a flagpole that fielders had to navigate in the rare instances balls were hit that far.

On this early April day in 2000, with the temperature in the high seventies, the roof remained open, allowing the sellout crowd of forty-one thousand to experience baseball the way it was meant to be played—outdoors.

The stadium's creative design shared civic accolades with another Houston company that also sought to be different: Enron Corporation. Headquartered in a fifty-story building a short trip from the ballpark, Enron had quickly become a Wall Street favorite, riding an updraft of fawning articles and surging profits. The company embraced the fashionable new concept of creative destruction, where corporations are encouraged to periodically renew themselves. Under this philosophy stability and teamwork become less important in a marketplace that rewards risk today, not tomorrow. The individual rather than the corporation now reigns supreme, with rewards going to those least afraid of failure, a philosophy described in the widely praised book on Enron, *The Smartest Guys in the Room.*

These individuals needed no group validation, only the courage to act.

It seemed fitting that this innovative company, a symbol of booming Houston, would be connected to the sparkling new stadium. So on opening day, baseball fans watched their first game in a stadium called Enron Field. The naming rights cost Enron $100 million, a manageable sum for America's seventh-largest publicly traded corporation. Several months later, Enron stock hit an all-time high of $90.56.

The union, however, did not last. Late the following year, Enron collapsed into what was then the biggest bankruptcy in U.S. history. Enron signs, suddenly an embarrassment, were removed from the stadium. The company's two leaders went to prison, and a third was headed there when he died. As Enron's grand plan unraveled, its auditors, the venerable Arthur Andersen, were caught shredding company records, forcing the company to surrender its license to operate. All told, more than seventy thousand people lost their jobs, most of them at Andersen. Many Enron employees lost their retirement savings as well.

The Astros suffered a different kind of ignominy. Years later, the team cheated to win the World Series, resulting in baseball's biggest scandal since White Sox players took money a century earlier to throw the World Series. The Astros' general manager and field manager were fired.

Enron and the Astros were done in by hubris, but also by their unquestioning belief in the supremacy of technology. Enron used it to cloak fraudulent activity in ways that the public could not understand, allowing it to report false profits and keep its stock price rising. The Astros used technology to steal signs and turn players—and the game itself—into bloodless data sets, altering the beauty and drama of the nation's most treasured sport. "The smartest guys in *the clubhouse,*" is how one magazine referred to them, a nod to the Enron crew. Their smug arrogance turned the Astros into the most disliked team in the majors.

Enron and the Astros shared another important bond. They put their trust in McKinsey & Company. Both organizations were run by a former McKinsey consultant, aided by a stable of consultants still at the firm, a short ten-minute walk from the stadium. After Enron became synonymous with scandal, Paul Krugman, a *New York Times* columnist, explained McKinsey's role in the company's demise. "Other companies hired business gurus as consultants," he wrote. "Enron, in effect, put the gurus in charge. . . . What they created was a company so trendy that investors were dazzled. And that let executives get away with financial murder."

The title of Krugman's column: "Death by Guru."

McKinsey wasn't implicated in anything illegal, a relief to the firm's managing partner, Rajat Gupta, who was so worried he dispatched McKinsey's lawyer Jean Molino to assess the situation.

In his personal life, Gupta wouldn't be so fortunate. After leaving the firm, he was sent to prison for insider trading.

Before Enron, McKinsey's Houston office had been nothing more than a small, inconsequential outpost in the firm's global empire. Paris on the bayou it was not, but it did offer the opportunity for risk takers to cash in on the city's boomtown growth.

One McKinsey consultant who seized that opportunity was Jeffrey Skilling, who, after just six months in the Dallas office, moved to Houston as the firm's third employee there. It was a place where a brilliant graduate of Harvard Business School could roll out his vision of how American corporations should work.

Enron, originally a natural gas company, gave him that opportunity, first as a consultant and later as an executive, during what McKinsey called "the dawning age of industry deregulation." Skilling set out to reorder the gas business. Believing that the best returns would come not from transporting gas but by trading it, Skilling invented the concept of a "gas bank," where Enron could buy gas and resell it, capturing the spread between the two, much as banks take in low-interest deposits, then lend that money out at higher rates.

Before long, Enron—the former stodgy gas company—was trading everything from power, steel, petrochemicals, plastics, water, and paper. It became a technology player in the broadband market. For several years running, a major financial magazine called Enron

America's most innovative company. McKinsey's Houston office became a hot spot, pulling in $10 million in fees a year from Enron alone, as the number of consultants there quickly grew.

Consultants burrowed into the company like armies of carpenter ants, staying weeks, sometimes months. In an uncirculated history of the firm, McKinsey wrote that its Enron team worked "year in and year out at both the strategic and operational levels of the company." A McKinsey partner even attended Enron board meetings.

As Enron's stock kept rising, so did the number of favorable articles, often written by McKinsey consultants who did not disclose to readers that their firm was pulling in tens of millions of dollars from the company they were praising. This undercut the firm's lofty pronouncements that it would never discuss a client's business or the advice it rendered. The *McKinsey Quarterly* praised Enron's "purported successes and ingenuity no less than 127 times" over a six-year period.

Skilling infused Enron with ideas he had learned at McKinsey, including the importance of periodically culling the herd. Either advance in the firm or leave. McKinsey called it "up or out." At Enron it was "rank and yank." McKinsey validated Enron's strategy, including risk taking, securitizing loans to gas purchasers, and its "asset light" approach. As the *McKinsey Quarterly* explained, Enron became a world leader in private power generation "because it saw that profit did not depend on construction and operation skills, but on deal structuring and risk allocation."

Skilling had been enamored of securitization since his earliest days at Enron, so in 1990 he set out to find a banker who knew how to structure a securitization deal. He found that person, a young banker named Andrew Fastow, at Chicago's Continental Bank, a pioneer in securitization. Fastow was keen to move to Houston, his wife's hometown.

"That is why I was contacted, specifically to figure out a way to securitize oil and gas reserves," Fastow recalled three decades later.

Fastow helped Skilling's unit with its first securitization, which involved the creation of a special purpose vehicle called Cactus, which removed debt from the company's balance sheet. Enron bundled $900 million in loans that it had promised to pay natural gas producers, securitizing the lot and selling it off to investors, including General Electric. Another off-balance-sheet entity, JEDI, was designed by Fastow and partnered Enron with California's Public Employees' Retirement System to find energy investments.

Skilling's early work at Enron drew praise from four McKinsey colleagues, who in a 1999 book, *Race for the World: Strategies to Build a Great Global Firm,* singled out Skilling's Enron Capital & Trade Resources, the division that carried out the securitizations. "ECT was able to hedge itself against market fluctuations and shortages through skillful financial engineering using instruments such as commodity swaps and over-the-counter options to offset the risk assumed for each agreement," they wrote.

JEDI was just one of hundreds of special purpose vehicles Fastow created at Enron, which inflated profits and hid losses, especially after he became the company's CFO in 1998. Fastow says that McKinsey consultants were not involved in any of his projects.

Ensuring that earnings rose quarter after quarter was important to Enron executives. It made them enormously wealthy while validating their actions in the eyes of investors. But meeting Wall Street's expectations became increasingly difficult, so Enron began cutting corners, using a variety of schemes to report higher profits and to cover up losses. Their victims were not just investors or banks but also consumers. When electricity prices dropped, Enron withheld electrical power, causing brownouts in California. Full service was restored when prices rose.

While McKinsey was never implicated in Enron's illegal activity, many inside the firm and out wondered why such smart people could not grasp the danger of becoming so deeply involved with a company that had difficulty explaining exactly how it earned money. Keeping Enron as a client also raised questions about the quality of the firm's risk managers, a vulnerability that would surface over and over in the following years.

In time, Enron's remarkable success was revealed to be little more than an illusion. The company collapsed after the public learned that its finances were based "on a web of fraudulent partnerships and schemes, not the profits it reported to investors and the public." McKinsey's official history put the best face on the scandal, calling it "a black comedy, in which the firm begins as a sober advisor, becomes enthusiastic advocate and ends up as one of the many unwitting victims." The difference between Enron and McKinsey, the firm wrote, was McKinsey's "values."

Veteran business reporters who have autopsied Enron's carcass were not sold on the victim part. "McKinsey didn't just cash the checks," Duff McDonald wrote in his history of the firm. "It fully believed in the cult and helped spread the gospel."

Soon after Enron imploded, a book called *Moneyball* became a bestseller, ushering in what one prominent sportswriter called the biggest change to professional baseball since integration half a century earlier. It told the story, later made into a movie with Brad Pitt, of how the frugal Oakland Athletics nearly won the pennant in 2002 by making game decisions based on data analysis—analytics for short—rather than on unscientific beliefs passed down through generations of baseball players.

For McKinsey, the book's popularity made it easier for the firm to use its data skills in the sports world. McKinsey designated Dan Singer, a Harvard Business School graduate and a nationally ranked expert at solving crossword puzzles, to lead the way. Broadly speaking, Singer oversaw two forms of entertainment—sports and gambling—which coexisted side by side, though sometimes uncomfortably.

Over the years, sports leagues had engaged in a careful dance with the gambling industry, fearful on the one hand of compromising the integrity of their games while recognizing that gambling intensifies interest, particularly as technology greatly expanded entertainment choices available to the public. The success of illegal internet gambling, a multibillion-dollar industry, was not lost on entrepreneurs who sought a *legal* slice of that market. The result was fantasy sports, where players are picked based on past performance and bets are placed over the internet on how they will perform in actual games. Because players are usually drawn from many teams, fixing games would be difficult, if not impossible. Even so, it was still gambling, just under a different name.

Betting on individual teams is another matter, and that's a side of McKinsey's business rarely discussed. The firm advised one of the world's most famous sports books, William Hill, which paid the firm in recent years almost $40 million, according to company records. In that same period McKinsey also took in $14 million for advising Caesars Entertainment, the giant casino operator. Caesars eventually bought William Hill, expanding its mobile betting operation to eight states with the prospect of more coming online.

McKinsey has boasted of helping the "leading casino gaming companies" expand their business through loyalty programs aimed at inducing gamblers to wager more. Under one plan, called "frontline empowerment," McKinsey said an attendant could offer players $50 just when they are about to walk away. Also "high-value customers can get tickets to Celine Dion shows and/or room upgrades, while low-value customers get free airport rides."

Singer, who was instrumental in reorganizing fantasy sports when its practices came under fire, had a foot in both sports and gambling. According to his official McKinsey bio, he served as "a strategic advisor to seven of the ten largest sports leagues in the world as well as numerous sports teams, conferences, and government bodies." He also consulted for gaming companies, including casinos, sports books, horse racing, and e-sports.

While Singer's name rarely surfaced in news accounts of games, his insights were valued by data analysts who don't make their living scoring runs or touchdowns.

McKinsey deepened its expertise in data science by buying a small, elite consulting company called QuantumBlack, which used data to evaluate athletes in the United States and Europe. One of its specialties was injury prediction—an obvious area of interest to gamblers. Knowing whether certain players were prone to injury might influence betting odds, though there is no evidence this type of information was leaked to gamblers.

According to QuantumBlack's home page, it helped a soccer team assess the "health of its players and identify the physical metrics that might signal impending injuries." QuantumBlack's evaluations were so detailed they included taking saliva samples. "Using objective medical markers and information from prior injuries, we identified the features that correlate to injury onset in the hamstring, upper leg, and lower leg," the company said. As if to differentiate its work from the speculative chatter of sports radio and TV analysts, the company reported that its blind historical testing "correctly forecast 170 out of 184 non-impact muscle injuries."

The company is more circumspect in discussing its work in the United States.

In September 2013, players on the New York Knicks were startled to see unidentified people taking notes at closed practices and on team flights. The team's owner, James Dolan, eventually acknowledged that the strangers were McKinsey consultants and that their advice led him to fire the team's general manager, Glen Grunwald, after the Knicks had reached the second round of the playoffs, a high-water mark that hasn't been duplicated since. Dolan wanted McKinsey to reorganize the team, emphasizing technology, without specifying what that meant.

This mandate confounded Dave Hopla, a Knicks shooting coach, who told *The Athletic,* "I wouldn't have a problem if a consulting firm came in and it was Hubie Brown and John Thompson or something, but not a consulting firm with some girl from MIT and some guy from Stanford that don't even know the first thing about basketball."

During one stretch coaches were instructed not to watch game film with players. Their priority became filling out detailed reports on players' performance and attitudes. Hopla became so frustrated with what he considered a mostly worthless exercise he once deposited his reports in the men's bathroom, where he thought they belonged, rather than on the desk of a McKinsey employee.

That season, the Knicks missed the playoffs by a single game and didn't make the playoffs until 2021, when they lost in the first round.

Had the players known all that McKinsey was doing, there might have been greater dissension not only on the team but around the league. Former QuantumBlack employees told the authors of this book that they were secretly using medical information to predict lower-body injuries. "It was very hush-hush internally at the team, working directly with the team doctor," one former consultant said. "They didn't want the players to know." Should a player be identified as likely to be injured, the consultant said, that could impact contract negotiations.

The findings ultimately proved of marginal value, but they did underscore a lingering concern about whom team doctors are supposed to serve—owners or players. This issue would become hugely controversial in the National Football League when some team doctors downplayed very real evidence of permanent brain damage from concussions.

But it was Major League Baseball, specifically the Houston Astros, where McKinsey had its biggest impact.

A new generation of video equipment produced massive amounts of granular data on every pitch and every batted ball. As a result, some long-held assumptions about how to win games were challenged. Now batters were instructed to pull the ball, to change their swing plane to produce more home runs, rather than line drives. Pitchers were told to throw more curves, fewer sinkers, and more four-seam fastballs high in the strike zone rather than at a batter's knees. The most extreme practitioners of baseball analytics believed that the entire game could be reduced to numbers, uncontaminated by human sentiment, emotions, or, as it would turn out, even ethics.

The question lurking beneath all this was at what point does data analysis cross over from helping athletes perform better to dehumanizing their sport. That issue took on new significance because of what a man named Jeff Luhnow—a former McKinsey consultant—was doing down in Houston.

A Wharton School graduate with an MBA from Northwestern, Luhnow had a fan's interest in baseball and statistics but did not initially aspire to work in sports. During his five years at McKinsey, his duties included working on the firm's much-maligned Allstate account. As a junior member of the Allstate team, Luhnow is unlikely to have played a role in devising that scheme, but it does make one wonder what lessons, if any, he might have taken from the experience.

Then *Moneyball* came along, and it piqued his curiosity and prompted the St. Louis Cardinals to rethink their baseball operation. With the help of a former McKinsey colleague—the son-in-law of the Cardinals' owner—Luhnow got a job as the team's vice president for scouting and player development, a surprisingly important position for a newcomer with no formal background in baseball.

Luhnow quickly signaled his commitment to analytics by hiring Sig Mejdal, a former blackjack dealer who had also worked as an engineer for Lockheed Martin and NASA. He changed careers after reading *Moneyball.* Mejdal's description of modern baseball did not evoke memories of Casey Stengel or Yogi Berra. "You are going to need database, you are going to need persons with database skills, you are going to need servers, you are going to need analysts to analyze that data, and then you are going to need analysts or others with skills to present it to the decision makers."

Luhnow's arrival upset baseball traditionalists. Behind his back, Cardinals employees called him "Harry Potter" or "the accountant." Yet Luhnow vastly improved the quality of players drafted by the Cardinals and established himself as a transformative voice in the baseball world.

Luhnow's belief in the magical powers of numbers eventually caught the attention of the Houston Astros. They, too, wanted more analytics, so the Astros hired Luhnow as general manager, the most important position in a baseball organization. His job: define the team's mission, make the necessary but controversial decisions, and ensure that everyone acted in harmony with the team's guiding principles. Which were, quite simply, to win.

Mejdal, the NASA scientist, came with him. Another early hire was Brandon Taubman, a numbers-savvy investment banker. He, too, had no background in baseball, but believed there must be a more logical way to make decisions on player personnel and in-game strategy. Taubman would be promoted four times in five years, ascending to the job of assistant general manager, Luhnow's top aide. Other tech guys were invited aboard, with nary a tobacco spitter among them.

Luhnow brought with him the ethos of his old employer McKinsey, where achieving higher profits was the standard by which the firm's success was measured. McKinsey had an expansive view of the value of analytics. "We can use it to ensure that we're recruiting the right people," said Dominic Barton, McKinsey's former managing partner. "We have a better sense of predicting who will leave. We've got a better sense of who creates value within organizations. We can be much more granular about that. The whole analytics around people has changed."

Like many former consulting colleagues, Luhnow embraced the concept of "disruption," a word increasingly used to describe systemic change. He spoke of wanting to be on the "bleeding edge" of that change. Luhnow did more than channel McKinsey's teachings; he hired the firm to guide the Astros on its new journey. More Ivy League grads telling baseball people how to play the game.

As with Enron, the *McKinsey Quarterly* became the church choir. In a two-part interview with Luhnow, the *Quarterly* promised to show "how analytics, organization, and culture combine to create competitive advantage in a zero-sum industry." If you don't win, you lose. The *Quarterly* did not mention that the Astros were also a McKinsey client. Luhnow told the interviewer where baseball was headed:

> Big data combined with artificial intelligence is the next big wave in baseball, and I think we're just starting to scratch the surface. It's an area that I consider to be highly proprietary, so I don't discuss it in front of my competition. But we're making a big investment in this area. I think other clubs are as well. There's so much being captured. There's radar and video at every facility in baseball now, not just the major leagues but the minor leagues, colleges, starting to go into high schools. We know what every person is doing on the field at all times. We know what the bat and ball are doing on the field at all times.

Baseball is a business, and as the *McKinsey Quarterly* noted, "the business is to win." Jeff Luhnow wanted to win. "If we're not making some mistakes along the way, we're not being aggressive enough," he said.

Luhnow's fascination with numbers extended to the study of players' bodies and their propensity for injury, a specialty of McKinsey's QuantumBlack, which also worked for the Astros. "We often measure asymmetries in players' bodies, because those are areas most likely to break down," Luhnow told two hundred people at the Singh Center for Nanotechnology at the University of Pennsylvania. "We need to anticipate injuries, rather than wait for them to happen before reacting." The point of merging sports medicine and technology, he said, was "to maximize players' performance."

Soon, another method of improving player performance would be revealed not by the Astros but by the media. And that method would cost the jobs of three major-league field managers and a general manager—Luhnow.

On a toasty Houston evening in September 2017, the White Sox pitcher Danny Farquhar took the mound, attempting to protect a 3–1 lead over the Astros. The teams were moving in different directions. The Sox were rebuilding; the Astros were charging ahead to an eventual 101-win season.

The retractable roof over Minute Maid Park, né Enron Field, was closed, and with the stadium only slightly more than half full sound traveled well, a fact that became important for what was about to happen.

In the eighth inning, Evan Gattis of the Astros stepped in the batter's box. "There was a banging from the dugout, almost like a bat hitting the bat rack every time a changeup signal got put down," Farquhar said. "After the third one, I stepped off. I was throwing some really good changeups and they were getting fouled off. After the third bang, I stepped off."

Farquhar believed that someone, somehow, was using the banging as a way to signal to the batter what pitch to expect. Teams usually try to steal signs—legally—by looking in from second base to see what pitch the catcher is signaling for and then communicating that to the batter. But in this case no runner was on second base.

Pitching from the stretch, Farquhar abruptly stopped and walked toward the catcher. They conferred and agreed to use more complex signals. Another changeup was called, but this time there was no banging. Farquhar's account was later confirmed by video posted on the internet by Jomboy Media Corp.

It was all there for anyone to look at or investigate. But no one did. Farquhar was angry that no reporters covering the game asked him what had happened. The Astros went on to win the World Series, the first in franchise history, in what *The Washington Post* called "the moment the analytics movement conquered the game for good."

In 2018, more disquieting incidents occurred involving Houston. One of the most serious took place in what would be the third playoff game between the Cleveland Indians and Houston.

No team had gone longer without winning the World Series than Cleveland. Two years earlier, the Chicago Cubs beat the Indians in extra innings of the seventh and final game of the World Series. Nineteen years before that, Cleveland became the first team to take a lead into the ninth inning of game 7 and lose—again in extra innings.

But Cleveland—the hard-luck city with vanishing jobs, bad schools, and government corruption—believed that 2018 would be the year to break the curse, restoring pride in the city. The Indians were a great team, having set an American League record the previous year of twenty-two straight wins. The Indians also had the league's best pitcher, the Cy Young Award winner Corey Kluber.

And that's where matters stood in 2018 when Cleveland met Houston in the best-of-five playoffs. The first two games were in Houston, and Cleveland lost them both. But the third would be in their home ballpark. Win or be eliminated.

Then something strange happened. A man with Houston credentials gained unauthorized access to the media-only camera pit immediately next to Cleveland's dugout. Once inside, he used his cell phone to surreptitiously record activity in the dugout. That brazen act startled Andre Knott, a veteran on-air field reporter who covers Indians games. "I was looking at his credentials and wondering what is someone from the Houston Astros doing here?" Knott said. Was it to steal signs from the bench coach, Brad Mills, or to see information that the manager, Terry Francona, taped to the dugout wall, showing pitcher-hitter matchups?

Knott said he is not a snitch but nonetheless thought the man's conduct so unusual he snapped a picture of him in the act and transmitted it to Indians officials, who informed MLB security. The spy, identified as Kyle McLaughlin, was escorted from the field and his credentials confiscated. Then Houston tried it again during the game, an Indians executive said.

As word got around the Indians dugout that Knott caught an Astros representative spying, the players were furious. The incident confirmed their suspicions—and those of other teams—that the Astros would do anything to win. When playing the Astros, players said they sometimes heard whistles, claps, and banging before pitches, possibly signaling what pitch was coming. After Cleveland's first game in Houston, Corey Kluber and his catcher, Yan Gomes, both told teammates they were shocked that no one had swung at Kluber's best pitch, a darting slider. Not one to make excuses or complain, Kluber said privately that he never had batters lay off every slider he threw.

Cleveland lost the final game and was eliminated. After the game, the Indians' starting pitcher, Mike Clevinger, was asked why Houston won.

"I'm going to keep it really short," he said. "We . . . kind of had our backs against the wall before this series started when it came to the analytical side." His cryptic remarks became the subject of much speculation over the following weeks. What he meant, Knott said, was that the Astros cheated, something many major leaguers already suspected. In fact, during the game, Clevinger had to be restrained while screaming at a Houston player, "We know you are cheating."

The Indians filed a formal protest with MLB and alerted the Astros' next opponent, the Boston Red Sox. For good reason. In their first game, Boston caught the same Astros official, Kyle McLaughlin, attempting what he had done in Cleveland.

Major League Baseball investigated both incidents and issued a short statement that exonerated Houston. "A thorough investigation concluded that an Astros employee was monitoring the field to ensure that the opposing Club was not violating any rules." It provided no details.

Few people believed the explanation. Knott called it "b.s." Paul Hoynes, a call-it-like-he-sees-it reporter who has covered the Indians for three decades, agreed. "No, I don't buy that," he said. "I can't believe nothing was ever done about it." And that was a shame, he added, because the incidents were a harbinger of things to come.

The Astros stuck to their story. "We were playing defense," Luhnow said. "We were not playing offense. We want to make sure it's an even playing field."

If MLB's investigation was as thorough as it claims, then investigators talked to the wrong people or asked the wrong questions. The rules prohibit using electronic equipment during games to steal signs, yet *The Athletic*'s Ken Rosenthal and Evan Drellich later discovered that an Astros executive sent an email to scouts in August 2017, *encouraging* them to steal signs—with cameras if necessary:

> One thing in specific we are looking for is picking up signs coming out of the dugout. What we are looking for is how much we can see, how we would log things, if we need cameras/binoculars, etc. So go to game, see what you can (or can't) do and report back your findings.

A year later, Houston's Kyle McLaughlin pointed his camera—without penalty—inside the dugouts of Cleveland and Boston during the sport's holiest of times, the playoffs. Houston did not go to the World Series this time, losing to Boston in the playoffs.

The Astros did win the pennant again in 2019. But during the raucous postgame celebration, Houston's carefully choreographed image as the smartest, toughest organization in the majors began to disintegrate faster than anyone could have imagined. It began when Brandon Taubman, the former banker turned assistant general manager, expressed his contempt for anyone foolish enough to question the wisdom of Luhnow trading for Roberto Osuna, an elite closer, while serving a seventy-five-game suspension for domestic violence.

"Thank God we got Osuna. I'm so fucking glad we got Osuna," Taubman yelled in the locker room, directing his comments toward three female reporters, one of whom wore a domestic violence awareness bracelet. Taubman said it six times. "Thank God we got Osuna. I'm so fucking glad we got Osuna."

Most of the Astros' front office objected to the trade, according to Ben Lindbergh and Travis Sawchik, authors of *The MVP Machine,* but "Luhnow . . . rammed it through regardless," with the support from the Astros' owner, Jim Crane. While other teams passed on

Osuna, Luhnow's culture of winning without regard to the morality of his actions—an attitude exhibited sometimes by McKinsey consultants—set the Astros apart. If the numbers screamed "sign him," then sign him they did. Luhnow earlier had to be talked out of drafting a convicted child molester.

After an outpouring of criticism, the Astros fired Taubman, and the team went on to lose the World Series to the Washington Nationals. Then the really bad news hit. Ken Rosenthal and Evan Drellich of *The Athletic* broke the story that Houston cheated to win games. In violation of league rules, the team used live video to steal signs from the catcher, which they decoded and communicated to batters by banging on a trash can in the tunnel leading to the dugout.

Major League Baseball investigated and found that the sign stealing occurred throughout 2017—including the World Series when the Astros beat the Dodgers—and in 2018. Major League Baseball's commissioner, Rob Manfred, suspended Luhnow and the team manager, A. J. Hinch. Although Luhnow denied knowing about the cheating, "there is both documentary and testimonial evidence that Luhnow had some knowledge of those efforts," Manfred wrote. Hinch disapproved of the scheme but did not stop it. Shortly after the suspensions were announced, both were fired, as were two other field managers who knew of the scheme when they were with the Astros.

The report's most damning conclusion was not the cheating per se but what happens when an analytics driven preoccupation with winning goes too far:

> It is very clear to me that the culture of the baseball operations department, manifesting itself in the way its employees are treated, its relations with other Clubs, and its relations with the media and external stakeholders, has been very problematic. At least in my view, the baseball operations department's insular culture—one that valued and rewarded results over other considerations, combined with a staff of individuals who often lacked direction or sufficient oversight, led, at least in part, to the Brandon Taubman incident . . . and finally, to an environment that allowed the conduct described in this report to have occurred.

McKinsey's name did not appear in Manfred's report, and no evidence emerged linking it to the scandal. But the firm's role in shaping the culture of the Astros was undeniable. "The Astros did not hire McKinsey to review ticket sales, concessions or merchandise," one veteran baseball writer from *The Athletic* concluded. "This was about baseball operations and baseball operations only, a willingness to open up the most essential and insular area of the team to complete outsiders."

Mejdal, the former Astros official, said in an interview that McKinsey's work was not as important as some people believed. "My general sense was they were taking a look at our processes, how do we develop players, what's our infrastructure for our data systems, and the backups we had for them, how is our front office organized. Things like that." Mejdal was not involved in the cheating scandal and now works for the Baltimore Orioles.

One baseball insider said McKinsey mostly used its ties to the Astros to impress clients and potential clients, rather than to score big fees.

There's no disputing that Luhnow's stewardship of the Astros reflected poorly on McKinsey as well as on the lessons he might have taken from his time at the firm. Had he not been fired, the commissioner would have ordered Luhnow to participate in "an appropriate program of management/leadership training to ensure no incidents of the type described in this report occur in the future."

Rather than ending the controversy, the commissioner's report created a new one. Players who competed and lost to Houston, including some of the quietest, biggest names in the game, complained angrily that no Astros players were disciplined. The team kept its World Series title, and the Astros' short but powerful second baseman, José Altuve, kept his American League Most Valuable Player award.

"Contempt for the Astros runs deep—and has well before this incident," ESPN's Jeff Passan wrote. "Jealousy breeds some of it. The organization's arrogance accounts for the rest. The Astros painted themselves as a disrupter and reveled in the commotion."

The scandal went way beyond just bragging rights. It affected players' livelihoods. "It's sad for baseball," said Mike Trout, baseball's best and least controversial player. "Guys' careers have been affected. A lot of people lost jobs."

The cheating hurt young pitchers fighting to stay in the majors after poor outings. And it might have kept the Yankees star, Aaron Judge, from winning the Most Valuable Player award, and the earnings that come with it. "Baseball has lost its soul under a growing technocracy," the veteran baseball writer Tom Verducci concluded. "The Astros are the warning shot of what happens when it goes too far."

Houston's analytics revolution undermined two traditional pillars of the game—scouts and Minor League Baseball. The Astros gutted their scouting department by placing a higher value on numbers to the exclusion of human observation. And it eased the way for the Houston-led plan to eliminate dozens of minor-league teams, often the economic and social center of small-town America, as well as the gateway through which generations of young people have developed a sustaining interest in the game.

How much McKinsey might have contributed to these decisions isn't known, but it was no secret that McKinsey met with Astros scouts—some of whom barely knew what the firm did. And at the behest of Commissioner Manfred, McKinsey also undertook a "full-scale" review of Major League Baseball that produced changes to the league structure and personnel.

Analytics led pitchers to increase spin rates to produce more movement, batters to hit more home runs, and fielders to reposition themselves to choke off base hits. One thing it hasn't done is to find a way to bring more people to the ballpark. Attendance at major-league games had fallen in six of the last seven pre-COVID years. Baseball writers who once glorified analytics are now questioning whether it made the game less exciting. Now baseball emphasizes home runs and strikeouts, rather than pitchers throwing complete games or runners advancing from first to third on singles.

One McKinsey consultant bemoaned Luhnow's approach of "eviscerating" poorly paid labor in the minors for the benefit of a multibillion-dollar industry.

Meanwhile, McKinsey, recognizing that it had saddled the wrong horse, retracted the article praising Luhnow's "analytics, organization, and culture." Rather than own up to its poor judgment, the *McKinsey Quarterly* offered this lame and largely fact-free explanation: " 'How the Houston Astros are winning through advanced analytics' was removed in light of subsequent developments suggesting that factors beyond data analytics were significant contributors to the Astros' success."

In other words, they cheated.

Chapter 12

"Clubbing Seals"

The South Africa Debacle

Shaped by an elite boarding school in the forested foothills of the Himalayas, Vikas Sagar was indoctrinated early in the values that McKinsey ostensibly espoused: social justice, equality, and leadership. His coed school, one of the oldest and most prestigious in Asia, expected students to live by the motto inscribed in the school crest: "Never give in." As if to prove fealty to those words, some students actually scaled Mount Everest.

Years later, Sagar brought that mindset to his job as a consultant in McKinsey's Johannesburg office. He ran. He swam. He cycled. McKinsey values athletes for their ability to endure long hours of work, travel, and lack of sleep. Sagar's athleticism made him fit in.

In other ways, though, he was different from the rest. His exuberance—quick to hug almost anyone—stood out in a company defined by numbers, spreadsheets, and PowerPoint slides. Bianca Goodson, an executive in a small consulting company, remembers Sagar well. One evening after a long business meeting inside McKinsey's Johannesburg office, Goodson said Sagar suddenly climbed atop the conference room table and danced. No one who knew him found that story surprising.

Because he was popular and fun to be around, Sagar's personality helped him develop and nurture client relationships. His ability to secure business impressed senior McKinsey executives, fueling his rise in the organization, first as a partner, then as a senior partner with a base salary of at least $1 million a year, not including bonuses.

He joined the Johannesburg office at an opportune time. South Africa was opening its wallet to McKinsey, and the firm eagerly spent that money. It moved into new twin glass towers, connected by elevated walkways. Free drinks on Fridays flowed to those not already invited to private, wine-soaked dinner parties. One partner drove a yellow Ferrari, others Porsches or BMWs.

This did not go unnoticed among government officials whom McKinsey depended on for contracts. "When am I going to get my Porsche?" asked one.

When apartheid reigned as the law of the land, a UN trade embargo sought to pressure South African leaders into changing their racial policies. The temptation to break that embargo was great. The country had an advanced economy and a bounty of natural resources, including diamonds, gold, coal, and platinum. McKinsey almost succumbed to the temptation. Three years before the stain of apartheid was removed, Standard Bank of South Africa tried to hire McKinsey. Intrigued, but aware of the reputational damage that would result, McKinsey sent a team to Johannesburg to investigate. Separately, the firm asked a new hire, Susan Rice, the future national security adviser to Obama, for her opinion. The firm ultimately declined the bank's offer.

Years later, the senior partner David Fine, a white native South African, spoke with pride of his firm's refusal to take clients there until free multiracial elections were held. When that finally happened in 1994, consultants at the firm clamored to be a part of South Africa's rebirth.

Yet working in South Africa was not as simple as helping Allstate sell more insurance or Philip Morris sell more cigarettes.

Nelson Mandela's political party, the African National Congress, decided that a strong central government should lead the way in transforming society, an approach that placed a heavy burden on a country with no democratic traditions and an untested legal system. It did not help that McKinsey built its reputation advising companies, not governments.

For years McKinsey had approached government work cautiously after an embarrassing episode in 1970 when a newspaper reported that the firm had profited from New York City contracts while a McKinsey partner worked pro bono in the city budget office. New York responded by halting $1 million in payments to McKinsey. No charges were filed and the city eventually resumed payments, but the episode taught the firm that government work carried heightened scrutiny and reputational risk.

McKinsey's attitude, however, softened over the years as the firm recognized that to retain its perch atop the consulting business, a larger client pool was needed. By the early years of the twenty-first century, the firm had reentered the public sphere in a major way—not just in America, but around the world.

In South Africa, McKinsey felt it had no choice but to take on government work and the risk that came with it. "If you want to be relevant in a country like South Africa, you have to get involved in the public sector," a former manager of the Johannesburg office observed.

But the early good feelings that came from helping Black South Africans began to fade as Mandela's vision of a kinder, more equitable nation gave way to corruption and violence in the ANC. Party operatives were siphoning vast sums of public funds meant to lift up Black South Africans. At first this lawlessness remained in the background, but that changed as ANC politicians began assassinating each other to hide their thievery. After it was revealed that the ANC's national spokesperson, Smuts Ngonyama, stood to make up to $10 million through a public contract, he responded, "I did not join the struggle to be poor."

Western companies were not innocent bystanders.

Bell Pottinger, one of London's most influential public relations firms, fanned racial divisions in South Africa in a ploy to divert attention from a client's corrupt public contracts. The publicists did this through fake Twitter accounts and by stirring anger about "white monopoly capital" in South Africa.

The giant German software firm SAP paid a middleman $9 million dollars in connection with obtaining contracts with state-owned agencies. KPMG, the auditing firm, helped President Jacob Zuma disembowel the state tax agency, paving the way for him to fire the finance minister, a critic of a powerful Zuma ally.

McKinsey entered the fray in 2005 when it began advising Transnet, the state-owned rail and port agency. To consult for a state-owned enterprise, McKinsey had to follow a government directive requiring contractors to share a portion of their business with a Black-owned subcontractor, a form of economic redistribution. If the relationship was properly handled, these subcontractors would eventually develop the skills needed to go out on their own. It functioned like an arranged marriage with all the attendant problems of two strangers learning to live together.

It was important for McKinsey to follow the rules and do it quickly because Transnet urgently needed upgrading. A vital part of the nation's economy, Transnet employed 60,000 workers and supported another 200,000 to 300,000 jobs. The mining industry needed freight trains to transport minerals around a country nearly twice the size of Texas. Power plants depended on regular shipments of thermal coal to generate electricity. And the port city of Durban needed Transnet to deliver cargo for export.

McKinsey's first Transnet subcontractor was a small consulting company called Letsema. For the most part that marriage was a happy one, though conflicts did arise over how much work Letsema contributed and how some McKinsey consultants treated Letsema employees. In 2013, McKinsey parted ways with Letsema after learning that it was advising General Electric—a potential bidder for a locomotive supply contract that McKinsey was overseeing for Transnet.

McKinsey now had to find another partner at a time when these Black economic empowerment companies were increasingly used as fronts for corrupt activities. The country was headed for trouble, and most everyone knew it, threatening South Africa's fragile democracy and McKinsey's growing business.

To avoid becoming ensnared in these corrupt schemes, McKinsey needed to thoroughly vet its new Black empowerment partner and clients as well. That did not happen. Instead, the firm mistakenly treated Transnet as though it were a private company, not government owned, which would have triggered a higher level of due diligence. So when Transnet recommended that McKinsey hire Regiments Capital as its partner, the firm did a mostly cursory review and found no significant problems.

To improve Transnet's services, McKinsey assembled a team that eventually swelled to a hundred consultants, assisted by ninety-four international experts and dozens of Transnet employees. The firm's consultants burrowed so deep into the agency that one Transnet official wondered how the agency could ever operate without them.

For such an important, far-flung industry, McKinsey had wanted a strong team leader who knew the country. That person turned out to be David Fine, the South African–born consultant. Smart, righteous, but not especially popular, Fine did not behave like Sagar, his more mischievous colleague. No one could imagine him impetuously hugging strangers or dancing on a conference table. A few colleagues called him socially awkward.

Transnet turned out to be an unruly client.

The rail agency had rehired its former freight rail chief, Siyabonga Gama, who had been fired earlier for contracting irregularities. And Jürgen Schrempp, a former DaimlerChrysler chief executive, abruptly resigned from the Transnet board because the agency failed to consult him before appointing a new chief executive, Brian Molefe. The decision to bypass him, Schrempp said, was "totally inappropriate" and a reflection of "poor corporate governance"—words that should have resonated with McKinsey, especially since Schrempp was well known to the firm's German partners.

While Schrempp remained in the dark, the appointment came as no surprise to Ajay, Atul, and Rajesh Gupta—three émigré brothers from India who were fast becoming the nexus of alleged schemes to raid the public treasury through front companies. A Gupta-owned newspaper reported the appointment months before it was publicly announced.

Since arriving in South Africa in the mid-1990s, the Guptas had used people close to President Zuma to help build a business empire that included mining, transportation, computers, and the media. The family even hired two of Zuma's children.

Their most brazen display of wealth and influence came in 2013 when the Guptas staged "the wedding of the century" for a relative, a multiday affair for which the bride's parents booked every room in one of South Africa's most luxurious resorts in Sun City. South Africans were angered by how a Gupta-chartered jet with two hundred guests from India had been given permission to bypass Johannesburg's commercial airport so it could land at a highly secure military base closer to Sun City. As reported by *The New York Times,* the guests were ferried to the wedding site at the Palace of the Lost City "in luxury vehicles accompanied by a sprawling security escort, sirens blaring."

The Guptas invited prominent South Africans to the wedding, including McKinsey's David Fine, who said he did not attend, adding that he had never met the Guptas and had no idea why he was invited. McKinsey executives insisted they were unaware of the Guptas' political influence.

Others were more observant.

In late February 2011, a South African newspaper quoted Sdumo Dlamini, a powerful trade union president, expressing concern about the Guptas. "We are worried that we are increasingly witnessing big deals happening in a suspicious manner," Dlamini said. A couple of weeks later, South Africa's *Mail & Guardian* reported similar worries about possible Gupta influence in state-owned agencies.

Unconcerned, McKinsey took on the responsibility of overseeing a risky new infrastructure plan inside Transnet's freight rail division run by none other than Siyabonga Gama, the same executive who had been fired for contracting irregularities and then inexplicably rehired.

Transnet's plan was a huge gamble.

Rather than invest in infrastructure based on current orders, Transnet planned to invest *without* confirmed orders, essentially betting hundreds of millions of dollars on business that did not yet exist. To succeed, the program needed McKinsey to accurately predict future economic activity. The firm's optimistic forecast led Transnet to order the biggest capital procurement in its history—the purchase of 1,064 locomotives.

For an idea of what might lie ahead, Transnet needed to look no further than its sister agency, the Passenger Rail Agency of South Africa. In March 2013, PRASA paid roughly $200 million for locomotives in a deal that, according to court documents, "was steeped in corruption and bid-rigging." The final product proved comical. The overpriced locomotives were too tall for the South African rail system or were never delivered. One derailed during a test, and those remaining were put up for auction.

Transnet's locomotive purchase was bigger and more consequential for the nation's economy. McKinsey pegged the value of Transnet's purchase at around $2.6 billion. After a series of delays, Transnet abruptly decided in early 2014 that the procurement had to be made immediately. Uncomfortable with the short deadline, McKinsey stopped advising on that procurement just as the winning bidders were about to be selected.

Almost overnight, the purchase price jumped nearly $1 billion. Fine said the higher payments involved "extraneous factors which in many cases are impossible to explain." In fact, he added, "they are not explainable." Another McKinsey senior partner was incredulous. "I've never heard that the price goes up after negotiations," he said. "You have an offer on the table and the executive negotiates the price upwards?"

McKinsey was not blameless in this fiasco. The firm had overestimated consumer demand for the locomotives, causing Transnet to buy overpriced locomotives that it didn't need. Unlike Transnet, however, McKinsey actually profited off its flawed forecast by securing the job of fixing the problem it helped to create. Its new assignment: cut costs and boost revenues.

Matthew Chaskalson, a constitutional law expert and a member of a judicial commission investigating what it called "state capture"—essentially a silent coup—said McKinsey began bagging big Transnet contracts after hiring a subcontracting partner, Regiments, which turned out to have links to the politically powerful Gupta family. "There is an extraordinary succession of sole-source contracts," Chaskalson said, pointing to the firm's seven sole-source contracts in less than eighteen months. During that period, he noted, McKinsey's fees grew "exponentially."

—

Questions were raised, quietly at first, inside McKinsey's Johannesburg office about those contracts.

Colin Douglas was at his home in Cape Town when he learned that McKinsey had been asking around if anyone knew of suspicious behavior at the firm involving Transnet. An early hire in McKinsey's Johannesburg office, Douglas had served as the resident writer and communications specialist for six years before leaving to freelance in 2004. While at the firm, he got to know Sagar, so when he learned of McKinsey's inquiry about Transnet, Douglas recalled something unusual and he contacted the firm.

The result was full-scale panic in the Johannesburg office and across McKinsey's global empire.

Douglas told of a bizarre request a couple of years earlier from Vikas Sagar to help write someone's MBA thesis. That someone turned out to be Siyabonga Gama, the notorious chief of the freight rail group when McKinsey worked on the locomotive procurement. Although Douglas expressed reservations, he went ahead and wrote at least two chapters with assistance from McKinsey personnel.

For his work, Douglas received around $7,000 billed to two different Transnet accounts, not including the value of contributions from other McKinsey employees. McKinsey immediately recognized the specter of a possible violation of the U.S. Foreign Corrupt Practices Act—for giving what could be viewed as a bribe, prompting a frenzied internal investigation.

The firm concluded that the value of its services to Gama had to be reported as a possible FCPA violation. But the U.S. government took no action after McKinsey said it found no link between helping Gama and contract awards.

If McKinsey's elders had taken the time to really get to know Sagar, they might have seen this coming.

Sagar had cultivated relationships with leaders at Regiments and Transnet, and his success in managing those relationships—and the money that flowed from them—impressed his McKinsey partners so much that they elected him a senior partner.

He had prepped for his job at McKinsey in the United States, receiving an undergraduate degree at the University of Michigan and an MBA from the Wharton School. After a brief stint in McKinsey's

Chicago office, Sagar started a small information management company in Kuwait, then rejoined McKinsey in Africa in 2001. Sagar landed in the firm's Johannesburg office several years after Fine.

A female business executive who attended meetings with Sagar described him as arrogant but Bollywood handsome, adorned with a Hermès belt, Montblanc cuff links, and a Louis Vuitton briefcase. "The only time Vikas ever spoke to me," the executive said, "was when I took my brand-new Prada bag to a meeting and he whispered 'stunning bag'—before adding that I should have bought a Celine."

Fine and Sagar approached work differently. Fine followed company procedures, consulting partners on major decisions. He rose quickly from partner to senior partner to manager of the Johannesburg office and later to a regional manager. Sagar, by dint of his personality, preferred to deal one-on-one with clients, excluding even his colleagues. Office elders warned Sagar that acting alone was irresponsible, but they mostly looked the other way. If Sagar's methods contributed to higher year-end bonuses for partners, then they were willing to accept his unorthodox practices.

McKinsey's troublesome but profitable work for Transnet served as a warm-up for the firm's next big score: fixing the state-owned power company, Eskom. If all went well, McKinsey stood to collect more money from Eskom than from virtually any other company in the world, with a potential value of $700 million. The optics were bad enough—a predominantly white firm seeking that amount of money without competitive bidding from an impoverished government. In the United States or Britain, this fee might attract little attention, but not in South Africa, with an income gap wider than most anywhere in the world and youth unemployment topping 50 percent. To extract that kind of money from a state-owned company sinking in debt with a history of mismanagement was unconscionable.

Eskom's problems boiled down to this: the continent's most advanced economy could no longer count on the power company to keep the lights on. In the first half of 2015, South Africa experienced blackouts or power reductions on more than half of the days. Each week seemed to bring new problems. Eskom fired a thousand workers at one power plant. Twenty-one thousand contract workers went on strike protesting poor living conditions and low pay. Four executives were suspended, prompting Standard & Poor's to cut Eskom's credit rating to junk. The previous year a major boiler blew up.

Desperate to right the ship, Eskom hired a new chief executive, Brian Molefe, who had presided over the locomotive fiasco at Transnet.

Sagar knew Molefe from Transnet. Another senior partner, Alexander Weiss, had advised Eskom since 2005. Weiss's credentials included two doctorates, one in civil engineering and another in business administration. Although he lived in Berlin, Weiss thought little of making twenty-six-hour round-trip flights, sometimes weekly, to Johannesburg, where he consulted alongside more than a dozen chief executives and chief financial officers at Eskom.

To reach an agreement on what needed to be done—and how much it would cost—Eskom and McKinsey negotiated for more than twenty days spread over nearly six months. The talks caused a stir inside McKinsey's glass tower in Sandton, Johannesburg's financial center, said to be the richest square mile in all of Africa.

Interviews with more than sixteen current and former McKinsey employees, including partners and senior partners, told of a sharp divide in the office between those who wanted to bet the long shot, believing they could reform Eskom, and those who saw the power company as fool's gold and a major reputational risk. The long-shot team won, the risk justified by the prospect of a mammoth payout.

Officially, McKinsey characterized the negotiations as arduous with a lot of back-and-forth. But in private, at least one former partner suggested McKinsey easily got what it wanted. "These negotiations were like clubbing seals," the partner said. A colleague added, "Greed had overtaken common sense."

Other concerns centered on the absence of competitive bidding and a controversial result-based fee structure, known as an at-risk contract. Unlike standard fixed-fee agreements, the final bill for an at-risk contract is unknown until the job is completed. McKinsey could work for years and receive no pay if agreed-upon goals were not achieved. On the other hand, the payout could be enormous. "You are betting the office," one partner warned colleagues. If the final payout becomes public, the partner added, "you are going to be slaughtered just for the size."

A result-based contract carried other risks. In the late 1980s, Jeffrey Skilling of Enron fame sat on a committee considering whether McKinsey should get paid based on the impact, such as a percentage of achieved cost reductions. The panel called that unwise, because it might incentivize the firm to tell clients to reduce costs when that was not in the client's interest. "Doing that," Skilling said, "could destroy" the firm. McKinsey eventually rejected that view because clients asked for it and competitors were using it.

"Trying to do a 100 percent at-risk contract at Eskom is trying to play God," a former South African consultant said. "You are guaranteeing that I can turn around everything, no problem." To do that, McKinsey might need more political clout and expertise than it had. "It is definitely way beyond what McKinsey can produce."

Still, the prospect of a major windfall made the Eskom project popular in Johannesburg and in other McKinsey offices. Supporters included two senior partners with oversight in energy and power—Moscow's Yermolai Solzhenitsyn, the novelist Aleksandr Solzhenitsyn's eldest son, and Thomas Vahlenkamp in Düsseldorf, Germany.

The big Eskom project began in January 2016 but quickly ran into trouble. The McKinsey team failed to confirm Eskom's assurances that the National Treasury had approved the unorthodox fee arrangement as required by law. It wasn't until many months later that McKinsey learned it had been working illegally.

McKinsey also had to find a trustworthy Black empowerment subcontractor after dumping Regiments in February 2016 over the quality of its work. Based on Sagar's recommendation, the firm chose Trillian, a new company that had been spun off from Regiments. McKinsey erred again—this time by starting work without a contract and without confirming that Trillian was Black owned and free from undesirable individuals.

Trillian's own behavior made the situation worse. While advising Eskom on buying a new boiler, it was also advising the seller, a Chinese company. "What was particularly concerning about this was that Trillian had not disclosed the potential conflict," Weiss said, noting that McKinsey only learned of the conflict during a meeting at Eskom.

Trillian had its own reasons for being angry at McKinsey. Bianca Goodson, who ran Trillian's management consulting unit, said McKinsey treated her and her company as unwanted baggage. At a leadership meeting one evening at McKinsey headquarters—the one where Goodson saw Sagar dance on the conference room table—Goodson waited several hours to speak, but when her time came, Weiss left the room. A McKinsey partner, Lorenz Jüngling, told her not to worry because Trillian "will still get their 30 percent." Goodson said that the following day Jüngling intimated that Trillian just wanted money "in return for not much work."

These exchanges reminded Goodson of advice she received from a man who had considerable influence inside Trillian.

"These McKinsey dicks—if they give you any trouble, call me," he told her. That man was Salim Essa, a Trillian owner and a shadowy figure who would emerge as a key conduit through which the Gupta family allegedly sought to "capture" South Africa's government.

The next day Sagar called to apologize for the conduct of his colleagues.

Meanwhile, Fine had grown increasingly concerned about Sagar's private meetings with officials at Trillian and Eskom. "This was an issue I raised with him, and my other colleague Norbert Doerr raised with him as well. We even had a dinner to discuss this matter."

Sagar did not take the criticism well. "You are not trusting enough," he said.

Confronting Sagar carried a risk, given his popularity and his success as a revenue generator at Eskom and Transnet. According to one estimate, those two accounts represented nearly half of the Johannesburg office's income.

Although Fine did not work on the Eskom account, as a manager he wanted to know who owned Trillian. "I had asked multiple times, well, who is Trillian?" he said. "There was no answer forthcoming." The only person Fine knew at the company was Eric Wood, Trillian's chief executive, whom he described as "a white South African starting a black advisory firm."

To press the issue, Fine arranged two meetings with Sagar and Wood at Tashas, a restaurant in Melrose Arch, an island of high-fashion retail stores, alfresco dining, a hotel, a gym, and business offices. "Who are the investors?" Fine demanded. Wood responded with a few names. Upon googling those names later, Fine became even more concerned. They were politically connected, he concluded.

The idea that McKinsey's due diligence on one of its biggest projects consisted of a partner googling names showed how ill-prepared the firm was to take on this assignment. Eventually, McKinsey hired investigators to examine Trillian's background, and the evidence they found pointed to the involvement of Salim Essa, the Gupta family associate.

Sagar had assured his colleagues that he had never met or spoken to Essa. That was untrue.

In fact, McKinsey found that Sagar had been communicating regularly with Essa and that Sagar had tried to hide it. He installed a program to wipe clean his computer memory and used a private email to communicate with Essa's own clandestine account. He also sent Eskom a letter bearing McKinsey's logo that authorized the power company to pay Trillian directly for subcontracting work, citing an "agreement" that McKinsey had with the company.

McKinsey informed Eskom in March 2016 that after three months of partnering with Trillian, it had cut ties with the company. The firm had finally taken a stand, but quickly undercut that decision by continuing to work alongside Trillian.

McKinsey had thus far managed to tamp down news of its involvement in tainted contracts by saying little or nothing. But in June, just six months into its three-year contract, Eskom terminated McKinsey, citing serious contracting irregularities.

McKinsey partners, who thought they had largely contained reputational damage, were in for a big surprise.

McKinsey had long profited from government contracts without accepting the responsibility to account for how it spent the public's money. In the United States, its prestige and political connections, as well as the country's favorable regulatory laws, often insulated the firm from questions about those contracts. It is surprising, then, that it took South Africa, a fragile democracy barely two decades old, to teach McKinsey lessons about accountability that it hadn't learned in the United States.

That education began in October 2016 after authorities launched a series of investigations into "state capture," defined as when private individuals and companies take over state agencies to redirect public resources into their own hands, while weakening the institutions responsible for ferreting out that corruption.

The first investigation was by the public protector, Thuli Madonsela, who released her findings three months after McKinsey stopped advising Eskom. She cited contract irregularities involving McKinsey's work at Transnet and Eskom, but provided few granular details because, as she wrote, the transactions "remain a mystery as all parties refuse to release details of the deals." The report scratched but didn't wound McKinsey.

The following month, another investigation began, this one by Advocate Geoff Budlender, a widely respected human rights activist. With more time, he dug deeper into the contracts. Budlender asked to interview McKinsey, but the firm declined, saying it would only answer written questions. One sentence in McKinsey's answers caught Budlender's attention: "McKinsey did not work on any projects on which Trillian worked as SDP [supply development partner] or a subcontractor to McKinsey."

Budlender knew more than he was letting on and had laid a trap for McKinsey. Upon receiving McKinsey's denial, he produced the letter from Sagar to Eskom stating the exact opposite. "As you know," Sagar wrote, "McKinsey has subcontracted a portion of the services to be performed under the agreement to Trillian." Sagar also authorized Eskom to pay Trillian directly.

Budlender demanded an explanation. Benedict Phiri, a McKinsey lawyer, said he would discuss the matter with his colleagues and get back to him. Week after week went by with no reply, despite frequent reminders from Budlender. Finally, two and a half months later, McKinsey said it would be "inappropriate" to respond to Budlender's "informal" inquiry.

"Why that would be 'inappropriate' has not been explained," Budlender wrote. "I have to say that I find this inexplicable, particularly having regard to the fact that McKinsey presents itself as an international leader in management consulting and given the widespread public interest in this matter." Budlender's final judgment: McKinsey had submitted false information.

By implying that McKinsey was dishonest, Budlender's report inflicted more than a surface wound. It cut deep, and the firm realized that. With more investigations lining up, McKinsey's silence was becoming untenable. Waiting in ambush were investigators from the National Treasury, the Parliament, the media, and the biggest of all, the Commission of Inquiry into State Capture, chaired by Raymond Zondo, deputy chief justice of South Africa.

McKinsey's reluctance to engage about public contracts carried over to the media. In an article about McKinsey's partnership with Regiments, amaBhungane, the country's premier investigative news unit, wrote, "Over two months, amaBhungane has sent six requests to McKinsey asking whether it was aware of the lavish fees Regiments paid to various 'business development partners.' McKinsey dodged the question each time."

The National Prosecuting Authority turned up the heat by publicly condemning McKinsey for enabling corruption. The NPA concluded that the firm had been instrumental "in creating a veil of legitimacy in what was otherwise a manifestly unlawful arrangement." The NPA, referring to McKinsey's Eskom work, delivered this judgment when Parliament was already deep into its hearings on government corruption.

McKinsey decided the time had come to make a stand, and to do so not through a faceless corporate statement but through a sympathetic McKinsey partner, David Fine, its loyal South African consultant who had risen to lead the firm's global public- and social-sector practice. Now living in Europe, Fine flew down to tell Parliament of McKinsey's deep regret for not talking to Advocate Budlender and to acknowledge a plethora of other mistakes.

"I understand it caused severe consternation internally about how we would or should cooperate with an investigation without our client's consent," Fine said. "We should have had a conversation with him to explain these matters and I'm embarrassed that we did not do that." Presumably, Budlender was less interested in McKinsey's reasoning for not talking and more interested in what it did or didn't do to enable state capture.

The public's right to know how the government spends its money is vital in a thriving democracy. That right, generally speaking, does not transfer to McKinsey's private clients, and the firm surely knew that government consulting carried additional responsibilities. McKinsey's experience in South Africa brought that difference into sharp focus: Should the firm discuss government clients when there is an expectation of confidentiality?

There are only two credible responses: don't take government business, or answer the questions. McKinsey offered a third, saying consultants are encouraged to raise difficult questions internally, but that fell far short of public accountability.

In South Africa at least, McKinsey changed its mind. Facing the loss of clients and most likely the closing of its South African office, the firm made a financial decision. It agreed to answer questions in a public forum—not once, but four times—a situation not yet encountered in the United States.

Fine was first, answering questions for four hours before a parliamentary committee. He admitted mistakes but no crimes. He apologized on behalf of the firm and announced that it would refund the entirety of its Eskom fees. "We should have absolutely had a fee structure that was capped," Fine said.

McKinsey officials offered up Sagar—not the firm—as a sacrifice, saying he caused the firm's troubles and announcing that he had left the firm while under suspension. The firm did not mention that he left with full benefits. The firm also sanctioned his co-leader on the Eskom team, Alex Weiss, without disclosing the nature of that sanction. Weiss kept his job. Sagar now runs a software company in London.

With a rapidly shrinking client base, McKinsey transferred dozens of employees to posts outside South Africa. The managing partner, Dominic Barton, based in New York City, made six tiring trips to South Africa to stop the hemorrhaging.

But another investigation into corruption and "state capture"—

the biggest yet—began in June 2018 and before it ended would take testimony from more than four hundred individuals. Led by Deputy Chief Justice Raymond Zondo, the commission continued its work well into 2021.

While witnesses were being called, Barton's successor, Kevin Sneader, thought it was important to visit Johannesburg, where he hoped to extinguish any remaining embers of anger. Speaking to a business group early on a Monday morning in July 2018—two weeks after *The New York Times* published a critical article about the firm's work in South Africa—Sneader used the word "sorry" eleven times. "The stories written about us in South Africa hurt deeply as they strike at what we value more than anything else—the trust we have built with our clients through the judgment, character, and reputation of our people."

Sneader admitted that McKinsey was too distant to grasp the rising anger in South Africa. "Our governance processes failed. Our commercial approach led to a fee that was too large. We did not admit we were wrong. And worse, we did not say sorry quickly enough and clearly enough." Sneader also acknowledged that McKinsey should not have continued to "interact" with Trillian at Eskom after the company had failed its due diligence review.

South Africa, though, wasn't done with McKinsey.

After Sneader's speech, more bad news emerged in the Zondo Commission hearings. Toward the end of 2020, the commission surprised the firm by finding two more tainted McKinsey contracts with state-owned enterprises.

One was with South African Airways, where McKinsey and Regiments were hired to "unlock" the airline's working capital. This time, no sole-source contract was necessary because Regiments bribed the airline's treasurer to get the work. According to the judicial commission, Regiments obtained the contract specifications in advance, then changed the evaluation criteria before the request for proposal was issued. Regiments also received "confidential information" on the evaluation process, including bids from its competitors. The airline ensured that the contract amount did not exceed a value that would have triggered a board review.

Forty percent of Regiments' share of the airline contract—

6.2 million rand, or roughly $420,000—went to a shell company that laundered payments to the Gupta family. McKinsey said it didn't know that the contract was secured through a bribe.

The second tainted McKinsey contract was with Transnet, where Regiments diverted millions of dollars to front companies controlled by the Guptas.

McKinsey again took the position that it knew nothing about these payments. Its investigators had said they reviewed more than one million emails, financial records, and other documents and conducted 115 interviews. The firm did lack subpoena power, but McKinsey's denials called to mind Claude Rains in the movie *Casablanca:* "I'm shocked, shocked to find that gambling is going on in here."

The commission raised another embarrassing issue: Weiss testified that he had insisted that Trillian provide documented proof of its ownership. "I asked for this in a very painful, highly frequent way," he said. If documentary proof was so important, the commission wanted to know, why then did he backdate his signature by almost nine months on McKinsey's Eskom contract. Weiss suggested that deception was insignificant.

The commission disagreed, saying a properly dated signature "would have flagged something that would have come out as an irregularity that may have triggered greater scrutiny of the contract." Weiss apologized for any confusion he might have caused. Not to be forgotten, he said, was that in a short time McKinsey "had a real, visible impact on Eskom's operational performance," including improved availability of electricity.

McKinsey sought to defuse the discovery of the two additional tainted contracts by agreeing to a commission request to refund more than $40 million from those contracts—even though the firm and the commission asserted it was not complicit. That elicited praise from the commission for being a "responsible corporate citizen." Together with the Eskom refund, McKinsey was now on the hook for more than $100 million.

The commission's praise angered David Lewis, executive director of Corruption Watch, a South African advocacy group. "To pay back your fee simply because you were caught with your bloody hands in the till is, frankly, not restitution," Lewis said. "They are involved in such dodgy activity across the world that I think there are grounds to remove their license to operate, certainly in this country. That would be the appropriate level of reparation."

McKinsey's troubles in South Africa prompted much soul-searching in the firm. Could the firm's managers have found a way to defuse the crisis sooner? What did they do wrong? Some of the harshest criticism came from former colleagues in the Johannesburg office. "It was a car crash in slow motion," one employee said.

Everyone seemed to agree that the firm took too long to recognize the depth of South Africa's anger. Dominic Barton, managing partner while the crisis unfolded, said senior partners had "a bit of a tin ear" in their early response. His predecessor, Ian Davis, criticized the firm for apologizing, equating it to an admission of guilt, according to a source with direct knowledge of what was said. (Davis declined to speak on the record about whether this account is accurate.) Others thought Kevin Sneader, who succeeded Barton, went too far in his apology.

In South Africa, the judicial commission lawyer, Matthew Chaskalson, asked the firm's new chief risk officer, Jean-Christophe Mieszala, why nobody at McKinsey questioned the firm's "astronomical increase in the fees."

"To my knowledge it was not something that was picked up," Mieszala answered.

The commission found no evidence suggesting that McKinsey as a firm had engaged in corrupt conduct, but Mieszala did admit that it is "morally wrong" to appear greedy when your client is struggling.

The picture was less clear for Sagar, a fact highlighted by the commission. "A relationship between Sagar and Essa went way beyond improper relationship," Chaskalson told Mieszala. "It actually involved impropriety toward Eskom." He concluded the evidence "does implicate Sagar in state capture." Sagar was no low-level number cruncher, but a trusted senior partner operating on behalf of McKinsey.

McKinsey asserts that it has addressed problems in South Africa by strengthening its internal governance, including more scrutiny of public-sector work. Chaskalson pushed back, saying the mistakes reflected McKinsey's culture more than weak governance.

The Economist seemed to agree. Under the headline "The Smuggest Guys in the Room," the publication opined,

> For almost 95 years, McKinsey has sought to portray itself as a genteel professional services company, not a grubby business. Unlike, say, a profit hungry Goldman Sachs banker, who walks into a room aware she may be hissed at, a McKinsey consultant expects his halo to be noticed. However much its senior partners insist that they are not motivated by outsized profits, they can earn as much each year as that Goldman banker.

Indeed, the firm's revenues almost doubled in a decade to more than $10 billion, prompting *The Economist* to conclude, "The firm's employees revel in the aura of the old McKinsey—of autonomy, discretion and intellectual prestige—while embracing the growth, profits and power that have come in more recent years. Rarely do they doubt whether they can have it all."

McKinsey's Mieszala seemed to acknowledge that reality.

"When you have people who are overachievers, it can generate bad behavior and this is why we have to be vigilant," he said. "It is pretty clear that the South Africa situation has taught us a lesson and we are very humbled by that lesson."

Eskom presumably learned a lesson as well. In January 2020, the company was forced to cut so much power that mines and factories shut down and households went dark. Weeks earlier, South Africa's president had cut short a diplomatic visit to the Middle East to deal with the crisis. One year later, more of the same.

The media reported that 2021 could be the worst year for power cutbacks in nearly a century.

Chapter 13

Serving the Saudi State

In the 1970s, Saudi Arabia was booming. Crude oil prices doubled, then quadrupled, in the wake of the Arab oil embargo. The kingdom, awash in cash, had big plans—new cities, new industries, new airports, new refineries—but needed foreign expertise to pull it off. Tens of thousands of expats flooded the country, often bringing their families.*

Among the many Americans who came was a star McKinsey consultant and former army intelligence officer, Sandy Apgar. The recession that the oil embargo helped to spark had gutted the work he'd been doing in London on real estate, so he headed to Saudi Arabia and "knocked on doors and tents."

Apgar found plenty of work. He advised the state-owned oil company, Aramco, as it underwent a massive expansion and also won business to help the kingdom plan its transition from a nation of Bedouin nomads to a modern, urban economy. More than forty years later, McKinsey's work in Saudi Arabia still revolves around those two pillars, the closest thing in consulting to a perfect hedge: advising Aramco and the Energy Ministry and helping the government move away from an economy totally dependent on Aramco's oil.

Apgar, who went on to be an assistant secretary of the army under

* Among those expats was the co-author Mike Forsythe, who spent much of his childhood in the Red Sea port city of Jeddah, from 1970 to 1981.

President Bill Clinton, quickly discovered that economic power in the country was, as he put it, "relatively centralized in the hands of government ministers, senior officials, and an entrepreneurial elite, most of whom are either members of or close to the royal family." His successors took extraordinary steps to build ties to that elite, hiring their sons and daughters.

Opportunity beckoned for American consultants. To get closer to the action, in 1996 McKinsey set up an office in Dubai, the Persian Gulf trading hub. Saudi rulers wanted to replicate the success of Dubai, then emerging as a multicultural global transport and financial center. The Saudi consulting surge was on.

Winning the biggest contracts in Saudi Arabia was dependent on the government, the driving force behind all of the Persian Gulf economies. That wasn't lost on Kito de Boer, the Dutch McKinsey partner and avid art collector who oversaw the region and later went on to serve as head of mission for the Quartet, the group made up of the United Nations, the European Union, the United States, and Russia, that mediates between Israelis and Palestinians. De Boer kept a unique kind of organization chart on the office walls of McKinsey's Dubai office: posters laying out who was who in the region's royal families.

In 2009, McKinsey opened an office in Riyadh, the Saudi capital, and business inside the kingdom really took off. The firm landed one of the biggest construction companies in the Middle East—one with a name instantly recognizable around the world because of its infamous family member—the Saudi Binladin Group. It also stepped up work with Aramco, advising on its restructuring ahead of its eventual IPO.

From only 2 jobs in 2010 in Saudi Arabia, the firm took on 47 projects the following year, according to internal McKinsey figures on "Know," the firm's intranet, where consultants can draw on the collective work of their colleagues, such as ready-made slide decks. By 2016, McKinsey had 137 projects in Saudi Arabia.

So ingrained was McKinsey into the kingdom's affairs that the Planning Ministry became known as the Ministry of McKinsey. Some of the firm's consultants who worked for a Saudi subsidiary acquired in 2017 even used government email addresses, one former consultant said. McKinsey said it was not aware of any consultants who were given Saudi government email addresses.

One force that drove McKinsey's explosive growth in Saudi Arabia was a political phenomenon the royal family wanted desperately to ward off: the Arab Spring. The wave of revolutions and revolts that swept through Egypt, Libya, Bahrain, Yemen, Syria, and Tunisia in 2011 and 2012 was potentially an extinction-level event for the royal family. "The consulting boom happened because dictators didn't want to become the next Mubarak," one former Dubai-based McKinsey consultant said, referring to the late Egyptian leader who was ousted in the unrest after decades of anemic growth and widespread corruption.

The eventual solution, in which McKinsey and its competitors played a central role, was to relax some of the kingdom's infamous social restrictions, such as the ban on women driving and movie theaters, while at the same time increasing repression of dissident voices.

Some McKinsey consultants, especially younger ones, were bothered that the firm would so willingly help the House of Saud, a family from Riyadh whose patriarch conquered much of the Arabian Peninsula in the 1920s and whose sons have overseen a ruthless theocratic autocracy ever since. They argued that the firm should reduce, or possibly even end, its work there. Said one, "Saudi Arabia is a country that shouldn't exist."

They were overruled by the partners, who argued that it wasn't McKinsey's job to pass judgment on the values of its clients. Left unsaid was the impact on annual bonuses if the Saudi work vanished. In defending McKinsey's decision to stay in Saudi Arabia, its senior partners inevitably rely on political arguments, saying its work helps keep Saudi Arabia from going the way of Syria or other failed states, despite the firm's oft-repeated claim that it doesn't involve itself in politics.

"If you take a country like Saudi, and you project it forward if nothing changes, the consequences for that region are just dire," said one senior partner who oversees work in the region. The problem is that after 2015, McKinsey's work in Saudi Arabia was beholden to a man who was building, as Ben Hubbard of *The New York Times* wrote, "a laboratory for a new kind of electronic authoritarianism."

McKinsey was helping him do it.

The five-member delegation from the Saudi Royal Court was making the rounds in Washington, visiting think tanks like the Brookings Institution and defense contractors like Lockheed Martin and Raytheon, the supplier of the bombs the Saudis were using to kill thousands of civilians during the war in neighboring Yemen.

It was February 2016, and the Saudis were there to talk about the new political reality in Saudi Arabia following the death of King Abdullah a year earlier. It came in the form of the heavyset young man Mohammed bin Salman, who was the favorite son of the octogenarian king.

At this point, enough was known about MBS to have made McKinsey or any Western company question the wisdom of doing business in the kingdom. MBS was ruthless. One story has him sending a single bullet in an envelope to a land-registry official who wouldn't sign over a parcel of land to him, earning him the nickname Abu Rasasa, or "father of the bullet." He even detained his own mother, for reasons that aren't clear. Anyone tuned in to Saudi politics knew the stories. Soon, the entire world would know just how far he would go to silence his perceived enemies.

But that wasn't the message his emissaries were bringing to the American capital. They told their hosts about MBS's grand goals to remake Saudi life. Their tour guides—McKinsey and its chief rival, Boston Consulting Group—outnumbered the Saudis. The consultants sat quietly, taking notes.

Four years later, McKinsey filed a very tardy disclosure with the Justice Department under the Foreign Agents Registration Act for that work. It is the only filing by McKinsey on the agency's website. The filing established McKinsey as more than just consultants to the kingdom. They were now representing that country's interests in the United States. The firm had earlier told reporters that it saw no reason to make a FARA filing.

McKinsey was working with the Saudi government to strengthen its diplomatic outreach, helping set up what became the Saudi Center for International Strategic Partnerships, which, McKinsey said, was "an entity whose purpose would be to help manage and improve Saudi Arabia's relationships with numerous countries around the world." Some of McKinsey's biggest stars were involved, including Gary Pinkus, then the managing partner for North America. McKinsey received $4.8 million for its work, paid by its client of almost half a century, Aramco.

These were busy days for American consultants in Saudi Arabia. The young prince was enamored of them. And he thought he needed their expertise to turn his big dreams into reality, such as the city of the future. In case there was any question about that, the city's name, NEOM, is an acronym for "new future," derived from the Greek word *neo* and the Arabic word for future, *mustaqbal.* Such an undertaking was so ambitious that "mega-project" just wouldn't do. This was a giga-project. Plans call for flying drone taxis, an artificial moon, and robotic *Jurassic Park*–style dinosaurs for this space-age city on the Red Sea. McKinsey billed millions of dollars to advise on the project, internal company records show.

The lobby of the Riyadh Ritz-Carlton was full of McKinsey men. Dominic Barton, then McKinsey's managing partner, made regular appearances in Riyadh, surprising McKinsey's local consultants with the frequency of his visits. Even taxi drivers could identify individual consultants and their firms.

In years past, consultants cultivated relationships in the myriad ministries, controlled by various fiefdoms of the sprawling royal family. Now MBS was consolidating power, and he brought the consultants into the Royal Court, a rare privilege under previous kings, one longtime consultant in the region said. "There was no question about working with MBS," one former McKinsey consultant told Ben Hubbard. "They were all in."

Early in MBS's rise to power, McKinsey landed a big job—a national transformation project, aimed at weaning the kingdom off its dependence on oil. In December 2015, McKinsey's think tank, the McKinsey Global Institute, rolled out the product of some of that work, "Saudi Arabia Beyond Oil." The report warned that by 2030, Saudi Arabia faced mass unemployment that could be averted by a $4 trillion investment splurge in areas such as mining, tourism, and finance. The reward: a doubling of GDP and six million new jobs. Oversight of this ambitious project would by design rest with the Ministry of Economy and Planning.

Yet McKinsey was not all-powerful in Saudi Arabia. A rival, Boston Consulting Group, had cultivated the young prince years earlier, advising his foundation, MiSK, which says it is "devoted to cultivate and encourage learning and leadership in youth for a better future in Saudi Arabia." It was BCG that got some of the biggest jobs, such as working with the country's sovereign wealth fund as well as the Ministry of Defense. And it was BCG's "Vision 2030" that won the day, not McKinsey's plan.

But McKinsey would not give in to its rival so easily. One way McKinsey could cement its influence was through politically connected hires. This it did with gusto.

Back in 2003 the firm hired Mazen Al-Jubeir, the younger brother of Adel Al-Jubeir, the future Saudi ambassador to the United States and the smooth-talking public face of the kingdom in Washington in the wake of the September 11, 2001, attacks. Mazen Al-Jubeir was, like so many McKinsey consultants, a graduate of Harvard Business School and was named a Baker scholar. As competition heated up with BCG, McKinsey went back to this playbook, though this time some of its hires didn't have such glittering academic résumés.

In 2017, *The Wall Street Journal* reported that over the previous two years McKinsey employed two children of the former Aramco chief as well as the son of a finance minister, two children of a former central bank chief, and the head of a state-owned mining company. Highlighting the closeness of McKinsey to the regime, at least five former McKinsey employees have gone on to work at MiSK, MBS's foundation, according to their LinkedIn profiles. One of those was Sarah Alkhedheiri, the daughter of a former information and culture minister. She and her brother worked at McKinsey after they finished their undergraduate studies at Northeastern University in Boston.

By 2017, two years into the age of MBS, McKinsey took a very bold move to cement its place in Saudi Arabia and strike back at BCG's dominance: it bought a well-connected Saudi consulting company.

In 2005, Hani Khoja, a former Procter & Gamble executive, founded his own consulting company, Elixir, at the urging of a McKinsey partner. Khoja had close ties to the planning minister, and Elixir's employees, based in Jeddah and Riyadh, had burrowed deep into the ministry, winning major contracts.

On April 1, 2017, McKinsey announced that it had bought Elixir. It was a very rare acquisition by McKinsey, which for the first nine decades of its existence had mainly relied on "organic" growth, eschewing mergers and acquisitions, even though it often advised and advocated for them for its clients.

McKinsey "never buys anything like this anywhere in the world," said one former McKinsey partner who worked in the region, speaking about Elixir. "The word was that it was purely for the relationships." In an instant, McKinsey's staff in Saudi Arabia ballooned by 140 people, adding almost 50 percent to its staff in the region.

"Four or five months in, you kind of realize it for what it is, which is a temp agency for the government," a former Saudi Elixir employee said.

Elixir's consultants are so close to the Saudi ministries that they're often indistinguishable from government employees, said a former Elixir employee, a Saudi hired after the McKinsey takeover. "When you come at them with a government email, they will talk to you," the person said, referring to government bureaucrats.

That put McKinsey consultants very close to their client. Another former McKinsey consultant in Saudi Arabia described the relationship as one of employer-employee: gone was the traditional relationship that—at least in theory—allowed McKinsey consultants to speak hard truths to their clients. The consultant recalls Ian Davis, then McKinsey's managing partner, telling young hires that they should view themselves as modern-day "courtiers and viziers."

Instead, it was, this person said, "Don't think as much; just do as I tell you."

McKinsey employees acting essentially as government officials would be problematic enough in a democracy. To be doing it in an absolute monarchy where its de facto leader jails or kills his political enemies made McKinsey unusually vulnerable to the whims of a despot.

Within months of the acquisition, that would be manifestly obvious.

In the first week of November 2017 more than 350 princes, ministers, and businessmen converged on the Saudi capital. They were invited there, under various pretexts, in the name of the king or his son MBS.

When they arrived in Riyadh, security officials confiscated their cell phones, pens, and wallets. They were confined to the Ritz-Carlton. The rooms were luxurious, but sharp objects—anything they could use to harm themselves—were nowhere to be found. One by one, they were presented with evidence of their crime—corruption—and many were offered deals that involved signing huge portions of their assets over to the Saudi state. Some were beaten, and at least one was bludgeoned to death.

Among those detained was Hani Khoja, the co-founder of Elixir and newly minted McKinsey partner. He was held for more than thirteen months, and according to a report in *The Wall Street Journal* he was also beaten.

Another casualty of the Ritz purge: the planning minister in charge of "the Ministry of McKinsey." He was charged with corruption.

Going into business with middlemen in a deeply corrupt country can imperil the reputation of American companies. McKinsey knows this from experience. In South Africa, it faced a similar dilemma and chose to jump in anyway, regardless of the risks. But unlike South Africa, where the taint of corruption devastated its business, that didn't happen in Saudi Arabia, apparently because McKinsey's work was seen by MBS and his government as important to the very survival of the House of Saud.

Collapsing crude oil prices were devastating the Saudi budget, and officials there were considering whether to cut oil subsidies, possibly raising the price of fuel in the kingdom. Because they didn't want to spark protests that might bring the Arab Spring into the country, Saudi leaders wanted to gauge the attitude of the masses toward cutting subsidies. To do that, they turned to McKinsey, Boston Consulting, and a third firm, the London-based SCL Group, better known through its subsidiary, Cambridge Analytica, notorious for influencing elections across the globe for any candidate willing to pay its fees. Cambridge Analytica's CEO, Alexander Nix, boasted to undercover journalists from Britain's Channel 4 News that the company could "send some girls around to the candidate's house" to entrap them, saying he liked to use Ukrainian "girls" for the job. The company also improperly accessed Facebook data to help the Trump campaign create psychological profiles of millions of voters who were then bombarded with targeted content.

In Saudi Arabia, SCL and Cambridge Analytica were essentially interchangeable: the work there was overseen by the person who succeeded Nix as Cambridge Analytica's CEO. The aim was to conduct focus groups across the kingdom, asking people how they would feel if the price of fuel increased. McKinsey and BCG would then process that information and present it to senior officials at the ministry. This deeply political work went far beyond the traditional McKinsey remit of providing advice to private companies on how to save money by being more efficient. One former Cambridge Analytica executive involved in the Saudi work with McKinsey said the purpose behind it was "to reduce the risk of unrest."

McKinsey was helping ensure the viability of a brutal, authoritarian regime. "Putting the bits and pieces together, in hindsight I don't feel good about it," said another former Cambridge Analytica consultant whose work intersected with McKinsey's. "It is a sort of reinforcement, or adding to their consolidation of power."

McKinsey said it did not work with Cambridge Analytica or the SCL Group for the Saudi Ministry of Economy and Planning.

McKinsey's work with the Saudis went far beyond focus groups. Saudi Arabia's population is one of the youngest in the world and one of the most engaged on platforms like Twitter and Facebook. A new technique—"sentiment analysis"—mined social media posts for keywords, allowing companies to measure attitudes about their products. McKinsey got excited about the technique, mentioning it in multiple reports. So did the Saudis; a group of Saudi scholars called it "opinion mining."

The Saudis latched onto the fact that sentiment analysis had potential way beyond determining how people felt about their pizza delivery experience. In a country like Saudi Arabia, where it seemed everyone was chatting on Facebook, Instagram, or Twitter, it could be used by the government to take the public's temperature and smoke out influential malcontents.

Around the same time McKinsey was working alongside SCL, one of its Dubai-based senior partners, Enrico Benni, was seeking out people across the firm for a new potential Saudi assignment: to perform sentiment analysis in Arabic, one former employee said. McKinsey's Saudi-based employees highlighted this work on their public profiles. One Saudi-based Elixir employee, Ahmad Alattas, listed "social media monitoring to conduct and study public sentiment analysis" among his jobs. Soon, this new line of work yielded results, but perhaps not the kind McKinsey had in mind.

In early 2018 a person from Saudi Arabia phoned Omar Abdulaziz to check up on him. He hadn't seen much from him recently on social media; Abdulaziz had hundreds of thousands of followers on Twitter and YouTube. Was he okay?

Abdulaziz, a Saudi national who had been living in Montreal for almost a decade, replied that he was fine. But the person had good reason to be worried. He told Abdulaziz that he had been working with McKinsey on a project for MBS. McKinsey had prepared a report about how the kingdom's subjects were reacting to government policies. The report identified Abdulaziz, along with some other Saudis, as being highly influential in shaping the public's opinion, and not in a positive way.

"I thought, 'Oh, that's great,'" Abdulaziz recalled more than two years later. "In the beginning I didn't know that it would be such an important thing. I couldn't imagine how MBS would be interested in my work. So I thought nothing would happen."

The banal title of the nine-page report, "Austerity Measures in

Saudi Arabia," belies its explosive content. It was sentiment analysis: weaponized. "Omar has a multitude of negative tweets on topics such as austerity and the royal decrees," read one McKinsey bullet point.

That May, Saudi emissaries traveled to Montreal to urge Abdulaziz to return to his homeland. As a young, hip YouTube star, he'd be a celebrity, they told him. As an added incentive, they brought along his brother to help to convince him.

Abdulaziz demurred. The following month, his phone was hacked, though he was unaware of it for months, according to a report by the Citizen Lab, an organization at the University of Toronto that investigates digital espionage against civil society. In August, Abdulaziz's two brothers were thrown in jail. Another influential online critic highlighted in the McKinsey report was also arrested, and a third account deemed negative by McKinsey disappeared from Twitter.

The phone hack also compromised Abdulaziz's communications with a prominent Saudi journalist. The two had been hatching a plan to counter MBS's emerging techno-authoritarian state, which used armies of internet trolls, called flies, to identify and overwhelm any dissenting online voices.

In September, the journalist had wired Abdulaziz $5,000 to get the project started. The plan was to counter the flies with a swarm of "bees"—people focused on countering the Saudi trolls.

The journalist's name was Jamal Khashoggi.

On October 2, 2018, Khashoggi, a columnist for *The Washington Post,* entered the Saudi consulate in Istanbul to pick up some paperwork for his marriage. His Turkish fiancée waited outside for him.

A Saudi assassination squad, alerted that he was set to visit the legation, was in place. Upon entering, Khashoggi was told he was going back to Saudi Arabia. An agent told him to write a message to his son, telling him not to worry "if you don't hear from me in a while." He refused. "We will anesthetize you," he was told. There were sounds of a struggle, Khashoggi saying, "I can't breathe, I can't breathe," then silence after Khashoggi was injected with a drug. Then came the buzzing sound of a saw as his corpse was dismembered.

American intelligence agencies concluded that MBS was behind the murder.

The existence of the McKinsey report targeting his colleague Omar Abdulaziz became public in the weeks after Khashoggi's murder, included in a *New York Times* story about the Saudi army of online trolls. The story provoked outrage the world over: in the United States, Senator Elizabeth Warren of Massachusetts sent a letter to McKinsey's managing partner, Kevin Sneader, asking him to give her office information about who might have seen the report.

"I am concerned that McKinsey's report on public perception may have been weaponized by the Saudi government to crush criticism of the Kingdom's policies, regardless of McKinsey's intended purpose for the information," Warren wrote.

At the time, McKinsey said it was "horrified by the possibility, however remote, that it could have been misused in any way." The firm said the report's "intended primary audience was internal" and that it was put together by a researcher in Riyadh. "Like many other major corporations including our competitors, we seek to navigate a changing geopolitical environment," the company said, "but we do not support or engage in political activities."

One former McKinsey consultant gave a very different response. "The firm's response to the social media mining stuff in Saudi is utter horseshit," the former consultant said. "I was involved in the conversations that led up to that work with Saudi, and it was much larger and more known about by the leaders in the region than that ridiculous 'it was only one analyst' story they released."

McKinsey says that the report was "composed entirely of publicly available information" and that it has "seen no evidence that the document in question was misused."

In fact, McKinsey's "internal" report was very much external. Abdulaziz's source, who was working with McKinsey on the project, told him it had been presented in 2017 to MBS's associates, and he sent Abdulaziz an electronic version, which was made public in a lawsuit. The *Times* got a copy from another source.

McKinsey had been working with the Saudi government since 2015 on exactly what was in the report—an analysis of how the public would react to cuts in subsidies. *It was an intensely political activity,* aimed at preserving the Saudi monarchy, working on core political tasks for one of the world's most repressive regimes.

Kevin Sneader, McKinsey's managing partner at the time, defended the work in Saudi Arabia on CNBC, framing it in terms of geopolitics, not business. "The world does not want Saudi Arabia to descend into a place where there aren't jobs, and where it gets really tough in a very nasty way," he told CNBC in March 2019, adding that he believes the firm makes "a positive contribution" there.

The revelation led to gallows humor among McKinsey's staffers around the world, most of whom, because of the purposefully stovepiped nature of McKinsey's work, were caught off guard by the *Times* story. In one office, a training session took a very dark turn:

> Your client is the Saudi Arabian Government. They have hired McKinsey to look into ways that they can suppress journalists and dissidents who criticized the Kingdom's autocratic policies.
>
> You've been asked to determine how many dissidents you can put into a vat of acid to dissolve and hide their bodies. Assuming that you have a 10' x 10' x 10' vat of hydrochloric acid, how many dissidents would fit? Explain your approach.

Abdulaziz eventually sued McKinsey, with his lawyers writing in the complaint that "McKinsey effectively put a target on Plaintiff's back." McKinsey persuaded the judge to dismiss the case, filed in California, on jurisdictional grounds. McKinsey said in court papers that Abdulaziz was a well-known critic of the regime for years who had been granted political asylum in Canada and that the report was citing publicly available tweets.

Abdulaziz sued McKinsey again in 2021, this time in federal court in New York, alleging that the slide deck that identified him as a regime critic was seen by representatives of MBS and that after its publication he "was forced into hiding and had to move from hotel to hotel for months to avoid being kidnapped or harmed." McKinsey again asked the judge in the case to dismiss it, and in September 2021 she did, citing, among several reasons, a lapsed statute of limitations and a failure on Abdulaziz's part to show McKinsey had any control over how the Saudi government would use the information in the slide deck.

After Khashoggi's murder, Saudi Arabia was radioactive. Big names such as Blackstone's CEO, Stephen Schwarzman, Jamie Dimon of JPMorgan Chase, and Christine Lagarde, then head of the IMF, pulled out of a Riyadh conference championed by MBS—dubbed Davos in the Desert—that happened just weeks after the murder.

McKinsey and some of the other consulting companies chose to stay. The firm led panels on money and energy, according to the program.

In 2019, the year after Khashoggi's killing, McKinsey's revenue in Saudi Arabia appears to have increased from the previous year, according to one internal measure. The list of clients, and the hours billed, are dominated by government agencies.

Internal records from 2018 and 2019 show McKinsey's work in Saudi Arabia centered on assignments for the country's Finance, Economic, Health, and Education Ministries, including many jobs related to NEOM, the planned city of the future on the Red Sea. There were no records of any work with the Interior, Justice, or Defense Ministries that are central to the government's suppression of dissidents and its ability to maintain power. But according to one former McKinsey employee familiar with the firm's work in Saudi Arabia, it wasn't for lack of trying. McKinsey had pitched for such work but lost out. "It went to BCG," the person said.

In 2019 internal records show that McKinsey took on work for a government-owned company, the Al-Elm Information Security Company, which contracts with the Interior and Justice Ministries. McKinsey said it doesn't do work for these ministries and doesn't advise private companies "as to how to engage with these ministries."

"I feel so naive now looking back," a former McKinsey consultant involved in the Saudi work on sentiment analysis said via a secure messaging system. "With hindsight it's SO obvious what this work could be used for, but at the time it didn't even cross my mind. I thought we were doing a good thing, helping the government get feedback from their people, maybe a tiny step towards democracy."

When asked on CNBC in March 2019 what McKinsey would do

if it found out its client was a murderer, Sneader, the firm's managing partner, had a two-word response: "You walk."

In Saudi Arabia, McKinsey most definitely did not walk.

The Saudi and China-related work is part of a larger pattern at McKinsey that's taken hold in recent years. The firm is increasingly working with authoritarian governments the world over or for the state-owned companies that undergird their power. And, like in Saudi Arabia, the elites of those nations can be found working inside McKinsey's offices.

In Russia, the state-owned VTB Bank, which has operated under U.S. and EU sanctions since 2014, ranked among McKinsey's top clients by revenue in recent years, as did Gazprom, the state-controlled energy giant, McKinsey records show. The head of Russia's sovereign wealth fund, Kirill Dmitriev, is a McKinsey alum.

In Ukraine, the country's richest oligarch hired McKinsey to advise the pro-Russian president, Viktor Yanukovych, helping in the effort to recast this profoundly corrupt man as an economic reformer. At the same time, Paul Manafort, Trump's former campaign manager, was burnishing Yanukovych's political image. McKinsey has also worked directly with other authoritarian regimes, including the governments of Azerbaijan and Kazakhstan, records show.

In 2019, following reports in *The New York Times* about the firm's work in South Africa, China, Ukraine, and Saudi Arabia, McKinsey introduced new rules adding layers of oversight in the client-selection process.

Chapter 14

Chumocracy

Half a Century at Britain's NHS

THE NEWS CRACKLED through radio sets across Britain. Victory over the Nazis in Egypt. After enduring defeats on battlefields in Europe and Asia, after the Blitz reduced English cities to rubble, the news that day in November 1942 was nothing short of glorious. Church bells—silent across the country for more than two years—rang in celebration.

With the Americans now in the war and Field Marshal Erwin Rommel's Afrika Korps in full retreat, there was hope. Winston Churchill, the wartime prime minister, expressed it as only he could: "Now this is not the end. It is not even the beginning of the end, but it is, perhaps, the end of the beginning."

Days later, Britons learned what might await them when victory finally came: a more just society. A government report laid out a plan for a welfare state, with support for the poor and, as its centerpiece, free health care for all. In the words of Aneurin "Nye" Bevan, the Welsh coal miner turned Labour Party politician who envisioned what would become the National Health Service: "No society can legitimately call itself civilized if a sick person is denied medical aid because of lack of means."

Before the NHS came into being in July 1948, Britain's health-care system reflected the unequal class-addled society built on the backs of factory workers where having money was the way to get "whatever rudimentary medical services were available." By September of that year, 93 percent of the British population had signed up for the service. The inadequacies of the previous system were borne out by what people were lining up for. Before the NHS, millions of Britons couldn't afford to see the dentist. In the first nine months of the service's existence, some thirty-three million sets of dentures—or two for every three Britons at the time—were ordered. Eyeglasses—until then seen as a luxury by the poor—were another popular item.

The NHS wasn't a national health insurance system. Medical care was free at the point of delivery; taxpayers funded it, and the government nationalized most of the hospitals as well. It wasn't perfect, but it worked. Nye Bevan, then the health minister, said that the NHS "must always be changing, growing and improving; it must always appear to be inadequate."

Since 1948 the NHS has served Britain well. For a smaller percentage of GDP than the United States spends, the NHS gets far better results. Maternal mortality rates are about a third of what they are in the United States. Britain's life expectancy, in lockstep with most of the world, has been steadily rising. In America—alone among developed nations—people are dying younger.

Polls have shown the NHS to be the most beloved institution in Britain: more popular than the army or the queen. It's so admired that it was showcased at the opening ceremonies for the 2012 London Olympics. Like Social Security in the United States, the NHS is the third rail of British politics, or, as two historians of postwar Britain put it, the "holy of holies."

And yet, in recent years, Britain's leaders have enacted major changes to the NHS, channeling a small but increasing share of the country's health-care spending to the private sector and opening the door for American companies to enter the market.

McKinsey played an outsized role in shaping and implementing these changes. Two of its biggest American clients benefited from them. The story of how the firm took center stage in overhauling the NHS says as much about the U.K. as it does about the firm.

For in Britain, McKinsey had found a perfect host.

—

More than six decades ago, McKinsey entered the British bloodstream with stunning speed and took hold of the nation's psyche in a way that never happened in the United States.

By the late 1950s, European companies were emerging from the ravages of World War II and were keen to learn the secrets of big American corporations like General Motors and GE, at the time the unquestioned leaders of the business world. For McKinsey, it was time to go global, and, true to form, it framed its decision in the most high-minded terms.

In a memo that opened with quotations from the French political thinker Alexis de Tocqueville, Charles H. Lee, a McKinsey senior partner, wrote that the world had entered "an era in which America has been given a world role of leadership."

"Our activities now transcend national frontiers and they are geared to a global stage," Lee wrote. "Our civic responsibilities have been enlarged, and our new role calls for us to exercise these responsibilities in this broader setting."

In 1957, McKinsey had taken on an assignment with Royal Dutch Shell—the Dutch and British oil company—to help it develop a multidivisional business structure pioneered by GM, which gave divisions within corporations more autonomy. Measured in fees, it was a big success, bringing in about $720,000, a huge amount in that era. That spurred the firm to set up a London office in hopes of landing more big clients.

McKinsey opened an office on King Street, an address at the heart of the power structure of the rapidly fading British Empire. It was steps from the clutch of social clubs where matters of state were often decided and a short walk from the government offices and the Houses of Parliament.

More important was the man McKinsey chose to lead the office: Hugh Parker, an American, who had graduated from Cambridge University, which along with Oxford has for centuries educated Britain's elite. While at Cambridge, Parker rowed crew. He turned to the ranks of the Leander Club, one of the world's oldest rowing clubs, for some of McKinsey's first British consultants. Parker looked and sounded the part, dressed in quintessentially British pinstripes, his American accent infused with a British precision.

"Of course the first thing I had to do was to try to get to be known in England. And I devoted the next ten years of my life intensively to doing just that," Parker, who died in 2008, recalled in an interview for *Masters of the Universe,* a documentary about consultants that aired on Britain's Channel 4 in 1999. "I made it my business to be seen and heard, I made speeches, I wrote articles, my whole time was spent getting to be known and recognized. And after several years this began to work."

McKinsey's combination of new American management thinking delivered by "clubbable" young consultants was a hit. The grandees of British industry came rushing to McKinsey for advice. After its success at Shell, a parade of other big companies wanted to learn the secrets of American managerial prowess. The chemicals group ICI, one of the country's largest manufacturers, signed on in 1961, followed by other heavyweights like Rolls-Royce, Cadbury Schweppes, Unilever, Rio Tinto, and Tate & Lyle.

Then came the state sector: the BBC, the Atomic Energy Authority, and, significantly, the Bank of England. McKinsey even helped with the nationalization of British Steel (and with its subsequent privatization years later).

McKinsey was everywhere and people noticed. "If God were to remake the world, he would call upon McKinsey for assistance," wrote the London correspondent for the journal *Science.* The journalist Stephen Aris, who in 1968 profiled Hugh Parker for *The Sunday Times,* said that the name McKinsey was "becoming as synonymous with managerial reform as Hoover is with vacuum cleaning." He even offered a definition: "McKinsey: n & v.t. 1. To shake up, reorganise, declare redundant, abolish committee rule. Mainly applied to large industrial companies but also applicable to any organisation with management problems."

With startling speed, McKinsey had conquered Britain. By the early 1970s, it had helped restructure twenty-five of Britain's top one hundred companies. "Once we really got going in England—this would be the mid- to late 1960s, ten years after we opened an office there—we were really on a roll," Parker said.

McKinsey hadn't just joined the club; it became, in a sense, *the* club. Parker and another McKinsey partner, Roger Morrison, inaugurated what they called "Chairman's Dinners" in the penthouse suite of the Dorchester hotel, the art deco landmark in London's affluent Mayfair district. The idea was for Britain's captains of industry to converse with McKinsey people and "not be presented to," according to McKinsey's in-house history book. It evolved into a mini-prototype of the World Economic Forum, where business leaders could gather to talk among themselves.

But one agency—the biggest employer in Britain—eluded McKinsey. The NHS. That was about to change.

By 1970, after more than two decades of operation, the NHS needed an overhaul. Because England's health system had three branches—primary care, NHS-run hospitals, and local services such as nursing home and mental health care—coordinating treatment proved difficult and wasteful. This "tripartite monster" led to irrational decisions, such as housing the elderly in overcrowded hospitals rather than in nursing homes.

Both main British parties—Labour and Conservative—recognized the problem, though they didn't agree on how to fix it. The government turned to McKinsey. As one official put it decades later, "You were the management gurus. You knew about management and the Department did not know about management."

McKinsey helped produce what was called the "Grey Book," published in 1972, laying out a plan to integrate the three segments of the health-care system along geographic lines. Overseeing it all were teams of doctors, nurses, and hospital managers who would make decisions by consensus. But, as one participant noted, "when everyone is responsible, no one is responsible."

The overhaul, rolled out in 1974, proved largely ineffective. McKinsey lamented a "proliferation of paper" and the confusing, overlapping bureaucracies. But it also marked an important milestone in McKinsey's global expansion—a job at the NHS, one of the world's largest organizations. The firm would stay for five decades, demonstrating its ability to adapt to the country's changing political views.

One big change would come soon. The U.K., widely regarded

as the "sick man of Europe," lagged behind most other European countries economically. A respected columnist speculated that Britain could become the first country in modern history to transition from a developed nation to an underdeveloped one. In 1979, voters chose a radical break, ushering into office a fervent disciple of free-market economics: Margaret Thatcher.

For McKinsey, the Thatcher years were very good. Her philosophy fit perfectly with the firm's own emerging worldview—that public problems can often be solved by the private sector.

Thatcher pushed to privatize the vital state-owned industries—steel, shipbuilding, aviation, and telecommunications, which, over preceding decades, had been nationalized by Labour governments. And McKinsey was there to help. "It was open season for them," said Andrew Sturdy, a professor at the University of Bristol who studies McKinsey and other management consulting companies.

Britain's best and brightest free marketers clamored to work at McKinsey. There was William Hague, future leader of the Conservative Party and foreign secretary, and Adair Turner, head of Britain's financial regulator, roughly akin to America's Securities and Exchange Commission.

Though controversial, privatization garnered popular support as the media championed the government's campaign to expand share ownership among the masses. Millions of Britons bought shares in newly privatized monopolies such as British Telecom, British Gas, and British Airways, while other state-owned companies were sold off to private owners.

But for some industries, especially those that were essentially public utilities, privatization backfired, leading to costs far in excess of what they had been under national control. One notable disaster was British Rail, the country's railroad system privatized under Thatcher's successor, John Major.

Transforming a system with more than ten thousand miles of track in a country that gave birth to the railroad nearly two centuries earlier was no small task. McKinsey immodestly called this assignment "Project Destiny." In 1994, with advice from McKinsey, the country's rail infrastructure was put under the control of a new company, Railtrack, which sold shares in 1996.

McKinsey's strategy included advice to reduce maintenance spending and replace infrastructure like rails and signals only when broken or about to break. The essential tasks would no longer be done in-house but be outsourced. "They are trying to sweat more use out of existing asset[s]," one contractor said.

Then, in August 1999, Railtrack's top official overseeing track maintenance took a walk along a stretch of the busy East Coast rail line that ran from London in the south to Edinburgh in the north. He found it was poorly maintained. That November he warned his superiors, in classic British understatement, that the track's condition was "heading towards the boundary of acceptability," adding that the "balance between commercial drivers and safety are currently overwhelmingly towards the commercial."

His superiors should have listened. On October 17, 2000, a passenger train derailed on that line near the town of Hatfield, killing four people and injuring more than seventy. A government investigation found the track riddled with cracks, undermining its structural integrity. The report blamed Railtrack for failing to properly maintain it, with several contemporaneous reports citing McKinsey's Project Destiny. Railtrack was soon renationalized.

Planes, trains, and gas stations were challenging enough to privatize, but Britain's beloved NHS stood as a far bigger and more politically fraught target for any political party.

Unlike Thatcher, who had waited until her eighth year of office before making small changes at the NHS, such as privatizing janitorial and catering work, Major dove right in. His government introduced competition, allowing patients to choose their medical providers. Poorly performing hospitals would, in theory, lose out.

In reality, competition didn't work well in a hospital setting. That wasn't a secret: one of the most praised economists of the twentieth century, Kenneth Arrow, had concluded decades earlier that the magic of markets didn't function for health care in the way it would for selling bread, cars, or plane tickets. Patients just didn't have the information to intelligently price health-care services, and more often than not their priority was getting the best care as soon as possible, not finding the cheapest oncologist.

Major's changes, however, did create new layers of bureaucracy overseeing this new internal market. As a result, administration costs for the NHS soared. In the 1970s they soaked up about 5 percent of the agency's budget. By 2003 that number had risen to 13 percent, according to one study.

Major also introduced a policy, known as the Private Finance Initiative, which allowed the NHS to contract with private companies to build hospitals. It led to massive cost overruns, saddling the NHS with £80 billion in debt for projects that were originally supposed to cost £11.4 billion.

When the Labour Party ended Conservative rule, there was the expectation that the NHS would largely be left alone—if for no other reason than Labour gave birth to the NHS in 1948. But the Labour leader, Tony Blair, like his contemporary Bill Clinton in the United States, did not fit any rigid ideological mold. Under Blair, top NHS hospitals were further reconfigured, with McKinsey's help, to operate like businesses. To guard against profiteering, a new watchdog agency called Monitor was set up to oversee NHS hospitals.

At times, McKinsey consultants and government officials seemed like interchangeable parts. A young doctor, Penny Dash, helped Blair to shape NHS policy before joining McKinsey two years later in 2002. Heading in the opposite direction was David Bennett, a McKinsey senior partner, who in 2005 became Blair's head policy adviser. Blair's successor, Gordon Brown, also leaned heavily on McKinsey for health policy advice.

Then the financial crisis hit. After years of more money being pumped into the NHS, which had sharply boosted staffing levels and reduced patient waiting times, the money flow came to a halt. Faced with a huge budget shortfall, the government turned to McKinsey to trim the NHS budget. In March 2009, McKinsey delivered its plan in a 123-slide PowerPoint presentation.

The proposal outlined a pathway to save the NHS as much as £20 billion ($32 billion at the time) by cutting about 10 percent of its workforce, or almost 140,000 jobs, in the midst of the sharpest economic downturn in decades.

The people who remained would have to work harder. McKinsey calculated that 1.7 percent of a doctor's time was lost to tea breaks and said £400 million in savings could be realized if weak medical providers "achieve standard performance."

But slashing jobs wasn't enough. McKinsey also called for the end of "low value added healthcare interventions." Translation: cutting back on what McKinsey deemed unnecessary medical procedures. For example, reducing certain hysterectomies by 70 percent could yield £80.6 million in savings; another £118 million could be saved by cutting knee joint surgeries by 30 percent.

One McKinsey slide praised Kaiser Permanente, the American health maintenance organization, as a model of austerity. But the very next slide showed that the average hospital stay in the U.K. cost just over a third of what it did in the United States.

Some of Britain's leading doctors joined politicians in criticizing McKinsey's proposed cuts. "Many of these procedures may be of apparently small or even marginal direct benefit at the time they are performed, but will prevent potentially serious medium and long-term problems," John Black, president of the Royal College of Surgeons, said at the time.

The Conservative Party's health spokesman, Andrew Lansley, jumped on the chance to skewer Labour, which for years had denounced attempts to cut the NHS budget.

The Labour government disavowed the McKinsey slide deck. But the ideas in the slides were far from dead.

On Monday, May 10, 2010, London was a city in transition. The Labour Party—in power for the previous thirteen years, had been thoroughly crushed in the national election four days earlier. Within forty-eight hours David Cameron would be prime minister.

At 1:18 p.m., McKinsey's London office sent an email to two government officials, offering them complimentary tickets to a performance the following week of Verdi's *La traviata* at the Royal Opera House. The two officials were no paper-pushing bureaucrats. They held senior posts at Monitor, the watchdog organization that oversaw the performance of NHS hospitals—the same hospitals that were subject to McKinsey's policy recommendations. One of those officials, Adrian Masters, had worked at McKinsey before becoming Monitor's head of strategy.

Soon another invitation came, this time tickets for their families to attend a performance of Cirque du Soleil, the Canadian acrobatic troupe, accompanied by the McKinsey senior partner Nicolaus Henke. McKinsey had good reason to lay on the charm. The new health secretary, Andrew Lansley, would soon talk about making changes to the NHS "big enough to be seen from space." The Tory's big new idea: introduce even more competition into the NHS through an act of Parliament.

McKinsey, by virtue of its connections, was in a prime position to help shape that legislation, providing the government with its phalanxes of Oxford- and Harvard-educated health-care experts.

Just days after the new government formed, McKinsey landed a £330,000 contract to advise Monitor, the government regulatory agency. It later won a far bigger, £6 million contract, for "services to the NHS leadership team." By May 31, a McKinsey consultant sent an email to two Monitor officials, letting them know that the firm has "been gathering our thinking on the implications of the new Government programme for the NHS [and] *have started to share this with clients*" (italics added) and asking if the two officials would "like to meet to discuss it."

The officials on the receiving end of that email were Adrian Masters and his boss, David Bennett, the former McKinsey senior partner, who was now Monitor's executive chairman.

It spoke to the coziness in Britain between government officials and corporate executives. "You cannot get a cigarette paper between the beliefs of many government ministers and multinational CEOs," the British journalist Tamasin Cave, who unearthed the McKinsey emails, wrote in a 2014 book.

McKinsey bombarded the in-boxes of Monitor officials with speaking invitations. Masters accepted an offer that June to speak at McKinsey's Chief Strategist Roundtable Dinner at St. Stephen's Club, once a members-only club for Conservative Party members.

Emails show that he accepted at least two other invitations to speak at McKinsey events in the run-up to the passage of the NHS legislation.

The firm was so close to Monitor that it helped pick speakers for the government watchdog's own events. In October 2010, a McKinsey consultant invited Ian Dalton, a senior official in the department of health and future head of Monitor, to speak at one such event. The following year, Dalton accepted a speaking gig at a McKinsey health-care event in Paris. Participants were booked at the luxurious Westin Paris and at Restaurant le Meurice Alain Ducasse, featuring two Michelin stars. McKinsey said it would pick up the tab for the hotel and meals.

All this attention came in the midst of meetings with the same officials—at government ministries and even at times at McKinsey's own office—as the Conservative government's plans for the NHS began to take shape.

Gaining a second lease on life was the McKinsey study from 2009, made under the Labour government and widely panned. Now the Conservatives were touting its cost-saving potential.

Nick Seddon, a top official in the right-wing think tank Reform, who would soon join Cameron's government as an adviser, recommended that the NHS reduce staffing by 150,000, eliminate up to 32,000 hospital beds, and reduce discretionary procedures "such as coronary bypass or mastectomy."

Writing in *The Guardian,* Seddon said McKinsey had found that these measures, among others, could lead to annual savings of over £20 billion in 2014–2015.

Seddon contended that the solution to the post-financial-crisis fiscal squeeze was more private health-care spending. "A commitment to national health is not the same as a commitment to the NHS, or every country would have an NHS, which they don't," he wrote. "It's time we caught up with the rest of the world."

The McKinsey study was then baked into a new government report that outlined ways to trim £20 billion from the NHS budget.

Two months after taking power, the new government issued a fifty-seven-page white paper laying out its proposals. The paper envisioned doctors taking charge of the lion's share of the $100 billion–plus annual NHS budget and deciding where the money should be spent or, in NHS-speak, "commissioned." Previously, another set of government bodies had made those decisions.

The idea of doctors deciding where health-care money is best spent may seem reasonable, but they are also notoriously busy, with neither the time nor the inclination to fine-tune budgets. Someone—or some firm like McKinsey—would have to help them. Once again, more privatization seemed to offer a solution, according to Monitor's CEO, Bennett, who joined McKinsey during Thatcher's privatization spree.

"We, in the UK, have done this in other sectors before. We did it in gas, we did it in power, we did it in telecoms," he said as the legislation was taking shape. "We've done it in rail, we've done it in water. So, there is 20 years of taking on monopolistic monolithic markets and providers and exposing them to economic regulation."

One way to introduce market forces was for private companies to buy NHS hospitals, particularly underperforming ones. Dalton, the British health official who was the focus of intense McKinsey politicking, met with McKinsey consultants on December 17, 2010, to sort through their options. They had a prospective buyer in mind—Helios—a private German hospital chain. Internal records showed that the parent company of Helios had been a McKinsey client in recent years.

But privatizing NHS hospitals, which would have a free hand in managing employees, might stir opposition. So the decision was made to start slowly. The goal: privatize ten to twenty hospitals but start "at the mindset of 1 at a time with various political constraints," a McKinsey consultant wrote to Dalton.

By the time lawmakers and bureaucrats began to consider the new NHS law, consultants were deeply embedded in Britain's government. In 2010 the NHS alone spent £313 million on management consultants. Decades earlier, the British government rolled out a national health-care program without the help of consultants. But, much like their American counterparts, that changed over time and their influence grew.

On February 14, 2011, McKinsey distributed a forty-seven-page slide deck, bearing the NHS logo, that described the government's plan to revamp the agency.

One slide appeared to suggest that the inspiration for the new NHS model came from the United States, noting similarities to the HMO Kaiser Permanente, for many years a McKinsey client. Kaiser seeks to contain costs by capping payments for medical services and paying doctors salaries, instead of the fee-for-service model. The Kaiser system has its fervent supporters in the United States, but also its detractors who say it lacks transparency and spends excessively on administration.

Six graphics-filled slides were devoted to laying out the Kaiser model. Two other options received less attention.

As the legislation took shape, McKinsey worked with a familiar audience—Paul Bate, a former McKinsey consultant and the head of the prime minister's health policy group, and Nicolaus Henke, the McKinsey senior partner and a prominent member of what was called Cameron's kitchen cabinet on health care.

Now the government—and McKinsey—had to sell the plan to lawmakers who would vote for it and the officials who would implement it.

Bring on the war games.

Some of London's most senior health officials were invited to join McKinsey consultants on March 4, 2011, at a conference center next to the Tower of London to participate in a simulation exercise on how the new system would work. According to a slide deck McKinsey prepared for the event—this time with the McKinsey logo—participants were given "role cards" representing the agency they would play as they simulated "the future of the London health economy."

The slide deck praised the proposed law, noting that the NHS overhaul would "put patients first" and improve health outcomes. McKinsey envisioned a system where large groups of private doctors covered hundreds of thousands of patients.

McKinsey also amplified the conceit that Britain, with one of the world's most cost-effective health-care systems, still needed to cut its health budget. "The current system will no longer be affordable soon—real transformational change is needed rapidly," it said.

The reality was that the Conservative government had chosen a path of fiscal austerity amid an economic downturn, a decision that ran counter to the writings of Britain's own John Maynard Keynes. And with the NHS in its sights, one group critical of the Conservative agenda said, "Those who maintain that we cannot afford the NHS must be made to answer the most important question—if we can't afford the most cost-effective health service in the world what can we afford?"

McKinsey threw its lot in with the Conservatives, who, like David Bennett, the former McKinsey senior partner, wanted to bring the magic of the free market to health care. As if to drive home that point, on June 8, 2011, McKinsey was the corporate sponsor for a conference at the Royal College of Nursing, which had turned its stunning Georgian mansion on Cavendish Square into a venue available for corporate events.

The conference, put on by the right-wing think tank Reform, was titled "A Lot More for a Lot Less: Disruptive Innovation in Healthcare." "Disruptive" meant a wider berth for private companies. The group argued that "for-profit companies and not-for-profit organizations are delivering healthcare successfully around the world and doing so at greater value and with equal, if not better, quality."

The McKinsey senior partner Nicolaus Henke, the firm's representative on the prime minister's kitchen cabinet on health, took part in the one-day conference, joined by two other McKinsey consultants. They again touted the benefits of the Kaiser Permanente model and suggested the NHS "empower patients to undertake more of their own care themselves." "Whether in online check-in for airlines or self-service tills at supermarkets, customers in other sectors are taking on greater roles leading to both more efficient businesses and higher satisfaction," Henke and a colleague wrote.

The McKinsey duo cited the treatment of chronic diseases like diabetes, which could be managed by patients "in partnership with professionals" through phone calls rather than through visits.

As the health-care bill drew closer, the many McKinsey veterans ensconced in Britain's health bureaucracy continued to receive a steady stream of emails to attend events for McKinsey "alumni." On September 14, 2011, it was an invitation to the London office's annual party, held at the National Gallery on Trafalgar Square. The guest of honor: the managing partner, Dominic Barton, who would be speaking about his recent article in the *Harvard Business Review,* "Capitalism for the Long Term."

Written in the wake of the global financial crisis, Barton's essay urged business leaders to look beyond short-term goals and think about the higher purpose of capitalism, quoting the eighteenth-century Scottish economist Adam Smith: "The wise and virtuous man is at all times willing that his own private interest should be sacrificed to the public interest."

The new bill—the Health and Social Care Act—became law in early 2012. The vast majority of Britain's health-care spending would now be routed through new doctor-led groups. Section 75 of the bill mandated that those doctors' groups put out their contracts for tender: meaning private companies would get a crack at the biggest budget item in the country.

As predicted, the doctors' groups needed help managing their new role as budget masters. It came as no surprise that McKinsey was part of a group of consultants that won a £7.1 million contract to advise the doctors.

McKinsey helped the government mold the legislation and, simultaneously, was paid by the groups most affected by it. "So they were picking pockets on both sides of the divide," said Jacky Davis, a doctor who campaigned against privatization of the NHS.

Other American companies were also advising the doctors' groups, including UnitedHealth Group, the giant American insurer, which operates in the U.K. as Optum. In recent years, UnitedHealth was among the top 10 percent of McKinsey clients in terms of revenue. It directly benefited from McKinsey's work in helping to shape the 2012 law.

By 2014, Simon Stevens, a former executive vice president of UnitedHealth, was running the NHS in England. In Washington, he had made a case against more government involvement in Obamacare, arguing that the United States didn't need a system like the NHS.

As the 2012 law took hold, the share of NHS money going to private companies increased, partly due to the requirement that the work of the doctors' groups be put out for bids, a policy decision that McKinsey helped to shape. When John Major served as prime minister in the 1990s, the government spent about £96 million on health-care services from private companies each year. Under Labour, that figure rose to £8.4 billion. After a decade of Tory rule, it stood at £14.4 billion, according to figures published in 2021 by the Labour Party.

Still, privatization has its limits. So much of what the NHS provides, such as emergency room services, isn't attractive to the private sector. Scores of companies with NHS contracts abandoned them after failing to turn an substantive profit. One company even took over management of an NHS hospital, only to abandon the project in 2015 amid deteriorating care and cost overruns.

"All these private companies, they want to know they can get a guaranteed return," said John Lister, an expert on the NHS who monitors efforts to siphon public health funds into private hands. "The last place you can get a guaranteed profit is running a full range of NHS services."

McKinsey said its work with the NHS was to support the agency's "strategic objectives." "McKinsey did not advocate or lobby to influence the government's stance, and categorically does not have an agenda for the privatization of the NHS," McKinsey said in response to questions about its work.

At the NHS, the use of consultants had its limits. According to one authoritative study, consultants made the NHS *less* efficient, and the average amount of money each hospital spent on consultants could have paid the salaries for thirty-five nurses or ten doctors.

Even Stevens, with his background at UnitedHealth, saw the limits of privatization and proposed scrapping section 75. In 2015, as head of NHS England, he tried a different approach, inviting McKinsey to help put together the "sustainability and transformation partnership" system. The aim was to set up a health-care bureaucracy that brought together the NHS, local doctors, mental health facilities, and the local government—in every geographic area of the NHS in England. In other words, McKinsey was being asked to help sort out roughly the same problem the NHS faced when it first brought in the firm nearly half a century earlier and to reverse many of the provisions of the 2012 law that it had helped to craft.

London was a major test bed for this integrated system, and McKinsey's Penny Dash was at the center of it. In 2020 she was appointed nonexecutive chairman of the partnership in northwest London, where McKinsey had been working for years helping to set up a pilot project for the new system alongside a big doctors' group called AT Medics. Under the new law some of these doctors' groups had rapidly expanded. AT Medics oversaw care for more than 300,000 Londoners. McKinsey said Dash took the post only as she was preparing to leave the firm and that during the overlap period she didn't work on NHS projects for McKinsey and wasn't involved in any decisions that awarded contracts to consulting firms.

In February 2021, the news broke that AT Medics had been bought by Operose Health, a British subsidiary of Centene, the huge American health insurance company that has been one of McKinsey's top global clients. Local doctors, fearing the takeover of such a large part of the British medical infrastructure by a private American company, scrambled to oppose it. But the takeover was a fait accompli.

The COVID-19 epidemic provided a major test of the country's retooled health-care system. Prime Minister Boris Johnson entrusted the all-important test-and-trace effort to the former McKinsey consultant Dido Harding, now Baroness Harding. She and the country's top health officials turned to private companies, not the NHS, to run the program. McKinsey alone charged £563,400 to provide a "vision, purpose and narrative" of the Harding-led program.

Test and trace was a disaster. More than a quarter of people exposed to COVID-19 were not aware that they needed to self-quarantine, a serious shortcoming that contributed to the country's failure to control the spread of the coronavirus. The country's death rate exceeded even that of the United States for much of the pandemic.

The *Guardian* columnist George Monbiot lashed out against U.K. health officials. "The government has bypassed the lean and efficient NHS to create an outsourced, privatised system characterised by incompetence and failure," Monbiot wrote. "The system's waste is measured not just in pounds, but in human lives."

The government's "Anticorruption Champion," whose remit would include looking into the slew of no-bid contracts awarded to private firms, was John Penrose, a Conservative member of Parliament who is also Baroness Harding's husband. They met while both were working at McKinsey. Harding had attended Oxford, just like Johnson, David Cameron, and twenty-six other British prime ministers. The British old boys' network, which now included women, had a new name: the chumocracy.

By the spring of 2021, Johnson's popularity had risen. One reason: Britain's unquestioned success at getting its population vaccinated. The U.K. was a world leader in rolling out its COVID vaccination program, and it was largely thanks to the organizational abilities of the government's NHS, whose doctors and nurses gave the injections, free of charge.

Epilogue

Among the many challenges to writing a book about McKinsey, none is bigger than its culture of secrecy, the foundation upon which its business is built. Consultants in their first days at the firm are programmed to say nothing publicly about clients or their advice. Most take that vow seriously. Decades after employees leave, whether on good terms or bad, they are still reluctant to violate that pledge.

Unencumbered by government oversight, McKinsey is accountable only to its clients, who expect that their vulnerabilities, mistakes, and business strategies—in other words, their secrets—will remain just that, a secret. And it's hard to imagine any institution that knows more of those secrets than McKinsey. Under these circumstances, reporting on the consultancy is akin to chasing shadows, in the United States and around the world. But nothing beckons investigative reporters more than powerful institutions that believe they are exempt from public scrutiny.

One former McKinsey consultant wrote anonymously, "To those convinced that a secretive cabal controls the world, the usual suspects are Illuminati, Lizard People, or 'globalists.' They are wrong, naturally. There is no secret society shaping every major decision and determining the direction of human history. There is, however, McKinsey & Company."

The consultant used humor to make a point, a serious point:

McKinsey has an unseen presence at the table inside the world's most consequential companies and governments.

Despite the firm's information lockdown, buttressed by nondisclosure agreements, we were able to interview nearly one hundred current and former McKinsey employees. They chose to speak not because they were disloyal but because they were exactly the types of consultants McKinsey seeks: smart people of principle, drawn to the company because of its stated values.

McKinsey goes to great lengths to emphasize its good deeds, and there are many. In a 2018 report titled "Creating Change That Matters," the firm's global managing partner wrote, "Protecting our planet, enabling meaningful work in our communities, and creating inclusive societies that honor our diversity are fundamental."

But as the firm discovered, hiring people with a purpose greater than earning bundles of money can have a downside. When these idealists see too much daylight between McKinsey's words and actions, they become disenchanted; they ask questions. Some even agreed to talk to us.

This book is based on much more than the spoken word. We became the first outsiders to peek inside McKinsey's secret vault of clients and billings—information off-limits to governments, clients, competitors, and even its own employees. With this information, we were able to uncover layer after layer of potential conflicts of interest, including its "long-standing policy" to serve competing clients with conflicting interests, "as well as counter-parties in merger, acquisition and alliance opportunities."

Bain & Company, a competitor, believes that is the wrong approach, and says it accepts only one client at a time in the same sector. McKinsey defends its decision, saying that an internal wall prevents the passing of confidential information.

McKinsey's laissez-faire style of management has allowed its consultants to reap big paydays promoting addictive products, recommending policies that expand income inequality, and serving bad actors on the international stage, including major polluters. There is no questioning McKinsey's desire to do good, to give back. But, as one former consultant said, McKinsey should also find a way to do less harm.

A Note on Sources

Our reporting on McKinsey began in earnest in early 2018, amid the uproar over the firm's work in South Africa. Our work was helped immeasurably by the aggressive South African press, particularly the investigative journalists at amaBhungane. McKinsey consultants were feeling the heat, and they began to talk. McKinsey itself, for this initial story, made several senior partners available to us as well, including its soon-to-depart managing partner, Dominic Barton. They had a story to tell: what happened in South Africa was sui generis, mostly due to a few bad actors but with wider lessons for the firm. McKinsey said measures were taken to make sure it never happens again.

After that initial article, published in late June 2018, McKinsey as an organization closed ranks. While their spokesman continued to be responsive, getting interviews with top McKinsey consultants was not going to happen. The South Africa story also mentioned McKinsey's work with ICE, spawning outrage within the firm at a time when the tragedy on America's southern border was dominating headlines. More people came forward. Other articles followed. They included reports about McKinsey's work with Saudi Arabia and with corrupt and authoritarian leaders in pre-Zelensky Ukraine and China. Still more people opened up. With many of these sources, we communicated through encrypted voice and messaging applications.

While we called the South African debacle the biggest controversy in the firm's nearly century-long history, it took less than a year for that crisis to be superseded. In early 2019 details emerged about McKinsey's extensive work with Purdue Pharma and its campaign to "turbocharge" sales of the highly addictive painkiller OxyContin.

That news story was not driven by sources, but rather by the subpoena power of the Massachusetts attorney general, Maura Healey. Suddenly hundreds, soon thousands, of pages of emails, spreadsheets, and slides became public, chronicling McKinsey's work with Purdue and other opioid makers.

In story after story, McKinsey's own words played a central role, often in the form of slide decks never intended for public consumption. A nine-page presentation made in Riyadh, the Saudi capital, explained how to identify influential voices on social media who might be critical of the government. Hundreds of documents, going back sixty years, showed its close relationship with Big Tobacco. Others showed its work with Juul, the dominant vaping company. Thousands of pages of documents detailed McKinsey's close relationship with government officials in Britain who oversaw the National Health Service.

While researching the book, we came across an unexpected source of information: closely guarded internal records that listed McKinsey's clients as well as billings that helped us understand the extent of McKinsey's consulting empire. What stood out: the prominence of the big American health-care companies and the government agencies that regulate them.

We approached McKinsey numerous times over the course of the years to request interviews. Most were denied. We also presented the firm with a comprehensive list of queries.

The book reflects McKinsey's responses, especially where the firm takes issue with specific findings from our reporting. Some of the answers were revelatory: McKinsey, for example, said it recently stopped consulting for tobacco companies, though the firm did not answer the question of exactly when it stopped or why it had continued to serve Big Tobacco decades after cigarettes were widely known to be deadly.

Responding to our section on safety issues, U.S. Steel said it operates differently today than in the past. "Our overall transformation efforts have improved our company's performance, created a sustainable maintenance program, and improved employee safety over time," the company said. As for McKinsey, the steelmaker said the firm had no decision-making authority. Disney declined to comment.

McKinsey also addressed questions about potential conflicts of interest, including serving multiple companies in the same industry and their government regulators. "We inform our clients about our confidentiality and conflict policies," McKinsey said. "Clients work with us because they trust that we will keep their confidential information safe."

McKinsey acknowledged that it has a "long-standing policy to serve competing clients and clients with potentially conflicting interests as well as counter-parties in merger, acquisition and alliance opportunities, and to do so without compromising McKinsey's professional responsibility to maintain the confidentiality of client information." "If an employee violates our policies, we can and do take appropriate disciplinary action including termination where warranted," McKinsey said. Asked how many times this had happened, the firm didn't answer.

As for questions surrounding its work for drugmakers and the Food and Drug Administration, McKinsey said that since it didn't advise the agency on specific pharmaceutical or tobacco products, then its work with these private clients posed no conflict. Nevertheless, McKinsey said its contract proposals "frequently" mentioned its work with the pharmaceutical industry.

Acknowledgments

Several years ago, the executive editor of *The New York Times,* Dean Baquet, stopped by a meeting of our investigative unit to find out what was in the pipeline. Before leaving, Dean said in so many words that he'd be interested in a deep, granular look at a major corporation as a way to help readers understand how power is wielded in our society. We took Dean's advice and chose to examine McKinsey, the secretive counselor to not one but *thousands* of companies worldwide.

We owe Dean our thanks for planting the seed that became this book and for his unwavering support of investigative reporting in all corners of the newsroom.

There are many steps between idea and book. With the help of two of the nation's best news editors, Paul Fishleder and Matt Purdy, we began our McKinsey reporting for the *Times.* Backing us up was David McCraw, the *Times*'s lawyer, a hero to every investigative reporter in our company. And for good reason. He has a spine of steel, exquisite judgment, and a devotion to First Amendment principles second to none. When our investigation moved overseas, we benefited from the wisdom of Michael Slackman and Greg Winter, editors on our international desk.

Among the thousands of people who read and commented on our McKinsey stories were two literary agents at ICM Partners, Alexandra Machinist and Amelia Atlas, who believed there was a larger story to tell. Perhaps a book? We were not ready for that, but we kept talking because of their enthusiasm—and they were just plain fun to be around. When M&A, as we affectionately call them, told us that one of the publishing world's most distinguished editors, William Thomas, editor and publisher of Doubleday, wanted a McKinsey book, we recognized this as an extraordinary opportunity, especially since he had edited several of our favorite writers. Bill's devotion to this project never wavered. He kept us focused, offering encouragement and guidance when we needed it. It came as no surprise that his editing made our book immeasurably better. Daniel Novack, our fearless Doubleday lawyer, leavened our legal review with well-timed humor, a quality not always present in either of our professions. A special shout-out to Nicole Pedersen, who did her best to convince readers that we received passing grades in English. Others at Doubleday to whom we owe thanks include Michael Goldsmith, Todd Doughty, Kathy Hourigan, and Khari Dawkins, along with all those who played vital roles in publishing this book.

Many people contributed in one way or another to our reporting. First and foremost is Kate Bakhtiyarova, our chief researcher and a graduate of the Columbia Journalism School. We could not have imagined anyone whom we'd rather have by our side. Another Columbia student, Bridget Hickey, co-wrote one of our articles for the *Times.* We also want to thank the former Columbia students Champe Barton, Sachi McClendon, Caterina Elly Barbera, Natasha Rodriguez, Eileen Marie Grench, and Grace Ashford.

Duff McDonald, the foremost chronicler of McKinsey's secret history, was unfailingly helpful. His work inspired us. Other writers who broke through McKinsey's sanitized version of events included Bethany McLean, Anita Raghavan, Anand Giridharadas, Garrison Lovely, Erik Edstrom, and Ian MacDougall of ProPublica.

There's an old saying in the newspaper business: don't bury the lead. On this, we plead guilty, for this book could never have been written without the help of courageous McKinsey consultants who broke their vows of silence because they thought the firm must do better. Three stand out in particular, but one person, whose assistance went above and beyond the call, gave us a pseudonym just for this occasion. Thank you, Cooper G. Duncan.

People with a conscience and a capacity for outrage are vital to truth seekers everywhere. Without them, democracy doesn't stand a chance. We are deeply grateful that we found so many of them at McKinsey.

—Walt Bogdanich and Michael Forsythe

W.B.'s Acknowledgments

I didn't know Mike Forsythe personally when I asked if he wanted to join me in taking a deep dive into McKinsey. I certainly knew his reputation as a reporter who courageously investigated China's autocratic leadership and didn't back down under threats. But as I would learn, Mike is much more than that. He is kind and generous, willing to do most anything to help a colleague in need. I know that because I was one of them. I needed a strong partner who wouldn't shrink from the monumental challenge of investigating the ghostly presence of McKinsey in all of our lives. Mike had the fortitude and skill to do just that. His reporting enriched this book far beyond anything I could have done. Thanks, Mike, for teaching me new skills and keeping this train upright and on time.

This book would never have happened had I not been at *The New York Times,* the best platform for investigative journalism in the universe. For that I thank Arthur Sulzberger, A. G. Sulzberger, Joe Lelyveld, Bill Keller, Jill Abramson, and Dean Baquet. I am especially grateful to Glenn Kramon, who hired me to oversee business investigations. Others who helped me along the way include Phil Zweig and Hank Gilman, dear friends going back to our *Wall Street Journal* days. Also, Ellen Pollack, who encouraged me to write about McKinsey; Joseph Pete and James Lane, who reintroduced me to my long-departed hometown of Gary, Indiana; and Mark Rachkevych who showed me around Kyiv while I reported on McKinsey's clients there. I also absorbed the wisdom of my talented colleagues in the *Times*'s investigative unit, including Willy Rashbaum, Mike McIntire, Michael LaForgia, Rebecca Corbett, Dean Murphy, Rory Tolan, Lanie Shapiro, Rebecca Ruiz, Jo Becker, Susan Beachy, and all of my Zoom regulars who reminded me there was life outside the bunker where I holed up for more months than I care to count. Also, Bojan, a bright light in these dark times and a well-known presence in the *Times* building.

Others who deserve more thanks than I can give them here include my friends John Martin, a former ABC News colleague who stuck by me in good times and bad, Dave Capp, Jim Procter, John Lawler, Frank Koughan, Rick Tulsky, Jacqueline Williams, Sheila Kaplan, Brent Larkin, Burt Graeff, James Neff, Tyler Kepner, the late Bob Green, my brother George, who first suggested that I try journalism, Sid Wolfe, Paul Steiger, and our profession's most respected educational group—Investigative Reporters and Editors.

Most of all, I thank my family. My wife of four decades, Stephanie Saul, a reporter of extraordinary skill and drive, helped in ways big and small to get this book across the finish line. She'll understand what I mean when I say she also acted as my catalytic converter. My sons, Nicholas, a talented fiction writer, and Peter, a lawyer-to-be, fill me with endless fatherly pride.

M.F.'s Acknowledgments

There's no way I'd have been able to take part in this years-long project without the advice, support, and encouragement of my wife, the writer and scholar Dr. Leta Hong Fincher. Leta made invaluable suggestions on multiple chapters.

Early in the writing process, Walt and I were guests at the lovely high desert home of Russ and Mary Roberts in Santa Fe, New Mexico. Russ, a former management consultant, spent two long days with us downloading everything he knew about McKinsey's relationship with Allstate Insurance. Russ and his writing partner Don Phillips were exceedingly generous with both their time and their binder after binder of documents.

I also want to thank my dear friend Nerys Avery, with whom I had worked at Bloomberg News in Beijing. An accomplished editor and reporter, she has the distinct advantage of being British, of the Welsh variety. She carefully went through the NHS chapter, removing all the Yankee howlers.

I felt more comfortable writing about Saudi Arabia because I had spent most of my childhood there. For that I must thank my parents, Dr. Dale Forsythe and Dr. Sandra Forsythe. The Saudi chapter would never have happened without the reporting prowess of our *New York Times* colleagues Katie Benner, Mark Mazzetti, Ben Hubbard, and Mike Isaac, who told the world in October 2018 about an explosive McKinsey slide deck. We also relied on Ben's superb book, *MBS: The Rise to Power of Mohammed bin Salman.*

Audrey Jiajia Li helped with early research for what became the China chapter, and Richard Heede of the Climate Accountability Institute was generous in providing us with copious data sets that formed the backbone of the environment chapter, " 'Turning a Coal Mine into a Diamond.' " One of McKinsey's most storied consultants, the late Carter Bales, helped provide the moral certainty that the firm's work with the world's worst polluters was an issue that needed to be written about. Walt's friend and former colleague Phillip L. Zweig wrote two stunningly researched books on banking that were important for helping to frame chapter 9, "Toxic Debt."

Thanks to my primary editors at the *Times,* Rebecca Corbett and Dean Murphy, who gave us the freedom to pursue a multiyear project, and to the steady hands of the editors Rory Tolan and Lanie Shapiro. Rebecca Corbett provided crucial advice on how to frame our coverage of McKinsey's work with Purdue Pharma when, as often happened during the course of writing this book, we were confronted with breaking news.

Last but not least, I'd like to thank my colleague, friend, and co-author, Walt. To me, the best thing about working at *The New York Times* is, without a doubt, being surrounded by fine colleagues delighted to impart their wisdom and experience. And Walt is the finest of them all.

Notes

Introduction

1 the world's biggest, most profitable company: U.S. Steel was the first billion-dollar corporation. Ohio State University Department of History, "1912: Competing Visions for America," "Gentlemen's Agreements," ehistory.osu.edu.

1 two hundred miles of railroad tracks: Operational communications lead at U.S. Steel.

1 book of the dead: Author visit to Gary Works in May 2021.

2 closed-casket affairs: Joseph S. Pete, "The Human Toll of the Steel Mill," in *The Gary Anthology,* ed. Samuel Love (Cleveland: Belt, 2020), 17.

2 two Nobel Prize winners: Paul A. Samuelson won the Nobel Prize in Economic Sciences in 1970; Joseph E. Stiglitz won it in 2001.

2 the Jackson Five: Charlie Burton, "Inside the Jackson Machine," *GQ,* Feb. 7, 2018.

2 workforce dropped below eight thousand: Jonathan P. Hicks, "An Industrial Comeback Story: U.S. Is Competing Again in Steel," *New York Times,* March 31, 1992.

2 "a triumph of scientific planning": James B. Lane, *City of the Century: A History of Gary, Indiana* (Bloomington: Indiana University Press, 1978), 38.

2 postapocalyptic and horror movies: Ben Clement (director of Gary Office of Film & Television), interview by author.

2 Crime spiked: Paul Sloan, "Gary Takes Over as Murder Capital of U.S.," *Chicago Tribune,* Jan. 3, 1994.

2 Gary's population dropped: Dan Carden, "NWI Population Steady over Past Decade; Gary's Plummets 14%, Census Finds," *Times of Northwest Indiana,* Aug. 12, 2021. Gary's population was 78,000 in 2014 per the U.S. Census.

2 "Shackled by Lust?": Billboards on Indiana toll road just outside U.S. Steel property. Author visit to Gary, Indiana, in May 2021.

2 Longhi, hired: *Christakis Vrakas et al. v. United States Steel Corporation,* W.D. Pa. (2017) No. 17-579, 2.

3 CIA, the FBI, and the Pentagon: Walt Bogdanich and Michael Forsythe, "How McKinsey Lost Its Way in South Africa," *New York Times,* June 26, 2018.

3 "a relentless focus": U.S. Steel 10-K Form for the Securities and Exchange Commission, 2016.

3 the company's chairman: Edwin Bierschenk, "Gary's Roots Founded in Steel," *Times of Northwest Indiana,* March 19, 2016.

3 the efficiency and profitability: James B. Lane, *Gary's First Hundred Years* (Home Mountain Printing, 2006), 19.

3 Renaissance art: *Art Collection of the Late Elbert H. Gary* (New York: American Art Association, 1928).

3 "a brutal system of industrial slavery": Lane, *Gary's First Hundred Years,* 37.
3 labor leaders his social inferiors: Ibid., 25.
3 the firm's biggest client: Duff McDonald, *The Firm* (New York: Simon & Schuster, 2013), 37.
4 special unit to advise corporate executives: George David Smith, John T. Seaman Jr., and Morgan Witzel, *A History of the Firm* (New York: McKinsey, 2011), 52. The book is a private, noncirculating history of the firm published internally.
4 the two companies moved apart: Ibid., 59.
4 CEO of U.S. Steel: Longhi's bio per UGI Corporation, where he has been director since April 2020.
4 not turned an annual profit in years: Len Boselovic, "The Outlook for U.S. Steel: Bleak and Bleaker," *Pittsburgh Post-Gazette,* Nov. 1, 2015.
4 bought a mansion: 9121 SW Sixty-Second Court, Pinecrest, Fla., Zillow listing.
4 sold the complex for $9.8 million: Brian Bandell, "Former U.S. Steel Corp. CEO Mario Longhi Sells Pinecrest Mansion," *South Florida Business Journal,* May 13, 2021.
4 property on Fisher Island: Longhi's Fisher Island address is listed in *Bieryla v. United States Steel Corp.,* W.D. Pa. (2019) 2:19-cv-00468-CB.
4 "long time trusted adviser": *Christakis Vrakas et al. v. United States Steel Corporation,* W.D. Pa. (2017) No. 17-579, 28.
4 "The Carnegie Way": U.S. Steel 10-K Form for the Securities and Exchange Commission, 2014.
4 "phenomenal" success: Vera Blei, "Mario Longhi: 'Phenomenal Change,'" *Metal Bulletin Magazine,* Dec. 2015/Jan. 2016.
5 stock began rising: Tom Taulli, "U.S. Steel: 'Carnegie Way' Is More Than a Slogan," *InvestorPlace,* Oct. 29, 2014.
5 first annual profit in six years: John W. Miller, "U.S. Steelmakers Take Hit from Drilling Cutbacks," *Wall Street Journal,* Jan. 27, 2015.
5 $75 million loss: Len Boselovic, "U.S. Steel Reports $75 Million First Quarter Loss," *Pittsburgh Post-Gazette,* April 28, 2015.
5 roving labor gangs: Joseph S. Pete, "USW Says U.S. Steel Layoffs Jeopardize Safety," *Times of Northwest Indiana,* Aug. 31, 2016.
5 jeopardized their safety: Ibid.
5 The coroner ruled: Coroner's report on Kremke's death provided by the Office of the Lake County Coroner.
5 four safety violations: Safety Order following Kremke's death filed by the Indiana Occupational Safety and Health Administration, Oct. 4, 2016.
5 raised $482 million: U.S. Steel "Questions and Answers" for the Securities and Exchange Commission, Third Quarter 2016.
6 Union members carried signs: Protest photos provided by Joseph S. Pete, Aug. 26, 2016.
6 "He was constantly complaining": Joseph S. Pete, "Steelworker Who Died Told Wife Mill Was Getting Less Safe," *Times of Northwest Indiana,* Oct. 3, 2016.
6 contact with 480 volts: Inspection Detail filed by the Occupational Safety and Health Administration, Oct. 3, 2016.
6 Friends and well-wishers raised: Pete, "Human Toll of the Steel Mill," 17.
6 "U.S. Steel made all these moves": McCall, interview by author.
7 reduced to $14,500: Inspection Detail filed by the Occupational Safety and Health Administration, Oct. 3, 2016, and June 16, 2016.
7 ten corrective actions: List of actions provided by the Indiana Occupational Health and Safety Administration.
7 "The fine is bigger": Interview with Finkel, who now teaches at the University of Michigan's School of Public Health.
7 U.S. Steel misled them: *Christakis Vrakas et al. v. United States Steel Corporation,* W.D. Pa. (2017) No. 17-579, 79. McKinsey is not a defendant in the lawsuit.
7 "up to 90 hours per week": Ibid., 3. A

fuller account of their allegations are under seal by court order in the lawsuit.

7 "jury-rig" failing machines: Ibid., 19–22. The eleven confidential U.S. Steel employees worked in a variety of departments and facilities at the company.

7 McKinsey and the plant manager: Ibid., 45.

7 because of the cost: Ibid., 47.

7 of what U.S. Steel purportedly saved: McCall, interview.

8 sold a combined $25 million in stock: *Christakis Vrakas et al. v. United States Steel Corporation,* W.D. Pa. (2017) No. 17-579, 6.

8 restore ten thousand jobs: Michelle Fox, "US Steel Wants to Accelerate Investments, Bring Back Jobs, CEO Says," CNBC, Dec. 8, 2016.

8 Longhi as one of twenty-eight business leaders: Howard Burns, "Longhi Included in Trump Manufacturing Jobs Initiative," *Pittsburgh Business Times,* Jan. 27, 2017.

8 27 percent drop in the stock price: *Christakis Vrakas et al. v. United States Steel Corporation,* W.D. Pa. (2017) No. 17-579, 7.

8 "given that it occurred": Ibid.

8 a $4.54 million bonus: Ibid., 13.

8 not a single mention: U.S. Steel 10-K Form for the Securities and Exchange Commission, 2017.

9 "S.T.E.E.L.": Ibid.

9 a surplus gift: McCall, interview.

9 at least $13 million in fees: McKinsey records.

9 consultants even wrote an article: Matt Gentzel, Brian Green, and Drew Horah, "Save Money, Raise Asset Productivity: Why Maintenance Staffing Matters," McKinsey & Company, April 1, 2018.

9 "I don't want the public": Disney quoted by the official Walt Disney Family Museum via Twitter on March 15, 2017.

9 died in 1966: Harry Trimborn, "Wizard of Fantasy Walt Disney Dies," *Los Angeles Times,* Dec. 16, 1966.

9 industry leader for safety: David Koenig, *More Mouse Tales* (Irvine, Calif.: Bonaventure Press, 1999).

9 Khrushchev, tried to visit: Alistair Cooke, "From the Archive: 21 September 1959: Mr. Khrushchev Banned from Disneyland," *Guardian,* Sept. 21, 2012.

10 became Disneyland's top executive: Chris Woodyard, "After a Successful Stint at Disney Stores, Paul Pressler Is Becoming . . . : the New Mayor of Disneyland," *Los Angeles Times,* Nov. 20, 1994.

10 favorite of Disney's chief executive: James B. Stewart, *Disney War* (New York: Simon & Schuster, 2005), 320.

10 a confidential report: "Transforming Maintenance: Defining the Disney Standard," McKinsey memo to Pressler, May 13, 1997.

11 "The reason they don't fail": Mike Anton and Kimi Yoshino, "Disney Ride Upkeep Assailed," *Los Angeles Times,* Nov. 9, 2003. Klostreich repeated this account in an interview with the author.

11 "As you know": *Torres v. Walt Disney Company,* SCOC (2004) No. 04CC10092, 12–13.

11 no response: Ibid.

11 Disneyland experienced a fatal accident: Aitken Aitken Cohn, "$25,000: Husband Killed and Wife Disfigured by Disney's Sailing Ship Columbia," June 3, 2010. The law firm represented the injured. In this press release, the supervisor is referred to as an assistant manager.

12 confidential settlement: Ibid.

12 cost-saving measures directly contributed: Aitken, interview by author.

12 higher-paid expert managers: Aitken Aitken Cohn, "$25,000: Husband Killed and Wife Disfigured by Disney's Sailing Ship Columbia." The ride leads were eventually restored, though it was alleged that they had less experience than the people they replaced.

12 "getting forced into graveyard shifts": Aitken, interview.

12 "I am concerned": Klostreich sent his internal memo "Attraction Maintenance" to Scott Smith, his superior, on Oct. 28, 1997. He resent the memo to Cynthia Harris, the president of Disneyland Resort, on Feb. 17, 1999.

13 Klostreich filed suit: *Robert Klostreich v. Disneyland Resort,* C.D. Cal. (2000) No. 00CC09137.

13 A wheel assembly fell off: *Torres v. Walt Disney Company,* SCOC (2004) No. 04CC10092, 13.

13 Brandon died at age thirteen: Kimi Yoshino, "Brandon Zucker Dies at 13; Injury at Disneyland Brought Focus to Amusement Park Safety," *Los Angeles Times,* Jan. 27, 2009.

13 "They encouraged the Disneyland management": Interview with Koenig, who estimates that over nearly three decades, he has talked to eight hundred or so Disneyland employees.

13 consultants mainly serve to legitimize: Lawler, interview by author.

14 "enjoyed a meteoric rise": Jerry Hirsch, "Mr. Pressler's Wild Ride at Disney," *Los Angeles Times,* Feb. 8, 2001.

14 A yellow tag was placed: *Torres v. Walt Disney Company,* SCOC (2004) No. 04CC10092, 4–5.

14 did not remove the roller coaster: Ibid., 5.

14 fall unnoticed onto the track: Amusement Ride Unit of the Division of California Occupational Safety and Health, "Accident Investigation Report Narrative" following the Thunder Mountain derailment, Sept. 5, 2003, 1.

14 forty-one feet per second: Ibid., 4.

15 parts of the ride scattered: Ibid., 6.

15 not follow proper procedure: Ibid., 11.

15 Machinists were also forbidden to sign: Ibid., 19–20.

15 "run to failure" philosophy: *Torres v. Walt Disney Company,* SCOC (2004) No. 04CC10092, 10.

15 confidential settlement: Aitken Aitken Cohn, "Confidential Settlement Involving Disneyland's Big Thunder Mountain," 2003.

15 He lasted four years: Michael Barbaro and Andrew Ross Sorkin, "Under Fire, Gap Chief Steps Down," *New York Times,* Jan. 23, 2007.

1. Wealth Without Guilt

17 the firm's vast alumni network: McKinsey operates what it calls the McKinsey Alumni Center, the firm's official contact point for former employees spread around the world.

17 an opportunity for young recruits: An analysis by Menlo Coaching B.V., a Netherlands-based MBA admissions advising firm, found that McKinsey—which hired 5.9 percent of all MBA graduates from the top twenty-four business schools in 2018, 2019, and 2020—outpaced any other employer.

17 make the world a better place: McKinsey touts its role as an agent for social change on its website: mckinsey.com.

18 internal company documents: The search by the authors of this book included highly confidential records that have never been publicly reported.

18 including *The New York Times:* Edmund Lee, "New York Times' Digital Subscription Growth Story May Be Ending," *Recode,* Aug. 25, 2014.

18 "armored personnel carriers": Walt Bogdanich and Michael Forsythe, "How McKinsey Lost Its Way in South Africa," *New York Times,* June 26, 2018.

18 island tax haven in the English Channel: See MIO Partners Inc. SEC Form ADV, filed July 29, 2021, sec.report.

18 McKinsey's reputation is enhanced by: Other prominent former McKinsey consultants include Susan Rice, Barack Obama's national security adviser, and Lael Brainard, a Federal Reserve governor who was among the candidates to be Fed chair.

19 "The very word *commercial*": George David Smith, John T. Seaman Jr., and Morgan Witzel, *A History of the Firm* (New York: McKinsey, 2011), 7.

19 "it is easier and more effective": Marvin Bower, *Perspective on McKinsey* (New York: McKinsey, 1979), 177–78.

19 top 5 percent of their graduating class: Baker scholars, those Harvard Business School students awarded top honors, are named after the late financier George F.

Baker (1840–1931). Known as the dean of American banking, Baker endowed the Harvard Business School in 1924.

19 Goldman Sachs, Google, and Microsoft: Duff McDonald, *The Golden Passport: Harvard Business School, the Limits of Capitalism, and the Moral Failure of the MBA Elite* (New York: HarperCollins, 2017), 199.

19 "Wedge yourself in and spread": Manish Chopra, *Learning Curve: Tips and Tricks I Learned, Often the Hard Way, in Navigating the Firm During My Years from Associate to Partner* (New York: McKinsey, 2011), 45. The guide was written for McKinsey employees and was not intended to be circulated outside the company.

20 "That's not Goldman Sachs's pitch": Karma, interview by author.

20 "there was never ever, ever an attempt": Author interview with McKinsey employee who declined to be identified.

21 "No one grows up and dreams": Author interview. Subject requested anonymity.

21 as much as $195,000, bonus included: Marco De Novellis, "Consulting Salaries for MBA & Master's Graduates," *BusinessBecause,* March 2, 2021.

22 "When I was a first-year associate": Chopra, *Learning Curve,* 23.

22 employs about thirty-four thousand people: "What's Ahead for McKinsey? A Conversation with Bob Sternfels," McKinsey Blog, July 1, 2021.

22 It simultaneously consults for companies: McKinsey says it takes special precautions to prevent confidential information from passing from one cohort to another.

22 "Whenever the firm has made mistakes": Smith, Seaman, and Witzel, *History of the Firm,* 454.

23 harm or kill people: Erik Edstrom's farewell email, July 18, 2019.

23 "Regardless of an individual's field": Notes on the election of a new managing director, March 30, 1968, in Smith, Seaman, and Witzel, *History of the Firm,* 171.

23 fifteen specific values: The fifteen values are explained in a video available at www.youtube.com/watch?v=6aDPocw72JY.

24 that word appeared unseemly: Smith, Seaman, and Witzel, *History of the Firm,* 85.

24 more than $120 million in two years: Billing records.

24 "The language around client service": Rosenthal, interview by author.

24 "you are also going to have": Karma, interview.

24 second value: Under the firm's updated policies, the second value is now the third.

25 "If you want to do ethical work": Rosenthal, interview.

25 "If we don't bring a moral purpose": Green, interview by author.

25 "Would having the courage": Seth Green, "I Worked at McKinsey. Here's How the Firm Needs to Change," *Fortune,* Dec. 11, 2019.

25 "I came to my job": Garrison Lovely, "McKinsey & Company, Capital's Willing Executioners," *Current Affairs,* Sept. 2019. When originally published, Lovely's essay carried the byline "Anonymous." He agreed to be identified as its author for this book. Part of his anonymous essay is also quoted in the epilogue.

25 "At a time when democracies": Walt Bogdanich and Michael Forsythe, "How McKinsey Has Helped the Stature of Authoritarian Governments," *New York Times,* Feb. 3, 2021.

25 pay more than $600 million: Michael Forsythe and Walt Bogdanich, "McKinsey Settles for Nearly $600 Million over Role in Opioid Cases," *New York Times,* Feb. 3, 2021. (The original settlement was under $600 million, but it subsequently increased with payments to additional states.)

26 "This is the banality of evil": Walt Bogdanich and Michael Forsythe, "McKinsey Proposed Paying Pharmacy Companies Rebates for OxyContin Overdoses," *New York Times,* Nov. 27, 2020.

26 "It was a great firm": Author interview with former McKinsey partner who declined to be identified.

26 his work as a McKinsey consultant: Sydney Ember, Reid J. Epstein, and Trip Gabriel, "Buttigieg Struggles to Square

Transparency with Nondisclosure Agreement," *New York Times,* Dec. 7, 2019.

27 "It was a phenomenal learning opportunity": "Pete Buttigieg on How He Plans to Win the Democratic Nomination and Defeat Trump," *New Yorker,* April 2, 2019.

27 "That's not good enough": Michael Forsythe, "When Pete Buttigieg Was One of McKinsey's Whiz Kids," *New York Times,* Dec. 5, 2019.

27 one of the bestselling business books: Thomas J. Peters and Robert H. Waterman Jr., *In Search of Excellence: Lessons from America's Best-Run Companies* (New York: Harper Business, 1982).

27 "It's nauseating": Peters, interview by author.

28 "not because it was struggling": Karma, interview.

28 An orientation booklet: Chopra, *Learning Curve.*

29 "I found it unethical": Ibid., 26.

29 "He was livid": Ibid., 25.

29 "I'll never forget when a young punk": Pechman in author interview and in a Facebook posting in response to "The Smuggest Guys in the Room: McKinsey Suffers from Collective Self-Delusion," *Economist,* Feb. 25, 2018.

29 In February 2018, McKinsey disclosed: "Kevin Sneader Elected Global Managing Partner of McKinsey & Company," press release, Feb. 25, 2018.

30 more than one million dollars in fees: The money was eventually repaid.

30 "We remain committed to": "Kevin Sneader Elected Global Managing Partner of McKinsey & Company."

30 McKinsey adopted a new code: McKinsey & Company, "Living Our Values: McKinsey's Code of Professional Conduct."

30 "Roughly half of those engagements": The authors obtained access to a recording of the discussion.

31 "In line with policy": Pjotr Sauer, "McKinsey Bans Moscow Staff from Attending Pro-Navalny Protest," *Moscow Times,* Jan. 23, 2021.

31 "Our Moscow office's communication": Ramiro Prudencio (partner and global director of communications, McKinsey), letter to the editor, *Financial Times,* Feb. 4, 2021.

31 after just one three-year term: Michael Forsythe, "Head of McKinsey Is Voted Out as Firm Faces Reckoning on Opioid Crisis," *New York Times,* Feb. 24, 2021.

31 joined Goldman Sachs: Goldman Sachs Group Inc. announced on Sept. 8, 2021, that Sneader would join the firm as co-president of Asia Pacific Ex-Japan.

2. Winners and Losers

32 "The Treaty of Detroit": Walter W. Ruch, "G.M., Auto Workers, Reach 5-Year Pact on Pensions, Wages," *New York Times,* May 24, 1950.

32 open a five-and-ten: Sam Walton's store in Bentonville, Walton's 5&10, was opened on May 9, 1950. See www.walmartmuseum.com.

33 study executive compensation: George David Smith, John T. Seaman Jr., and Morgan Witzel, *A History of the Firm* (New York: McKinsey, 2011), 106.

33 CEOs made at least 351 times: Lawrence Mishel and Jori Kandra, "CEO Pay Has Skyrocketed 1,322% Since 1978," Economic Policy Institute, Aug. 10, 2021.

33 The McKinsey study: Arch Patton, *Men, Money, and Motivation: Executive Compensation as an Instrument of Leadership* (New York: McGraw-Hill, 1961), lx.

33 "People just came from far and wide": Smith, Seaman, and Witzel, *History of the Firm,* 107.

33 "set our industry back": Patton, *Men, Money, and Motivation,* 46.

34 "the debilitating effect of the graduated income tax": Ibid., 197.

34 "was no doubt an attempt": Smith, Seaman, and Witzel, *History of the Firm,* 52.

34 "The traditionally paternalistic Marshall Field": Ibid., 59.

34 10 percent of the firm's billings: Ibid., 107.

35 "Then I would do the study": Ibid.

35 "with the general objective": Ibid., 233.

35 "You've got to understand": Ibid.

35 prosperous career at the firm: Ibid., 299.

35 As John Kenneth Galbraith wrote: John Kenneth Galbraith, *The New Industrial State* (Boston: Houghton Mifflin, 1967), 189.

36 "Paper pushers of the middle class": Louis Hyman, *Temp: How American Work, American Business, and the American Dream Became Temporary* (New York: Viking, 2018), 4.

36 "a new, strictly financial view": Louis Hyman, "It's Not Technology That's Disrupting Our Jobs," *New York Times,* Aug. 19, 2018.

36 investors over society: Author interview.

36 "The corporation under the consultants' helm": Hyman, *Temp,* 7.

36 To keep in step: Smith, Seaman, and Witzel, *History of the Firm,* 188.

36 who believed that managers: Thomas J. Peters and Robert H. Waterman Jr., *In Search of Excellence: Lessons from America's Best-Run Companies* (New York: HarperBusiness Essentials, 2006), 14.

37 Peters acknowledged that McKinsey: Duff McDonald, *The Firm: The Story of McKinsey and Its Secret Influence on American Business* (New York: Simon & Schuster, 2013), 151.

37 seek help from McKinsey, Ford also hired McKinsey, but according to David Halberstam's book *The Reckoning,* Ford's visionary president, Lee Iacocca, "loathed the McKinsey people" from the moment they arrived. "What is this shit?" he asked. "What the hell do we need outsiders coming in to tell us who we are?" The consultants, he believed, didn't realize how little they knew about building a car because they had never done it. Iacocca lost that battle, among others, prompting him to leave Ford, only to enjoy great success at Chrysler as its chief executive. See David Halberstam, *The Reckoning* (New York: William Morrow, 1986), 539.

37 on a massive corporate reorganization: McDonald, *Firm,* 183–84.

37 "Billions could be made": Les Leopold, *Runaway Inequality: An Activist's Guide to Economic Justice* (New York: Labor Institute Press, 2015), 53.

37 "This is not the invisible hand": Leopold, interview by Bogdanich.

37 "It was the corporate downsizing": Ed Michaels, Helen Handfield-Jones, and Beth Axelrod, *The War for Talent* (Boston: Harvard Business School Press, 2001), 7.

38 "When management consulting untethered": Daniel Markovits, "How McKinsey Destroyed the Middle Class," *Atlantic,* Feb. 3, 2020.

38 "Outstanding corporations do win the right": Sarah Kaplan and Richard N. Foster, *Creative Destruction: Why Companies That Are Built to Last Underperform the Market—and How to Successfully Transform Them* (New York: Currency/Doubleday, 2001), 10.

38 "There is a distinct possibility . . . that McKinsey": McDonald, *Firm,* 8.

39 In 2020, just 10 percent: U.S. Bureau of Labor Statistics, *Union Members Survey,* Jan. 22, 2021.

39 "We have unparalleled experience": Digital McKinsey, *Sourcing,* n.d.

39 "Globalization used to hurt": Steven Greenhouse, *The Big Squeeze: Tough Times for the American Worker* (New York: Alfred A. Knopf, 2008), 203.

39 "Offshore-istan": Anita Raghavan, *The Billionaire's Apprentice: The Rise of the Indian-American Elite and the Fall of the Galleon Hedge Fund* (New York: Grand Central Publishing, 2013), 139–41.

39 two senior leaders in the firm: Gupta and Kumar shared a blind spot when it came to ethics. After Gupta left the firm, he was convicted and imprisoned on charges related to insider trading. Gupta's crime did not involve McKinsey business. Not so for Kumar, who profited by sharing confidential client information with a $7 billion hedge fund. He escaped prison by testifying against Gupta.

40 an offshoring facilitator: The name of the offshoring facilitator is 31 West. Its website identified the five companies.

40 McKinsey praised offshoring: Diana Farrell, ed., *Offshoring: Understanding the Emerging Global Labor Market* (Boston: Harvard Business Review Press, 2006). Farrell served as director of the McKinsey Global Institute.

40 "By leveraging cheap labor": "Offshoring: Is It a Win-Win Game?," McKinsey Global Institute, 2.

40 "Companies aren't getting the most": Michael Bloch, Shankar Narayanan, and Ishaan Seth, "Getting More out of Offshoring the Finance Function," McKinsey & Company, April 1, 2007.

40 as independent and highly regarded: McKinsey said the University of Pennsylvania ranked the firm's think tank as the best.

41 "neutral public intellectuals": Bivens, interview by author.

41 Congress held hearings on outsourcing: House of Representatives, Committee on Ways and Means, *Promoting U.S. Worker Effectiveness in a Globalized Economy,* June 14, 2007.

41 Courtney cited one published report: Testimony of Marcus Courtney, representing Washington Alliance of Technical Workers, Committee on Ways and Means, June 14, 2007.

41 "Focusing the offshoring debate": "Who Wins When Jobs Move Overseas?," McKinsey & Company, Oct. 26, 2003.

41 It also produces new revenue: Farrell, *Offshoring,* 57.

41 "job losses must be seen": Ibid., 59.

41 "Even in the best of circumstances": Joseph E. Stiglitz, "On the Wrong Side of Globalization," *New York Times,* March 15, 2014.

42 "Talent is a seductive word": Michaels, Handfield-Jones, and Axelrod, *War for Talent,* xiii.

42 "Data provide compelling evidence": Ibid., 6.

42 Enron's top five executives: "Pay Madness at Enron," *Forbes,* March 22, 2002, based on an analysis by Charas Consulting.

42 "CEOs don't just get salaries": Opening statement of Representative Henry A. Waxman, Democrat of California, House of Representatives, Committee on Oversight and Government Reform, *Executive Pay: The Roles of Compensation Consultants,* Dec. 5, 2007.

43 Roughly 80 percent: Mishel and Kandra, "CEO Pay Has Skyrocketed 1,322% Since 1978."

43 "as passing insider information": Kevin P. Coyne and Jonathan W. Witter, "Taking the Mystery out of Investor Behavior," *Harvard Business Review,* Sept. 2002.

43 "While shareholder capitalism": Anne Gast et al., "Purpose: Shifting from Why to How," *McKinsey Quarterly,* April 22, 2020.

43 "There's a however": Peter Coy, "Globalization 'Cheerleader' McKinsey Global Institute Has Second Thoughts," Bloomberg, July 15, 2016.

43 Cheaper products and market power: Charles Fishman, *The Wal-Mart Effect: How the World's Most Powerful Company Really Works—and How It's Transforming the American Economy* (New York: Penguin, 2006). Walmart, as the company is currently known, was previously called Wal-Mart.

44 median household income in the United States was almost $50,000: Census data, www2.census.gov/library/publications/2008/acs/acs-09.pdf. Household income includes the possibility of more than one person working. Even so, two people working full-time at Walmart would not come close to the median household income.

44 confidential memo: Steven Greenhouse and Michael Barbaro, "Wal-Mart Memo Suggests Ways to Cut Employee Benefit Costs," *New York Times,* Oct. 26, 2005.

45 "Moreover, because we pay": Twenty-five-page memo, with exhibits, from Susan Chambers to Walmart's Board of Directors, obtained by the authors.

45 Walmart's insurance did not cover: Andy Miller, "Wal-Mart Employees Have Highest Number of Kids on Supplemental Health Insurance," Cox News Service, Feb. 29, 2004.

45 "misguided, destructive assault on a business": Fishman, *Wal-Mart Effect,* 245.

46 "If my McKinsey buddies were here": Walker, interview by Tucker Carlson, *Tucker Carlson Tonight,* Fox News.

46 Fishman reminded readers: Fishman, *Wal-Mart Effect,* 227.

46 "Wal-Mart can't seem to grasp": Ibid., 269.

47 Walmart banned the sale of handguns: Abha Bhattarai, " 'The Status Quo Is Unacceptable': Walmart Will Stop Selling Some Ammunition and Exit the Handgun Market," *Washington Post,* Sept. 3, 2019.

47 Walmart began testing a plan: Melissa Repko, "Walmart Ends Quarterly Bonuses for Store Employees as It Raises Employees' Hourly Pay," CNBC, Sept. 9, 2021.

47 $5 million in fees: Confidential source.

47 "These are 7,000 jobs of people": Julia La Roche, "AT&T CEO Says They'll Invest 'at Least $1 Billion' and Create 7,000 New Jobs If Tax Reform Passes," *Yahoo News,* Nov. 29, 2017.

47 "If the President signs the bill": Tomi Kilgore, "AT&T to Pay $1,000 Bonuses over Holidays If Trump Signs Tax Bill by Christmas," *MarketWatch,* Dec. 20, 2017.

48 Three days before Christmas: Jane C. Timm, "Trump Signs Tax Cut Bill, First Big Legislative Win," NBC, Dec. 22, 2017.

48 A spokeswoman for AT&T said the bonuses: Author interview with spokeswoman for AT&T.

48 more than $35 million: McKinsey records.

48 AT&T eliminated nearly eleven thousand jobs: Communications Workers of America, press release, June 16, 2020.

48 reorganizing parts of the company: Confidential source.

48 Stephen Smith had worked: Michael Sainato, "Bosses Pocket Trump Tax Windfall as Workers See Job Promises Vanish," *Guardian,* June 16, 2019.

48 Cindy Liddick had worked: Michael Sainato, " 'They're Liquidating Us': AT&T Continues Layoffs and Outsourcing Despite Profits," *Guardian,* Aug. 28, 2018.

48 "It looks like AT&T is pushing": Communications Workers of America, press release, June 16, 2020, based on a review of Securities and Exchange records.

48 the company paid McKinsey $96 million: McDonald, *Firm,* 197. The five-year period was between 1989 and 1994.

48 $120 million in 2018 and 2019: Confidential source. This payment has not been previously reported.

49 Nearly two hundred McKinsey consultants: Author interview.

49 "The fastest way to get there": Geiser, interview by author.

49 "Many millions of Americans": Anand Giridharadas, *Winners Take All: The Elite Charade of Changing the World* (New York: Alfred A. Knopf, 2018), 4.

49 A study by the Federal Reserve Board: Isabel Cairo and Jae Sim, *Market Power, Inequality, and Financial Instability,* Board of Governors of the Federal Reserve System, July 2020.

49 "of tensions that have been boiling over": Gast et al., "Purpose: Shifting from Why to How."

50 "boom and bust cycles": André Dua, McKinsey partner and author of "The Zip Code Reality," speaking at McKinsey's Ideas Festival, as reported in the McKinsey Blog, Jan. 31, 2019.

50 "Even at its best": Anand Giridharadas (@anandwrites), Twitter, Nov. 12, 2019.

50 "What is your company's core reason for being?": Gast et al., "Purpose: Shifting from Why to How."

50 "Guilty": Dana Canedy, "Arch Patton, 88; Devised First Survey of Top Executives' Pay," *New York Times,* Nov. 30, 1996.

3. Playing Both Sides

51 McKinsey consultants descended: Gary MacDougal, *Make a Difference: A Spectacular Breakthrough in the Fight Against Poverty* (New York: St. Martin's Press, 2005), 274.

51 left the firm: Ibid., 24.

51 1988 presidential campaign: Ibid., 33.

51 welfare too often perpetuated poverty: Ibid., 29.

51 MacDougal persuaded Illinois's governor: Ibid., 3.

51 Norwood became a trusted confidante: Ibid., 105.

52 the organizational shortcomings: Ibid., 274–75. The information detailed is also sourced from author interviews.

52 "The fact that the firm was volunteering": Ibid., 275.

52 dropped 22 percent: Ibid., 285.

52 chair the Illinois Republican Party: Rick Pearson, "GOP Taps a Conservative; Gary MacDougal Is Charged with Mending Party," *Chicago Tribune,* July 27, 2002.

52 an additional 650,000 people: The State of Illinois Medicaid Managed Care Organization Request for Proposals, Feb. 27, 2017.

52 as his deputy governor: Kim Geiger, "Rauner Names Former Comptroller Munger to Deputy Governor Post," *Chicago Tribune,* Feb. 3, 2017.

53 for a McKinsey client, Aetna: Internal McKinsey records.

53 managed care division: Felicia Norwood's LinkedIn page and her testimony to the Appropriations–Human Services Committee Hearing, Illinois House of Representatives, March 9, 2017, 2.

53 The state had no budget: Susana A. Mendoza, "Consequences of Illinois' 2015–2017 Budget Impasse and Fiscal Outlook," Illinois Office of the Comptroller.

53 The state owed $800,000: State of Illinois Comptroller, "Comptroller Mendoza Prioritizes Payments to Senior Care Givers," press release, March 28, 2017.

53 "They were screaming for help": Mendoza, interview by author.

53 "the people who are sick": Julie Bosman and Monica Davey, "Everything's in Danger: Illinois Approaches 3rd Year Without Budget," *New York Times,* June 29, 2017.

53 she froze $21.6 million: State of Illinois Comptroller, "Comptroller Mendoza Freezes Spending on ERP Pending Answers from Rauner Administration," press release, March 14, 2017. The frozen funds were eventually released to McKinsey three years later.

53 deadline came and went without answers: Illinois Office of the Comptroller.

54 pay McKinsey more than $75 million: Public contract data from Illinois comptroller.

54 totaling roughly $24 million: Ibid.

54 The state awarded both to McKinsey: Appropriations–Human Services Committee Hearing, Illinois House of Representatives, Nov. 30, 2017, 13.

54 Norwood, whose office had awarded the contracts: Norwood awarded the contracts as head of the Illinois Department of Family and Health Services. Ibid., 19.

54 "When you talk about a sole source contract": Ibid., 5.

54 Strategizing organizational change was deemed: Ibid., 12.

54 worth $12 million: John O'Connor, "Illinois Procurement Chief Cancels Rauner Consulting Pact," Associated Press, Dec. 5, 2017.

54 froze payments on a second McKinsey contract: "Illinois Comptroller Nixes Pay on a 2nd Rauner Contract," Associated Press, Dec. 6, 2017.

54 with McKinsey's guidance, arranged to pay $63 billion: Appropriations–Human Services Committee Hearing, Illinois House of Representatives, Nov. 30, 2017, 1.

54 "That means this proposal is not": Appropriations–Human Services Committee Hearing, Illinois House of Representatives, May 10, 2017, 2.

55 "That does not seem to be very conducive": Appropriations–Human Services Committee Hearing, Illinois House of Representatives, Nov. 30, 2017, 16. McKinsey has inserted similar language in contracts with other governmental agencies. When the authors of this book filed a Freedom of Information Act request seeking details of a McKinsey contract with the Food and Drug Administration, the agency—after waiting a year to respond—replied that it would first need to check with McKinsey about what information it could release.

55 She explained that the giant managed care contracts: Appropriations–Human

Services Committee Hearing, Illinois House of Representatives, March 9, 2017, 2. State officials said they were prohibited from disclosing the names of the contract evaluators.

55 McKinsey helped state employees prepare them: Ibid., 5.

55 more than $200 million: Internal McKinsey records.

56 "a hefty investment to recoup": Eddie Baeb, "Consulting Firm McKinsey Signs Big Lease at Blue Cross Building," *Crain's Chicago Business,* June 22, 2011.

56 "deliverables": Appropriations–Human Services Committee Hearing, Illinois House of Representatives, Nov. 30, 2017, 15–19.

56 people began to laugh: Harris, interview by author.

56 "Do we have a cadence defined?": Appropriations–Human Services Committee Hearing, Illinois House of Representatives, Nov. 30, 2017, 16–19.

56 Norwood left her state job: Norwood's LinkedIn indicates that she joined Anthem in June 2018; the last Appropriations–Human Services Committee hearing was in Dec. 2017.

56 billed Anthem more than $90 million: Internal McKinsey records.

56 nine other insurance company clients: Internal McKinsey records.

57 a clean record: Appropriations–Human Services Committee Hearing, Illinois House of Representatives, Nov. 30, 2017, 29–30.

57 Eric Greitens: Jack Suntrup and Kurt Erickson, "Embattled Missouri Gov. Eric Greitens Resigns; Prosecutor Drops Computer Tampering Charge," *St. Louis Post-Dispatch,* May 30, 2018. Greitens resigned before completing his term amid allegations of impropriety, none involving McKinsey.

57 new position specifically for Drew Erdmann: Benjamin Peters, "Greitens Names Drew Erdmann as New COO," *Missouri Times,* Jan. 11, 2017.

57 Missouri hired McKinsey: Email from Joel M. Walters (Missouri director of revenue) to the staff of the Missouri Department of Revenue, reproduced in a PowerPoint by the Department of Revenue about McKinsey's "Organizational Health Index," 6.

57 McKinsey's pro bono work: Will Schmitt, "Missouri Revamps HR Policy for State Workers After Research Project by COO's Former Firm," *Springfield News-Leader,* Jan. 6, 2018; Agreement signed between Commissioner Sarah Steelman, Missouri Office of Administration, and McKinsey & Company, June 14, 2017.

57 McKinsey and four other consulting firms: Memorandum from Stacia Dawson to the Missouri Office of Administration Division of Purchasing, "Cooperative Contract Award Memo."

57 combat waste, fraud, and abuse: Statement of Work issued by the Missouri Department of Social Services on April 2, 2018, "Rapid Response Review—Assessment of Missouri Medicaid Program."

57 blacked out entirely or mostly blacked out: Technical Proposal to the Missouri Department of Social Services for the "Rapid Response Review" published initially to the public. A non-redacted version has since been made publicly available in compliance with Missouri's Sunshine Law, and the redacted version is no longer available for public view.

57 No other consulting firm: Original bids by four competing firms (Deloitte, KPMG, Navigant, Accenture) published on the Missouri Office of Administration Awarded Contract and Bid Documents Search, Bid CPPS30034901802660.

58 "Since Erdmann was hired": Tony Messenger, "Missouri COO's Former Company Wins Medicaid Bid Despite Being 3 Times Higher Than Others," *St. Louis Post-Dispatch,* June 18, 2018.

58 new rating system that de-emphasized cost: Commissioner Sarah Steelman's testimony to the Missouri House Budget Committee Hearing, July 17, 2018.

58 *three times higher* than the lowest bid: Original bids by four competing firms (Deloitte, KPMG, Navigant, and Accenture) published on the Missouri Office of Administration Awarded

Contract and Bid Documents Search, Bid CPPS30034901802660. The lower bids were KPMG for $750,000, Navigant for $898,725, and Deloitte for $981,000. The contract was important beyond its dollar amount, because McKinsey's recommendations affected a large swath of the state's health-care apparatus.

58 identical evaluations: Evaluation Narrative, "Rapid Response Review—Assessment of Missouri Medicaid Program," 4.

58 Competitors were judged more harshly: Ibid., 2–11.

58 McKinsey requested a meeting: Karen Boeger (director of the Missouri Office of Administration Division of Purchasing) to David Mosley (Navigant Consulting), Sept. 27, 2018.

58 "was afforded the opportunity": Bid protest by Navigant against awarding of Rapid Response contract to McKinsey & Company, June 12, 2018, 2.

58 blocked competitors from reviewing the plan: Ibid., 3.

58 State officials rejected Navigant's protest: Boeger to Mosley, Sept. 27, 2018.

58 rigging the selection process: Blake Nelson and Summer Ballentine, "Gov. Parson Stands By Contract for COO's Former Employer," Associated Press, June 18, 2018.

59 "I don't trust them for a second": Merideth, interview by author.

59 "We cannot know if McKinsey": Missouri Health Care for All, "The McKinsey Report on Missouri's Medicaid Program: The Good, the Bad, and the Ugly for Consumer Health," March 2019, 9.

59 or soon-to-be McKinsey clients: Internal McKinsey records.

59 "faced serious charges of mismanagement": Jason Clayworth, "Iowa's New Private Medicaid Manager Has Paid Millions of Dollars in Penalties in a Dozen States," *Des Moines Register,* July 1, 2018. McKinsey was not accused of wrongdoing in connection with Centene's work.

59 billed Centene more than $50 million: Internal McKinsey records.

59 already known to state officials: Missouri Health Care for All, "McKinsey Report on Missouri's Medicaid Program," 5.

59 "Anybody could have gone": D'Abreu, interview by author.

59 "Nearly all of the major recommendations": Missouri Health Care for All, "McKinsey Report on Missouri's Medicaid Program," 9.

59 "The report seems to blame": Ibid., 1.

60 "When we see over 50,000 children": Phil Galewitz, "Shrinking Medicaid Rolls in Missouri and Tennessee Raise Flag on Vetting Process," *Kaiser Health News,* Feb. 8, 2019.

60 closer to 100,000: Merideth, interview.

60 "Because of its focus": Report obtained by author. Joel Ferber, director of advocacy for Legal Services of Eastern Missouri, said in an interview with the author that McKinsey's report was "primarily about finding ways to save money."

60 "They sold us on saving money": Merideth, interview.

60 "I am not opposed": Sharfstein, interview by author.

61 "an emergency" sole-source contract: Arkansas Legislative Audit, "Review of Selected Software Procurements and Cooperative Purchasing Agreements," June 24, 2015, 12–13.

61 "A McKinsey partner was sitting": Allison, interview by author.

61 more than $100 million: Arkansas Legislative Audit, "Review of Selected Software Procurements and Cooperative Purchasing Agreements," June 24, 2015, 14.

61 Later, a legislative audit: Ibid., 13.

61 "Innovation and payment reform requires": Allison, interview.

61 firm hired him in 2015: Arkansas Legislative Audit, "Review of Selected Software Procurements and Cooperative Purchasing Agreements," June 24, 2015, 14.

62 The firm promoted its proprietary analytics: For example, McKinsey's approved proposal to be placed on Missouri's statewide Qualified Vendor List for "Management Consulting Services," 1.

62 signature domestic achievement: Robert

Pear and David M. Herszenhorn, "Obama Hails Vote on Health Care as Answering 'the Call of History,'" *New York Times,* March 21, 2010.

62 privately tried to kill it: A former Obama official said the companies disliked the requirement that they spend 80 percent of their premium income on health care and return the rest to customers. Rick Ungar, "Busted! Health Insurers Secretly Spent Huge to Defeat Health Care Reform While Pretending to Support Obamacare," *Forbes,* June 25, 2012.

62 remove the "public option": Wendell Potter, "Elimination of 'Public Option' Threw Consumers to the Insurance Wolves," Center for Public Integrity, Feb. 16, 2015.

63 McKinsey shocked Washington by releasing: Shubham Singhal, Jeris Stueland, and Drew Ungerman, "How US Health Care Reform Will Affect Employee Benefits," McKinsey & Company, June 1, 2011.

63 McKinsey's findings clashed with other studies: Jonathan Cohn, "McKinsey Insider: Survey 'Not a Good Tool for Prediction,'" *New Republic,* June 14, 2011.

63 "The findings of this survey": U.S. House of Representatives Ways and Means Committee, "Key House Democrats Ask McKinsey to Release Methodology of Potentially Biased Health Reform," press release, June 16, 2011.

63 Senator Max Baucus: U.S. Senate Committee on Finance, "Baucus Calls on McKinsey to Release Methodology Behind Survey Results," press release, June 16, 2011.

63 "It isn't every day": Greg Sargent, "Incoming: Dems Dropping Bombs on McKinsey," *Washington Post,* June 16, 2011.

63 McKinsey finally bowed: U.S. House of Representatives Ways and Means Committee, "McKinsey Changes Its Tune, Acknowledges Survey Is Not Predictive," press release, June 20, 2011.

64 "is filled with cherry-picked facts": U.S. Senate Committee on Finance, "Baucus Blasts McKinsey for Unjustifiable Explanations, Efforts to Back Away from Claims," press release, June 20, 2011.

64 skewered McKinsey's report: Nancy-Ann DeParle, "Not a Prediction," Summary blog on President Barack Obama's White House website, June 20, 2011.

64 DeParle declined to speculate: DeParle, phone call with author.

64 "to track and model the impact": "Center for US Health System Reform," McKinsey & Company Healthcare Systems & Services.

64 "leading retail pharmacies": McKinsey & Company's bid to the Missouri Department of Social Services for the "Rapid Response Review—Assessment of Missouri Medicaid Program," April 16, 2018, 2.

65 Together they accounted for nearly half: Author analysis of publicly available campaign donation records compiled by the Washington-based Center for Responsive Politics.

65 nearly $1 million to Democrats: Elling's contributions overwhelmingly favored Democrats. They made up about one-quarter of all the political donations to federal candidates and committees by McKinsey employees, according to Federal Election Commission figures compiled by the Washington-based Center for Responsive Politics.

65 favorable accommodations: Emails titled "Convention packages," from Daniel Parrish to Elling, May 4, 2016, and "Thank you" from Parrish to Judith Hazlewood, May 4, 2016.

65 Vivian Riefberg, a senior partner: Vivian Riefberg's LinkedIn page.

65 an influential voice on health: Wes Venteicher, "Paul Mango Appointed to Trump Administration Post at CMS," Associated Press, July 29, 2018.

66 McKinsey grabbed more FDA business: Annual amounts obligated to McKinsey by the FDA, usaspending.gov.

66 at least $400 million: Confidential source. McKinsey has also counseled the FDA on medical devices, medical radiation, smoking, vaping, and a variety of organizational and regulatory issues.

66 "have knowledge of, and relationships with": Job solicitation publicly posted on McKinsey's website.

66 McKinsey posted a biography: Evgeniya Makarova's partner biography publicly posted on McKinsey's website.

66 But it was the agency's close collaboration: Michael A. Carome (director of Public Citizen's Health Research Group) to Christi A. Grimm (principal deputy inspector general of the Office of Inspector General), Dec. 9, 2020, 1.

67 The eleventh member was "uncertain": Pam Belluck, "FDA Panel Declines to Endorse Controversial Alzheimer's Drug," *New York Times,* Nov. 6, 2020.

67 "probably the worst drug approval": Thomas M. Burton, "FDA's Approval Decision of Alzheimer's Drug Leads to Third Adviser's Resignation," *Wall Street Journal,* June 10, 2021.

67 cost of $56,000 per patient: Rebecca Robbins and Pam Belluck, "In a Reversal, FDA Calls for Limits on Who Gets Alzheimer's Drug," *New York Times,* July 8, 2021.

67 "indefensible" and "reckless": Public Citizen letter, June 16, 2021.

67 "first-in-class disease-modifying therapy": McKinsey document, April 15, 2021.

68 Carome, said he was unaware: Carome, interview by author. Carome was informed of this fact by the author.

68 billed the FDA $11.6 million: Records obtained through the Freedom of Information Act and public contracts databases.

68 "with the speed and agility": Records obtained through the Freedom of Information Act and public contracts databases.

68 McKinsey's ties to FDA officials: BioNJ event: "Cell and Gene Therapy Manufacturing 'Crack the Code,'" Sept. 20, 2019.

68 "the safety, purity, potency": U.S. Food and Drug Administration, Center for Biologics Evaluation and Research Responsibilities Questions and Answers. Dr. Marks's unit was not involved in the Biogen evaluation.

69 "Please note, no walk-ins": BioNJ event, "Cell and Gene Therapy Manufacturing 'Crack the Code,'" Sept. 20, 2019.

69 "We recognize that rigorous clinical endpoints": "Helping to Accelerate Cures," Pharmaceuticals & Medical Products, McKinsey, Jan. 2019.

69 at least $130 million with the FDA: Records obtained through the Freedom of Information Act.

69 without bidding for it: The agreement is called a Federal Supply Schedule Contract. Office of Audits, Office of Inspector General, U.S. General Services Administration, "Improper Pricing on the McKinsey Professional Services Contract May Cost the United States an Estimated $69 Million," July 23, 2019, 10.

69 This contract, with renewal options: This is called a Blanket Purchase Agreement, which is similar to a charge account. Federal agencies have the option of buying from multiple vendors or a single one. U.S. General Services Administration, "Blanket Purchase Agreements and the GSA MAS Program."

70 get the records or cancel the contract: Office of Audits, Office of Inspector General, U.S. General Services Administration, "Improper Pricing on the McKinsey Professional Services Contract May Cost the United States an Estimated $69 Million," i.

70 as much as 193 percent: Ibid., 8. Neither McKinsey nor the GSA official was charged in connection with the contracts.

70 *an additional 10 percent rate increase:* Ibid., 3.

70 an estimated $69 million: Ibid., 5.

70 "any potential costs related": Interview with inspector general spokesperson.

70 What made these requests so unusual: Office of Audits, Office of Inspector General, U.S. General Services Administration, "Improper Pricing on the McKinsey Professional Services Contract May Cost the United States an Estimated $69 Million," 11.

70 "We really would appreciate": Ibid., 12.

71 McKinsey was allowed to resubmit its offer: Ibid., 11. The IT contract was canceled.

71 "abandoned his role": Ibid., 13.

71 The GSA refused to identify: An extensive record search uncovered the man's name—Jacob Bertram. In an interview with the author, he denied acting improperly.

71 McKinsey made a bold: All information about McKinsey-hosted events obtained through the Freedom of Information Act.

72 killed more than 900,000: "Coronavirus in the U.S.: Latest Map and Case Count," *New York Times,* April 7, 2022.

72 "From surviving to thriving": Kevin Sneader and Bob Sternfels, "From Surviving to Thriving: Reimagining the Post-COVID-19 Return," McKinsey & Company, May 1, 2020.

72 his five *R*s: Ibid.

72 Within months of the pandemic's arrival: Ian MacDougall, "How McKinsey Is Making $100 Million (and Counting) Advising on the Government's Bumbling Coronavirus Response," ProPublica, July 15, 2020.

72 in California, Washington, Tennessee, New York, and New Jersey: State public contracting databases.

72 "Our first concern": Senators Elizabeth Warren, Richard Blumenthal, and Thomas R. Carper to Scott Gast (senior counsel to the president and designated ethics official of the White House), April 15, 2020.

73 It did not lead the fight: After years of promoting opioid sales, McKinsey belatedly acknowledged that it had erred. Michael Forsythe and Walt Bogdanich, "McKinsey Settles for Nearly $600 Million over Role in Opioid Crisis," *New York Times,* Feb. 3, 2021.

73 Five drug company clients: Nicholas Florko, "Are You an American, Sir? Lawmakers Interrogate Amgen, Novartis, Mallinckrodt Executives on Why U.S. Prices Are So High," *Stat+,* Oct. 1, 2020.

4. McKinsey at ICE

74 For a company accustomed to always being *in control:* The articles on McKinsey's work in South Africa, with opioid makers, and with autocrats were published in *The New York Times* and written by the authors of this book. *The Wall Street Journal* published stories about McKinsey's bankruptcy practice, as did the *Times.* See Gretchen Morgenson and Tom Corrigan, "McKinsey Is Big in Bankruptcy—and Highly Secretive," *Wall Street Journal,* April 27, 2018.

74 In June 2018: Walt Bogdanich and Michael Forsythe, "How McKinsey Lost Its Way in South Africa," *New York Times,* June 26, 2018.

75 "We will not, under any circumstances": Sneader note to McKinsey alumni cited in Michael Forsythe and Walt Bogdanich, "McKinsey Ends Work with ICE amid Furor over Immigration Policy," *New York Times,* July 10, 2018.

75 One reporter obtained an audio recording: Ginger Thompson, "Listen to Children Who've Just Been Separated from Their Parents at the Border," ProPublica, June 18, 2018.

76 The article revealed some uncomfortable truths: Ian MacDougall, "How McKinsey Helped the Trump Administration Detain and Deport Immigrants," ProPublica, Dec. 3, 2019.

76 "a notable decrease in the time": Emailed statement from ICE press office, forwarded to authors on March 4, 2020.

76 The article reverberated outside the firm: Michael Forsythe, "When Pete Buttigieg Was One of McKinsey's 'Whiz Kids,'" *New York Times,* Dec. 6, 2019. Andy Slavitt, in a Dec. 4, 2019, Twitter post, said, "@McKinsey recommendations to cut food, supervision, and medical care to immigrants in custody were so cruel they made the staff at ICE uncomfortable."

77 "When Mexico sends its people": Donald Trump Presidential Campaign Announcement Full Speech (C-SPAN), June 16, 2015, www.youtube.com/watch?v=apjNfkysjbM.

77 Five days into his presidency: Executive Order: Enhancing Public Safety in the Interior of the United States, Jan. 25, 2017, www.whitehouse.gov.

78 "ICE is changing direction": Elder quotation is a recollection from an interview with a former McKinsey employee who was on the call and wished to remain anonymous. Elder, who left McKinsey in 2019, did not respond to an emailed request asking for comment and seeking verification.

78 During the late 1960s: George David Smith, John T. Seaman Jr., and Morgan Witzel, *A History of the Firm* (New York: McKinsey, 2011), 176.

79 "Transformation design to increase arrests": The client for the ICE work on McKinsey's "Know" internal website was anonymized, as are all such job descriptions, as "Police—Service Operations," but a McKinsey employee confirmed that the work was for ICE.

79 On February 13, 2017, less than a month: MacDougall, "How McKinsey Helped the Trump Administration Detain and Deport Immigrants."

79 "The hiring system can work better": ICE FOIA production to ProPublica, 323.

79 "With Trump, who is going to work there now?": Interview with a former McKinsey consultant who wished to remain anonymous.

79 McKinsey fought back: "McKinsey Statement on New York Times and ProPublica Article Regarding ICE and CBP," Dec. 4, 2019.

80 Its consultants claimed ICE could save: ICE FOIA production, 289.

80 The consultants found six areas: Ibid., 296.

80 "ICE spends so much": Interview with former senior ICE official, March 8, 2020.

80 That drew the ire: This is a recollection of what D'Emidio told the senior ICE official. D'Emidio was sent a summary of how we would characterize him in the book via a LinkedIn direct message. Subsequently, through a McKinsey spokesman, he denied that these events took place.

81 "They are cheaper because they are shitty": Interview with former Department of Homeland Security official, Feb. 25, 2020.

81 At one point in 2018: "One Detained Baby Remains in ICE Custody," CBS News, March 6, 2019.

81 ICE was paying CoreCivic: ICE FOIA production, 74.

81 Dilley was where, in March 2018: Federal Tort Claims Act—Form 95—claim on behalf of Yazmin Juárez, dated Nov. 27, 2018, www.arnoldporter.com.

82 Her mother filed a $60 million wrongful death claim: Arnold & Porter, press release, Nov. 27, 2018, www.arnoldporter.com.

82 "I never saw anyone as helpless": Garbus, interview by author, Feb. 28, 2020.

82 "I saw the South African police": Martin Garbus, "What I Saw at the Dilley, Texas, Immigrant Detention Center," *Nation,* March 26, 2019.

82 Another of McKinsey's "deliverables": ICE FOIA production, starting on page 309.

82 By October 2017, McKinsey's contract: Ibid., 642.

83 The ICE spokesman Bryan D. Cox: Statement was made to ProPublica for inclusion in its Dec. 3, 2019, article, "How McKinsey Helped the Trump Administration Detain and Deport Immigrants."

83 McKinsey had been trying to speed deportation: "McKinsey Statement on New York Times and ProPublica Article Regarding ICE and CBP."

84 It was, Elfenbein recalled: Scott Elfenbein, "The Best Story I Know," blog post on Medium.com, May 24, 2018.

84 "Apparently a bunch of teens": Ibid.

84 They got a senator: Terry Aguayo and Julia Preston, "Students' Family Members Are Deported," *New York Times,* Oct. 31, 2007.

85 The case got national attention: Julia Preston, "In Increments, Senate Revisits Immigration Bill," *New York Times,* Aug. 3, 2007.

86 "Many of us share": This account is

constructed from a recording of the meeting made by a participant.

90 A few days later, D'Emidio: D'Emidio email to colleagues, Dec. 12, 2019.

5. Befriending China's Government

91 In late 2013 a fleet: Various blogs have published the position of the *Tian Jing Hao* in the South China Sea in late 2013 and into 2014, citing ship's positioning data analyzed by IHS Jane's. See garudamiliter.blogspot.com/2014/06/world-news-china-goes-all-out-with.html. For a description of the vessel and its ownership, see Charles Clover, "South China Sea Island-Maker Seeks Foreign Flotation," *Financial Times,* June 11, 2015.

91 The respected *Jane's Defence Weekly:* James Hardy and Sean O'Connor, "China Completes Runway on Fiery Cross Reef," *IHS Jane's Defence Weekly,* Sept. 25, 2015.

92 To help guide him: For a list of the *zhongyang qiye,* see the website of the State-Owned Asset Supervision and Administration Commission of the State Council. Figures of McKinsey clients are derived from open-source research on Chinese-language websites and McKinsey internal records.

92 In all, 702 people: "公司召开'十三五'战略咨询视频会" (Company holds thirteenth five-year-plan strategic consulting video conference), China Communications Construction Company, Sept. 29, 2015, www.ccccltd.cn/xwzx/gsyw/201509/t20150929_41727.html.

93 In one incident: Luis Martinez, "Chinese Warship Came Within 45 Yards of USS Decatur in South China Sea: US," ABC News, Oct. 1, 2018.

93 A Washington think tank: Michael Forsythe, "Possible Radar Suggests Beijing Wants 'Effective Control' in South China Sea," *New York Times,* Feb. 24, 2016. The think tank is the Center for Strategic and International Studies.

93 "China, with its authoritarian system": "SECNAV Nominee Del Toro's Written Statements to the Senate," USNI News, July 13, 2021.

93 In 2015, the same year: McKinsey's work with the U.S. Army on the ammunition industrial base is well documented. See "Franz's Efforts Backstop Contract Award" on the Joint Program Executive Office for Armaments & Ammunition, Jan. 21, 2016. Also see agenda for an Oct. 2017 meeting of the National Defense Industrial Association: www.ndia.org/-/media/sites/ndia/meetings-and-events/divisions/munitions-technology/proceedings/final-icap-108-hilton-nj-16-apr-18-distro-a.ashx.

93 McKinsey has also worked with: See U.S. DOD contract award numbers N001789D8088 and N0017819F8088.

93 In 2019, the navy awarded: "McKinsey Wins $15M for Six Months' Work to Lower F-35 Costs," Defense-Aerospace.com, Feb. 11, 2019, www.defense-aerospace.com.

94 McKinsey even set up: "不同寻常的入党礼物" (Unusual gift for joining the party), *People's Daily Online,* June 1, 2016.

94 "in each case on the grounds": George David Smith, John T. Seaman Jr., and Morgan Witzel, *A History of the Firm* (New York: McKinsey, 2011), 347.

95 Meanwhile, to master Chinese: Author attended an intensive Chinese-language program at Tsinghua University in 1998–1999 with three McKinsey-bound students.

95 McKinsey consultants were there: Kayser, telephone interview by author, July 8, 2021.

96 "The genie of freedom": Excerpts, speech by President Bill Clinton at the Paul H. Nitze School of Advanced International Studies, *New York Times,* March 9, 2000.

96 So they set up talks: Kayser, telephone interview.

97 McKinsey took on Ping An: For details on McKinsey's early work with Ping An, see Smith, Seaman, and Witzel, *History of the Firm,* 389–91. Telephone interview with Beijing-based former McKinsey consultant who requested anonymity to share client information, Sept. 3, 2018.

97 The Ping An IPO: Liu's hiring by McKinsey was detailed by the authors in "Turning Tyranny into a Client," *New York Times,* Dec. 16, 2018. The wealth of Premier Wen's family was the subject of a 2012 Pulitzer Prize–winning article by David Barboza, "Billions Amassed in the Shadows by the Family of China's Premier," *New York Times,* Oct. 26, 2012. In 2021, a firsthand account by the then husband of the Wen family's business partner in acquiring the Ping An shares corroborated Barboza's article. See Desmond Shum, *Red Roulette: An Insider's Story of Wealth, Power, Corruption, and Vengeance in Today's China* (New York: Scribner, 2021).

97 The fact that Premier Wen's son-in-law: The connections were even deeper. Yu Jianming, a business partner of Wen Jiabao's son, Winston Wen, was an alum of the firm.

98 From starting out: Smith, Seaman, and Witzel, *History of the Firm,* 348.

98 Davis's tart reply: Ibid., 435.

98 For multinational companies: David Barboza, "China Passes Japan as Second-Largest Economy," *New York Times,* Aug. 16, 2010.

99 Local governments and Beijing ministries: For Shanghai work, see Zhang Lulu, "Foreign Consulting Firms in China," on the China.org website, posted Feb. 19, 2014. Davis agreement with MOFCOM, see "3月20日，易小准副部长在京会见麦肯锡公司总裁戴颐安" (March 20, Vice-Minister Yi Xiaojun meets McKinsey president Ian Davis in Beijing), posted March 21, 2009, on the ministry's website.

99 That same year: Barton spoke about this work at a 2016 panel at the Council on Foreign Relations in New York. See www.cfr.org.

99 One former McKinsey consultant: Telephone interview with former Beijing-based McKinsey consultant who requested anonymity, Aug. 9, 2021.

99 The ruse fooled: See "隐身'十二五'背后的'洋外脑'：章鱼麦肯锡" (The "foreign brain" behind the stealth "twelfth five-year plan": Octopus McKinsey), *China Economic Weekly,* Nov. 10, 2010, www.chinanews.com.

100 "nobody was man enough": "Leaked Speech Shows Xi Jinping's Opposition to Reform," *China Digital Times,* Jan. 27, 2013.

101 "adhering to party leadership": See CCTV report from the Communist Party's meeting with SOEs, Oct. 10–11, 2016, in Beijing, tv.cctv.com/2016/10/11/VIDEvVXA50DJio6WTkuNjUKv161011.shtml.

101 "These roads cannot be those": Michel Rose, "China's New 'Silk Road' Cannot Be One-Way, France's Macron Says," Reuters, Jan. 8, 2018.

101 McKinsey took a different view: Barton's speech is available in Chinese, but he delivered it in English, so his remarks at the forum are not in quotation marks, but rather paraphrased. For his public comments about the Belt and Road Initiative not being a threat, see "专访麦肯锡董事长鲍达民：建议设立'一带一路'风险防范机制" (Exclusive interview with McKinsey chairman Dominic Barton: Proposal to establish a "Belt and Road" risk prevention mechanism), Yicai, April 9, 2015.

101 McKinsey convened senior government officials: See discussion between McKinsey senior partner Zhang Haimeng and Chinese officials (in Chinese) on McKinsey China's website: "'一带一路'圆桌论坛：倾听一线的声音" ("One Belt One Road" roundtable forum: Listening to the voice of the front line), posted Aug. 10, 2015. Comment from the China Development Bank's Cao Honghui.

101 "The world is waiting": For Barton's comments on BRI (Chinese), see "多赢的'一带一路'：让梦想化作现实" (Multi-win "One Belt One Road": Turning dreams into reality), posted on the McKinsey China website, May 27, 2015.

102 In a slide presentation: McKinsey slide presentation: "East Coast Rail Line." Slide 7 focuses on how the rail line can boost ties with China. Slide 17 focuses on financing.

102 In 2016, China Communications Construction: Rozanna Latiff and Joseph Sipalan, "Malaysia Had Plan to Use Chinese Money to Bail Out 1MDB, Court Hears," Reuters, Sept. 4, 2019.

102 McKinsey said that its role: See McKinsey statement on *New York Times* article, Dec. 16, 2018, www.mckinsey.com/about-us/media/statement-on-new-york-times-article.

102 For McKinsey, touting the Belt and Road: Figures on top BRI contractors compiled by Washington-based RWR Advisory Group as of Aug. 2021.

103 In March 2021 the Biden administration: See U.S. Trade Representative, *2021 National Trade Estimate Report on Foreign Trade Barriers,* 96, ustr.gov.

103 people like Chen Guang: Information from Chen Guang's LinkedIn profile.

103 In December 2017, Chen spoke: See "集团领导力专项培训在深圳举行" (Group leadership training held in Shenzhen), China Merchants Group statement, www.cmhk.com.

104 McKinsey took part in a 2018: For details on the conference, including McKinsey's involvement, see *Hexun News,* m.hexun.com/news/2018-08-15/193787173.html; McKinsey featured Sha Sha's remarks on its website. See "打开智慧城市2.0时代的想象空间" (Open up the range of imagination for Smart Cities 2.0 era), posted on the McKinsey China website, June 21, 2019; Ping An's work with McKinsey is detailed in "平安智慧城市，新旅程新机遇" (Ping An's smart cities: New journeys, new opportunities), posted on the Sohu.com website, Sept. 7, 2018, www.sohu.com.

104 A report issued by a U.S. congressional panel: Katherine Atha et al., "China's Smart Cities Development" (research report prepared on behalf of the U.S.-China Economic and Security Review Commission, Jan. 2020), 2, www.uscc.gov.

104 "virtual cage": Christopher Buckley and Paul Mozur, "How China Uses High-Tech Surveillance to Subdue Minorities," *New York Times,* May 23, 2019.

105 Usually corporate retreats: Bogdanich and Forsythe, "Turning Tyranny into a Client."

105 Days before the McKinsey Xinjiang gathering: See letter from the Committee on the Elimination of Racial Discrimination concluding observations on the combined fourteenth to seventeenth periodic reports of China (including Hong Kong, China, and Macao, China), Aug. 30, 2018, 7–8. For more on how the mass detention system evolved, see Megha Rajagopalan, Alison Killing, and Christo Buschek, "Built to Last," *BuzzFeed News,* Aug. 27, 2020. Part of a series of stories on Xinjiang that won the Pulitzer Prize in 2021.

105 "a climate of terror": "China Cuts Uighur Births with IUDs, Abortion, Sterilization," Associated Press, June 29, 2020.

105 A March 2021 U.S. State Department: See *2020 Country Reports on Human Rights Practices: China,* U.S. State Department, www.state.gov.

106 Peter Walker, the former McKinsey senior partner: See Walker's website, peterbwalker.com, where he is described as an expert on U.S.-China issues.

106 Walker told Tucker Carlson: To view Walker's interview with Tucker Carlson, which aired on April 24, 2020, see video.foxnews.com/v/6151714336001#sp=show-clips.

106 In response to the *Times* account: McKinsey statement, Dec. 16, 2018.

107 "Kevin Sneader is based in Hong Kong": Interview with McKinsey consultant who requested anonymity, July 1, 2020.

107 In a June 2020 letter: Rubio to Sneader, June 17, 2020.

107 Rubio's office said that McKinsey: A spokesman at Rubio's office confirmed on July 14, 2021, that McKinsey did not give the office any information about its China clients.

108 McKinsey was invited: "省国资委邀请麦肯锡咨询公司与部分省属企业开展战略规划编制交流工作" (The provincial SASAC invited McKinsey Consulting Co. to carry out strategic planning and work with some provincial enterprises), Sohu.com, June 30, 2020.

108 Also on the list: Shenhua merged with another company and as of 2021 is part of China Energy Investment Corporation (国家能源投资集团).

108 In the wake of reporting: See "Client Selection" on McKinsey's website, www.mckinsey.com.

6. Guarding the Gates of Hades

110 Rayburn House Office Building: Hearing on Oversight of Tobacco Products, House of Representatives Committee on Energy and Commerce, Subcommittee on Health and the Environment, 113th Congress, April 15, 1994. Testimony came from seven tobacco industry executives: Donald S. Johnston, chief executive of American Tobacco Company; Thomas Sandefur Jr., chief executive of Brown and Williamson Tobacco Company; Edward A. Horrigan Jr., chief executive of Liggett Group Inc.; Andrew H. Tisch, chief executive of Lorillard Tobacco Company; Joseph Taddeo, president of United States Tobacco Company; James W. Johnston, chief executive of R. J. Reynolds; and William I. Campbell, chief executive of Philip Morris. The industry leaders testified that they did not believe cigarettes were addictive.

110 The hearing followed new revelations: David A. Kessler (commissioner of Food and Drug Administration) to Coalition on Smoking or Health, Feb. 25, 1994.

111 High-nicotine tobacco plants: Testimony of David A. Kessler, commissioner of Food and Drug Administration, Subcommittee on Health and the Environment, June 21, 1994.

111 "to be able to control": Amended Final Opinion, U.S. District Judge Gladys Kessler, Aug. 17, 2006, Civil Action No. 99-2496, *United States of America and Tobacco-Free Kids Action Fund, American Cancer Society, American Health Association, American Lung Association, Americans for Nonsmokers' Rights, and National African American Tobacco Prevention Network v. Philip Morris USA Inc. et al., defendants,* 383 (hereafter cited as Judge Gladys Kessler's ruling).

111 "Think of the cigarette pack": William L. Dunn Jr., Motives and Incentives in Cigarette Smoking, R107, 1972, Philip Morris Records, Master Settlement Agreement, Truth Tobacco Industry Documents, hosted by the University of California, San Francisco, library. Available at www.industrydocuments.ucsf.edu (hereafter cited as UCSF tobacco archives).

111 filing a $10 billion lawsuit: *Philip Morris Co., v. American Broadcasting Co.,* 36VA Circuit, Richmond, Va. (1994) LX-816-3.

111 their landmark investigation of nicotine manipulation: "Smoke Screen," *Day One,* ABC News, Feb. 28, 1994, John Martin, correspondent, Walt Bogdanich, producer.

111 "played to a deep popular anger": Allan M. Brandt, *The Cigarette Century: The Rise, Fall, and Deadly Persistence of the Product That Defined America* (New York: Basic Books, 2007), 368.

111 largest civil litigation settlement in U.S. history: The Master Settlement Agreement between forty-six states and four major tobacco companies, Nov. 23, 1998, provided for payouts of $206 billion over twenty-five years, among other concessions. Available at publichealthlawcenter.org.

111 "The hearing ushered in": "Getting Answers on Drug Prices," *New York Times,* Feb. 25, 2019.

111 two major books totaling fourteen hundred pages: Richard Kluger, *Ashes to Ashes: America's Hundred-Year Cigarette War, the Public Health, and the Unabashed Triumph of Philip Morris* (New York: Alfred A. Knopf, 1996); and Brandt, *Cigarette Century.* Kluger won the 1997 Pulitzer Prize for General Nonfiction.

112 "I'll tell you why": Transcript, Berkshire Hathaway annual meeting, May 5, 1997.

112 fourteen million pages of industry documents: UCSF tobacco archives.

112 Among McKinsey's recommendations: "Planning Facilities for Profitable Growth Philip Morris, Incorporated 56100," report by McKinsey & Company, Oct. 11, 1956, UCSF tobacco archives.

112 McKinsey produced another report: "Plan of Organization Research Division," chart recommending Philip Morris restructuring, McKinsey & Company, Aug. 19, 1957.

112 By the mid-1950s: The landmark study that opened the floodgates was published in 1950. Ernest L. Wynder and Evarts A. Graham, "Tobacco Smoking as a Possible Etiologic Factor in Bronchiogenic Carcinoma: A Study of Six Hundred and Eighty-Four Proved Cases," *Journal of the American Medical Association,* May 27, 1950. Many more would follow.

113 "I think continuous attempts": Andrew C. Britton memo regarding "Five Year Research Program—McKinsey Report," March 21, 1957, UCSF tobacco archives.

113 Any lingering doubts about the safety: Terry's news conference on Jan. 11, 1964, announced the findings of the U.S. Public Health Service in *Smoking and Health: Report of the Advisory Committee to the Surgeon General of the Public Health Service* (Washington, D.C.: U.S. Department of Health, Education, and Welfare, 1964).

113 Recognizing the impact: National Library of Medicine Profiles, Reports of the Surgeon General, National Library of Medicine.

113 In 1985, McKinsey wrote: "Building Competitive Advantage in Key Channels," confidential memo from McKinsey & Company to William Campbell (executive vice president of marketing, Philip Morris) and Vincent Buccellato (vice president of sales, Philip Morris), UCSF tobacco archives.

114 "the merchandising and display programs": Ibid., 4.

114 The firm added two senior partners: Ibid., 13.

114 "We crunched the numbers": LeDoux, interview by author.

115 "We put client interests": "Developing RJR's Program to Build a Sustainable Competitive Position," McKinsey discussion with RJR executive management team, March 27, 2003, UCSF tobacco archives.

115 "All too often in the choice": U.S. District Judge H. Lee Sarokin order and opinion, Feb. 6, 1992, in *Susan Haines v. Liggett Group Inc.,* Civil Action 84-678, District of New Jersey, 140 F.R.D. 681, 683 (D.N.J. 1992).

115 In 1990 a *Fortune* magazine survey: Faye Rice et al., "Leaders of the Most Admired," *Fortune,* Jan. 29, 1990.

116 "What do you think smokers would do": Brandt, *Cigarette Century,* 430.

116 "renowned for their ability": Andrew H. Tisch memo to staff announcing that Lorillard had retained McKinsey, June 16, 1993, UCSF tobacco archives.

116 "Newport is a whole new bag": Stephanie Saul, "A Flavoring Seen as a Means of Marketing to Blacks," *New York Times,* May 13, 2008.

117 "Offshoring parts of products": "Developing RJR's Program to Build a Sustainable Competitive Position," 36.

117 Joe Camel: Stuart Elliott, "Camel's Success and Controversy," *New York Times,* Dec. 12, 1991.

117 "trendy 20s in urban areas": "Developing RJR's Program to Build a Sustainable Competitive Position."

117 In Germany, where RJR's Camel: "Building RJR International's Position and Capabilities in Germany," McKinsey memo to RJR International, Jan. 7, 1993, UCSF tobacco archives.

118 first global public health treaty: During the 1990s, the World Health Organization began global strategies for tobacco control, which ultimately became effective in 2005, as described in Ruth Roemer, Allyn Taylor, and Jean Lariviere, "Origins of the WHO Framework Convention on Tobacco Control," *American Journal of Public Health* 95, no. 6 (2005): 936–38.

118 even Kissinger Associates: Project Cerberus: Regaining the Initiative Working Session Kickoff, Jan. 10, 1999, at Grosvenor House featured speakers from Kissinger Associates, UCSF tobacco archives.

118 McKinsey helped organize strategy sessions: McKinsey developed a work plan for a meeting the week of Jan. 11, 2000, according to a McKinsey document on that date, UCSF tobacco archives.

119 "This lesson is particularly important": Hadii M. Mamudu, Ross Hammond, and Stanton A. Glantz, "Project Cerberus: Tobacco Industry Strategy to Create an Alternative to the Framework Convention on Tobacco Control," *American Journal of Public Health* 98, no. 9 (2008): 1630–42.

119 RICO: Marc Lacey, "Tobacco Industry Accused of Fraud in Lawsuit by U.S.," *New York Times,* Sept. 23, 1999.

119 In August 2006: Judge Gladys Kessler's ruling.

119 "marketed and sold their lethal product": Ibid., 4.

119 "Defendants have known many of these facts": Ibid.

120 As of 2019, McKinsey's tobacco clients: Internal McKinsey records show the following people worked on the Altria account: Ford Halbardier, Brandon Brown, Ignacio Felix, Travis Reaves, Matt Deimund, Jonathan McClain, Jeffrey Salazar, Megan Pacchia, Brian Henstorf, and Robert Levin. The records did not indicate what they did for Altria.

120 $30 million in 2018 and 2019: McKinsey records.

120 "We have served the FDA": Food and Drug Administration records.

120 "risk identification and mitigation": Ibid.

121 The percentage of young smokers: Teresa W. Wang et al., "Tobacco Product Use and Associated Factors Among Middle and High School Students—United States, 2019," *MMWR Surveillance Summaries* 68, no. 12 (2019): 1–22.

121 President Obama sought to build: Jeff Zeleny, "Occasional Smoker, 47, Signs Tobacco Bill," *New York Times,* June 22, 2009.

122 It was called Juul: For a more detailed account of Juul's history, there are two excellent books on the topic: Lauren Etter, *The Devil's Playbook: Big Tobacco, Juul, and the Addiction of a New Generation* (New York: Crown, 2021); and Jamie Ducharme, *Big Vape: The Incendiary Rise of Juul* (New York: Henry Holt, 2021).

123 "Other schools across the country": Sheila Kaplan, "Juul Targeted Schools and Youth Camps, House Panel on Vaping Claims," *New York Times,* July 25, 2019.

123 "Losing precious market share": Testimony of Senator Richard J. Durbin, Democrat of Illinois, before the House Committee on Oversight and Reform, Subcommittee on Economic and Consumer Policy, *Examining JUUL's Role in the Youth Nicotine Epidemic: Part 1,* July 24, 2019 (hereafter cited as Durbin testimony).

123 roster of Juul employees: Spreadsheet, compiled by Walt Bogdanich's investigative reporting class at Columbia University Graduate School of Journalism.

123 "JUUL's massive nicotine content": Written testimony of Dr. Jonathan P. Winickoff on behalf of the American Academy of Pediatrics, before the House Committee on Oversight and Reform, Subcommittee on Economic and Consumer Policy, *Examining JUUL's Role in the Youth Nicotine Epidemic,* July 24, 2019.

123 "More than 20 percent of children": Durbin testimony.

124 In 2013, two years before Juul: The letter to Margaret Hamburg, the commissioner of the Food and Drug Administration, was sent April 16, 2013, by five Senate Democrats: Richard J. Durbin of Illinois, Frank Lautenberg of New Jersey, Richard Blumenthal of Connecticut, Sherrod Brown of Ohio, and Jack Reed of Rhode Island.

124 "Pediatricians are reporting": American Academy of Pediatrics, news release, Jan. 2, 2020.

124 "full-blown catastrophe": Joshua M. Sharfstein, "Why the FDA Was Unable to

Prevent a Crisis of Vaping Among Kids," *Stat,* Nov. 21, 2019.

124 "delaying commonsense regulation": Durbin testimony.

125 "In dozens of interviews": Katie Thomas and Sheila Kaplan, "E-cigarettes Went Unchecked in 10 Years of Federal Inaction," *New York Times,* Nov. 1, 2019.

125 By the end of 2017: FDA statistics.

125 5.4 million in 2019: Wang et al., "Tobacco Product Use and Associated Factors Among Middle and High School Students—United States, 2019."

125 Not a single Juul device: Mitch Zeller, director, Center for Tobacco Products, testimony before the House Committee on Oversight and Reform, Subcommittee on Economic and Consumer Policy, *Examining JUUL's Role in the Youth Nicotine Epidemic: Part 1,* July 24, 2019.

125 Juul's sales of e-cigarettes: Thomas and Kaplan, "E-cigarettes Went Unchecked in 10 Years of Federal Inaction."

125 Juul and the tobacco giant Altria: "Juul Labs, Marketing, Sales Practices and Products Liability Litigation," Case No. 19-md-2913-WHO. Alfonso Pulido, McKinsey senior partner in a deposition marked "Highly Confidential."

126 In less than two years of work: Ibid.

126 the marijuana market: Pulido deposition. Pulido said the flavor name survey was done to inform Juul's "youth prevention activity as well as introduce a specific set of flavors to the market."

126 "Oh my God, McKinsey": Author interview with McKinsey employee who asked not to be identified.

126 "awareness of youth use": Pulido deposition.

127 In a wrongful-termination lawsuit: *Siddharth Breja v. Juul Labs,* civil action number 3:19-cv-07148-WHO, U.S. District Court of Northern California.

127 "split between mission and money": Author interview.

127 Chui did not single out: Chui did not respond to LinkedIn messages.

128 Foundation for a Smoke-Free World: On Sept. 28, 2021, the World Health Organization issued a statement on the organization, saying, "When it comes to the Foundation for a Smoke-Free World, there are a number of clear conflicts of interest involved with a tobacco company funding a purported health foundation, particularly if it promotes sales of tobacco and other products found in that company's brand portfolio. WHO will not partner with the Foundation. Governments should not partner with the Foundation and the public health community should follow this lead."

128 $8.4 million: Internal Revenue Service Form 990 filed by Foundation for a Smoke-Free World, 2017 and 2018.

128 $400,000 went to McKinsey: Internal Revenue Service Form 990, Foundation for a Smoke-Free World, 2017.

128 "does not match the picture": Tess Legg et al. correspondence, "The Philip Morris–Funded Foundation for a Smoke-Free World: Tax Return Sheds Light on Funding Activities," *Lancet* 393, no. 10190 (2019): 2487.

128 "curiosity, creativity and innovation": Food and Drug Administration records obtained by the authors.

129 Two months later, he backed off: Annie Karni, Maggie Haberman, and Sheila Kaplan, "Trump Retreats from Flavor Ban for E-cigarettes," [illegible] 2019.

129 Altria said it had devalued: Katie Robertson, "Juul's Meltdown Cost Tobacco Giant Altria $4.5 Billion," *New York Times,* Nov. 20, 2019.

129 Trump reversed himself again: Abby Goodnough, "With Partial Flavor Ban, Trump Splits the Difference on Vaping," *New York Times,* Jan. 2, 2020.

129 Addiction researchers criticized: R. J. Wickham, "How Menthol Alters Tobacco-Smoking Behavior: A Biological Perspective," *Yale Journal of Biology and Medicine* 88, no. 3 (2015): 279–87. See also Shakir Alsharari et al., "Effects of Menthol on Nicotine Pharmacokinetic, Pharmacology and Dependence in Mice," *PloS One* 10, no. 9

(2015), doi:10.1371/journal.pone.0137070.

129 "The idea that menthol": American Academy of Pediatrics statement on June 2, 2020, criticizing President Trump's decision not to ban menthol.

7. Turbocharging Opioid Sales

130 McKinsey planned to stimulate interest: Martin E. Elling et al., "Making More of Pharma's Sales Force: Pharmaceutical Companies Have Lost Their Focus on Doctors. The Key to Higher Sales Is Regaining It," *McKinsey Quarterly,* no. 3 (2002).

131 McKinsey assembled a formidable team: The two medical doctors were Pasha Sarraf, who holds an MD and a PhD from Harvard, and Arnab Ghatak, who holds an MD and MBA from the University of Pennsylvania.

131 In the end, the casualties included: Michael Forsythe and Walt Bogdanich, "McKinsey Settles for Nearly $600 Million over Role in Opioid Crisis," *New York Times,* July 20, 2021.

131 Purdue filed for bankruptcy: Jan Hoffman and Mary Williams Walsh, "Purdue Pharma, Maker of OxyContin, Files for Bankruptcy," *New York Times,* Sept. 15, 2019.

132 the 750,000 people who died in an epidemic: "Understanding the Epidemic," Centers for Disease Control and Prevention, National Center for Injury Prevention and Control. Available at www.cdc.gov.

132 Upwards of five thousand physicians: Art Van Zee, "The Promotion and Marketing of Oxycontin: Commercial Triumph, Public Health Tragedy," *American Journal of Public Health* 99, no. 2 (2009): 221–27, doi .org/10.2105/AJPH.2007.131714.

132 "From a sales perspective": Beth Macy, *Dopesick: Dealers, Doctors, and the Drug Company That Addicted America* (New York: Little, Brown, 2018), 31.

132 The U.S. attorney in Maine: Testimony of Jay P. McCloskey, U.S. Attorney, Maine, before the Committee on the Judiciary, U.S. Senate, "Evaluating the Propriety and Adequacy of the OxyContin Criminal Settlement," July 31, 2007.

133 editor he knew at *The New York Times:* The editor was Walt Bogdanich.

133 The editor asked a reporter: Francis X. Clines and Barry Meier, "Cancer Painkillers Pose New Abuse Threat," *New York Times,* Feb. 2, 2001.

133 "used money, job offers": Barry Meier, *Pain Killer: An Empire of Deceit and the Origin of America's Opioid Epidemic* (New York: Random House, 2018), 140.

133 forty-five hundred projects: McKinsey & Company, "About This Practice," www .mckinsey.com.

133 McKinsey had already been advising: Walt Bogdanich, "McKinsey Advised Johnson & Johnson on Increasing Opioid Sales," *New York Times,* July 25, 2019.

133 In PowerPoint slides: Ibid. McKinsey said its work for Johnson & Johnson "was designed to support the legal use of a patch that was then widely understood to be less susceptible to abuse."

134 "embarking on a cunning": Closing statement of Mike Hunter, attorney general of Oklahoma, in the state's case against Johnson & Johnson, CJ-2017-816, District Court of Cleveland County, Oklahoma.

134 "false, misleading, and dangerous": Jan Hoffman, "Johnson & Johnson Ordered to Pay $572 Million in Landmark Opioid Trial," *New York Times,* Aug. 26, 2019. (The penalty was later revised to $465 million by the Oklahoma district judge Thad Balkman.)

134 The Oklahoma Supreme Court: Jan Hoffman, "Oklahoma's Top Court Throws Out $465 Million Opioid Ruling Against J&J," *New York Times,* Nov. 10, 2021.

134 J&J through its corporate "credo": Johnson & Johnson's credo can be viewed in full on its web page: www.jnj.com.

134 The company's legal team: Meier, *Pain Killer,* 183.

134 "grossly overstate the safety profile":

"FDA Warns OxyContin Maker over Ads," Associated Press, Jan. 22, 2003.
135 Their union merited a breezy article: Weddings/Celebrations, "Anu Gupta and Arnab Ghatak," *New York Times,* Nov. 27, 2005.
136 "We believe that government officials": Macy, *Dopesick,* 70.
136 "an incendiary catalog of corporate malfeasance": Patrick Radden Keefe, *Empire of Pain: The Secret History of the Sackler Dynasty* (New York: Doubleday, 2021), 273.
136 So in June 2009: First Amended Complaint, *Commonwealth of Massachusetts v. Purdue Pharma,* Civil Action No. 1884-cv-01808, Suffolk Superior Court, Jan. 31, 2019, 249.
136 Purdue decided to reformulate OxyContin: Reuters, "Harder to Break OxyContin Pill Wins Approval," *New York Times,* April 5, 2010.
137 "had a very good FDA rehearsal": Document 2012-1, Maria Gordian, email to McKinsey colleagues Rob Rosiello and Martin Elling, U.S. Bankruptcy Court for the Southern District of New York, Purdue Pharma Case No. 19-23649-RDD, filed Nov. 18, 2020.
137 "The real problem with opioids": Matthew Perrone, "Revamped OxyContin Was Supposed to Reduce Abuse, but Has It?," Associated Press, July 24, 2015.
137 One suggestion was to promote: *Massachusetts v. Purdue Pharma,* First Amended Complaint, Jan. 31, 2019, 97.
138 "They have the greatest sales rep access": Memo from McKinsey & Company to John Stewart and Russell Gasdia (Purdue Pharma), July 13, 2013, cited in affidavit of Jenny Wojewoda, assistant attorney general, in *Commonwealth of Massachusetts v. Purdue Pharma,* Exhibit 4 (hereafter cited as Wojewoda affidavit).
138 "Despite a national decline": Ibid.
138 At a Fort Wayne pain clinic: Complaint in *United States of America v. $67,906.43 in U.S. Currency et al.,* case 2:16-cv-362-JEM, filed Aug. 11, 2016, by U.S. Attorney David A. Capp in Hammond, Ind. Capp's office sought to seize cash, gold, and guns received by Cozzi as payment for controlled substances. The U.S. magistrate judge John E. Martin ordered the items forfeited to the federal government on Aug. 13, 2019. By that time, Cozzi was deceased—killed in a tractor accident in 2018.
138 The sales boom benefited: Complaint in *State of Indiana v. Purdue Pharma,* No. 49D01-1811-PL-045447, Circuit Court for Marion County, Indiana, Nov. 14, 2018, 16.
139 "knew the identities, practices": Ibid., 10.
139 They did ride-alongs with sales reps: McKinsey memo to Purdue, July 18, 2013, cited in complaint, *Commonwealth of Massachusetts v. McKinsey & Company Inc.,* No. 21-0258H, Suffolk Superior Court, Feb. 4, 2021.
139 "Lastly our work builds upon": McKinsey & Company memo cited in exhibit 4 to Wojewoda affidavit.
140 "The retail channel": Ibid.
140 "to loosen up": Michael Forsythe and Walt Bogdanich, "McKinsey Advised Purdue Pharma to 'Turbocharge' Opioid Sales, Lawsuit Says," *New York Times,* Feb. 1, 2019.
140 The most audacious recommendation: Maura Healey, Massachusetts Attorney General, press release, Feb. 4, 2021, www.mass.gov/news/ags-office-secures-573-million-settlement-with-mckinsey-for-turbocharging-opioid-sales-and.
140 "turbocharge" Purdue's sales engine: Forsythe and Bogdanich, "McKinsey Advised Purdue Pharma to 'Turbocharge' Opioid Sales, Lawsuit Says."
141 "Arnie, some venting": Purdue Pharma bankruptcy case, document number 2012-2, 24.
141 "FYI . . . think it is just stress": Ibid., 23.
141 "The findings were crystal clear": Ibid., 32.
141 $2.6 million consulting contract: This book's authors discovered this contract.

141 targeting the heaviest prescribers: Purdue Pharma bankruptcy case, document 2012-2, 17.

141 using patient advocacy groups: Forsythe and Bogdanich, "McKinsey Advised Purdue Pharma to 'Turbocharge' Opioid Sales, Lawsuit Says."

142 "Evolve to Excellence": Wojewoda affidavit, 13.

142 McKinsey made a suggestion: Walt Bogdanich and Michael Forsythe, "McKinsey Proposed Paying Pharmacy Companies Rebates for OxyContin Overdoses," *New York Times,* Nov. 27, 2020.

142 As the decade came to a close: McKinsey statement, www.mckinseyopioidfacts.com.

142 400,000 Americans had died: CDC numbers, representing overdoses between 1999 and 2018, www.cdc.gov/drugoverdose/epidemic/index.html.

142 "an unstable and challenging situation": Purdue Pharma bankruptcy case, document 2012-1, 48–49.

142 Doubtful she'd put that on her résumé now: Gordian left McKinsey to work for a competitor, Bain & Company.

143 "It probably makes sense": Bogdanich and Forsythe, "McKinsey Proposed Paying Pharmacy Companies Rebates for OxyContin Overdoses."

143 "Indeed, while our past work": Confidential memo from Sneader to McKinsey colleagues, Feb. 4, 2021.

143 A McKinsey lawyer said: Jeff Overley, "McKinsey Opioid MDL Has a Need for Speed, Judge Say," *Law 360 Legal News,* July 29, 2021.

143 In 2018, Tom Latkovic: Sarun Charumilind et al., "Why We Need Bolder Action to Combat the Opioid Epidemic," McKinsey & Company, Sept. 6, 2018.

144 "with known or potential risk factors": Sarun Charumilind, Elena Mendez-Escobar, and Tom Latkovic, "Ten Insights on the US Opioid Crisis from Claims Data Analysis," McKinsey & Company, June 5, 2018.

144 Gary Mendell: Franklin Crawford, "Man on a Mission," *Cornell Alumni Magazine,* Sept./Oct. 2017.

144 For years no one at McKinsey dared: Latkovic did not respond to requests for comment.

144 Purdue is not solely to blame: Purdue was dissolved as a company as a result of bankruptcy proceedings. Jan Hoffman, "Purdue Pharma Is Dissolved and Sacklers Pay $4.5 Billion to Settle Opioid Claims," *New York Times,* Sept. 1, 2021.

144 "We didn't get ahead of it": Jayne O'Donnell, "FDA Chief Supports Opioid Prescription Limits, Regrets Agency's Prior Inaction," *USA Today,* Oct. 23, 2019.

144 The FDA official who led: Dr. Andrew Kolodny (senior scientist at Brandeis and an addiction expert who has testified before multiple government committees), interview by author.

145 "that placed the financial interests": Emails with author.

145 A *New York Times* headline: Abby Goodnough and Margo Sanger-Katz, "As Tens of Thousands Died, F.D.A. Failed to Police Opioids," *New York Times,* Dec. 30, 2019.

145 "the design of the program": James Heyward et al., "Evaluation of the Extended-Release/Long-Acting Opioid Prescribing Risk Evaluation and Mitigation Strategy Program by the US Food and Drug Administration: A Review," *JAMA Internal Medicine* 180, no. 2 (2020). Alexander was also a paid expert in litigation against opioid manufacturers and distributors.

145 the agency's extensive contracts with McKinsey: Author analysis of USAspending.gov.

145 "It is a very obvious conflict": Kolodny, interview by author.

145 a bipartisan group of six senators: Senators Margaret Wood Hassan (Democrat of New Hampshire), Charles Grassley (Republican of Iowa), Sheldon Whitehouse (Democrat of Rhode Island), Joe Manchin III (Democrat of West Virginia), and Edward J. Markey and Elizabeth Warren (Democrats of Massachusetts), to Janet Woodcock (acting commissioner, U.S. Food and Drug Administration), Aug. 23, 2021.

146 influential health-care official, Alex Azar: Chris Hamby, Walt Bogdanich, Michael Forsythe, and Jennifer Valentino-DeVries, "McKinsey Opened a Door in Its Firewall Between Pharma Clients and Regulators," *New York Times,* April 13, 2022.

147 *Deaths of Despair:* Anne Case and Angus Deaton, *Deaths of Despair and the Future of Capitalism* (Princeton, N.J.: Princeton University Press, 2020).

147 "We all but load the weapons": Atul Gawande, "The Blight: How Our Economy Has Created an Epidemic of Despair," *New Yorker,* March 23, 2020.

148 Healey was the first attorney general: Danny Hakim, Roni Caryn Rabin, and William K. Rashbaum, "Lawsuits Lay Bare Sackler Family's Role in Opioid Crisis," *New York Times,* April 1, 2019.

148 Healey called the governor's decision: Matt Stout, "Maura Healey Attacks Charles Baker for Contracts with McKinsey in Wake of Opioid Settlement: 'It's Outrageous,'" *Boston Globe,* March 25, 2021.

8. "Turning a Coal Mine into a Diamond"

150 "can generate ideas capable": ExxonMobil, "Five Big Ideas from the Aspen Ideas Festival," press release, July 9, 2019.

150 He quickly pivoted to the topic: "This Is Not Rocket Science: Rutger Bregman Tells Davos to Talk About Tax—Video," *Guardian,* Jan. 29, 2019. The 2020 World Economic Forum at Davos took place before the global onset of COVID-19.

150 In June 2019: For a description of the McKinsey partners speaking at Aspen, see "A Festival of Ideas, Shaped by McKinsey Insight" on the McKinsey website, posted July 31, 2019, www.mckinsey.com.

151 "We are not on the right path": Quotations in this section from Pinner, Tett, and Waldeck are taken from a video of their Aspen panel posted by McKinsey, in Dickon Pinner, "Dispatch: Climate Breaking Points at the Aspen Ideas Festival," McKinsey.com, July 30, 2019.

151 The world was running out of time: Five of the six biggest fires California had seen until that point occurred in 2020, with a massive fire in 2021 then taking second place. See the state's list of top fires at www.fire.ca.gov. For more on the Russian fires of 2021, see "Russia's 2021 Wildfires Now Largest in Its Recorded History," *Moscow Times,* Sept. 7, 2021. One point seven million hectares is 170,000 square kilometers. Tunisia, by comparison, is 163,610 square kilometers.

151 With warmer air: Details on the 2021 New York storms and the record rainfall at "Flooding from Ida Kills Dozens of People in Four States," *New York Times,* Sept. 2, 2021. Also see Olivia Rosane, "Greenland's Ice Sheet Has Reached 'Point of No Return,'" *EcoWatch,* Aug. 17, 2020.

152 McKinsey even calculates its own: From McKinsey's website under the topic "Sustainability." In 2018 McKinsey's emissions were 743 $ktCO_2e$ (kilotons of carbon dioxide equivalent).

152 "As a firm, we take seriously": McKinsey Code of Conduct, www.mckinsey.com.

152 Those McKinsey reports don't downplay the crisis: "GHG Emissions and Climate Change," McKinsey discussion document, March 2019.

153 "You are the caretaker": Pilita Clark, "The Job Interview of the Future Is Already Here," *Financial Times,* Dec. 15, 2018.

153 Pinner and his colleagues argued: "Climate Math: What a 1.5-Degree Pathway Would Take," *McKinsey Quarterly,* April 30, 2020.

153 "Our challenge to our clients": Naina Dhingra, Robin Nutall, and Matt Stone, "Embedding Purpose: Fewer Slogans, More Action," post on McKinsey's Strategy & Corporate Finance blog, Aug. 28, 2019.

154 "the Aspen Consensus": Anand Giridharadas, "The Thriving World, the Wilting World, and You" (speech, Aspen Institute's Action Forum, July 29, 2015), posted on Medium.com.

155 ExxonMobil said it was "all the buzz": See "Five Big Ideas from the Aspen Ideas Festival," on the ExxonMobil website, published July 9, 2019. ExxonMobil has been talking about the potential of carbon capture and storage since at least 2008. That year the company started a project to capture carbon dioxide at a natural gas plant in Wyoming. See Josie Garthwaite, "Exxon to Spend $170M on Carbon Capture, Storage Technology," *New York Times,* Dec. 29, 2008.

155 Months before he spoke: Kevin Crowley and Akshat Rathi, "Exxon's Plan for Surging Carbon Emissions Revealed in Leaked Documents," *Bloomberg Green,* Oct. 5, 2020.

155 Edstrom fits the profile: Biographical material on Edstrom comes from his public LinkedIn profile and his autobiography.

155 "If a millennium of the dead could speak": Erik Edstrom, *Un-American: A Soldier's Reckoning of Our Longest War* (New York: Bloomsbury, 2020).

156 Mobil Oil was McKinsey's first megaclient: George David Smith, John T. Seaman Jr., and Morgan Witzel, *A History of the Firm* (New York: McKinsey, 2011), 127–98.

157 Although Edstrom had hoped: Either Australia or Indonesia is, depending on the year and which organization is doing the measuring, the world's biggest coal exporter. For per capita carbon emissions, see the website of the Union of Concerned Scientists, "Each Country's Share of CO_2 Emissions," updated Aug. 12, 2020.

157 "one of the most profitable projects": Taken from multiple interviews with Edstrom after he left McKinsey and his July 2019 departure email from McKinsey.

158 McKinsey says it is working: Figures on McKinsey's work with clean energy companies and big polluters come from internal records and interviews with current and former McKinsey employees.

158 "They can't invent billable hours": Shahinian, interview by author, June 29, 2018.

158 Australia is one of the few: A new coal mine in the Galilee Basin was set to begin exporting coal in late 2021. See Nickolas Zakharia, "Bravus Breaks First Coal Milestone at Carmichael," *Australian Mining,* June 25, 2021.

159 "It was dying out incredibly fast": Screenshot of text message from Edstrom.

160 "Fuck you, I won't do what you tell me": Lyrics from "Killing in the Name," by Rage Against the Machine. Released in 1992.

160 The following year: McKinsey's comment on being "more thoughtful" about its choices of corporate retreats in "Statement on New York Times Article on McKinsey Work in Southeast Asia, China, Eastern Europe, and the Middle East," Dec. 16, 2018, www.mckinsey.com. Account of the Australian Values Day based on interviews and emails with Edstrom.

162 McKinsey consultants were enabling: One megaton is 1,000 kilotons. Big coal mines supply enough coal to put *gigatons* (1 million kilotons) of carbon dioxide into the atmosphere over their lifetimes. A gigaton is about the weight of three Empire State Buildings. For example, some of the proposed mines in Wyoming's Powder River Basin have estimated lifetime CO_2 emissions of more than 2 gigatons. See www.nwf.org. The Empire State Building weighs about 331 million metric tons.

162 In the hours after he sent: Responses to Edstrom's July 18, 2019, farewell email provided by Edstrom.

162 Since 2010, McKinsey has worked: See the Climate Accountability Institute's Carbon Majors Report, updated in 2020. The number of top polluters McKinsey has worked for is compiled from internal records, open-source material available on the internet (particularly in China), and interviews with current and former McKinsey consultants.

163 In 2019, energy-related emissions: International Energy Agency, "Global CO_2 Emissions in 2019," Feb. 11, 2020.

163 Other top McKinsey fossil fuel clients:

List of companies from McKinsey internal records.

163 If McKinsey was advising: Details on McKinsey's work with Chevron from McKinsey internal records.

163 In July 2020, just as the global pandemic: Kevin Crowley and Bryan Gruley, "Chevron's Answer to Climate Change Is to Keep Drilling for Oil," *Bloomberg Businessweek,* Aug. 13, 2020.

164 Teck, one of the world's biggest exporters: For the size of Teck compared with other steelmaking coal exporters, see "Teck: Fact Sheet: Steelmaking Coal." For Teck Resources' "Scope 3" emissions in 2019, see Teck Resources, "Climate Change and Energy Use," 59. Canada emitted 730 megatons of CO_2 in 2019. See Environment and Climate Change Canada, "National Inventory Report 1990–2019: Greenhouse Gas Sources and Sinks in Canada: Executive Summary," 1.

165 Scientists say the runoff: Chloe Williams, "From Canadian Coal Mines, Toxic Pollution That Knows No Borders," *Yale Environment 360,* April 1, 2019.

165 In 2019, McKinsey: Details on McKinsey's work with Teck from internal McKinsey records.

165 China's sovereign wealth fund: Quan Chong, who rose to a vice-ministerial post in China's trade ministry, is a director as of Oct. 2021. It is highly unusual for former Chinese government officials to serve on boards of North American companies. In Chinese, his last name comes first, so he is Chong Quan. See www.teck.com. Teck announced on Sept. 4, 2019, that Barton was stepping down. Barton, via Canadian government press officers, was asked to comment on his role at Teck. He didn't respond. In a statement sent on Oct. 25, 2021, Teck's spokesman Chris Stannell said, "Teck is committed to supporting global action on climate change and we are taking action to reduce our GHG emissions, including setting the goal of being carbon neutral across our operations by 2050."

166 In China, McKinsey was advising: Chinese clients derived from internal McKinsey records and Chinese-language announcements by the client companies. See the CNOOC 2019 Annual Report (Chinese language edition), 12.

166 One of the firm's major clients: See Banpu, "Sustainability Report, 2018," 15.

166 American coal exports: For U.S. coal export figures, see www.eia.gov.

167 Among 465 people responding: Internal survey seen by the authors. The survey might have also included some former McKinsey consultants as well as some prospective hires.

167 "The climate crisis is the defining issue": Open letter dated March 23, 2021, seen by the authors.

168 "Without senior partners from the Middle East": Readout of conference call provided to authors by a former McKinsey employee.

168 Two weeks after the letter came out: Email from Sneader and Sternfels, Subject: "Climate Action at McKinsey," April 5, 2021.

168 on June 30, a massive fire: The all-time high temperature in Las Vegas is 117 degrees Fahrenheit.

168 An Asian power company was planning: Email from Praveen, Subject: "EPC Contractors for Building a Coal Power Plant," July 26, 2021.

169 "Just reading our own publishing": Email from Naveed to colleagues, Subject: "Goodbye, and a call to action on our posture towards client emissions," July 30, 2021.

169 "Companies can't go from brown to green": Sternfels was issuing a rebuttal to the *New York Times* article in the opinion section of *The Wall Street Journal.* Bob Sternfels, "Why McKinsey & Co. Does Business with Greenhouse-Gas Emitters," *Wall Street Journal,* Oct. 27, 2021. He was responding to this article: Michael Forsythe and Walt Bogdanich, "At McKinsey, Widespread Furor over Work with Planet's Biggest Polluters," *New York Times,* Oct. 27, 2021.

170 "It's a long-term terrible idea": Bales,

interview by author, May 14, 2018, at his residence on Park Avenue in New York City.

9. Toxic Debt

172 "I'm obsessed with this issue": Jeffrey Toobin, "The Senator and the Street," *New Yorker,* July 26, 2010.

172 Home prices in the hottest markets: Martin Crutsinger, "Existing Home Sales Plunge in 2006," Associated Press, Jan. 25, 2007.

172 Goldman Sachs bankers were scrambling: Bethany McLean and Joe Nocera, *All the Devils Are Here* (New York: Portfolio/Penguin, 2010), 274–76.

172 Schumer, as a New York senator: See Toobin, "The Senator and the Street."

173 McKinsey veterans occupied top positions: Ian Lowitt, the CFO of Lehman when it collapsed, was a Rhodes scholar and a McKinsey veteran; James P. Gorman, the CEO of Morgan Stanley who was co-president during the financial crisis, was a former McKinsey senior partner; Peter Wuffli, a former McKinsey partner, was CEO of UBS until mid-2007.

173 The firm concluded that Europe: McKinsey & Company, *Sustaining New York's and the US' Global Financial Services Leadership,* Jan. 2007, 13, graphics8.nytimes.com/images/2008/12/12/business/SchumerBloomberg.pdf.

174 In its early years: George David Smith, John T. Seaman Jr., and Morgan Witzel, *A History of the Firm* (New York: McKinsey, 2011), 30. To this day, McKinsey, as well as its rivals Bain and BCG, draw in big fees writing "due diligence" reports—basically kicking the tires of investment or takeover targets for securities firms, venture capitalists, and private equity firms.

174 Big New York City lenders: Phillip L. Zweig, *Wriston: Walter Wriston, Citibank, and the Rise and Fall of American Financial Supremacy* (New York: Crown, 1995), 133.

174 bankers operated on the 3-6-3 rule: For an explanation, see John R. Walter, "The 3-6-3 Rule: An Urban Myth?," *Economic Quarterly* (Winter 2006): 51–78.

175 In 1980, the highest-paid banker: In 1980, Anderson passed Citibank's Walter Wriston for the top spot with his $710,440 pay package. See *American Banker,* "Banking as a Career," UPI Archives, May 28, 1981.

175 made $35 million: Sridhar Natarajan, "Goldman Sachs CEO David Solomon's Pay Rockets to $35 Million," Bloomberg News, Jan. 28, 2022.

175 "You don't have the guts": Zweig, *Wriston,* 244.

175 On Christmas Eve 1968: Ibid., 245.

175 The system was called "matrix management": Ibid., 249.

176 In 1972, Citibank: Ibid., 365.

176 Wriston fired McKinsey: Smith, Seaman, and Witzel, *History of the Firm,* 113.

177 Continental Illinois was once the largest bank: Continental's work with McKinsey and the bank's history come in large part from an account of the bank's rise and collapse by one of its former officers, James P. McCollom. See James P. McCollom, *The Continental Affair* (New York: Dodd, Mead, 1987). The history of the bank under Cummings begins on page 28.

177 "The McKinsey people seemed a little wistful": Ibid., 185.

177 By January 1977 the bank: See Phillip Zweig, *Belly Up: The Collapse of the Penn Square Bank* (New York: Crown, 1985), 75.

177 *Dun's Review* lauded Continental: Federal Deposit Insurance Corporation, *History of the Eighties—Lessons for the Future* (Washington, D.C.: Federal Deposit Insurance Corporation, 1997), 1:237.

178 Until McKinsey's matrix changed his life: Zweig, *Belly Up,* 73.

178 Owing to its small size: Ibid., 72.

178 It was the biggest bank failure: "Failure of Continental Illinois," Federal Reserve History website, www.federalreservehistory.org.

179 Lytle got three and a half years in prison: Allan Johnson and John Gorman, "Ex–Bank Executives Get Prison Terms," *Chicago Tribune,* Aug. 31, 1988, 1.

179 McKinsey's banking work earned the ire: Gillian G. H. Garcia, "Failing Prompt Corrective Action," *Journal of Banking Regulation,* June 9, 2010.

179 "the modish but quite obviously": Thomas J. Peters and Robert H. Waterman Jr., *In Search of Excellence: Lessons from America's Best-Run Companies* (New York: HarperCollins Ebooks), 49.

179 "McKinsey had sold us matrix management": McCollom, *Continental Affair,* 233.

179 It was one of the safest jobs: Michael Quint, "A Bank Expert's Plan for Change," *New York Times,* Aug. 22, 1990.

180 Bryan regarded McKinsey's banking work: Smith, Seaman, and Witzel, *History of the Firm,* 189.

180 "I was just shocked": Oral interview with Bryan in 1997 cited in ibid.

180 When he was hired, the firm's banking practice: Smith, Seaman, and Witzel, *History of the Firm,* 302.

180 "There was a growing sense of frustration": Ibid., 268.

180 To make a McKinsey career more attractive: Ibid., 269–73.

181 "They were on a highway": Feiger, interview by telephone with author, Dec. 4, 2020.

181 "We can't just be a Firm": Smith, Seaman, and Witzel, *History of the Firm,* 277.

182 In 1968, Fannie Mae: For a very readable discussion of the origins of the mortgage-backed securities market, read chapter 1 of McLean and Nocera, *All the Devils Are Here.*

182 "to improve McKinsey's ability": Lowell L. Bryan, *Breaking Up the Bank* (Homewood, Ill.: Dow Jones–Irwin, 1988), xiii.

183 The *Journal of Applied Corporate Finance* devoted: *Journal of Applied Corporate Finance* 1, no. 3 (Fall 1988). The journal was published by Continental Bank, which at the time was government supported following the Fed's 1984 rescue.

183 "Securitization's potential": Bryan cited in Bethany McLean and Peter Elkind, *The Smartest Guys in the Room: The Amazing Rise and Scandalous Fall of Enron* (New York: Portfolio, 2003), 66–67.

183 These credit guarantees: Bryan, *Breaking Up the Bank,* 72.

183 "In the securitized credit process": Ibid., 87.

184 "Over time this will lead": James A. Rosenthal and Juan M. Ocampo, *Securitization of Credit: Inside the New Technology of Finance* (New York: Wiley, 1988), 227.

184 Bryan acknowledged that securitization: Bryan, *Breaking Up the Bank,* 87.

184 "Back in the '80s and '90s": Kravitt, telephone interview by author, Nov. 19, 2020.

184 "The McKinsey book helped": Mark Pittman, "Evil Wall Street Exports Boomed with 'Fools' Born to Buy Debt," Bloomberg News, Oct. 27, 2008.

185 "We helped them get": Feiger, interview by author, Dec. 4, 2020.

185 "The largest banks in the world": Interview with former McKinsey partner who spoke on condition of anonymity, Nov. 16, 2020.

185 "informational in nature": Board of Governors of the Federal Reserve System, *An Introduction to Asset Securitization* (Washington, D.C.: Federal Reserve System, Supervision and Regulation, Task Force on Securitization, 1990), vol. 1 of 2. Quotation is on page 1 of the bibliography.

185 "given advice to industrial companies": George M. Feiger, "Why a Bank or Building Society Should Want to Securitise Its Assets," paper delivered at "The Market in Asset-Backed Securities," a conference organized by the *Financial Times* in London, June 19–20, 1991.

186 "displace completely the classic banking system": Bryan, *Breaking Up the Bank,* 65.

186 "The longer we at McKinsey": Ibid., 66.

186 Bryan's core bank idea: Restructuring of Banking Industry, House hearing, June 18, 1991, www.c-span.org/video/?18461-1/restructuring-banking-industry.

186 The measure was defeated: Roll call vote for H.R. 6, Nov. 4, 1991.

186 "Going forward, loan securitization": Lowell Bryan and Diana Farrell, *Market Unbound: Unleashing Global Capitalism* (New York: Wiley, 1996), 67.
187 Skilling had been "deeply influenced": McLean and Elkind, *Smartest Guys in the Room,* 66.
187 Between 2001 and 2008 more than $27 trillion: Securitization figures in Pittman, "Evil Wall Street Exports Boomed with 'Fools' Born to Buy Debt."
188 Weeks after Schumer and Bloomberg: New Century Financial said in early March 2007 that it was the subject of federal probes and filed for Chapter 11 bankruptcy protection on April 2, 2007. See Julie Creswell and Vikas Bajaj, "Home Lender Is Seeking Bankruptcy," *New York Times,* April 3, 2007.
188 "In theory, securitization should serve": Timothy Geithner and Lawrence Summers, "The Case for Regulatory Reform," *Washington Post,* June 15, 2009.
188 $22 trillion in losses: This includes $13 trillion in lost output and $9.1 trillion in asset depreciation. Of course, the rise in asset values in the recovery from the financial crisis and in the years following needs to be considered. See "Financial Regulatory Reform: Financial Crisis Losses and Potential Impacts of the Dodd-Frank Act," Government Accountability Office, Jan. 2013.
189 *The New York Times* revisited some of the people: Ben Casselman, Patricia Cohen, and Doris Burke, "The Great Recession Knocked Them Down. Only Some Got Up Again," *New York Times,* Sept. 12, 2018.
189 "Securitization was based on the premise": Pittman, "Evil Wall Street Exports Boomed with 'Fools' Born to Buy Debt."
189 "If you look at securitization": Conversation between Professor Richard Rumelt and Lowell Bryan in "Weighing the US Government's Response to the Crisis: A Dialogue," *McKinsey Quarterly,* June 2009.
190 "What you're dealing with": Feiger, phone interview by author, Dec. 4, 2020.
190 "It's a powerful technology": Pittman, "Evil Wall Street Exports Boomed with 'Fools' Born to Buy Debt." Pittman died in 2009.

10. Allstate's Secret Slides

191 The Allstate adjuster on the case, Mary Greene: Jeff Bauer (one of Aldridge's attorneys), telephone interview by author, Jan. 10, 2020.
191 "I really thought my life was over": Aldridge, telephone interview by author, Jan. 27, 2020.
192 Only then did his lawyers: Bauer, interview.
192 Allstate had run up more than $7 million: Associated Press, "Allstate Settles Dispute on Claims Documents," *Chicago Tribune,* July 12, 2008, sec. 2, 3.
192 Manners later said he had never seen: Manners, interview by author, Dec. 31, 2019.
192 Berardinelli had learned of the slides: David J. Berardinelli, *From Good Hands to Boxing Gloves* (Portland, Ore.: Trial Guides, 2008), 6.
193 "a kind of holy grail": Joe Lombe, "Allstate Won't Produce Records Despite $25,000-a-Day Fine," *Kansas City Star,* Dec. 20, 2007, accessed on the North Carolina Trial Law Blog.
193 "They were willing to wait": Berardinelli, *From Good Hands to Boxing Gloves,* 13. Berardinelli died in 2018.
193 "If Allstate is willing to pay": Florida Insurance Commissioner Kevin McCarty, press release, Jan. 16, 2008, floir.com/PressReleases/viewmediarelease.aspx?ID=1630.
193 "You're in good hands": Mae Anderson, "53 Years Later, Still in Good Hands," *Adweek,* Feb. 3, 2003.
194 That changed in 1995: "Sears Formally Spins Off Allstate," *Chicago Tribune,* July 1, 1995.
194 As a new publicly listed company: Financialized economy is commonly defined as finance supplanting industry in economic importance.
194 "It worked. It paid off": Manners, interview.

194 "false and misleading": Email from Nicholas Nottoli, Allstate spokesman, Feb. 15, 2022.
195 "We were told at this meeting": Maureen Reed, sworn deposition given in Bernalillo County, New Mexico, April 12, 2003.
195 "More people without representation": Maureen Reed, sworn statement, April 12, 2003.
195 The "claims man" was an honorable: Jay M. Feinman, *Delay, Deny, Defend: Why Insurance Companies Don't Pay Claims and What You Can Do About It* (New York: Portfolio, 2010), 68.
196 "Insurance is the great protector": Ibid., 3.
196 In the 1980s the senior partner Peter Walker: Interview with former McKinsey partner, Dec. 16, 2019.
196 In 2018 the property and casualty industry: National Association of Insurance Commissioners, "U.S. Property and Casualty Insurance Industry: 2018 Full Year Results."
197 "After years of squeezing": "Factory and Firm: The Future of Claims Handling," McKinsey & Company.
197 "It has been common knowledge": Stephen Strzelec, affidavit, Aug. 4, 2008.
197 "The claims process was just evil": Interview with former McKinsey partner who requested anonymity to speak freely, Dec. 16, 2019.
198 The pay of Allstate's top five executives: Allstate proxy statement, March 28, 1997, www.allstateinvestors.com.
198 In 2020 the top five executives made: 2020 Allstate executive compensation from the salary.com website: www1.salary.com/ALLSTATE-CORP-Executive-Salaries.html; 2019 Allstate average salary from pay scale.com: www.payscale.com/research/US/Employer=Allstate_Insurance_Company/Salary.
198 In 1987, Allstate paid out 70.9 cents: J. Robert Hunter, "The 'Good Hands' Company or a Leader in Anti-consumer Practices? Excessive Prices and Poor Claims Practices at the Allstate Corporation," Consumer Federation of America, July 18, 2007, 11.
198 "The use of these products": J. Robert Hunter, testimony before the Senate Committee on the Judiciary, Regarding the McCarran-Ferguson Act, March 7, 2007.
199 had fallen by 10 percent: Slide presentation given by Liddy at 2006 investment conference.
199 Liddy shared in that wealth: Becky Yerak, "Allstate Outlines CEO Pay Package," *Chicago Tribune,* April 3, 2007.
199 "So much of this is driven": Roberts, interview by author, Aug. 26, 2019.
199 "simplistic and invalid": Email from Nicholas Nottoli, Allstate spokesman, Feb. 15, 2022.
200 "Delay, deny, defend violates the rules": Feinman, *Delay, Deny, Defend,* 5.
200 Shannon Brady Kmatz comes from an Allstate family: Brady, interview by author, Aug. 26, 2019. She prefers to use Brady, her last name when she worked at Allstate.
201 Brady, who became an expert witness: Shannon Brady, sworn statement, State of New Mexico, County of Bernalillo, 2003.
201 "Some people choose to hire an attorney": Feinman, *Delay, Deny, Defend,* 89.
202 "If you knew they were living paycheck to paycheck": Brady, interview.
[illegible] Romano, one of the people: Romano, telephone interview by author, Oct. 28, 2019.
203 "did not identify institutional issues": Email from Nicholas Nottoli, Allstate spokesman, Feb. 15, 2022.
203 Aldridge won his own settlement: *Deer v. Aldridge* is provided in this summary of a related case on the Leagle website: www.leagle.com/decision/inksco20100416250.

11. "The Enron Astros"

204 the sellout crowd of forty-one thousand: *Baseball Reference.*
204 Under this philosophy: Bethany McLean and Peter Elkind, *The Smartest Guys in the Room: The Amazing Rise and*

Scandalous Fall of Enron (New York: Portfolio/Penguin, 2013), 32.

205 seventh-largest publicly traded corporation: Associated Press, "Enron's Founder Oversaw Company's Rise and Collapse," *New York Times*, July 5, 2006.

205 the venerable Arthur Andersen: Jeffrey Zaslow, "How the Former Staff at Arthur Andersen Is Faring Two Years After Its Collapse," *Wall Street Journal*, April 8, 2004.

205 Enron employees lost their retirement: Richard A. Oppel Jr., "Employees' Retirement Plan Is a Victim as Enron Tumbles," *New York Times*, Nov. 2, 2001.

205 "The smartest guys in *the clubhouse*": David Roth, "The Smartest Guys in the Clubhouse," *New Republic*, Dec. 3, 2019.

206 "Other companies hired business gurus": Paul Krugman, "Death by Guru," *New York Times*, Dec. 18, 2001.

206 dispatched McKinsey's lawyer: George David Smith, John T. Seaman Jr., and Morgan Witzel, *A History of the Firm* (New York: McKinsey, 2011), 418.

206 One McKinsey consultant: McLean and Elkind, *Smartest Guys in the Room*, 32.

206 "the dawning age of industry deregulation": Smith, Seaman, and Witzel, *History of the Firm*, 416.

206 Before long, Enron: Ibid., 417.

207 McKinsey's Houston office became: Duff McDonald, *The Firm: The Story of McKinsey and Its Secret Influence on American Business* (New York: Simon & Schuster, 2013), 239.

207 "year in and year out": Smith, Seaman, and Witzel, *History of the Firm*, 417.

207 tens of millions of dollars: Author's conclusion after reviewing McKinsey quarterly reports, books written by McKinsey consultants, and McKinsey's policy of not disclosing client payments.

207 "purported successes and ingenuity": Smith, Seaman, and Witzel, *History of the Firm*, 508.

207 Skilling had been enamored: McLean and Elkind, *Smartest Guys in the Room*, 66–67.

207 "That is why I was contacted": Fastow, interview by author over LinkedIn messaging, Nov. 11, 2020.

207 Fastow helped Skilling's unit: McLean and Elkind, *Smartest Guys in the Room*, 67.

208 "ECT was able to hedge itself": Lowell Bryan et al., *Race for the World: Strategies to Build a Great Global Firm* (Boston: Harvard Business School Press, 1999), 292.

208 "on a web of fraudulent partnerships": Associated Press, "Enron's Founder Oversaw Company's Rise and Collapse."

209 "McKinsey didn't just cash the checks": McDonald, *Firm*, 242.

209 a book called *Moneyball:* Michael Lewis, *Moneyball: The Art of Winning an Unfair Game* (New York: Norton, 2003).

209 sports and gambling: For years the major sports leagues fought New Jersey's efforts to allow sports betting, claiming they would suffer "irreparable harm" if sports books opened in Atlantic City. But after the U.S. Supreme Court cleared the way for states outside Nevada to legalize sports betting, sports teams and their leagues have begun partnering with those same sports books, as ESPN's David Purdum reported on Nov. 1, 2018.

210 almost $40 million: Figures cited in this paragraph are based on records and author interviews.

210 "frontline empowerment": Confidential sources.

210 "a strategic advisor to seven of the ten": McKinsey biography.

210 Knowing whether certain players: Neither McKinsey nor QuantumBlack has been accused of passing inside information to gamblers.

211 In September 2013, players: Mike Vaccaro, "James Dolan Dishes on Knicks, Rangers, and Isiah," *New York Post*, Nov. 22, 2013.

211 "I wouldn't have a problem": Mike Vorkunov, " 'It Was Crazy': How a Famous Consulting Firm Contributed to the Chaos of the 2013–14 Knicks," *Athletic*, Nov. 25, 2019.

212 During his five years at McKinsey: Internal records obtained by the author.

213 engineer for Lockheed: Jake Kaplan, "Known as Astros Science Guy, Sig Mejdal to Experiment with Role as Minor League Coach," *Texas Sports Nation,* March 13, 2017.

213 "You are going to need database": "Analytically Speaking: Conversations with Thought Leaders," www.youtube.com/watch?v=p3HqSMhY46Q.

213 "We can use it to ensure": McKinsey podcast, May 15, 2017.

214 Luhnow told the interviewer: "How the Houston Astros Are Winning Through Advanced Analytics," *McKinsey Quarterly,* June 2018.

214 "We often measure asymmetries": "Astros GM Jeff Luhnow Explains How Data Analytics Helped Houston Win the World Series," *Wharton Stories,* March 29, 2018.

215 "There was a banging from the dugout": Ken Rosenthal and Evan Drellich, "The Astros Stole Signs Electronically in 2017," *Athletic,* Nov. 12, 2019.

216 "the moment the analytics movement": Dave Sheinin, "Astros World Series Win May Be Remembered as the Moment Analytics Conquered MLB for Good," *Washington Post,* Nov. 2, 2019.

216 "I was looking at his credentials": Knott, interview by author.

217 Houston tried it again: Author interview.

217 Not one to make excuses: Author interview with two clubhouse sources.

217 What he meant: Knott, interview.

217 "We know you are cheating": Author interview.

217 "No, I don't buy that": Hoynes, interview by author.

218 "We were playing defense": Bob Nightengale, "MLB Clears Astros of Cheating," *USA Today,* Oct. 17, 2018.

218 "One thing in specific": Ken Rosenthal and Evan Drellich, "Astros Executive Asked Scouts for Help Stealing Signs and Suggested Using Cameras, Email Shows," *Athletic,* Nov. 16, 2019.

218 "Thank God we got Osuna": Stephanie Apstein, "Astros Staffer's Outburst at Female Reporters Illustrates MLB's Forgive and Forget Attitude Toward Domestic Violence," *Sports Illustrated,* Oct. 21, 2018.

218 "Luhnow . . . rammed it through regardless": Ben Lindbergh and Travis Sawchik, *The MVP Machine: How Baseball's New Nonconformists Are Using Data to Build Better Players* (New York: Basic Books, 2019), 196.

219 "there is both documentary": Robert D. Manfred Jr., "Statement of the Commissioner," Jan. 13, 2020. Luhnow filed suit in Texas against the Astros alleging that he was made the scapegoat for the actions of others. Once again he denied knowing anything about the sign-stealing scheme. The lawsuit was dismissed after both sides resolved their differences.

220 "My general sense was": Mejdal, interview by author.

220 "Contempt for the Astros": Jeff Passan, "Inside the Astros Culture That Bred Brandon Taubman's Comments," ESPN, Oct. 25, 2019.

221 "It's sad for baseball": Marc Carig, "Mike Trout Uncharacteristically Takes Aim at Astros, Rob Manfred," *Athletic,* Feb. 17, 2020.

221 "Baseball has lost its soul": Tom Verducci, "Baseball's Fight to Reclaim Its Soul," *Sports Illustrated,* March 4, 2020.

221 undertook a "full-scale" review: Eric Fisher, "Changes Expected at MLB," *Street and Smith's Sports Business Journal,* Nov. 13, 2017.

12. "Clubbing Seals"

223 Shaped by an elite boarding school: "Vision Statement" brochure from the Lawrence School, Sanawar, Solan District, Himachal Pradesh, India. Sagar's LinkedIn biography indicates that he attended the school from 1977 to 1986.

223 As if to prove fealty: "Sanawar School Boys Become the Youngest Team to Scale Mount Everest," *India Today,* May 21, 2013.

223 He ran. He swam. He cycled: Sagar's

trustee biography on the Capital Kids Cricket website.

223 quick to hug almost anyone: Author interviews with McKinsey colleagues.

223 One evening after a long: Goodson, interview by author.

223 first as a partner, then as a senior partner: Sagar's LinkedIn.

223 at least $1 million a year: Interviews with current and former McKinsey partners.

224 He joined the Johannesburg office: Ibid.

224 "When am I going to get my Porsche?": Author interview with McKinsey consultant recalling what he heard.

224 UN trade embargo: Philip I. Levy, "Sanctions on South Africa: What Did They Do?," Yale University Economic Growth Center, Feb. 1999.

224 Three years before the stain of apartheid: George David Smith, John T. Seaman Jr., and Morgan Witzel, *A History of the Firm* (New York: McKinsey, 2011), 338, 339.

224 The firm ultimately declined: Ibid.

224 Fine, a white native South African: Fine's biography, McKinsey & Company website.

224 South Africa's rebirth: Smith, Seaman, and Witzel, *History of the Firm,* 339.

224 Nelson Mandela's political party: Saki Macozoma, "The ANC and the Transformation of South Africa," *Brown Journal of World Affairs* (Winter 1994).

225 pro bono in the city budget office: Martin Tolchin, "City Paid $75-Million in 1969 in Fees to Private Consultants," *New York Times,* July 1, 1970.

225 New York responded by halting: Martin Tolchin, "Beame Withholds Fee to Consultant; Questioning Ethics," *New York Times,* July 3, 1970.

225 No charges were filed: Michael C. Jensen, "McKinsey & Co.: Big Brother to Big Business," *New York Times,* May 30, 1971.

225 eventually resumed payments: Smith, Seaman, and Witzel, *History of the Firm,* 184.

225 "If you want to be relevant": One of the sixteen author interviews with partners or former partners who worked in South Africa or had ties to that country.

225 Party operatives were siphoning vast sums: Aodhan Beirne, "Corruption in South Africa: A Guide to Our Recent Reporting," *New York Times,* Dec. 22, 2018.

225 "I did not join the struggle": Martin Williams, "Mantashe Misses the Point, Rich People Can Steal," *Citizen,* Jan. 10, 2018. That is, $10 million in 2021 U.S. dollars.

225 Bell Pottinger, one of London's: Ed Caesar, "The Reputation-Laundering Firm That Ruined Its Own Reputation," *New Yorker,* June 18, 2018.

225 "white monopoly capital": Andrew Cave, "Deal That Undid Bell Pottinger: Inside Story of the South Africa Scandal," *Guardian,* Sept. 5, 2017.

225 The giant German software firm: Alexander Winning, "Exclusive: South Africa Tries to Recover $23 Million from SAP for 'Unlawful' Contracts," Reuters, August 7, 2020.

226 disembowel the state tax agency: Jeanette Chabalala, "Ntsebeza Inquiry: Claims That KPMG 'Rogue Unit' Report Was Cut-and-Paste Job," *News24,* June 27, 2018.

226 fire the finance minister: Joseph Cotterill, "KPMG South Africa Executives Dismissed over Gupta Scandal," *Financial Times,* Sept. 15, 2017.

226 McKinsey entered the fray: Statement of David Fine to the Parliamentary Monitoring Group, Eskom Corporate Governance Inquiry, Nov. 11, 2017, 3 (hereafter cited as Eskom Inquiry).

226 To consult for a state-owned enterprise: South African National Treasury, "Code of Good Practice for Black Economic Empowerment in Public-Private Partnerships."

226 Transnet employed 60,000 workers: Statement of Fine to Eskom Inquiry, Nov. 11, 2017, 3.

226 And the port city of Durban: Ibid., 3–5.

226 McKinsey's first Transnet subcontractor: Ibid., 5.

226 McKinsey now had to find another:

Simon Mantell, "BEE Inadvertently Became 'Prime Enabler of State Capture and Corruption in South Africa,'" *Daily Maverick,* April 3, 2019.

226 Instead, the firm mistakenly treated: Statement of David Fine to the Portfolio Committee on Public Enterprises, Nov. 15, 2017, 15.

227 McKinsey hire Regiments Capital: Statement of Fine to Eskom Inquiry, Nov. 11, 2017, 6–7.

227 To improve Transnet's services, McKinsey assembled: Ibid., 3.

227 A few colleagues called him: Interviews with current and former McKinsey partners.

227 The rail agency had rehired: "Gama Reinstated to Transnet Executive Committee," *Mail & Guardian,* Feb. 23, 2011.

227 And Jürgen Schrempp: Transnet Inquiry Reference Book, published by Commission of Inquiry into State Capture, 10.

227 was "totally inappropriate": Jürgen Schrempp's Letter of Resignation to Malusi Gigaba, Minister of Public Enterprises, Feb. 17, 2011.

227 A Gupta-owned newspaper: Testimony of Popo Simon Molefe to Commission of Inquiry into State Capture, May 7, 2019, 15.

227 Since arriving in South Africa: "The Guptas and Their Links to South Africa's Jacob Zuma," BBC, Feb. 14, 2018.

228 "in luxury vehicles": Lydia Polgreen, "South Africa Is Outraged by a Shortcut to a Wedding," *New York Times,* May 3, 2013.

228 The Guptas invited prominent: Testimony of David Fine to the Eskom Inquiry, Nov. 15, 2017.

228 McKinsey executives insisted: Statement of Fine to Eskom Inquiry, Nov. 11, 2017, 10.

228 "We are worried that we are": Matuma Letsoalo, "Cosatu Raises Red Flag on Guptas," *Mail & Guardian,* Feb. 25, 2011.

228 A couple of weeks later: Sam Sole, "Going off the Rails?," *Mail & Guardian,* March 4, 2011.

228 Unconcerned, McKinsey took on: Statement of Fine to Eskom Inquiry, Nov. 11, 2017, 4.

228 Rather than invest in infrastructure: Ibid.

228 1,064 locomotives: Ibid., 14.

229 "was steeped in corruption": Pieter-Louis Myburgh, "Come on Baby, Do the Locomotion," *Daily Maverick,* July 23, 2019.

229 $2.6 billion: Statement of Fine to Eskom Inquiry, Nov. 11, 2017, 14. Figure converted from rand into U.S. dollars.

229 Uncomfortable with the short deadline: Ibid., 15. McKinsey withdrew in Feb. 2014. The contracts were awarded the next month. Transnet blamed the higher price on an accelerated production schedule and the decision to split the contract among four different companies.

229 Fine said the higher payments: Statement of Fine to Eskom Inquiry, Nov. 11, 2017, 247–48.

229 "I've never heard that the price": Author interview.

229 The firm had overestimated: Lameez Omarjee, "Excessive Costs for 1064 Locomotive Contract Not Justifiable, Says Acting Transnet CEO," *New24,* May 15, 2019.

229 Its new assignment: Susan Comrie, "The McKinsey Dossier, Part 5—How Transnet Cash Stuffed Gupta Letterboxes," amaBhungane, Oct. 23, 2017.

229 "There is an extraordinary succession": Matthew Chaskalson, Testimony of David Fine to Commission of Inquiry into State Capture, Dec. 10, 2020, 143.

230 Questions were raised: Matthew Chaskalson, Testimony of Jean-Christophe Mieszala to Commission of Inquiry into State Capture, Dec. 10, 2020, 148.

230 An early hire: Internal McKinsey records.

230 While at the firm, he got to know Sagar: Ibid. Safroadu Yeboah-Amankwah of McKinsey said in a statement that the firm learned of Sagar's help in writing Gama's MBA thesis in July 2017. McKinsey said that it "found no link between the support of any work awarded to McKinsey" and that Gama contends he received help only with language.

230 McKinsey immediately recognized: Statement of Safroadu Yeboah-Amankwah to Commission of Inquiry into State Capture, April 8, 2019, 9.

230 Sagar had cultivated relationships: Interview with senior partner.

230 He had prepped for his job: Sagar's career time line described on his LinkedIn page.

231 "The only time Vikas": Mosilo Mothepu, *Uncaptured* (Cape Town: Penguin Books, 2021).

231 Sagar, by dint of his personality: Interviews with McKinsey colleagues.

231 $700 million: "The McKinsey Dossier Part 1—How McKinsey and Trillian Ripped R1.6bn from Eskom," amaBhungane and Scorpio, Sept. 14, 2017. The figure is converted using the 2017 rand into U.S. dollars rate.

231 income gap: The World Bank Gini index. Measured according to the ranked Gini coefficients assigned to each country.

231 youth unemployment topping 50 percent: The World Bank.

231 In the first half of 2015: Statement of Yeboah-Amankwah to Commission of Inquiry into State Capture, April 8, 2019, 12.

231 Eskom fired a thousand workers: "About 1,000 Workers at S. Africa's Eskom's Medupi Fired—Eskom," Reuters, March 26, 2015.

232 Eskom's credit rating to junk: Wendell Roelf, "South Africa's Eskom Chairman Under Fire as Power Crisis Deepens," Reuters, March 25, 2015.

232 The previous year a major boiler: Ted Blom of the Organisation Undoing Tax Abuse, "Unplugging Corruption at Eskom," submitted to the Parliamentary Monitoring Group, Oct. 18, 2017.

232 Desperate to right the ship: "Transnet CEO Brian Molefe Now Acting CEO of Eskom," *News24,* April 17, 2015.

232 Alexander Weiss, had advised Eskom: Statement of Alexander Weiss to Commission of Inquiry into State Capture, 2.

232 Weiss's credentials included: Weiss's biography on the McKinsey & Company website.

232 Although he lived in Berlin: Statement of Weiss to Commission of Inquiry into State Capture, 2.

232 To reach an agreement: Statement of Yeboah-Amankwah to Commission of Inquiry into State Capture, April 8, 2019, 22.

232 McKinsey's glass tower in Sandton: Address provided on McKinsey & Company's website.

232 richest square mile: "The History of Africa's Richest Square Mile," *Sun International,* Oct. 26, 2014.

233 "could destroy" the firm: Anita Raghavan, *The Billionaire's Apprentice: The Rise of the Indian-American Elite and the Fall of the Galleon Hedge Fund* (New York: Grand Central Publishing, 2013).

233 competitors were using it: Paul Solman, "Consulting Fees Based on Results Begin to Challenge Old-Style Bills," *Financial Times,* Nov. 10, 2014.

233 Supporters included two senior partners: Author interviews with current or former McKinsey employees.

233 It wasn't until many months later: McKinsey said it took Eskom's word that permission had been obtained. Statement of Yeboah-Amankwah to Commission of Inquiry into State Capture, April 8, 2019, 25.

233 McKinsey also had to find: Statement of Fine to Eskom Inquiry, Nov. 11, 2017, 8.

233 McKinsey erred again: Statement of Weiss to Commission of Inquiry into State Capture, 10–13.

233 "What was particularly concerning": Ibid., 12.

234 Bianca Goodson, who ran Trillian's management: Goodson, interview.

234 Salim Essa, a Trillian owner: Statement of Yeboah-Amankwah to Commission of Inquiry into State Capture, April 8, 2019, 42.

234 "This was an issue": Testimony of Fine to Eskom Inquiry, Nov. 15, 2017.

234 According to one estimate: Author interview with McKinsey official.

234 "I had asked multiple times": Testimony of Fine to Commission of Inquiry into State Capture, Dec. 10, 2020, 236.

234 The only person Fine knew: Testimony of Fine to Eskom Inquiry, Nov. 15, 2017.

235 He installed a program: Statement of Mieszala to Commission of Inquiry into State Capture, Dec. 10, 2020, 11–12.

235 He also sent Eskom a letter: Ibid., 10. McKinsey said the letter falsely stated that the firm had subcontracted with Trillian.

235 McKinsey informed Eskom in March 2016: Statement of Yeboah-Amankwah to Commission of Inquiry into State Capture, April 8, 2019, 46.

235 But in June, just six months: Eskom Annual Financial Statement, March 31, 2019, 120.

236 "remain a mystery as all parties refuse": Thuli Madonsela, "State of Capture: A Report of the Public Protector," Oct. 14, 2016, 57.

236 Budlender asked to interview McKinsey: Geoff Budlender, "Report on Allegations with Regard to the Trillian Group of Companies, and Related Matters," 33.

236 "McKinsey did not work": Ibid., 35.

236 "As you know," Sagar wrote: Ibid., 36.

236 McKinsey said it would be "inappropriate": Ibid., 37.

237 "I have to say that I find": Ibid., 38.

237 McKinsey had submitted false information: Ibid., 40.

237 Waiting in ambush were investigators: Statement of Mieszala to Commission of Inquiry into State Capture, Dec. 10, 2020, 2.

237 chaired by Raymond Zondo: Executive Committee page of the Commission of Inquiry into State Capture website.

237 "Over two months, amaBhungane has sent": Comrie, "McKinsey Dossier, Part 5."

237 "in creating a veil": Angelique Serrao, "NPA Concludes Eskom Payments to McKinsey and Trillian Were Criminal," *News24,* Jan. 17, 2018.

237 Parliament was already deep into its hearings: Meetings archive of the Public Enterprises National Assembly Committee of the Parliamentary Monitoring Group.

237 "I understand it caused": Testimony of Fine to Eskom Inquiry, Nov. 15, 2017.

238 McKinsey offered a third: Statement of Mieszala to Commission of Inquiry into State Capture, Dec. 10, 2020, 13.

238 Fine was first, answering questions: Testimony of Fine to Eskom Inquiry, Nov. 15, 2017.

238 McKinsey officials offered up Sagar: Statement of Mieszala to Commission of Inquiry into State Capture, Dec. 10, 2020, 11.

238 The firm did not mention: Athandiwe Saba, "Firms Shrug Off Corruption," *Mail & Guardian,* Dec. 8, 2017.

238 The firm also sanctioned his co-leader: Bogdanich and Forsythe, "How McKinsey Lost Its Way in South Africa."

238 Weiss kept his job: Weiss's biography on the McKinsey & Company website.

238 Sagar now runs a software company: Sagar's LinkedIn. Sagar did not respond to messages seeking his comments.

238 The managing partner, Dominic Barton: Bogdanich and Forsythe, "How McKinsey Lost Its Way In South Africa."

238 But another investigation into corruption: "Judicial Commission of Inquiry into Allegations of State Capture (Call for Evidence/Information)," Parliamentary Monitoring Group, June 22, 2018. The number of individuals who gave testimony is from the commission's statistics page.

239 Speaking to a business group: "Speech by Kevin Sneader, Global Managing Partner of McKinsey & Company, at Gordon Institute of Business Science Seminar, 9 July 2018," McKinsey & Company website.

239 Toward the end of 2020: "Media Statement Released at the Chairperson's Instance on Wednesday, 9 December 2020," Commission of Inquiry into State Capture, Dec. 9, 2020.

239 "unlock" the airline's working capital: "Report on the South African Airways Contract with McKinsey/Regiments Consortium," Commission of Inquiry into State Capture, Nov. 11, 2020, 5.
239 This time, no sole-source contract: Ibid., 4.
239 According to the judicial commission: Ibid., 5.
239 "confidential information": Ibid., 7.
239 The airline ensured that the contract amount: Ibid., 8.
239 Forty percent of Regiments' share: Ibid., 7.
240 McKinsey said it didn't know: Ibid., 4.
240 The second tainted McKinsey contract: "Report on Laundering of Regiments' Proceeds of Contracts Alongside McKinsey for the Benefit of Essa/the Guptas," Commission of Inquiry into State Capture, Nov. 13, 2020, 5.
240 McKinsey again took the position: Statement of Mieszala to Commission of Inquiry into State Capture, Dec. 10, 2020, 2.
240 Its investigators had said: Ibid., 4–5.
240 "I asked for this": Testimony of Alexander Weiss to Commission of Inquiry into State Capture, Dec. 10, 2020, 30.
240 If documentary proof was so important: Ibid., 52.
240 "would have flagged something": Ibid., 53.
240 "had a real, visible impact": Statement of Weiss to Commission of Inquiry into State Capture, 7.
240 McKinsey sought to defuse: "McKinsey & Company Makes Further Voluntary Commitment to Repay Fees," McKinsey & Company website.
240 being a "responsible corporate citizen": "Media Statement Released at the Chairperson's Instance on Wednesday, 9 December 2020," Commission of Inquiry into State Capture, Dec. 9, 2020.
240 "To pay back your fee": Melody Emmett, "Athol Williams on Why Companies Involved in State Capture Should Be Prosecuted," *Daily Maverick,* Jan. 18, 2021. McKinsey issued a statement that quoted Advocate Chaskalson saying: "I can confirm that certainly from the side of the Commission we have no complaints whatsoever about the way in which McKinsey has interacted with us. We found McKinsey to be very transparent in its interactions with us. Where we asked for materials we've always received them and sometimes whether we haven't asked for them, we've . . . received them too."
241 "a bit of a tin ear": Barton, interview by author.
241 Others thought Kevin Sneader: Author interviews.
241 "astronomical increase in the fees": Testimony of Mieszala to Commission of Inquiry into State Capture, Dec. 10, 2020, 163.
241 "To my knowledge it was not something": Ibid., 155.
241 The commission found no evidence: Statement of Mieszala to Commission of Inquiry into State Capture, Dec. 10, 2020, 2.
241 it is "morally wrong": Testimony of Mieszala to Commission of Inquiry into State Capture, Dec. 10, 2020, 142. Mieszala, a senior partner based in Paris, became chief risk officer in Jan. 2018 and did not work in South Africa.
241 "A relationship between Sagar and Essa": Ibid., 179.
242 McKinsey's culture more than weak governance: Ibid., 142. McKinsey has worked for corrupt individuals and governments in Ukraine, Malaysia, Azerbaijan, Angola, and Russia.
242 "For almost 95 years": "McKinsey's Partners Suffer from Collective Self-Delusion," *Economist,* March 4, 2021.
242 "When you have people": Testimony of Mieszala to Commission of Inquiry into State Capture, Dec. 10, 2020, 157.
242 In January 2020, the company was forced: "Eskom Misled Ramaphosa About Extent of Load-Shedding: David Mabuza," *TimesLIVE,* Jan. 9, 2020.
242 South Africa's president had cut short:

"President Cuts Short Egyptian Visit to Attend to Electricity Crisis," South African Government News Agency, Dec. 11, 2019.

242 The media reported that 2021 could: Jackie Cameron, "Loadshedding: 2021 to Be Worst Year Yet for SA Electricity Crisis—Chris Yelland, Energy Expert," *BizNews,* Jan. 20, 2021.

13. Serving the Saudi State

243 "knocked on doors and tents": "Interview with Sandy Apgar by Debbie Hepton," *Journal of Corporate Real Estate* 11, no. 4 (2009).

243 He advised the state-owned oil company: Biography of Apgar on Wilson Center website: www.wilsoncenter.org.

244 "relatively centralized in the hands": Mahlon Apgar IV, "Succeeding in Saudi Arabia," *Harvard Business Review,* Jan.–Feb. 1977.

244 De Boer kept a unique kind of organization chart: Two former McKinsey consultants in the region confirm that de Boer had these organization charts on the walls of the Dubai office. De Boer declined an interview request.

244 Saudi Binladin Group: McKinsey's work with the Binladin group comes from an interview with a former Saudi-based [illegible] consultant, April 2020.

246 "a laboratory for a new kind": Ben Hubbard, *MBS: The Rise to Power of Mohammed bin Salman* (New York: Tim Duggan Books, 2020), 140.

246 One story has him sending: Dexter Filkins, "A Saudi Prince's Quest to Remake the Middle East," *New Yorker,* April 2, 2018.

246 He even detained his own mother: Hubbard, *MBS,* 33.

246 The consultants sat quietly: Michael Forsythe, Mark Mazzetti, Ben Hubbard, and Walt Bogdanich, "Consulting Firms Keep Lucrative Saudi Alliance, Shaping Crown Prince's Vision," *New York Times,* Nov. 4, 2018.

247 McKinsey received $4.8 million for: FARA Registration filed with the Department of Justice, received Aug. 10, 2020.

247 This was a giga-project: NEOM-related websites list several "giga-projects" under construction or planned for NEOM. See www.neom-property.com.

247 Even taxi drivers could identify: Interview with former Dubai-based McKinsey consultant, April 14, 2020.

247 "There was no question": Hubbard, *MBS,* 65.

248 Mazen Al-Jubeir was: See Al-Jubeir's LinkedIn profile.

248 *The Wall Street Journal* reported: Justin Scheck, Bradley Hope, and Summer Said, "In Growing Saudi Business, McKinsey Hired Officials' Children," *Wall Street Journal,* Nov. 10, 2017.

249 In 2005, Hani Khoja: Hani Ibrahim Khoja, *A Global Nomad in Search of True Happiness* (Self-published, 2016), 199.

249 "The word was that it was purely": Telephone interview with former McKinsey partner who requested anonymity, April 13, 2020. See "McKinsey Has Acquired Elixir, a Saudi Arabian Consultancy," an announcement by McKinsey on April 1, 2017. On mckinsey.com.

249 "When you come at them": Interview with former Elixir consultant who requested anonymity, April 30, 2020.

250 When th[illegible] in Riyadh: [illegible] of the Ritz detention in Hubbard, *MBS,* starting on page 186.

250 Among those detained was Hani Khoja: Summer Said, Justin Scheck, and Bradley Hope, "Former McKinsey Executive Imprisoned by Saudis," *Wall Street Journal,* Dec. 28, 2018.

250 In South Africa, it faced: Walt Bogdanich and Michael Forsythe, "How McKinsey Lost Its Way in South Africa," *New York Times,* June 26, 2018; Michael Forsythe, Kyra Gurney, Scilla Alecci, and Ben Hallman, "How U.S. Firms Helped Africa's Richest Woman Exploit Her Country's Wealth," *New York Times,* Jan. 20, 2020.

251 To do that, they turned to McKinsey: Interviews with two former Cambridge

Analytica employees confirmed McKinsey's relationship with SCL, April–May 2020.

252 "opinion mining": Abdullah Alsaedi, Roobaea Alroobaea, and Sepi Chakaveh, "Twitter-Based Reporting System for Public Infrastructure in Saudi Arabia," *Journal of Technology Research* 8 (Jan. 2019).

252 "I thought, 'Oh, that's great' ": This account is drawn from an on-the-record interview with Abdulaziz in June 2020. Abdulaziz did not disclose the identity of his acquaintance out of concern that doing so would put that person in danger.

252 The banal title of the nine-page report: The *New York Times* reporter Katie Benner obtained a copy of this report in late 2018, and an identical version was entered as an exhibit in a lawsuit Abdulaziz filed against McKinsey. The PowerPoint presentation was reviewed by a former McKinsey consultant familiar with sentiment analysis who confirmed that this was the technique being employed.

253 The following month, his phone was hacked: Citizen Lab, "How a Canadian Permanent Resident and Saudi Arabian Dissident Was Targeted with Powerful Spyware on Canadian Soil," Oct. 22, 2018.

253 "We will anesthetize you": Account of Khashoggi's murder, based on audio recordings, from Hubbard, *MBS,* 262–64.

254 "horrified by the possibility": McKinsey comment in Katie Benner, Mark Mazzetti, Ben Hubbard, and Mike Isaac, "Saudis' Image Makers: A Troll Army and a Twitter Insider," *New York Times,* Oct. 20, 2018.

254 "The firm's response to the social media": Interview with former McKinsey consultant who requested anonymity, via secure messaging application, April 21, 2020.

254 Abdulaziz's source, who was working with McKinsey: Abdulaziz did not reveal the name of the acquaintance who was working with McKinsey out of concern this would put the person in danger of retaliation from the Saudi government.

255 "The world does not want": Sneader speaking on CNBC's *Squawk Box,* March 1, 2019.

255 "Your client is the Saudi Arabian Government": Email from former Australia-based McKinsey consultant, Sept. 26, 2019.

255 "McKinsey effectively put a target": *Omar Abdulaziz v. Twitter Inc., McKinsey & Co., and DOES 1-10, Inclusive,* 3:19 CV: 06694-LB. The case was dismissed in Aug. 2020, with the judge accepting McKinsey's argument that the case had no standing in California, where it was filed.

255 Abdulaziz sued McKinsey again in 2021: See *Abdulaziz v. McKinsey & Company Inc. et al.,* District Court for the Southern District of New York, 1:21-cv-01219-LGS.

256 McKinsey and some of the other: Forsythe, Mazzetti, Hubbard, and Bogdanich "Consulting Firms Keep Lucrative Saudi Alliance, Shaping Crown Prince's Vision."

256 "It went to BCG": For details of BCG's work with the Saudi Ministry of Defense, see ibid. In a statement for that article, BCG said it focused in Saudi Arabia on work that could "positively contribute to economic and societal transformation" and that the company had turned down work that went against that principle. The firm had declined projects that involved military or intelligence strategy, a spokesman said.

257 In Ukraine, the country's richest oligarch: Walt Bogdanich and Michael Forsythe, "Turning Tyranny into a Client," *New York Times,* Dec. 16, 2018. After Yanukovych was overthrown in 2014, Ukrainians were amazed at the opulence of his sprawling estate, which boasted a menagerie with exotic animals and had gold bathroom fixtures.

14. Chumocracy

258 "Now this is not the end": Churchill speech at Mansion House, London, Nov. 10, 1942, www.churchill-society-london.org.uk.

258 "No society can legitimately": From a 1952 essay by Bevan, "In Place of Fear."

258 "whatever rudimentary medical services": Susan Cohen, *The NHS: Britain's National Health Service, 1948–2000* (London: Bloomsbury, 2020), 15.

259 some thirty-three million sets of dentures: "The Story of NHS Dentistry." On the website of the British Dental Association.

259 "must always be changing": Michael Foot, *Aneurin Bevan: A Biography* (London: Davis-Poynter, 1973), vol. 2, 273.

259 Maternal mortality rates: In 2018, 6.5 British mothers died for every 100,000 live births. In America the figure was 17.4. See "Maternal Mortality and Maternity Care in the United States Compared to 10 Other Developed Countries," Commonwealth Fund website.

259 people are dying younger: In 2012 the United States spent 16.3 percent of its GDP on health, rising to 16.9 percent in 2018. In the U.K., the figures were 8.3 percent and 9.8 percent, respectively. U.S. life expectancy fell from 78.8 in 2012 to 78.6 in 2017, while the U.K.'s rose from 81 to 81.2 during that period. The U.S. life expectancy was the lowest among eleven countries surveyed. See Roosa Tikkanen and Melinda K. Abrams, "U.S. Health Care from a Global Perspective, 2019: Higher Spending, Worse Outcomes?," Commonwealth Fund, Jan. 30, 2020. In 2020, life expectancy in many countries, including the U.K., declined because of the COVID pandemic.

259 "Holy of holies": Alan Sked and Chris Cook, *Post-war Britain: A Political History* (London: Penguin Books, 1993), 523.

260 In a memo that opened: Until recently, senior partners were called "directors" and partners were "principals." For clarity, we use the present-day titles.

260 "Our activities now transcend": George David Smith, John T. Seaman Jr., and Morgan Witzel, *A History of the Firm* (New York: McKinsey, 2011), 126.

260 bringing in about $720,000: The fee was £267,000, converted at the exchange rate at the time.

260 That spurred the firm to set up: Smith, Seaman, and Witzel, *History of the Firm,* 130.

260 Parker looked and sounded the part: Ibid., 139.

261 "Of course the first thing": Interview with Parker in the 1999 Channel 4 series *Masters of the Universe* by the director Roger Graef.

261 Then came the state sector: Smith, Seaman, and Witzel, *History of the Firm,* 137.

261 "McKinsey: n & v.t. 1": *Times* (London), Sept. 1, 1968, cited in ibid.

261 "Once we really got going": Parker quotation from episode 1 of *Masters of the Universe.*

262 This "tripartite monster": Philip Begley and Sally Sheard, "McKinsey and the 'Tripartite Monster': The Role of Management Consultants in the 1974 NHS Reorganisation," *Medical History* 63, no. 4 (2019): 390–410.

262 "You were the management gurus": Recollection of Dr. Eric Caines in a transcript on a witness seminar, *The 1974 NHS Reorganization,* held at the University of Liverpool in London on Nov. 9, 2016, 34.

262 "when everyone is responsible": Ibid.

262 "proliferation of paper": Begley and Sheard, "McKinsey and the 'Tripartite Monster,'" 403.

263 A respected columnist speculated: The *Guardian* columnist Peter Jenkins, cited in Sked and Cook, *Post-war Britain,* 327.

263 "Project Destiny": Project Destiny appears to be a common code name for McKinsey assignments. This was also the name given to McKinsey's plan to overhaul the organization of the insurance giant AIG after the global financial crisis.

264 "They are trying to sweat more use": "Railtrack Rethinks Spending," *New Civil Engineer,* Oct. 22, 1998. Also Gerald Crompton and Robert Jupe, "'Basically a Halfway House': Not-for-Profit in British Transport" (working paper, Canterbury Business School, University of Kent, U.K.), citeseerx.ist.psu.edu/viewdoc/download?doi=10.1.1.198.3447&rep=rep1&type=pdf.

264 "heading towards the boundary of": *Train Derailment at Hatfield: A Final Report by the Independent Investigation Board,*

Office of Rail Regulation, July 2006, 114.

264 The report blamed Railtrack: Ibid., 10. See also Richard Thompson, "Time to Switch Track," *Construction News,* Oct. 26, 2000.

264 In reality, competition didn't work well: Kenneth J. Arrow, "Uncertainty and the Welfare Economics of Health Care," *American Economic Review* 53, no. 5 (Dec. 1963).

265 As a result, administration costs: See John Lister, *The NHS After 60: For Patients or Profits?* (London: Middlesex University Press, 2008).

265 It led to massive cost overruns: John Furse, "The NHS Dismantled," *London Review of Books,* Nov. 7, 2019.

265 A young doctor, Penny Dash: See Dash's LinkedIn profile.

265 McKinsey delivered its plan: "Achieving World-Class Productivity in the NHS 2009/10–2013/14: Detailing the Size of the Opportunity" (prepared for the Department of Health, March 2009), McKinsey slide deck.

266 "achieve standard performance": Ibid., slide 29.

266 reducing certain hysterectomies: Ibid., slides 51 and 52.

266 One McKinsey slide praised Kaiser Permanente: Ibid., slides 70 and 71.

266 "Many of these procedures": Randeep Ramesh, "Health Secretary, Lansley Publishes NHS Report Disowned by Labour," *Guardian,* June 3, 2010.

266 The Conservative Party's health spokesman: Owen Bowcott, "NHS Advised to Lose One in 10 Workers," *Guardian,* Sept. 2, 2009.

266 At 1:18 p.m., McKinsey's London office: This account is drawn from emails released under FOI requests by Tamasin Cave, an investigative journalist. Masters turned down the opera tickets, but he, along with Monitor's chief operating officer, Stephen Hay, did attend the Cirque du Soleil event with Henke, according to the emails.

267 "big enough to be seen": Polly Toynbee, "The Tories' Massive NHS U-Turn Won't Undo the Damage They Inflicted," *Guardian,* Feb. 8, 2021.

267 "been gathering our thinking": Email from McKinsey to David Bennett (CEO of Monitor and a former McKinsey partner), May 31, 2010. Subject line: "Future of the NHS." In emails obtained by Tamasin Cave via FOI. Link to the email cache: powerbase.info/images/6/6b/2010_Emails_-_redacted.pdf.

267 "You cannot get a cigarette paper": Tamasin Cave and Andy Rowell, *A Quiet Word: Lobbying, Crony Capitalism, and Broken Politics in Britain* (London: Bodley Head, 2014), loc. 1564, Kindle.

268 Emails show that he accepted: Masters sent his regrets for some events, such as the Health Investors Awards dinner. The details are from emails obtained by the journalist Tamasin Cave through Freedom of Information requests.

268 Writing in *The Guardian,* Seddon said: Nick Seddon, "Getting Value out of the Health Budget," *Guardian,* June 16, 2010.

268 The McKinsey study was then baked into: "Delivering Efficiency Changes in the NHS," Department of Health Briefing for the House of Commons Health Committee, Sept. 2011.

269 the $100 billion–plus annual NHS budget: NHS budget for the entire U.K. in 2010 was £120 billion, or $184 billion at the average exchange rate for that year. But some of this is for Scotland and Wales, which have separate NHS structures. See Nigel de Kare-Silver, "NHS Cuts and Services: Can We Afford It?," *British Journal of General Practice* 60, no. 572 (2010): 218–19.

269 The idea of doctors deciding: Jackie Applebee, a GP in East London, explained in an interview, "We're doctors, we want to be looking after patients, not running health services. We don't want to be doing the government's bidding."

269 "We, in the UK, have done this": Jane

Lewis, "Government and NHS Reform Since the 1980s," Working Paper 05-20, LSE Department of Social Policy, April 2020, citing "Gas and Power Markets Are a 'Model' for the Health Service," *Times,* Feb. 25, 2011.

269 "at the mindset of 1 at a time": Email from McKinsey to Dalton, Nov. 9, 2010. Subject: Collaboration. From emails from and to McKinsey employees and Ian Dalton, 2010–11. Obtained through a Freedom of Information Act request by Tamasin Cave.

269 In 2010 the NHS alone: That number would more than double to £640 million in 2014. Ian Kirkpatrick, Andrew Sturdy, and Gianluca Veronesi, "Using Management Consultancy Brings Inefficiency to the NHS," LSE Blog, March 10, 2018, blogs .lse.ac.uk.

270 McKinsey distributed a forty-seven-page slide deck: "NHS Commissioning Board: Organisational Design" (discussion draft—OD workshop, Feb. 14, 2011), McKinsey-prepared slide deck obtained by Tamasin Cave through FOI request.

270 McKinsey worked with a familiar audience: David Rose, "The Firm That Hijacked the NHS," *Mail on Sunday,* Feb. 12, 2012.

270 Some of London's most senior: This account is drawn from McKinsey slide deck, "Simulating the Future of the London Health Economy" (pre-read for simulation event, March 2011).

271 "Those who maintain that we": Jacky Davis, John Lister, and David Wrigley, *NHS for Sale: Myths, Lies, and Deception* (London: Merlin Press, 2015), loc. 916, Kindle.

271 The conference, put on by the right-wing think tank: Account drawn from conference program, "A Lot More for a Lot Less: Disruptive Innovation in Healthcare," Reform conference sponsored by McKinsey. Henke and the McKinsey consultant Tom Kibasi wrote a brief article for the program titled "Disruptive Innovation."

272 "The wise and virtuous man": Dominic Barton, "Capitalism for the Long Term," *Harvard Business Review,* March 2011.

272 It came as no surprise: Daniel Boffey, "NHS Reforms: American Consultancy McKinsey in Conflict of Interest Row," *Guardian,* Nov. 5, 2011.

272 "So they were picking pockets": Davis, telephone interview by author, May 11, 2021.

272 In Washington, he had made a case: Stevens cited in Chad Terhune and Keith Epstein, "The Health Insurers Have Already Won," *Bloomberg Businessweek,* Aug. 6, 2009.

273 When John Major served as prime minister: Major-era figure from John Lister, author interview. The 2010 and 2020 figures in Denis Campbell, "Non-NHS Healthcare Providers Given £96bn in a Decade, Says Labour," *Guardian,* May 3, 2021.

273 One company even took over management: "Hinchingbrooke Hospital Asks for £9.6 Million Bailout as Circle Withdraws," BBC, Feb. 10, 2015, www.bbc.com.

273 "All these private companies": Lister, telephone interview by author, May 12, 2021.

273 According to one authoritative study: Ian Kirkpatrick et al., "The Impact of Management Consultants on Public Service Efficiency," *Policy and Politics* 47, no. 1 (2019): 77–95. First published online Feb. 20, 2018.

274 McKinsey was being asked: See NHS website on ICS: www.england.nhs.uk.

274 London was a major test bed: See page 17 of agenda of Barnet, Enfield, and Haringey Mental Health NHS Trust Board Meeting, Jan. 27, 2020, on Dash's appointment. For AT Medics' role in the NW London ICP, see presentation of Dr. Aumran Tahir to Secretary of State for Health Andrew Lansley on June 21, 2012, on the AT Medics website. For details on McKinsey's involvement in the project, see Gerald Wistow et al., "Putting Integrated Care into Practice: The North West London

Experience," research paper by the Nuffield Trust and the LSE Personal Social Services Research Unit, Oct. 2015.

274 In February 2021, the news broke: See Nick Bostock, "US Company's Subsidiary to Hold Nearly 1% of GP Contracts in England," *GP Online*, Feb. 18, 2021.

274 McKinsey alone charged £563,400: See Andrea Downey, "McKinsey Bags £560K Deciding 'Vision' for New NHS Test and Trace Body," *Consulting Point*, Aug. 27, 2020.

274 Test and trace was a disaster: Ibid.

275 "The government has bypassed": George Monbiot, "The Government's Secretive Covid Contracts Are Heaping Misery on Britain," *Guardian*, Oct. 21, 2020.

275 The government's "Anticorruption Champion": Penrose's official bio on gov.uk lists his McKinsey background and role as anticorruption champion.

275 twenty-six other British prime ministers: For a list of British prime ministers who went to Oxford, see www.ox.ac.uk/about/oxford-people/british-prime-ministers.

Index